BEYOND MALE AND FEMALE?

T&T Clark Enquiries in Theological Ethics

Series editors
Brian Brock
Susan F. Parsons

BEYOND MALE AND FEMALE?

A Theological Account of Intersex Embodiment

Sam Ashton

LONDON • NEW YORK • OXFORD • NEW DELHI • SYDNEY

T&T CLARK
Bloomsbury Publishing Plc
50 Bedford Square, London, WC1B 3DP, UK
1385 Broadway, New York, NY 10018, USA
29 Earlsfort Terrace, Dublin 2, Ireland

BLOOMSBURY, T&T CLARK and the T&T Clark logo are trademarks of Bloomsbury
Publishing Plc

First published in Great Britain 2024

A catalogue record for this book is available from the British Library.

Library of Congress Cataloging-in-Publication Data
Names: Ashton, Sam, author.
Title: Beyond male and female? : a theological account of intersex embodiement /
by Sam Ashton.
Description: New York : T&T Clark, 2023. | Series: T&T Clark enquiries in theological ethics |
Includes bibliographical references and index.
Identifiers: LCCN 2023023839 (print) | LCCN 2023023840 (ebook) | ISBN 9780567713148
(hardback) | ISBN 9780567713186 (paperback) | ISBN 9780567713155 (pdf) |
ISBN 9780567713179 (epub)
Subjects: LCSH: Gender identity–Religious aspects–Christianity. | Intersexuality–
Biblical teaching. | Intersexuality.
Classification: LCC BT708 .A786 2015 (print) | LCC BT708 (ebook) |
DDC 241/.66–dc23/eng/20230731
LC record available at https://lccn.loc.gov/2023023839
LC ebook record available at https://lccn.loc.gov/2023023840

ISBN: HB: 978-0-5677-1314-8
ePDF: 978-0-5677-1315-5
ePUB: 978-0-5677-1317-9

Series: T&T Clark Enquiries in Theological Ethics

Typeset by Deanta Global Publishing Services, Chennai, India

To find out more about our authors and books visit www.bloomsbury.com and
sign up for our newsletters.

To my Aličé
מחמד עיני *(Ezek. 24:16)*

CONTENTS

ACKNOWLEDGMENTS

Once a year, on Whit Tuesday, the Luxembourg town of Echternach hosts a religious procession. Linked five abreast, rows of pilgrims hop three steps forward, then two steps back—five steps are taken to advance one—as they dance their way up to the basilica for worship. Writing a book has the feel of an Echternach procession. At the dénouement of the dance, I am deeply thankful to God for his enabling and sustaining grace, and for those he has brought to join the jig along the way.

To the doctoral committee at Wheaton College, thank you for inviting me to cross the pond and learn to dance. It is a delight to see you pursue your vocation "for Christ and his Kingdom." Long may God use you to bless the nations with "biblically rooted, theologically formed" servants. I highlight the salutary tutelage of Daniel Treier, whose concern for the reputation of his Lord bears the life-giving aroma of Christ (2 Cor. 2:15–16). Likewise, I have gained greatly from the theologically rich and pastorally motivated insights of Beth Felker Jones. I am especially grateful for the sapiential supervision of Marc Cortez. Marc's faithful ministry with middle-schoolers prepared him well to cope with a bumbling Brit. Marc embodies the gentleness of a mother and the encouragement of a father (1 Thess. 2:7, 11). An *Adeodatus*.

To my fellow students, particularly my dancing-cohort (Amy Allan, Heather Zimmerman, Stephen Wunrow, and Grant Flynn), thank you for bearing with me while I pontificated at lunch about everything from Brexit and Biden to bread and baseball (and why the *maths* says cricket is four times better). Even amid occasional "sharp disagreement," you spurred me on to know God more deeply in his scriptures. This specific project has benefited immensely from the patient wisdom of James Cuénod, Ty Kieser, and Matthew Levering. All have listened well, kept me from greater error, and helped me see and savor our savior.

To our church in America, Wellspring Alliance, thank you for welcoming us into your family. Alice and I left England trusting Matt. 19:29, and God has answered abundantly through you, particularly our homegroup (hosted by the extraordinarily kind and godly Peter and Margery Walters). We are indelibly marked by your emphasis on global frontier missions (Rom. 10:14–15). To our new church in England, St Paul's Hadley Wood, thank you for calling us to serve among you. May God be glorified as we share his life and love.

To our friends and family in England, your faithful prayers and generous support have sustained us in ways you cannot imagine. Throughout our sojourn to the States, your letters, chocolate biscuits, FaceTimes, and wonderful visits have buoyed us up. I extend further gratitude to the Sallberg fellowship, the Sola Trust, the Cross Trust, Church Society, the Latimer Trust, the Daily Prayer Union

Trust, the Andrew Anderson Trust, the Evangelical Trust, St. Andrew's PCC, St. Ebbe's UKMG, as well as individual supporters. You excel in the grace of giving (2 Cor. 8:7). I am deeply humbled by your gospel partnership. I am thankful for the permission from Church Society to reproduce in Chapter 5 a previously published article ("Beyond Male and Female? How Redemption's Relationship to Creation Shapes Sexual Ethics," *The Global Anglican* 136/1 [2022]: 19–35). Additional thanks to Brian Brock and Susan Parsons for graciously accepting this book into their series, and to the hardworking team at T&T Clark, particularly Anna Turton, Sophie Beardsworth, Vishnu Prasad, and Jack Curtin.

To my own family, and above all my wife, Alice, I am profoundly grateful. Three and a half years ago we left England with four bags. We now leave Chicago with three children (little Americans!), good friends, and too many bags (my books don't count). Alice, in the highs and lows, the joy of the LORD has been your strength (Neh. 8:10). That makes me love you, and our Triune God, more and more. Your sacrificial servant-heartedness shines, your fun-loving creativity delights, and your faithful friendship reassures. You are my woman of noble character. I dedicate this work to you.

Sam Ashton
Eastertide, 2023

ABBREVIATIONS

AARDS	American Academy of Religion Dissertation Series
AB	Anchor Bible
AcTSup	*Acta Theologica Supplementum*
ACW	Ancient Christian Writers
AJHB	*American Journal of Human Biology*
ANF	*Ante-Nicene Fathers*. Edited by A. Roberts and J. Donaldson. Buffalo, 1885–96. Reprint, Peabody, MA, 2004
AngS	Angewandte Sexualwissenschaft
AOAT	Alter Orient und Altes Testament
AOTC	Apollos Old Testament Commentary
AphQ	*American Philosophical Quarterly*
ARC	Ashgate Research Companion
ArsD	*Ars Disputandi*
ArV	*Archa Verbi*
ATD	Alte Testament Deutsch
AThR	*Anglican Theological Review*
AugStud	*Augustinian Studies*
A-L	*Augustinus-Lexikon*. Edited by Cornelius Mayer. 5 vols. Basel: Schwabe, 1986–
BECNT	Baker Exegetical Commentary on the New Testament
BDAG	*Greek-English Lexicon of the New Testament and Other Early Christian Literature*. Bauer, W., F. W. Danker, W. F. Arndt, and F. W. Gingrich. 3rd ed. Chicago: University of Chicago Press, 1999
BHGNT	Baylor Handbook on the Greek New TestamentBHHB Baylor Handbook on the Hebrew Bible
BHRG	*A Biblical Hebrew Reference Grammar*. van der Merwe, Christo H. J., Jacobus A. Naudé, and Jan H. Kroeze. 2nd ed. London: T&T Clark, 2018
BIS	Biblical Interpretation Series
BJS	Brown Judaic Studies
BLE	*Bulletin de littérature ecclésiastique*
BMO	Barcino Monographica Orientalia
BRMT	Blackwell Readings in Modern Theology
BTNT	Biblical Theology of the New Testament
BZA	Beiträge zur Altertumskunde
BZNW	Beihefte zur Zeitschrift für die neutestamentliche Wissenschaft
CBMW	*The Council on Biblical Manhood and Womanhood*
CBR	*Currents in Biblical Research*
CCR	Cambridge Companions to Religion

CCRel	Columbia Classics in Religion
CCSL	Corpus Christianorum: Series latina. Turnhout, 1953–
CCTheo	Contours of Christian Theology
CHANE	Culture and History of the Ancient Near East
ChrCent	*Christian Century*
CIT	Current Issues in Theology
Civ.	*De civitate Dei.* Augustine. Edited by Bernard Dombart and Alphonse Kalb. 2 vols. Turnhout, 1955
CLA	Christianity in Late Antiquity
CMG	Corpus Medicorum Graecorum
Comm	*Communio*
ConJ	*Concordia Journal*
COQG	Christian Origins and the Question of God
CSEL	Corpus scriptorum ecclesiasticorum latinorum
CSR	Church of Sweden Research
CTC	Christian Theology in Context
CTHP	Cambridge Texts in the History of Philosophy
CTJ	*Calvin Theological Journal*
DAI	*Deutsches Ärzteblatt International*
DBW	Dietrich Bonhoeffer Works
DLGTT	*Dictionary of Latin and Greek Theological Terms: Drawn Principally from Protestant Scholastic Theology.* Richard Muller. 2nd ed. Grand Rapids, 2017
DuqSt	Duquesne Studies
E&M	*Ethics & Medicine: An International Journal of Bioethics*
EBib	Etudes bibliques
ECF	Early Church Fathers
ECL	Early Christianity and its Literature
EKKNT	Evangelisch-katholischer Kommentar zum Neuen Testament
Épi	Épiphanie
ER	*Encyclopedia of Religion*
ES	Emerging Scholars
ESEC	Emory Studies in Early Christianity
ET	Ethics as Theology
ExpF	Expanding Frontiers: Interdisciplinary Approaches to Studies of Women, Gender, and Sexuality
FB	Forschungen zur Bibel
FC	Fathers of the Church
FET	Foundations of Evangelical Theology
FOTL	Forms of the Old Testament Literature
FP	*Faith and Philosophy*
FPS	Fundamentals of Philosophy Series
FR	Faith and Reason
FRLANT	Forschungen zur Religion und Literatur des Alten und Neuen Testaments
GBHS	*A Guide to Biblical Hebrew Syntax.* Arnold, Bill T., and John H. Choi. 2nd ed. Cambridge: Cambridge University Press, 2018

GLQ	*GLQ: A Journal of Lesbian and Gay Studies*
GSH	Genders and Sexualities in History
GTS	Gender, Theology and Spirituality
HALOT	*The Hebrew and Aramaic Lexicon of the Old Testament.* Koehler, Ludwig, and Walter Baumgartner. Revised by Walter Baumgartner and Johann Jacok Stamm. Translated by M. E. J. Richardson. 5 vols. Leiden: Brill, 1994–2000
HASNMA	Historical-Analytical Studies on Nature, Mind and Action
HCR	*Hastings Center Report*
HR	*History of Religions*
HT	Handbücher Theologie
HTA	Historisch Theologische Auslegung
HThKAT	Herders Theologischer Kommentar zum Alten Testament
HTR	*Harvard Theological Review*
HUT	Hermeneutische Untersuchungen zur Theologie
Hyp	*Hypatia*
ICC	International Critical Commentary
IJPR	*International Journal for Philosophy of Religion*
IJST	*International Journal of Systematic Theology*
ILELNM	International Library of Ethics, Law, and the New Medicine
ITC	International Theological Commentary
JAAR	*Journal of the American Academy of Religion*
JAHLS	John Albert Hall Lecture Series
JASA	*Journal of the American Scientific Affiliation*
JBL	*Journal of Biblical Literature*
JDR	*Journal of Disability & Religion*
JECS	*Journal of Early Christian Studies*
JFSR	*Journal of Feminist Studies in Religion*
JHSe	*Journal of the History of Sexuality*
JJS	*Journal of Jewish Studies*
JM	Joüon, Paul, and T. Muraoka. *A Grammar of Biblical Hebrew.* 2nd ed. 2 vols. Subsidia Biblica 27. Rome: Editrice Pontificio Instituto Biblico, 2006
JMFNM	*Journal of Maternal-Fetal & Neonatal Medicine*
JMT	*Journal of Moral Theology*
JOTT	*Journal of Translation and Textlinguistics*
JPSTCP	Jewish Publication Society Torah Commentary Project
JRDH	*Journal of Religion, Disability & Health*
JRE	*Journal of Religious Ethics*
JSCE	*Journal of the Society of Christian Ethics*
JSIRS	*Journal for the Sociological Integration of Religion and Society*
JSNT	*Journal for the Study of the New Testament*
JSOTSup	Journal for the Study of the Old Testament: Supplement Series
JSR	*Journal of Sex Research*
JTISup	Journal of Theological Interpretation Supplements
L/E	Latin/English Edition of the Works of St. Thomas Aquinas
LATC	Los Angeles Theology Conference

LCL	Loeb Classical Library
LD	Lectio divina
LHBOTS	Library of Hebrew Bible/Old Testament Studies
LNTS	Library of New Testament Studies
LTP	*Laval théologique et philosophique*
MFF	*Medieval Feminist Forum*
ModB	*Modern Believing*
MT	Masoretic Text
NAC	New American Commentary
NatGeo	*National Geographic*
NBf	*New Blackfriars*
NEJM	*New England Journal of Medicine*
NelSBT	Nelson Studies in Biblical Theology
Neot	*Neotestamentica*
NewRe	*New Republic*
NICNT	New International Commentary on the New Testament
NICOT	New International Commentary on the Old Testament
NIDOTTE	*New International Dictionary of Old Testament Theology & Exegesis.* Edited by Willem VanGemeren. 5 vols. Grand Rapids, 1997
NIGTC	New International Greek Testament Commentary
NovTSup	Novum Testamentum Supplements
NPNF²	*Nicene and Post-Nicene Fathers*, Series 2. Edited by Philip Schaff and Henry Wace. New York, 1890. Reprint, Peabody, MA, 2004
NSBT	New Studies in Biblical Theology
NSCE	New Studies in Christian Ethics
NTS	*New Testament Studies*
Numen Numen:	*International Review for the History of Religions*
NV	*Nova et Vetera*
OBT	Overtures to Biblical Theology
OEB	Oxford Encyclopedias of the Bible
OECT	Oxford Early Christian Texts
OH	Oxford Handbooks
OSAT	Oxford Studies in Analytic Theology
OSTE	Oxford Studies in Theological Ethics
OWC	Oxford World's Classics
P&S	*Psychology & Sexuality*
PC	*Philosophia Christi*
PCMR	*Pigment Cell and Melanoma Research*
PFL	Pastoring for Life
PG	Patrologia Graeca. Edited by J.-P. Migne. 162 vols. Paris, 1857–66
PhilS	*Philosophical Studies*
PiNTC	Pillar New Testament Commentary
PostM	*Postmedieval*
PPS	Popular Patristic Series
PracTheo	*Practical Theology*
PrinTMS	Princeton Theological Monograph Series
PTSDSSP	Princeton Theological Seminary Dead Sea Scrolls Project

QI	Queer Interventions
RA	Rewriting Antiquity
RC	Routledge Classics
RCIP	Routledge Contemporary Introductions to Philosophy
RD	*Reformed Dogmatics*. Herman Bavinck. Edited by John Bolt. Translated by John Vriend. 4 vols. Grand Rapids, 2003–8
ResQ	*Restoration Quarterly*
RNCTRTBS	Routledge New Critical Thinking in Religion, Theology and Biblical Studies
RTCAHD	Rethinking Theologies: Constructing Alternatives in History and Doctrine
SBJT	*The Southern Baptist Journal of Theology*
SBS	Stuttgarter Bibelstudien
SCB	*Science and Christian Belief*
SCC	Studies in Chinese Christianity
SCDS	Studies in Christian Doctrine and Scripture
SCE	*Studies in Christian Ethics*
SCG	*Summa Contra Gentiles*. Thomas Aquinas. Translated by Laurence Shapcote. 2 vols. Green Bay, WI, 2018
SCMCT	SCM Core Text
Scri	*Scriptura*
SD	Sexual Dimorphism
SemeiaSt	Semeia Studies
Sent.	*Commentary on the Sentences* III. Thomas Aquinas. Translated by the Aquinas Institute. Green Bay, WI, 2018–
SHANE	Studies in the History of the Ancient Near East
SHBC	Smyth & Helwys Bible Commentary
SHI	*Sociology of Health & Illness*
SHST	Studies in Historical & Systematic Theology
SMB	Spectrum Multiview Books
SNTSMS	Society for New Testament Studies Monograph Series
SP	Sexual Polymorphism
SR	*Studies in Religion*
SRTD	Studies in Religion, Theology, and Disability
ST	*Summa Theologiae*. Thomas Aquinas. Edited by John Mortensen and Enrique Alarcón. Translated by Laurence Shapcote. 10 vols. Lander, WY, 2012
STK	*Svensk Teologisk Kvartalskrift*
STS	Studies in Theology and Sexuality
STTA	Studi e testi tardoantichi
SVTQ	*St Vladimir's Theological Quarterly*
TBas	The Basics
TBN	Themes in Biblical Narrative
TCH	Transformation of the Classical Heritage
TDNT	*Theological Dictionary of the New Testament*. Edited by G. Kittel and G. Friedrich. Translated by G. W. Bromiley. 10 vols. Grand Rapids, 1964–76

TDOT	*The Theological Dictionary of the Old Testament*. Edited by G. J. Botterweck, H. Ringgren, and H.-J. Fabry. Translated by J. T. Willis, G. W. Bromiley, and D. Green. 15 vols. Grand Rapids, 1974–2006
Them	*Themelios*
Theol	*Theologica*
ThH	Théologie historique
ThS	*Theology & Sexuality*
TJ	*Trinity Journal*
TMB	*Theoretical Medicine and Bioethics*
TOW	Theologie Ost-West: Europäische Perspektiven
TRE	*Theologische Realenzyklopädie*. Edited by G. Krause and G. Müller. 26 vols. Berlin, 1977–2007
TRS	Thomistic Ressourcement Series
TS	*Theological Studies*
TTC	Transdisciplinary Theological Colloquia
TTCBS	T&T Clark Biblical Studies
TTCETE	T&T Clark Enquiries in Theological Ethics
TTCH	T&T Clark Handbooks
TTCSST	T&T Clark Studies in Systematic Theology
TTCT	T&T Clark Theology
TynBul	*Tyndale Bulletin*
VdM	Vérité des mythes
VE	*Vox evangelica*
VT	*Vetus Testamentum*
VTSup	Supplements to Vetus Testamentum
WBC	Word Biblical Commentary
WHS	Williams, Ronald J. *Williams' Hebrew Syntax*. Revised and expanded by John C. Beckman. 3rd ed. Toronto: University of Toronto Press, 2012
WSA	Works of Saint Augustine: A Translation for the 21st Century
WUNT	Wissenschaftliche Untersuchungen zum Neuen Testament
WUNT 2/	Wissenschaftliche Untersuchungen zum Neuen Testament 2. Reihe
ZECNT	Zondervan Exegetical Commentary on the New Testament
ZNSD	Zondervan New Studies in Dogmatics

Chapter 1

INTRODUCING INTERSEXUALITY

I. The Milieu of Intersex

Issues of sexuality cut to the psychosomatic bone.[1] As embodied creatures, all humans are biologically sexed.[2] While most humans are identifiably sexed as either male or female,[3] the sexed anatomy of some is atypical.[4] Toss a coin and it typically lands heads or tails. But what if the coin rests on its side? How should Christians interpret liminal embodiment?

1. Human sexuality is a complicated nexus that involves, at minimum, issues related to biology, culture, identity, philosophy, psychology, spirituality, and ethics. See further Adrian Thatcher, ed., *The Oxford Handbook of Theology, Sexuality, and Gender*, OH (Oxford: Oxford University Press, 2015).

2. Mirja Kutzer, "Mann/Frau (katholisch)," in *Handwörterbuch Theologische Anthropologie: Römisch-Katholisch/Russisch-Orthodox: Eine Gegenüberstellung*, ed. Bertram Stubenrauch and Andreï Lorgus (Freiburg im Breisgau: Herder, 2013), 74. All foreign language translations are my own unless otherwise indicated.

3. Biological sex refers to the primary sex characteristics of genetics, gonads, genitalia, and hormones, as well as a host of secondary sex characteristics. A typical female has 46,XX chromosomes, ovaries, a vulva and vagina, fallopian tubes and a uterus. A typical male has 46,XY chromosomes, testes, a scrotum and penis. I employ the terms "male" and "female" strictly in reference to sexed embodiment.

4. The incidence rate of sexually atypical bodies remains unclear. This is due to challenges of collecting data (e.g., some conditions are not visible until puberty or when testing for infertility) and disagreements over (dis)qualifying conditions (itself ideologically fraught). The most inclusive proposal suggests an occurrence rate of 1.7 percent (Melanie Blackless et al., "How Sexually Dimorphic Are We? Review and Synthesis," *AJHB* 12 [2000]: 151–66). The lowest estimates propose 0.018 percent (Leonard Sax, "How Common Is Intersex? A Response to Anne Fausto-Sterling," *JSR* 39 [2002]: 174–8). Given the theological nature of this project, the *existence* of sexed atypicality is more important than precise statistics. Yet, strikingly, if 1.7 percent is correct, the percentage of anatomically atypical Americans is higher than Down syndrome (0.14 percent), albinism (0.005 percent), and on par with having red hair (1–2 percent).

This book dissects the "hardware" of sexed anatomy to develop a theological interpretation of atypically sexed embodiment.[5] Different periods and cultures (e.g., medical, legal, identitarian) have labeled atypically sexed individuals as "hermaphrodites," "intersex," or persons with "differences/disorders/variations of sex development" (DSD/VSD).[6] While most today reject "hermaphrodite" as stigmatizing and offensive,[7] correct nomenclature remains highly contested. Some fear DSD language pathologizes a condition that does not need a medical "fix."[8] Others worry that "intersex" terminology burdens affected individuals with the baggage of identity politics.[9] Although both classifications exhibit advantages and disadvantages, I employ "intersex" vocabulary because it more precisely represents the *Hauptfrage* of this book: how should Christians interpret atypically sexed bodies that fall outside the statistically predominant pattern of male and female?[10] On the one hand, do such individuals remain resolutely female or male,

---

5. I assume a conceptual distinction between the "hardware" of biological sex and the "software" of culturally conditioned, interpreted, and performed gender. Since humans are social mammals, the terms "sex" and "gender" frequently bleed into each other. "Sex" and "gender" are often used synonymously in the literature, reflecting their correlativity. Nevertheless, it remains heuristically helpful to articulate a conceptual distinction between "sex" and "gender" to clarify that the purview of *this* project is exclusively humanity's anatomical sex. Thus, in this work I use "sex" as a *noun*, referring to one's biology, rather than as a *verb*, involving one's sexual gender-identity, sexual expression, or sexual orientation.

6. For a brief history of the terminology in different contexts, see Ellen K. Feder and Katrina Karkazis, "What's in a Name? The Controversy Over 'Disorders of Sex Development,'" *HCR* 38 (2008): 33–6. Although the majority world offers further nomenclature for atypically sexed individuals (e.g., "Hijras" in India), I limit my scope to my Western context. See further, Gilbert H. Herdt, ed., *Third Sex, Third Gender: Beyond Sexual Dimorphism in Culture and History* (New York: Zone, 1996).

7. E.g., Conrad Krannich, *Geschlecht als Gabe und Aufgabe: Intersexualität aus theologischer Perspektive*, AngS 4 (Gießen: Psychosozial-Verlag, 2016), 7 n.1; Susannah Cornwall, *Sex and Uncertainty in the Body of Christ: Intersex Conditions and Christian Theology*, GTS (London: Equinox, 2010), 243.

8. E.g., Katrina Karkazis, *Fixing Sex: Intersex, Medical Authority, and Lived Experience* (Durham, NC: Duke University Press, 2008); Hilary Malatino, *Queer Embodiment: Monstrosity, Medical Violence, and Intersex Experience*, ExpF (Lincoln: University of Nebraska Press, 2019). Some fear that VSD elevates the condition above the person.

9. Tove Lundberg, Peter Hegarty, and Katrina Roen, "Making Sense of 'Intersex' and 'DSD': How Laypeople Understand and Use Terminology," *P&S* 9 (2018): 161–73. See also the advocacy group Accord Alliance, "Our Mission," https://www.accordalliance.org/about-accord-alliance/our-mission/.

10. Note that DSDs include "abnormal" features that do not necessarily question the male-female binary (e.g., hypospadias in males or Turner's syndrome in females). Further, "intersex" is the preferred terminology among my identitarian interlocutors. E.g., Cornwall, *Sex and Uncertainty*, 17–20; Megan K. DeFranza, *Sex Difference in Christian Theology: Male,*

subsumed within a sexually dimorphic framework? Alternatively, do liminal lives suggest that humanity is truly sexually polymorphic? In answer, I construct a dogmatic account of intersexuality in conversation with contemporary theological interpretations of intersex embodiment.

While the contemporary conversation around intersexuality frequently blurs into identitarian issues,[11] I restrict my focus to atypical *sexed bodily conditions*. The concentration on atypical embodiment is neither a denigration nor a denial of the full personhood of each intersex individual. All humans, however sexed, are full bearers of the divine image (Gen. 1:26). With this theological cornerstone in place, I maintain a conceptual distinction between embodiment and personhood in order to devote specific attention to the intrinsic theological meaning and significance of sexed bodily atypicality. Bodies and personhood correspond, but they need not exhaust each other. Listening carefully to intersex testimony—their internal sense of self and external lived-experience—remains important.[12] Yet holding a procedural difference between the body and personhood allows for a richer analysis of the body per se. While focusing on the body does not diminish the need for much pastoral sensitivity (and robust pastoral theology), exploring intersex bodily conditions in themselves means that I reserve direct engagement with some of the concrete and complex challenges for intersex persons until the book's conclusion.

II. Introducing Intersex

Sexed bodily atypicality manifests itself in a variety of ways, affecting genetics, gonads, and genitalia. For example, people with Complete Androgen Insensitivity

---

Female, and Intersex in the Image of God (Grand Rapids: Eerdmans, 2015), 56–7. Cornwall also employs "intersex/DSD."

11. E.g., human rights advocacy and intersex activism. See Morgan Holmes, ed., *Critical Intersex*, QI (Farnham: Ashgate, 2009); Nikoletta Pikramenou, *Intersex Rights: Living Between Sexes* (Dordrecht: Springer, 2020). Although some co-opt intersex under the LGBTQ banner, this move is not strictly necessary. Intersex is primarily a physical phenomenon, whereas the initialism LGBTQ represents sexual orientations (Lesbian, Gay, Bisexual), gender incongruence (Transgender), and identity queering (Queer). Emi Koyama and Lisa Weasel suggest that "conflating or collapsing intersexuality into LGBT agendas fails to acknowledge the specific and urgent issues facing intersex people" ("From Social Construction to Social Justice: Transforming How We Teach About Intersexuality," in *A Guide for Teachers in Women's, Gender and Queer Studies*, ed. Emi Koyama, 2nd ed. [Portland, OR: Intersex Initiative Portland, 2003], 5).

12. For a good example, see Susannah Cornwall, "British Intersex Christians' Accounts of Intersex Identity, Christian Identity and Church Experience," *PracTheo* 6 (2013): 220–36. One should not forget that the primary agents of intersex interpretation are intersex individuals.

Syndrome (CAIS) are "born genetically male with XY chromosomes and feature internal testes and female appearing external genitalia."[13] Congenital Adrenal Hyperplasia (CAH) causes someone *in utero* who is genotypically female (46,XX) to develop phenotypically male (or uncertain) genitalia.[14] Others with Genetic Mosaicism possess "a mixture of chromosomes in their cells [typically 45,X/46,XY] . . . [and] may experience some extent of genital ambiguity."[15] Still others with Ovotestes have both testicular and ovarian cells. Genetically 46,XX, they "feature typical male appearing genitalia."[16] People with the preceding (or similar) conditions qualify as intersex because either their sexed phenotype is ambiguous (at least from a binary perspective)[17] or because they exhibit an atypicality between their genotypic and phenotypic sex.[18] Hence the lingering question: Is an intersex individual male, female, or something else?

III. Interpreting Intersex

Current intersex interpretation finds itself caught between the frameworks of sexual dimorphism (SD) and sexual polymorphism (SP). Should intersexuality be (self)interpreted within a sexually dimorphic model as *either* male *or* female? Or like the coin on its side, do liminal individuals open the door to a sexually polymorphic "third sex"?[19] While the existence of atypical embodiment was not unknown in the ancient world,[20] the "gender revolution" sweeping Western society had raised the public profile of such questions.[21] Precisely by giving due

---

13. Jay Kyle Petersen, *A Comprehensive Guide to Intersex* (London: Jessica Kingsley, 2021), 27.

14. Sax, "How Common Is Intersex?," 175–6.

15. Cornwall, *Sex and Uncertainty*, 242. See John C. Achermann and Ieuan A. Hughes, "Pediatric Disorders of Sex Development," in *Williams Textbook of Endocrinology*, ed. Shlomo Melmed et al., 13th ed. (Philadelphia, PA: Elsevier, 2016), 912.

16. Petersen, *Guide to Intersex*, 27. For more variations of intersex (conversant with much medical literature), see ibid., 57–117.

17. Although the language of "ambiguity" appears throughout intersex literature, atypical embodiment only becomes epistemically ambiguous when one presupposes a binary perspective. I privilege the nomenclature of "atypicality" over "ambiguity" until the latter can be theologically demonstrated.

18. Sax, "How Common Is Intersex?" 175.

19. Herdt, *Third Sex, Third Gender*. Herdt comments that the "code of 'thirdness' should not be taken literally" but is "emblematic of other possible combinations that transcend dimorphism" (ibid., 19–20).

20. See Chapter 2.

21. E.g., National Geographic Society, "Gender Revolution," *NatGeo* 231 (2017). One front cover displays a group photo with various superscriptions that include "intersex nonbinary."

"attention to the question of God," Christian theology contributes "things that would not otherwise be said," and so can further the current conversation.[22] Before expanding upon what it means to think *theologically* about intersexuality, I shall briefly narrate how Christian interpretations of intersexuality largely fall into two groups: traditional/traditionalist and innovational/innovationist or revisionist.[23]

Traditionalist interpretations of sexed embodiment emphasize the "givenness of maleness and femaleness" in Genesis 1–2.[24] "No dimension other than maleness and femaleness exists."[25] Jesus reaffirms "male and female" (Gen. 1:27) as "creational givens" in Matt. 19:4–6,[26] with "the fulfillment of creational designs" promised at the eschaton.[27] In a postlapsarian and pre-eschaton world, intersex bodies represent "anomalies and distortions" that "in no way undermine the creational norms."[28] Intersex conditions may be "traced to a malfunction at some point in the outworking of the either-or of chromosomal endowment."[29] Thus, traditionalists interpret intersexuality firmly within the grid of SD.

Innovationists denounce the traditional interpretation as dehumanizing. Marchal laments: "If humans were created male and female, by God no less, then

---

22. Colin E. Gunton, "The Indispensability of Theological Understanding: Theology in the University," in *Essentials of Christian Community: Essays for Daniel W. Hardy*, ed. David F. Ford and Dennis L. Stamps (Edinburgh: T&T Clark, 1996), 277.

23. Following Darrin W. Snyder Belousek, "Both terms bear positive connotation—'traditional/traditionalist' connotes holding fast to a valued heritage, 'innovational/innovationist' connotes advocating change toward a desired goal—and each term, albeit imperfectly, reflects how various proponents of each view have presented themselves" (*Marriage, Scripture, and the Church: Theological Discernment on the Question of Same-Sex Union* [Grand Rapids: Baker Academic, 2021], xiv). See further, Susannah Cornwall, "The Future of Sexuality Debates in the Church: Shared Challenges and Opportunities for Theological 'Traditionalists' and 'Revisionists,'" *ModB* 62 (2021): 10–23. Oliver O'Donovan reminds us that good tradition innovates and good innovation learns from tradition (*Church in Crisis: The Gay Controversy and the Anglican Communion* [Eugene, OR: Cascade, 2008], 108).

24. Dennis P. Hollinger, *The Meaning of Sex: Christian Ethics and the Moral Life* (Grand Rapids: Baker Academic, 2009), 77.

25. Gregg R. Allison, *Embodied: Living as Whole People in a Fractured World* (Grand Rapids: Baker, 2021), 44.

26. Hollinger, *Meaning of Sex*, 77.

27. Ibid., 90.

28. Ibid., 83, 84. The language of "anomaly" is also used by the Council on Biblical Manhood and Womanhood, *Nashville Statement: A Coalition for Biblical Sexuality*, 2017, Article 5. Cited November 3, 2020. https://cbmw.org/nashville-statement.

29. Oliver O'Donovan, *Transsexualism: Issues and Argument* (Cambridge: Grove, 2007), 7. O'Donovan and Hollinger often appear in innovationist literature as representative bulwarks of the traditional interpretation.

what kind of human is an intersex person?"[30] On the logic of SD, "Intersex persons cannot have a proper relationship with God or other people, as they cannot properly exist bodily as male or female."[31] SD relegates intersex to the sub-human, less in the image of God, more fallen, and even disqualified from baptism.[32] SD turns intersex *people* into *patients*—mere "pathological objects" until their "true sex" is surgically inscribed.[33] Such pressure to conform can suffocate intersex persons into silence, secrecy, stigma, shame, and even suicide.[34] The fetishized "golden calf" of SD "must be exposed" and exterminated,[35] for it is a "White European" ontology that "perpetuate[s] a hierarchical account of power that is part of what has led to human exploitation of other animals and White exploitation of Black people."[36] Elevating intersex embodiment in theological discourse disrupts "the entire taxonomy" of "male-and-female."[37]

Constructively, revisionists read nontheological and theological sources as opening space for SP and so for the full inclusion of intersex *as* intersex.[38] For example, innovationists interpret nontheological sources to argue that SD is scientifically unjustifiable. Evolutionary biology paints a rainbow of sexed diversity.[39] Second, SD is construed as historically novel. The ancient view of

---

30. Joseph A. Marchal, *Appalling Bodies: Queer Figures Before and After Paul's Letters* (New York: Oxford University Press, 2020), 69.

31. John Hare, "'Neither Male nor Female': The Case of Intersexuality," in *An Acceptable Sacrifice? Homosexuality and the Church*, ed. Duncan Dormor and Jeremy Morris (London: SPCK, 2007), 106.

32. Sally Gross recounts her experience in "Intersexuality and Scripture," *ThS* 11 (1999): 70.

33. J. David Hester, "Intersex(es) and Informed Consent: How Physicians' Rhetoric Constrains Choice," *TMB* 25 (2004): 37.

34. Sharon E. Preves, *Intersex and Identity: The Contested Self* (New Brunswick, NJ: Rutgers University Press, 2003).

35. Cornwall, *Sex and Uncertainty*, 23.

36. Susannah Cornwall, *Constructive Theology and Gender Variance: Transformative Creatures*, CIT (Cambridge: Cambridge University Press, 2023), 283.

37. Susannah Cornwall, "The Kenosis of Unambiguous Sex in the Body of Christ: Intersex, Theology and Existing 'for the Other,'" *ThS* 14 (2008): 193.

38. The distinction between nontheological and theological sources corresponds to the difference between "natural" and "super-natural" revelation. I say "natural" rather than "general" revelation to focus on the manner of God's revelation as opposed to the extent of its availability. See Steven J. Duby, *God in Himself: Scripture, Metaphysics, and the Task of Christian Theology*, SCDS (Downers Grove, IL: IVP Academic, 2019), 59 n.1. As I develop in Chapter 4, the book of nature is best read *through* the book of scripture.

39. Joan Roughgarden, *Evolution's Rainbow: Diversity, Gender, and Sexuality in Nature and People*, 2nd ed. (Berkeley: University of California Press, 2004).

the sexed body was monolithically one-sex.[40] All were male to a greater or lesser degree. Reading bodies as "two separate sexes was shockingly new in the modern period."[41] Thus, a "properly conservative mentality" should appropriate one-sex thinking.[42] Finally, SD is dismissed as culturally passé. Just as Western culture now reads self-expression, sexual orientation, and gender identity as a spectrum, so too with the sexed body.[43]

Theological sources also encourage interpreting intersex as disrupting SD in favor of SP. The doctrine of creation exults in an astonishingly diverse world, suggesting that "human biological sex (like that found in many other species) might best be thought of as polymorphic (even fluid), rather than rigidly dimorphic."[44] If we "condemn or attempt to eradicate these naturally occurring variations, we are working counter to the will of God for creation, which God has declared to be good."[45] Intersex bodies exhibit creational diversity rather than postlapsarian disorder. With a nod toward theology proper, such "difference in creation is always more than binary, . . . because it echoes the Trinitarian difference which is always at least tri-directional."[46]

The case for SD not only falsely privileges (and misreads) the "order of creation" but it undervalues the import of eschatologically redemptive newness in Christ.[47] Considering his work, Jesus "provided an important supplement to the binary model of human sex and gender" (by privileging the literal eunuch in

---

40. Thomas Laqueur, *Making Sex: Body and Gender from the Greeks to Freud* (Cambridge, MA: Harvard University Press, 1990).

41. Adrian Thatcher, *Gender and Christian Ethics*, NSCE 39 (Cambridge: Cambridge University Press, 2021), 27.

42. Adrian Thatcher, *Redeeming Gender* (Oxford: Oxford University Press, 2016), 104.

43. For an example of such logic being assumed, see Petersen, *Guide to Intersex*, 27. The influence of Michel Foucault and Judith Butler on contemporary attitudes cannot be overstated. See especially Michel Foucault, *The History of Sexuality*, 3 vols (New York: Vintage, 1980); Judith Butler, *Gender Trouble: Feminism and the Subversion of Identity* (New York: Routledge, 1990). For one suggested provenance of such attitudes, see Carl R. Trueman, *The Rise and Triumph of the Modern Self: Cultural Amnesia, Expressive Individualism, and the Road to Sexual Revolution* (Wheaton, IL: Crossway, 2020).

44. Patricia Beattie Jung, "Intersex on Earth as It Is in Heaven," in *Intersex, Theology, and the Bible: Troubling Bodies in Church, Text, and Society*, ed. Susannah Cornwall (New York: Palgrave Macmillan, 2015), 177.

45. Justin Sabia-Tanis, "Holy Creation, Wholly Creative: God's Intention for Gender Diversity," in *Understanding Transgender Identities: Four Views*, ed. James K. Beilby and Paul Rhodes Eddy (Grand Rapids: Baker Academic, 2019), 201, 204.

46. Susannah Cornwall, *Un/Familiar Theology: Reconceiving Sex, Reproduction, and Generativity*, RTCAHD 1 (London: Bloomsbury, 2017), 90.

47. Duncan Dormor, "Intersex in the Christian Tradition: Personhood and Embodiment," in *The Legal Status of Intersex Persons*, ed. Jens M. Scherpe, Anatol Dutta, and Tobias Helms (Cambridge: Intersentia, 2018), 119.

Matt. 19:12).[48] Concerning his person, a parthenogenetic virgin birth implies an intersex Christ—phenotypically male yet genotypically female.[49] Further, Christ, the true human, inaugurates a new human "continuum" that "accommodates everyone who does not straightforwardly identify with either of the sexual binaries," including "'third sex' people."[50] Methodologically, eschatology trumps creation.[51] The church prefigures the eschatological justice of "intersex on earth as it is in heaven."[52]

The "brute physical phenomenon" of intersexuality "challenges cherished assumptions about sex . . . within Western society."[53] Yet traditionalists' and innovationists' interpretations of the intersex challenge remain diametrically opposed. At its core, the dispute pits SD against SP. The traditionalist insists upon SD, relegating intersex to a post-fall disorder. The innovationist sees intersexuality as indisputable evidence for SP. Intersex is a SP bomb falling on the SD playground. Caught in-between are real people who feel "unknown, unwelcomed, unwanted" by Christian communities.[54]

As the fuse flickers, attention is imperative. Not only for the sake of those suffering collateral damage but also because tendrils from the innovational case reach multiple doctrinal *loci*, suggesting minimally their reconsideration and maximally their potential reconfiguration. For example, concerning the doctrines of creation and fall, to what extent does intersexuality participate in creational diversity or postlapsarian disorder? What counts as "natural"? How do we know? The doctrine of God: If God made humans in his image, and God is Trinity, is SP a better reflection of God's triune nature? Christology: Does the virgin birth imply an intersex Christ? Theological anthropology: What is the dogmatic function of human nature from creation to consummation? Hermeneutics: How does redemption relate to creation? Does eschatology trump creation? Ecclesial ethics: If intersex intimates SP, what are the repercussions for sexual ethics, particularly marriage and singleness? In short, intersex interpretation shoots tendrils into core Christian doctrines, provoking minimally their reassessment and maximally their reworking. The theological exploration of intersexuality is not some esoteric *adiaphoron*. Interpreting intersex embodiment can inform how we piece together the Christian mosaic so as to display a clear, coherent, and compelling picture of Christ.

---

48. DeFranza, *Sex Difference*, 106.

49. Virginia R. Mollenkott, *Omnigender: A Trans-Religious Approach*, rev. and exp. (Cleveland, OH: Pilgrim, 2007), 116.

50. Thatcher, *Redeeming Gender*, 141, 169.

51. Thatcher, *Gender and Christian Ethics*, 112.

52. Jung, "Intersex on Earth," 173.

53. Gross, "Intersexuality," 67.

54. Val Hiebert and Dennis Hiebert, "Intersex Persons and the Church: Unknown, Unwelcomed, Unwanted Neighbors," *JSIRS* 5 (2015): 31–44.

IV. Contribution

There currently exists no evangelical response to the best innovationist arguments that interpret intersex embodiment along sexually polymorphic lines.[55] I propose to fill this academic *lacuna* by developing a constructive theological account of intersexuality, in conversation with the best innovationist arguments for SP. I do not advance an account of the sexed body more generally,[56] nor do I look to mount a defense of SD per se, whether biblically,[57] theologically,[58] metaphysically,[59] or historically.[60] My concern is for the correct theological interpretation of intersexuality,[61] an exploration contoured by revisionist biblical-doctrinal proposals.[62] I do not offer a worked-out theological ethic of intersexuality. I merely develop a dogmatic account of intersexuality to help Christians interpret intersex embodiment *theologically*.

55. I use "evangelical" in its theological sense (as defined here), rather than referring to a sociocultural segment of the church. Jennifer Anne Cox offers a recent "evangelical" theology of intersexuality, considering intersex "through the lens of Christ" (*Intersex in Christ: Ambiguous Biology and the Gospel* [Eugene, OR: Cascade, 2018], 2). However, Cox does not engage the best arguments proposed by innovationists (the one-sex theory, objections to the fall, whether Jesus is intersex, different ways of formulating the relationship between redemption and creation, what constitutes numerical identity in the eschaton, etc.), nor does she read intersexuality as challenging SD. Cox's concern is to demonstrate how "intersex fits with the gospel of Christ" (ibid., 6). For a similar assessment of Cox, see Mary Elizabeth Zagrobelny Lofgren, "John Paul II's Theological Anthropology and the Intersexual Body" (PhD diss., The Catholic University of America, 2020), 77–9.

56. E.g., Nancy Pearcey, *Love Thy Body: Answering Hard Questions about Life and Sexuality* (Grand Rapids: Baker, 2018).

57. E.g., Richard M. Davidson, *Flame of Yahweh: Sexuality in the Old Testament* (Peabody, MA: Hendrickson, 2007).

58. E.g., Belousek, *Marriage.*

59. E.g., Alexander D. Hostoffer, "A Theory for the Metaphysical Foundation of the Complementarity of the Sexes" (PhD, Washington, DC: The Catholic University of America, 2020).

60. E.g., Christopher C. Roberts, *Creation and Covenant: The Significance of Sexual Difference in and for the Moral Theology of Marriage* (New York: T&T Clark, 2007); Prudence Allen, *The Concept of Woman*, 3 vols (Grand Rapids: Eerdmans, 1997–2016).

61. Of course, my conclusions regarding intersexuality will inform any deeper engagement with SD.

62. Investigating revisionist proposals limits opportunities to explore hypothetical arguments.

V. A Thick Theological Method

Stating with clarity what it means to think, speak, and in our case, read the sexed body *theologically* remains a difficult task.[63] In an exercise of meta-dogmatics, Sameer Yadav maintains that the minimum condition of Christian dogmatics is an "ontological commitment to a narrative" of creation and redemption.[64] Innovationist and traditionalist interpretations of intersexuality may disagree about the right "truthmaker," sources, tools, and shape of the Christian narrative, but all qualify as theological accounts because they all share an "ontological commitment" to the basic Christian story of creation and redemption.[65] This book will likewise be shaped by the narrative of creation and redemption.

Yadav then proposes a distinction between theological engagement "*simpliciter*" (i.e., committing to the creation and redemption narrative) and theology practiced "*properly*" (i.e., done well rather than badly).[66] Extending Yadav's distinction, if a commitment to the story of creation and redemption qualifies as a *thin* theological approach, this book expounds a *thick* theological method, shaped by three criteria: (i) God is the narrative's truthmaker; (ii) the narrative is coherent because God is coherent; (iii) reading the narrative as drama clarifies the narrative's coherence.[67]

First, as champagne is rightly called champagne because its source is *le terroir de Champagne*, so too are some theological interpretations theologically thick because their source (and end) is theology proper. Theological reading is practiced well when the "truthmaker" that grounds one's "ontological commitment" to the

---

63. John Webster, *Confessing God: Essays in Christian Dogmatics II* (London: T&T Clark, 2005), 22.

64. Sameer Yadav, "Christian Doctrine as Ontological Commitment to a Narrative," in *The Task of Dogmatics: Explorations in Theological Method*, ed. Oliver Crisp and Fred Sanders, LATC (Grand Rapids: Zondervan, 2017), 76.

65. By "ontological commitment" Yadav refers to the conviction that there is "something (or some things)" that grounds the narrative as "true" (ibid., 79). Here Yadav appropriates Bradley Rettler's thesis that "when one affirms a sentence, one is ontologically committed to there being something (or some things) that makes (or make) true the proposition expressed by the sentence" ("The General Truthmaker View of Ontological Commitment," *PhilS* 173 [2016]: 1405). Different theological readings may commit to diverse "truthmakers" for the truthfulness of the Christian narrative (e.g., feelings of dependence or existential orientations), but all *Christian* theology commits to the narrative of creation and redemption.

66. Yadav, "Christian Doctrine," 74, italics original.

67. These three criteria distinguish my use of "thick" from more cultural-anthropological definitions. E.g., Clifford Geertz, *The Interpretation of Cultures: Selected Essays* (New York: Basic, 1973), adapted literarily by Kevin J. Vanhoozer, *Is There a Meaning in This Text? The Bible, the Reader, and the Morality of Literary Knowledge* (Grand Rapids: Zondervan, 1998), 282.

Christian narrative as "true" is exclusively the triune God. Only God exegetes God (John 1:18). "God and God's actions," John Webster asserts, are the North Star for "theological theology."[68] God remains his own best witness.[69] A thick theological method lets *theos* dictate theology.[70]

Second, God as "first theology" provides clarity and coherence for the Christian narrative to which all theological reading is ontologically committed.[71] As trinitarian missions *ad extra* reflect inner-trinitarian processions *ad intra*, so there is an ordered structure and coherence to triune action in the world, what Webster calls the "divine economy" (cf. Eph. 1:10; 3:2).[72] This divine economy refers to the "comprehensive scope of God's dealing with creation and humanity—as creator, as savior, and as the one who will bring his purposes to perfection. The panorama of what the triune God does is the execution of God's being."[73] The ordered coherence of "God and God's actions" is displayed in the narrative of creation to consummation. Thus, whereas a thin theological reading minimally refers to the Christian narrative, perhaps pitting one dispensation against another (e.g., eschatology trumping creation), a thick theological reading takes the narrative of creation to consummation as a divinely ordered and coherent whole.

Third, reading the Christian narrative as *drama* clarifies such coherence.[74] Following Kevin Vanhoozer, the gospel of *Deus dixit* is "'theo-dramatic'—a series of divine entrances and exits, especially as these pertain to what God has done in Jesus Christ."[75] The theatrical metaphor focuses attention on God the protagonist and his actions, inviting the church (and watching world) to participate and perform "in the round."[76] The gospel drama of creation to consummation

---

68. Webster, *Confessing God*, 25.

69. Hilary of Poitiers, *De trinitate*, ed. Pieter Smulders, CCSL 62 (Turnholti: Brepols, 1979), 1.18.

70. For a similar approach informing a theology of gender, see Fellipe do Vale, "Gender as Love: A Theological Account" (PhD, Southern Methodist University, 2021).

71. Kevin J. Vanhoozer, *First Theology: God, Scripture & Hermeneutics* (Downers Grove, IL: IVP, 2002).

72. John Webster, *The Domain of the Word: Scripture and Theological Reason*, TTCT (London: T&T Clark, 2012), 117.

73. John Webster, *Holiness* (Grand Rapids: Eerdmans, 2003), 40.

74. For the notion of drama as a lens for reading the biblical narrative, see Hans Urs von Balthasar, *Theo-Drama: Theological Dramatic Theory*, 5 vols (San Francisco: Ignatius, 1988). Balthasar's *Theodramatik* has been developed by numerous scholars. Most systematically (and perhaps significantly) among evangelicals may be Kevin Vanhoozer. See further Daniel J. Treier and Douglas A. Sweeney, eds., *Hearing and Doing the Word: The Drama of Evangelical Hermeneutics in Honor of Kevin J. Vanhoozer* (London: T&T Clark, 2021).

75. Kevin J. Vanhoozer, *The Drama of Doctrine: A Canonical-Linguistic Approach to Christian Theology* (Louisville, KY: Westminster John Knox, 2005), 31.

76. Ibid., 28 n. 81.

"provides the overarching plot out of which humankind as a whole is defined."[77] A thick interpretation of intersex embodiment will thus require careful attention to each theo-dramatic act within the whole drama: creation, fall, redemption, and consummation.[78] Beth Felker Jones summarizes well the need for such consideration:

> No statement . . . on the body can ever be taken at face value without first understanding the place of that statement in God's work of salvation. Are we speaking of the body of Adam, good but able to sin? Are we speaking of the fallen body, plagued by the mutability which will bring it death? Are we speaking of the risen body, blessedly unable to do other than reflect the glory of God?[79]

To interpret intersexuality rightly, Jones's searching questions suggest a need (i) to consider the body's particular theo-dramatic location, (ii) to grasp the whole story, and (iii) to appreciate how God directs and transforms bodies along the way. Accordingly, I explore each theo-dramatic act to assess how different scenes depict the sexed body and God's involvement in directing the drama forward. The aim (and benefit) of stopping at each narrative "emplotment" is to explicate what is metaphysically essential or natural for the sexed body and what might be accidental or historically particular at *that* theo-dramatic act. In theatrical timbre, I foreground the narrative story to illuminate its metaphysical staging. Indeed, we need the complete divine drama in view to avoid mistaking the accidental for the essential (and vice versa).

Therefore, while I follow the theologically minimal condition of focusing on the Christian story, my thick theological approach reads the story by (i) privileging God and his actions, (ii) expecting narrative coherence, and (iii) appreciating its dramatic character. Procedurally, I track and trace the sexed body through the divine drama of creation to consummation to illumine the theological meaning and significance of intersex bodies. When the sexed body is "*narratively-indexed*

---

77. John Webster, "The Human Person," in *The Cambridge Companion to Postmodern Theology*, ed. Kevin J. Vanhoozer, CCR (Cambridge: Cambridge University Press, 2003), 224.

78. I explore these theo-dramatic acts because they serve as both a familiar heuristic and represent integral "emplotments" in the Christian narrative. For the concept of "emplotment" and its value for adjudicating what is essential and what is incidental for the fundamental coherence of the plot, see Paul Ricœur, *Time and Narrative*, trans. Kathleen McLaughlin and David Pellauer (Chicago: University of Chicago Press, 1984), 1:31–51. Of course, divine economic action is not limited to these narrative moments. As this project unfolds, "theo-dramatic" and "divine drama" terminology refer to the macro-narrative arc of creation to consummation. "Redemptive-history" denotes the inner-narrative arc of fall to redemption.

79. Beth Felker Jones, *Marks of His Wounds: Gender Politics and Bodily Resurrection* (Oxford: Oxford University Press, 2007), 36.

to the great story of what God is doing in Christ,"[80] we may discern whether certain sexed properties are universal to the "structure" of human nature or particular to its "direction" within a specific theo-dramatic act/dispensation.[81]

VI. Sources

The theo-dramatic arc of creation to consummation dictates the formal shape of this study. I explicate the material content of each theo-dramatic act by engaging nontheological and theological sources.

A. Nontheological

Many contemporary theologies of intersexuality draw deeply from nontheological sources, particularly the biological sciences,[82] cultural-historical studies,[83] ethnographic research,[84] and the lived experiences of intersex persons.[85] I, likewise, leverage nontheological sources where appropriate for two reasons.[86] First, they offer valuable insights into the current complexity of human life. For example, which sex characteristics should determine biological sex? Should we elevate genetics above gonads and genitalia?[87] If so, why? Second, nontheological

---

80. Fellipe Do Vale, "Cappadocian or Augustinian? Adjudicating Debates on Gender in the Resurrection," *IJST* 21 (2019): 193, italics original.

81. When this study uses "structure" terminology, it refers to what is metaphysically essential or natural for human nature. Language of "direction" pertains to what is commonly particular for human nature at certain historical dispensations. I appropriate insights from Oliver O'Donovan, among others, to develop the distinction and dynamic between the natural and the historical.

82. E.g., John Hare, "Hermaphrodites, Eunuchs, and Intersex People: The Witness of Medical Science in Biblical Times and Today," in *Intersex, Theology, and the Bible: Troubling Bodies in Church, Text, and Society*, ed. Susannah Cornwall (New York: Palgrave Macmillan, 2015), 79–96.

83. E.g., Thatcher, *Redeeming Gender*.

84. E.g., Stephanie A. Budwey, *Religion and Intersex: Perspectives from Science, Law, Culture, and Theology*, RNCTRTBS (Abingdon: Routledge, 2022).

85. E.g., Susannah Cornwall, "Laws 'Needefull in Later to Be Abrogated': Intersex and the Sources of Christian Theology," in *Intersex, Theology, and the Bible: Troubling Bodies in Church, Text, and Society*, ed. Susannah Cornwall (New York: Palgrave Macmillan, 2015), 147–71. Other nontheological sources utilized in theologies of intersexuality include psychology, history, legal studies, sociology, and philosophy.

86. Enlisting nontheological sources is also legitimate via an account of God's sovereignty and common grace (developed in Chapter 4).

87. Such as Denny Burk, "Asking the Right Questions about Intersex Athletes: Part 1." *CBMW* (August 22, 2016). Cited November 19, 2020. https://cbmw.org/2016/08/22/asking -the-right-questions-about-intersex-athletes-part-1/.

sources offer perceptive critiques of common assumptions regarding "natural" sexed embodiment. For instance, the one-sex theory advances a cultural-historical counter-narrative to the common claim that the ancient view of the sexed body was monolithically two-sex. If the one-sex thesis obtains, then an appeal to tradition ironically subverts the case for sexual dimorphism.

However, nontheological sources in themselves are insufficient for a thick theological reading of intersexuality. Not only is the triune God and his economy our "first theology," but our fallen thinking is "futile" (Rom. 1:21; Eph. 4:17) such that we often seek "to know created realities without reference to their creator."[88] Biological sciences, cultural-history, and personal experience may grasp by gracious natural revelation *some* aspect of given reality. But as Bonhoeffer underscores, "All things appear as in a distorted mirror if they are not seen and recognized in God."[89] Indeed, God has acted definitively in the life-death-resurrection-ascension of Christ. "Now he commands all people everywhere to repent, for he has established a day in which he intends to judge the world in righteousness by a man whom he has appointed" (Acts 17:30–31).[90] Given the absolute sovereignty of God (demonstrated supremely in the lordship of Christ), a theology of intersexuality must privilege theological sources.

B. *Theological*

A thick theological reading of intersexuality concerns itself principally with God and his actions. *Deus dixit.* The inherently self-communicative God has spoken *ad extra*, supremely in his Son (Heb. 1:2). *Deus dicet.* God continues to speak today (Heb. 3:7). God in his sovereign grace has set apart his divine discourse of scripture as "the medium of triune communicative activity and thus an extension of God's own personal communicative presence."[91] The "textual ontology" of scripture is *holy* because it is the divinely appointed means by which the perfect God is present with his people.[92] God speaks authoritatively through scripture as his appointed witness to the divine drama of creation to consummation.

Not only has God spoken, but he has spoken coherently. Inner-divine coherence demands coherence in the divine economy, which invites a hermeneutic of trust in

---

88. John Webster, *God Without Measure: Working Papers in Christian Theology: God and the Works of God*, TTCT (London: Bloomsbury, 2016), 1:222. Webster labels this endeavor as "curiosity."

89. Dietrich Bonhoeffer, *Ethics*, ed. Clifford J. Green, trans. Reinhard Krauss, Charles C. West, and Douglas W. Stott, DBW 6 (Minneapolis: Fortress, 2005), 48.

90. All Bible translations are my own unless otherwise indicated.

91. Kevin J. Vanhoozer, "Holy Scripture," in *Christian Dogmatics: Reformed Theology for the Church Catholic*, ed. Michael Allen and Scott R. Swain (Grand Rapids: Baker Academic, 2016), 47.

92. Darren Sarisky, "The Ontology of Scripture and the Ethics of Interpretation in the Theology of John Webster," *IJST* 21 (2019): 59. See, e.g., Webster, *Holiness*, 17.

the truthfulness and coherent nature of scripture's testimony to the divine drama of creation to consummation.[93] The divine drama summons ecclesial participation and worship in God's "economy of light" (cf. Ps. 36:9).[94] *Deus dixit et dicet* is a truly "evangelical" conviction.[95] It gives theology confidence to proceed humbly with scripture as its *norma normans*. My theological task is thus primarily exegetical— the "close and delighted reading of Holy Scripture as the *viva vox Dei*, the voice of the risen Jesus to his community."[96] I follow scripture as my primary source via the guidance of three criteria: Scripture's (i) plain sense, (ii) canonicity, and (iii) catholicity.

First, while all theological approaches are in some measure "biblicistic," thick theological exegesis aims to explicate the "plain sense" of scripture. This means prayerfully discerning the way the words run in individual texts, and then relating those passages "to the church's understanding of how the two-Testament canon of scripture is to be heard, interbiblically, according to the rule of faith."[97] Admittedly, Adrian Thatcher lambastes applying "the surface meaning of biblical texts to contemporary sexual problems [as] both naïve and dangerous."[98] However, Thatcher's barb neglects how divine ontology (God's perfect goodness, truthfulness, knowledge, etc.) undergirds our assurance in the perspicuous truthfulness and unity of scripture. We can have confidence in the clarity and applicability of scripture's "plain sense" because God sanctifies and inspires the text and illumines

93. Emphasizing a coherent theological logic to scripture need not suffer David H. Kelsey's criticism that such a "canon-unifying narrative" unavoidably simplifies or subsumes biblical diversity into its monolithic vision (*Eccentric Existence: A Theological Anthropology* [Louisville, KY: Westminster John Knox, 2009], 1:468; idem, *Human Anguish and God's Power*, CIT [Cambridge: Cambridge University Press, 2021], xi). Kelsey's caveat notwithstanding, Marc Cortez helpfully demonstrates how "Scripture itself begins to move toward integrating these various narratives [Kelsey's triple helix of creation, reconciliation, and consummation] through their emphasis on the one who is both Creator and Redeemer" (e.g., Col. 1:15–20) ("Election and Creation," in *The T&T Clark Handbook to Election*, ed. Edwin Chr. van Driel, TTCH [New York: Bloomsbury, forthcoming]).

94. Kevin J. Vanhoozer and Daniel J. Treier, *Theology and the Mirror of Scripture: A Mere Evangelical Account*, SCDS (Downers Grove, IL: IVP Academic, 2016), 85–90.

95. Vanhoozer, *Drama of Doctrine*, 26.

96. John Webster, *The Culture of Theology*, ed. Ivor J. Davidson and Alden C. McCray (Grand Rapids: Baker Academic, 2019), 64. Webster goes on to develop the necessary "anthropology of the reader" in her ecclesial context (ibid., 73). Similarly, see Oliver O'Donovan, *The Desire of the Nations: Rediscovering the Roots of Political Theology* (Cambridge: Cambridge University Press, 1996), 15–16.

97. Christopher Seitz, "Sexuality and Scripture's Plain Sense: The Christian Community and the Law of God," in *Homosexuality, Science, and the "Plain Sense" of Scripture*, ed. David L. Balch (Grand Rapids: Eerdmans, 2000), 177.

98. Adrian Thatcher, *Liberating Sex: A Christian Sexual Theology* (London: SPCK, 1993), 21.

the reader (cf. John 16:13).[99] Thus, following the "plain sense" requires sapiential sensitivity to scripture's "canonical sense," inflected with a "catholic sensibility."[100]

Appreciating "canon" as both *list* and *rule* clarifies the inherent unity and authority of the scriptures as the "*unus sermo dei.*"[101] Given the coherence of the divine drama, each scriptural unit must be situated and interpreted within its canonical location to discern divine authorial intent. As such, "canonical sense" liberates our hermeneutic from incommensurable fragmentation by enabling us to discern canonical coherence when biblical authors may employ different concepts to communicate similar judgments. In short, scripture interprets scripture.[102] This will be especially significant as I seek to chart and elucidate what is essential or accidental for the sexed body as it moves through the divine drama.

Finally, "catholic sensibility" acknowledges that one's theological reading is neither exhaustive nor neutral. At present, we are positively bound by place, time, culture, finitude, and negatively, by fallenness. Since the same Spirit anoints and teaches his church (1 John 2:18–29), we may learn from the church catholic, as the "seedbed of theology,"[103] how to receive and transmit the faith today (1 Cor. 15:3). Indeed, wisdom acknowledges that the "strangeness of the past" has much to teach us about the present,[104] a past that was well aware of sexed atypicality.[105] Accordingly, as I exegete the theo-dramatic acts recorded in the canon, I retrieve ancient, living voices extended in space and time (Luke 20:38).

Two recurring voices are Augustine and Thomas Aquinas (among others). One should not assume that their selection loads the deck in the traditionalist's favor. In innovationist literature, Augustine is the historical figure appealed to most

---

99. John Webster, *Holy Scripture: A Dogmatic Sketch*, CIT (Cambridge: Cambridge University Press, 2003), 10, 91.

100. Vanhoozer and Treier, *Mirror of Scripture*, 42. See further, Vanhoozer, *Drama of Doctrine*, 115–237.

101. Augustine, *In Psalmum CIII* 4.1, in *Enarrationes in Psalmos 101–109*, ed. Franco Gori and Adiuvante Claudio Pierantoni, CSEL 95/1 (Wien: OAW, 2011), 185. For one delimitation of the biblical canon and its sufficiency for salvation, see Article VI, in W. H. Griffith Thomas, *Principles of Theology: An Introduction to the Thirty-Nine Articles*, 4th ed. (London: Church Book Room, 1951), 103–33.

102. Article XX, in Thomas, *Principles of Theology*, 281–90.

103. Michael Allen and Scott R. Swain, *Reformed Catholicity: The Promise of Retrieval for Theology and Biblical Interpretation* (Grand Rapids: Baker Academic, 2015), 18. Our pneumatology and ecclesiology shape our historiography.

104. Rowan Williams, *Why Study the Past? The Quest for the Historical Church* (Grand Rapids: Eerdmans, 2005), 24.

105. E.g., Luc Brisson, *Le sexe incertain: Androgynie et hermaphrodisme dans l'Antiquité gréco-romaine*, 2e éd., VdM (Paris: Belles Lettres, 2008); Ilona Zsolnay, ed., *Being a Man: Negotiating Ancient Constructs of Masculinity*, SHANE (London: Routledge, 2017).

frequently,[106] with Aquinas given a significant supporting role.[107] Their choice may seem surprising, but their deep concern for the goodness and specificity of concrete embodiment captures a constant concern among innovationists.[108] Given the stated aim of developing a dogmatic account of intersexuality *in conversation with the best innovationist arguments*, analyzing revisionist appeals to Augustine and Aquinas seems most fitting. Here, I merely follow the innovationist lead.

More positively, my aim is to "think *with*" ancient voices "for the sake of mapping out a particular theological domain" that will "shed light" on current interpretations of intersexuality.[109] At times, "*thinking with*" will involve thinking "*beyond*" my historical sources, particularly where their insights need to be reapplied to a new context with new questions.[110] Thus, my retrieval theology is not limited to *de dicto* specifications *qua* historical theology, but looks to extend *de re* the conceptual content of ancient figures,[111] particularly where they illumine scripture.[112] Again, this is because "the primary theological task . . . is exegesis."[113] Any theological retrieval or attempt to explicate dogmatic coherence between various dogmatic loci serves as "handmaid[en] to the ecclesial task of exegesis."[114]

106. E.g., Cornwall, *Sex and Uncertainty*; Karen R. Keen, *Scripture, Ethics, and the Possibility of Same-Sex Relationships* (Grand Rapids: Eerdmans, 2018); Teri Merrick, "Can Augustine Welcome Intersexed Bodies into Heaven?" in *Gift and Economy: Ethics, Hospitality and the Market*, ed. Eric R. Severson (Newcastle: Cambridge Scholars, 2012).

107. E.g., Elyse J. Raby, "'You Knit Me Together in My Mother's Womb': A Theology of Creation and Divine Action in Light of Intersex," *ThS* 24 (2018): 98–109.

108. This may explain why intersex literature does not follow contemporary theologies of gender in appropriating Gregory of Nyssa, who is often lauded as a "Queer Father." See Virginia Burrus, "Queer Father: Gregory of Nyssa and the Subversion of Identity," in *Queer Theology: Rethinking the Western Body*, ed. Gerard Loughlin (Malden: Wiley-Blackwell, 2007), 147–62.

109. Darren Sarisky, "Tradition II: Thinking with Historical Text—Reflections on Theologies of Retrieval," in *Theologies of Retrieval: An Exploration and Appraisal*, ed. Darren Sarisky (London: Bloomsbury, 2017), 200, italics original. For different theologies of retrieval, see John Webster, "Theologies of Retrieval," in *The Oxford Handbook of Systematic Theology*, ed. John Webster, Kathryn Tanner, and Iain R. Torrance, OH (Oxford: Oxford University Press, 2007), 583–99.

110. Sarisky, "Tradition II," 201, italics original.

111. Robert Brandom, *Tales of the Mighty Dead: Historical Essays in the Metaphysics of Intentionality* (Cambridge, MA: Harvard University Press, 2002), 94–107.

112. The *de dicto/de re* distinction also means that my recourse for retrieving Augustine and Thomas is not a blanket endorsement of all they say (or are interpreted to say), especially regarding issues of sexuality.

113. Webster, *Holy Scripture*, 3.

114. R. Michael Allen, *The Christ's Faith: A Dogmatic Account*, TTCSST (London: T&T Clark, 2009), 3.

In sum, scripture is the primary theological source, exegeting its plain, canonical, and catholic sense the primary theological task.

VII. Overview

To recap, I aim to respond to the best biblical-doctrinal arguments for interpreting intersex along SP lines in order to construct a dogmatic account of intersexuality. By tracking and tracing the theo-dramatic movement of the sexed body from creation to consummation, I aim to elucidate what is essential and accidental for sexed embodiment. I ultimately contribute a thick theological set of glasses through which to read intersexuality,[115] salutary for academic, ecclesial, and worldly audiences.[116]

Since the proposed methodological approach prioritizes exegesis of the canonical scriptures, appreciating the "cognitive environment" of the biblical authors will prove beneficial.[117] Chapter 2 pursues this task, prompted by innovationist appeals to Thomas Laqueur's claim that the ancient view of the sexed body was monolithically one-sex. If all bodily sex exists on a single, slippery spectrum, then to read the "male and female" of Gen. 1:27 along sexually dimorphic lines smacks of an anachronistic imposition of post-Enlightenment values. Revisionists adapt Laqueur's thesis to disrupt SD and to propose a horizontally ordered, one-sex, "human continuum."[118] With the emphasis placed upon our common humanity, "*sexual* difference makes no difference."[119] In response, I scrutinize the viability of Laqueur's thesis, offering material and formal concerns that problematize its hermeneutical and theological appropriation. Nevertheless, even if the Bible's cultural-historical background was not monolithically one-sex, a one-sex "human continuum" may still be a legitimate interpretive option for explicitly exegetical and

---

115. The metaphor of reading glasses need not objectify intersex bodies, for the primary wearers of the proposed glasses are intersex persons.

116. This project whispers to a growing number of secular scholars who challenge the pervasive view that the body is malleable to self-expressive *poesis*. See e.g., Debra Soh, *The End of Gender: Debunking the Myths about Sex and Identity in Our Society* (New York: Threshold, 2020); Kathleen Stock, *Material Girls: Why Reality Matters for Feminism* (London: Little, Brown, 2021). To the disillusioned and discontent, Christian theology reenchants "reality" with its God-given mimetic coherence. We read reality rightly when we recognize *whose* it is, *what* it is, and *where* it fits within the divine drama of creation to consummation.

117. For the promise of attending closely to the "cognitive environment" of the Bible, see John H. Walton, *Ancient Near Eastern Thought and the Old Testament: Introducing the Conceptual World of the Hebrew Bible*, 2nd ed. (Grand Rapids: Baker Academic, 2018), 3–30.

118. Thatcher, *Redeeming Gender*, 169.

119. Adrian Thatcher, *Thinking About Sex* (Minneapolis: Fortress, 2015), 53, italics original.

theological reasons. Accordingly, Chapters 3–6 engage the biblical and theological material to discern the nature and nuances of the sexed body as it moves from creation to consummation.

Beginning with the theo-dramatic act of creation, Chapter 3 examines the extent to which Genesis 1–2 indicates intersex existence in creation, whether via primal androgyny or the hybrid argument.[120] Moving beyond the *event* of creation to consider its creational *intent*, I assess whether Adam and Eve should be read as parents of fecundity rather than prototypes of fixity. For DeFranza, their embodiment of the *apposite* sex sparks a trajectory of othering: "Other others are born from these parents [Adam and Eve]: other ages, other languages, other cultures, and even others whose sex does not match either parent."[121] In response, I construct a cumulative case, stressing the syntactically inseparable and mutually interpreting nature of Gen. 1:27–28, and noting further how the canonical context consistently interprets "male and female" (v.27) alongside "be fruitful and multiply" (v.28). To ascertain whether the procreative commission operates as an exclusive norm (or simply obtains for the statistical majority), I move "behind the scenes" of creation's event and intent to the metaphysical "staging," proposing a Thomistically inflected rubric of "form founds function—function fits form." The combination of biblical exegesis and theological reflection suggests that SD was likely the divine design in the event and intent of creation. SD participates in creation's divinely ordered *shalom*.

In Chapter 4, I explore the impact of the fall upon the sexed body. I develop from Genesis 3 a description of death as an all-pervasive decaying power. Death disorders the sexed body in both form and function. Such an austere account of the fall could undermine any appeal to a "natural" or "normal" sexed body. Here I argue via Augustine and Thomas that death is not a metaphysical substance but a privative evil. The structure of creation endures through the fall, such that the norm of male and female continues in theological intent, even if at times uncertain in empirical expression. Thus, the theological explanation for the existence of intersexuality from the perspectives of creation and fall remains that of impairment—disordered diversity in a diversely disordered world. Yet intersex persons are not more fallen than others. Every body is subject to "death because of sin" (Rom. 8:10). Every mortal body needs life from the Spirit of Christ (Rom. 8:11).

Chapter 5 considers redemptive life in Christ. Regarding Christ's person, I examine the possibility and significance that Jesus was intersex. Concerning Christ's work, I explore how the dogmatic locus of redemption relates to creation.

---

120. E.g., Gross, "Intersexuality"; Justin Tanis, *Trans-Gendered: Theology, Ministry, and Communities of Faith* (Cleveland, OH: Pilgrim, 2003).

121. DeFranza, *Sex Difference*, 182. The language of "othering" in this dissertation attempts to reflect DeFranza's emphasis on the good of creational diversification. "Othering" should not be confused with its pejorative usage in alternative discourses, e.g., theologies of race.

Does redemptive newness in Christ replace, expand, or restore creation? Following innovationist focus on Matt. 19:12 and Gal. 3:28, I maintain that newness in Christ refers to spiritual and social inclusion rather than sexed structural expansion or replacement. Yet the possibility of somatic transformation remains open in the eschaton.

Chapter 6 takes up the hypothesis of intersex in heaven, analyzing revisionist appeals to the normativity of Jesus' scars, conditions constituting numerical identity, and the proposal that the Trinity offers a blueprint for SP in glory. I respond from 1 Corinthians 15 that somatic transformation in the eschaton is contoured by creation. In sum, eschatological redemption restoratively transforms creation. As such, it is biblically and theologically fitting for the sexed body to be epistemically unambiguous in the consummation. Rather than decry "heavenly healing" as a form of "heavenly eugenics,"[122] Augustine offers resources for the fittingness of the "heavenly eulogization" of intersex conditions as "marks of honor" (*dignitas*) rather than "marks of deformity" (*deformitas*).[123]

I synthesize in Chapter 7 the theological argument developed in Chapters 3–6, highlighting the benefits of my theological glasses for a thick theological interpretation of intersexuality. I conclude by suggesting how one could move from fairly abstract dogmatic judgments about intersexuality to the moral-pastoral care of concrete intersex individuals, focusing on the complex challenge of connecting intersexuality with marriage. The aim is not to make comprehensive, definitive decisions, but to show how the proposed theological glasses could help navigate theological-ethical issues to cast a compelling vision of corporate holiness.

122. Candida R. Moss, *Divine Bodies: Resurrecting Perfection in the New Testament and Early Christianity* (New Haven, CT: Yale University Press, 2019), 26.

123. Augustine, *De civitate Dei* 22.19, in *De civitate Dei: Libri XI–XXII*, ed. Bernard Dombart and Alphonse Kalb, CCSL 48 (Turnhout: Brepols, 1955), 839; trans. William Babcock, under the title *City of God*, ed. Boniface Ramsey, WSA I/7 (Hyde Park, NY: New City, 2013), 530. Hereafter, *Civ.*

Chapter 2

HISTORICAL-CULTURAL BACKGROUND

THE ONE-SEX THEORY?

I. Making Sex *Appeal*

A thick theological account of intersex embodiment requires scripture as its magisterial *norma normans*. The dogmatic task of constructing a theology of intersexuality is foundationally exegetical. To aid faithful and fruitful biblical exegesis, Lawson Younger commends appreciating scripture as a collection of textual artifacts from the Ancient Near East (ANE), Ancient Semitic World (ASW), and Graeco-Roman World (GRW). As such, "It requires an effort on our part to understand the cultures that produced it."[1]

Recognizing the ministerial value of background studies, it is in vogue among some contemporary theologians advocating SP to appropriate the influential work of cultural historian Thomas Laqueur and claim that the ancient view of the sexed body was monolithically one-sex.[2] Accordingly, biblical references to "male and female" do not refer to two distinct yet complementary sexes (as traditionally conceived) but to a single-sex spectrum that allows for a multiplicity of sexed diversity. For innovationists, faithful and fruitful biblical hermeneutics and theological construction require careful attention to the Bible's one-sex cultural and historical context.

Nonetheless, while Laqueur's cultural-historical thesis has been widely accepted among revisionist scholars, the appeal to the one-sex theory to justify a complete elimination of the traditional two-sex reading of scripture remains open to investigation. What exactly is the one-sex theory, and how ubiquitous was it in the ancient world? To what extent does contemporary one-sex theological appropriation lead to more faithful and more fruitful readings of scripture? To answer such questions, I first explicate the logic of the one-sex theory, as presented

---

1. K. Lawson Younger, "The Old Testament in Its Cultural Context: Implications of 'Contextual Criticism' for Chinese and North American Christian Identity," in *After Imperialism: Christian Identity in China and the Global Evangelical Movement*, ed. Richard R. Cook and David W. Pao, SCC (Eugene, OR: Pickwick, 2011), 74.

2. See below for examples.

principally by Laqueur. Second, I chart how Laqueur's thesis has been appropriated for biblical hermeneutics and theological construction. Third, I query the universality of the one-sex view in the ancient world, incorporating critiques from scholars of comparative studies, ancient medicine, and classicists. I conclude that since the ancient view of the sexed body was not as monolithically one-sex as some innovationists claim, one-sex readings of scripture based on its putative historical and cultural background are unwarranted. However, even if the cultural context complicates one-sex hermeneutics, a continuum view of sexed bodies could remain a viable interpretive option if exegetical and theological reasons internal to scripture may be found. This conclusion necessitates a re-engagement with the biblical material, taken up in subsequent chapters.

A. Single-Sex Spectrum

In *Making Sex*, Laqueur explicates the one-sex model as an important act within the narrative of the sexed body's cultural history. For Laqueur, the premodern world understood all humans to share in a single sex "in which men and women were arrayed according to their degree of metaphysical perfection, their vital heat, along an axis whose telos was male."[3] All humanity existed on a single-sex, hierarchical continuum. Everyone was male to a greater or lesser degree, depending on one's internal heat. Laqueur draws on Hippocrates (*c.* 460–*c.* 370 BC), Aristotle (384–322 BC), Herophilus (325–255 BC), Soranus (*c.* first/second century AD), and Galen (*c.* AD 130–*c.* 210) to highlight the fungibility of bodily fluids (especially in sexual generation) and humanity's isomorphic genital anatomy. In short, a female was an inverted male: "The vagina an eternally, precariously, unborn penis, the womb a stunted scrotum."[4] Such genital homology remained commonplace "for thousands of years."[5]

The reason for female inversion is explained by the larger metaphysical context of hierarchical heat and perfection. "Now just as mankind is the most perfect of all animals," Galen opines, "so within mankind the man is more perfect than the woman, and the reason for his perfection is his excess of heat, for heat is Nature's primary instrument."[6] On Laqueur's reading, since a hierarchy of heat and perfection permeates and predominates the cosmic and cultural context, all anatomy (and any new data) should be explained through this metaphysical grid. Thus, from the ancient world right up to the Renaissance, there was a lack of exact

---

3. Laqueur, *Making Sex*, 5–6. Laqueur's premodern period runs from "classical antiquity" (seemingly starting with Hippocrates) through to "the end of the seventeenth century" (ibid., 25).

4. Ibid., 28.

5. Ibid., 4.

6. Galen, *On the Usefulness of the Parts of the Body*, trans. Margaret Tallmadge May (Ithaca, NY: Cornell University Press, 1968), 2:630, quoted in Laqueur, *Making Sex*, 28.

nomenclature for female genitalia: "The linguistic equivalent of the propensity to see the female body as a version of the male."[7]

Nevertheless, although a woman was a man manqué, she could still hope to ascend the single-sex spectrum toward male perfection. In the one-sex world, stories were regaled of women becoming men through the influence of excessive heat.[8] Yet, importantly, from Galen (second century) to Gaspard Bauhin (sixteenth century), "Men cannot be physically transformed into women" as "movement is always up the great chain of being."[9]

Interestingly, contemporary advocates for SP discern a two-way movement up and down a slippery single-sex spectrum. As Conway opines, in the ancient world a deep anxiety lingered over "the possibility of gender slippage, particularly from male to female."[10] Since one's location on the single-sex spectrum depended on gender performance rather than biological sex, even if one were legally classified as male at birth, growing up to be a man was not guaranteed. Hence the perennially haunting question for every ancient male, "If women were not different in kind, but simply a lesser, incomplete version of men, what was there to keep men from sliding down the axis into the female realm?"[11] Indeed, the specter of sex slippage was inscribed as a warning on the bodies of hermaphrodites: "Double-natured barely-men possessing a penetrating (masculine) penis and a penetrable (feminine) vagina."[12]

In summarizing Laqueur's presentation of the one-sex theory, two distinctive features are worthy of note. First, in the ancient world, "There existed many genders, but only one adaptable sex."[13] Everyone was male to a greater or lesser degree, depending on one's internal heat (the resultant complexion of one's cardinal humors). Thus, as Thatcher avers, "Earlier generations would have had no difficulty in extending the bounds of bodily normality to such people [intersex, 'third gender'], because their presence in the human world was explained by the unique combination of elements and humors."[14] Thatcher continues, "Within a

---

7. Laqueur, *Making Sex*, 96, italics original.

8. Ibid., 127.

9. Ibid.

10. Colleen M. Conway, *Behold the Man: Jesus and Greco-Roman Masculinity* (Oxford: Oxford University Press, 2008), 18.

11. Ibid.

12. Diane M. Swancutt, "Sexing the Pauline Body of Christ: Scriptural Sex in the Context of the American Christian Culture War," in *Toward a Theology of Eros: Transfiguring Passion at the Limits of Discipline*, ed. Virginia Burrus and Catherine Keller, TTC (New York: Fordham University Press, 2006), 78.

13. Laqueur, *Making Sex*, 35.

14. Adrian Thatcher, "The One Sex Theory and Why It Still Matters" (Research Seminar in the Theology and Religion Department, University of Exeter, November 2012), 6–7; accessed August 5, 2020. http://www.adrianthatcher.org/lectures.php?id=44.

one-sex, multigendered model of human bodies the presence of people with ambiguous genitals was unremarkable and indeed expected."[15]

Second, the sexed body was not the fixed foundation upon which gender characteristics were built. Rather, according to the one-sex theory of the ancient world, gender was the "primary or 'real' . . . part of the order of things."[16] Sex was simply epiphenomenal—a "sociological and not an ontological category."[17] The ancient world's "ideology" of hierarchical cosmology wrote a script for men, women, and everyone else in-between that the single-sex body acted out.[18] In nuce, gender was natural, whereas sex was performed on the cultural stage. Hence Laqueur's title, *Making Sex*. "Thus for hermaphrodites," Laqueur clarifies, "the question was not 'what sex they are really,' but to which gender the architecture of their bodies most readily lent itself."[19]

B. From One-Sex to Two-Sex

Laqueur continues that at "sometime in the eighteenth century, sex as we know it was invented. The reproductive organs went from being paradigmatic sites for displaying hierarchy, resonant throughout the cosmos, to being the foundation of incommensurable difference."[20] No longer were all humans regarded as male, arranged "along a vertical axis of infinite gradations."[21] Now humanity was organized into the ontologically distinct categories of male and female, set "along a horizontal axis whose middle ground was largely empty."[22] This effectively eliminated the atypically sexed. In the one-sex model, sex difference remained a matter of degree, not kind. Now, due to "a shrill call to articulate sharp corporeal distinctions"[23] (not via increased scientific knowledge but epistemological and political exigencies), sex difference was in kind, not degree. Women were portrayed as fundamentally different to men, "everywhere and in all things, moral and physical, not just in one set of organs."[24]

As the title *Making Sex* indicates, the transition from one-sex to two-sex denotes that sex is a fabricated artifact. "On the basis of historical evidence," whether in a one-sex or two-sex world, sex is situational: "It is explicable only within the context of battles over gender and power."[25] In short, no set of facts

---

15. Ibid., 14.
16. Laqueur, *Making Sex*, 8.
17. Ibid.
18. Ibid., 88.
19. Ibid., 135, italics original.
20. Ibid., 149.
21. Ibid., 148.
22. Ibid.
23. Ibid., 5.
24. Ibid., 149.
25. Ibid., 11.

about sex transcends history. Hence Laqueur's playful inversion of Freud's dictum: "Destiny is anatomy." Any claim that biology serves "as a sort of ontological granite for observable sexual differences" is "patently absurd."[26] The historical record demonstrates "the fundamental incoherence of stable, fixed categories of sexual dimorphism."[27] In sum, culture defines biology. In the ancient world, metaphysical, sociological, and political cultures shaped the interpretation of biological anatomy into a monolithically one-sex body.

II. One-Sex Appropriation

In 2016, Adrian Thatcher noted that "the one-sex theory was almost unknown in modern theological and sexual ethics at least until recently. . . . [Now] theologians are waking up to the insights the one-sex model can offer for an evolving understanding of sex in the history of Christianity."[28] As such, a growing number of contemporary theologians are increasingly persuaded by Laqueur's claim that the ancient view of the sexed body was monolithically one-sex. For example, Dale Martin asserts, "The ancient body . . . was a 'one-sex' body: a hierarchical spectrum or continuum along which all human bodies could be placed."[29] "Historians of medicine," avers Jane Shaw, "have convincingly shown that both [sexual difference and gender complementarity] are modern concepts."[30] For Gerard Loughlin, the "more ancient [view] thought there was really only one kind of body, of which male and female are variants, inversions of one another."[31] Indeed, Loughlin advances, "The one-sex model was operative in much ancient thought—we see something like it in the opening chapters of Genesis."[32]

Contemporary theological appropriation of Laqueur varies.[33] Yet the unifying theme pertinent here is the general consensus that Laqueur has convincingly

26. Ibid., 21, 22.

27. Ibid., 22.

28. Thatcher, *Redeeming Gender*, 12–13.

29. Dale B. Martin, *Sex and the Single Savior: Gender and Sexuality in Biblical Interpretation* (Louisville, KY: Westminster John Knox, 2006), 84.

30. Jane Shaw, "Conflicts Within the Anglican Communion," in *The Oxford Handbook of Theology, Sexuality, and Gender*, ed. Adrian Thatcher, OH (Oxford: Oxford University Press, 2015), 354.

31. Gerard Loughlin, "Gender Ideology: For a 'Third Sex' Without Reserve," *SCE* 31 (2018): 480.

32. Ibid.

33. A growing number of contemporary theologians are increasingly persuaded by Laqueur's underlying premise that culture not only shapes but defines biology. For example, see Gerard Loughlin, "Omphalos," in *Queer Theology: Rethinking the Western Body*, ed. Gerard Loughlin (Oxford: Blackwell, 2007), 117. We currently expect and read sexed bodies as dimorphic because that is what we are trained to see by our modern

demonstrated that the ancient view of the sexed body was monolithically one-sex. Thus, Thatcher concludes that "complementarity" (whether sexed or gendered) is a "conceit."[34] Conversely, a "properly conservative mentality would not dismiss the one-sex theory, but recognize it as part of the tradition."[35]

A. Biblical Hermeneutics

If the one-sex theory is correct, then as Loughlin intimates earlier, significant implications follow for how we should read biblical texts. One scholar who actively appropriates the one-sex theory for biblical hermeneutics is Adrian Thatcher. Focusing on Genesis 1–2, Thatcher offers several reasons why acknowledging the one-sex cognitive environment undermines the "traditional" assumption that this text teaches sexual dimorphism.[36] First, the one-sex theory helps us see that a sexually dimorphic reading of Genesis 1–2 wrongly assumes that a straight line exists from the world of Genesis to the twenty-first century.[37] Such a presupposition suffers the fallacy of "presentism," the "tendency to introduce present-day assumptions and ideas into analyses and interpretations of the past."[38]

Second, the one-sex theory forces us to adjust our biblical hermeneutic (and theology) in light of current research. Darwin's theory of evolution troubled pre-scientific assumptions about the duration of creation activity, causing Christians to "reclaim Genesis 1 as theological 'narrative' or 'story.'"[39] Similarly, Christians today should allow the one-sex view to queer the supposition that SD is "an essential, eternal rule, when other factual claims the narrative assumes, have long been abandoned."[40]

Third, recognizing that the cognitive environment of the ancient world was monolithically one-sex encourages us to translate and interpret Gen. 1:26–27 in light of the ten references in Genesis 1 to "kinds." "Male and female" in Gen. 1:26–27

Weltanschauung (e.g., Georgia Warnke, "Intersexuality and the Categories of Sex," *Hyp* 16 [2001]: 126–37). Moreover, Laqueur's charting of an historical shift from one-sex to two-sex has encouraged some theologians to call for a further shift toward a multiple-sex model. See Susannah Cornwall, "'State of Mind' Versus 'Concrete Set of Facts': The Contrasting of Transgender and Intersex in Church Documents on Sexuality," *ThS* 15 (2009): 8; DeFranza, *Sex Difference*, 144; Marvin Mahan Ellison, *Making Love Just: Sexual Ethics for Perplexing Times* (Minneapolis: Fortress, 2012), 20.

34. Thatcher, *Gender and Christian Ethics*, 96–118.

35. Thatcher, *Redeeming Gender*, 104.

36. Adrian Thatcher, *God, Sex, and Gender: An Introduction* (Chichester: Wiley-Blackwell, 2011), 42. Thatcher also interprets Matt. 19:1–12, Mark 10:1–12, and Heb. 11:11a as revealing one-sex thinking ("One Sex Theory," 6, 11).

37. Thatcher, *God, Sex, and Gender*, 42.

38. Thatcher, *Redeeming Gender*, 84.

39. Thatcher, *God, Sex, and Gender*, 42.

40. Ibid.

are not incommensurable opposites *qua* "malekind" and "femalekind." Rather, the text must be read as "let us make humankind" and "God created humankind in his image."[41] Just as every creature belongs to its kind, so all humans belong to humankind. The emphasis is on ontological solidarity rather than difference. God created diversity within humankind to fulfil his command to "be fruitful and multiply" (Gen. 1:28). This necessity does not valorize or prioritize sexual difference,[42] nor does it insist that every human without exception must fit within the male/female binary for the "procreative imperative" to be fulfilled.[43] The one-sex context helps us understand that the "male and female" of Gen. 1:27 should be read as a merism: "The very same thing as the one-sex continuum which moves from male to female."[44]

Moreover, Genesis 2 "massively supports the one-sex continuum."[45] Since the man is made first, he has priority over the woman. Further, "While the etymology of 'helper' need not imply inferiority (Gen. 2:18), the role does. The narrative emphasizes that the woman comes from the flesh of the man, that he recognizes her derivation: 'This at last is bone of my bones and flesh of my flesh' (Gen. 2:23)."[46] For Thatcher, modern science is backtracking fast on its past insistence on two sexes,[47] and the one-sex continuum can help theology do the same.[48]

B. Constructive Theology

While some directly adopt Laqueur's vertical one-sex spectrum to advance a more open and inclusive sexual ethic,[49] seamless appropriation introduces

41. Thatcher, *Redeeming Gender*, 175.

42. Ibid., 145.

43. Thatcher, *God, Sex, and Gender*, 42.

44. Thatcher, *Redeeming Gender*, 144, italics original. Thatcher further highlights the prevalence of the one-sex theory in church history, from Tertullian to Aquinas (ibid., 41–9), charting its legacy into the present-day Roman Catholic and Anglican churches (ibid., 84–112).

45. Thatcher, *Redeeming Gender*, 145.

46. Ibid.

47. Ibid., 176. Thatcher draws upon the work of Mary Hawkesworth, "Sex, Gender, and Sexuality: From Naturalized Presumption to Analytical Categories," in *The Oxford Handbook of Gender and Politics*, ed. Georgina Waylen et al., OH (Oxford: Oxford University Press, 2013), 31–56.

48. Thatcher, *Redeeming Gender*, 177.

49. E.g., Diane M. Swancutt argues that in Rom. 1:22–27 Paul is not condemning homosexuality *in toto*, but rather the "disease of effemination." To be passively penetrated was to slide down the slippery single-sex spectrum ("'The Disease of Effemination': The Charge of Effeminacy and the Verdict of God (Romans 1:18–2:16)," in *New Testament Masculinities*, ed. Stephen D. Moore and Janice Capel Anderson, SemeiaSt 45 [Atlanta, GA: SBL, 2003], 193–233).

significant problems.[50] Accordingly, Thatcher claims the one-sex model as the cultural context for biblical teaching on bodily sex difference and yet significantly redefines it. Thatcher constructively proposes "a refined version" of Laqueur's one-sex model that takes the ancient vertical spectrum (inherently androcentric) and flips it horizontally to envision "a common humanity with many differences, but without gender hierarchy or opposition."[51] As noted earlier, Thatcher asserts that the theological anthropology of prelapsarian Genesis 1–2 is a horizontally ordered, one-sex "human continuum."[52] While the fall might verticalize the human continuum epistemologically, resulting in the age-old performance of male dominance, the ontological ordering of the human continuum as horizontal remains metaphysically intact.[53] In redemption, where "all are one in Christ Jesus" (Gal. 3:28), the epistemological is reordered horizontally and the ontological is fulfilled, such that "within the androgynous body of Christ, sexual difference makes no difference."[54] Indeed, Thatcher suggests that a circle is a better image than a continuum, since "a circle indicates unbroken continuity," with Christ as "the centre around whom all humanity revolves."[55] "The divine image is now restored, revealed, and shared," Thatcher opines: "The essence of humankind is Christ. Christ for Christian faith is the Head of a transhistorical, transcultural body of people that relativizes all other human distinctions without eliminating them."[56]

What appears to drive Thatcher's reappropriation of the one-sex theory is not only the conviction that Laqueur's reading of the ancient world is correct, but also Thatcher's deep concern for important Christological and soteriological issues. Thatcher fears that the two-sex view asserts such an essential/ontological difference between men and women that in the incarnation we find a "malekind" Christ who necessarily excludes all non-"malekind." Following Gregory Nazianzen's dictum

---

50. For instance, the vertical nature of the one-sex model is inherently misogynistic. Women are not less perfect than men, bad enough as that is. Rather, in the one-sex theory, women *are* men. There remains only one sex—male. Thus, if the Bible's teaching is consonant with its one-sex cultural context, then it is hard to avoid the conclusion that the Bible is a misogynistic text from a misogynistic God. Even if Romans 1 does not condemn homosexual activity per se, the overall sexual ethic of the Bible would be androcentric, systemically abusive to women, the atypically sexed, and all those anxiously sliding down the slippery single-sex spectrum. Indeed, since the soteriological telos is perfect maleness, a direct one-sex appropriation would champion their ultimate obliteration.

51. Thatcher, *Redeeming Gender*, 4, 50.

52. Ibid., 169.

53. Thatcher makes no effort to explain the verticalization of the one-sex spectrum, let alone employ the dogmatic *locus* of the fall. My use of the terms "fall," "epistemological," and "ontological" are an attempt to explain (and strengthen) the logic of Thatcher's position.

54. Thatcher, *Thinking About Sex*, 53, italics original.

55. Thatcher, *Redeeming Gender*, 140.

56. Ibid., 178.

that "the unassumed is the unhealed,"[57] such a male Christ can only redeem men. This is not only bad news for women, but "intersex, third-sex, and transgender people are officially made to vanish."[58] Thus for Thatcher, the reclamation of the one-sex theory is not just about more faithful and fruitful biblical hermeneutics but has significant Christological and soteriological benefits for the church today.

III. *The Malaise of* Making Sex

Making Sex appeals to contemporary theologians advocating for SP. However, classicists and historians of ancient medicine raise serious material and formal concerns regarding Laqueur's thesis that the ancient, sexed body was monolithically one-sex. Given the focus on the historical-cultural background of the Bible, I limit my scope to critiques that pertain to the ancient world, notably (i) Laqueur's surprising omission of key sources, and (ii) his lack of care with the sources he does cite. These material critiques flow from and back into a more formal concern, namely (iii) Laqueur's ironic imposition of his own culture's sex/gender binary. These errors skew Laqueur's reading of the ancient, sexed body, particularly in terms of discerning what constitutes one's true sex, and how that relates to the telos of the sexed body. The identified inadequacies of Laqueur's project offer noteworthy caveats before any hermeneutical or theological appropriation.

A. Surprising Omissions

Laqueur argues that the one-sex body, particularly genital homology, was commonplace "for thousands of years."[59] To substantiate this claim, Laqueur limits his evidence to medical texts, and as will become clear here, a subset of even that. Certainly, medical texts provide important material for discerning ancient attitudes to the sexed body, and the sources that Laqueur highlights (Hippocrates, Aristotle, Herophilus, Galen, and Soranus) are significant in quality and quantity. Yet Laqueur's surprising omission of evidence from other genres (legal, theological, philosophical, myth, folklore, etc.) weakens his totalizing claim to reveal the one-sex body as the ancient view.[60]

---

57. Ibid., 98.

58. Ibid., 93.

59. Laqueur, *Making Sex*, 4.

60. Sally Shuttleworth notes how in *Making Sex*, "The dramatic shifts in ideas on gender and sexuality brought about by the rise of Christianity are given a mere three pages" ("Review of *Making Sex*: Body and Gender from the Greeks to Freud," *JHSe* 3 [1993]: 634). For the profound and radical difference Christianity made in the sexual economy of ancient Rome, see Kyle Harper, *From Shame to Sin: The Christian Transformation of Sexual Morality in Late Antiquity* (Cambridge, MA: Harvard University Press, 2013).

Although Laqueur repeatedly asserts the importance of hierarchical cosmology for discerning bodily sex difference, he leaves out key figures responsible for forming the very metaphysics he sees as so instructive, and how those figures related their cosmology to sex difference. One example is the eighth-century BC archaic poet Hesiod, who in his *Theogony* presents the creation of the feminine, the woman Pandora, as a radically asymmetrical "Other to the masculine norm."[61] In contrast to the one-sex theory where the woman is simply a lesser male, for Hesiod, the woman enters the world "as the bearer of difference tout court."[62] She is "a separate and alien being."[63] Indeed, "Hesiod insists not simply on sexual difference but on a form of difference that denies women a proper place in both the natural order and the human community."[64] As Loraux has mapped, Hesiod's asymmetry between the sexes was programmatic into the classical period.[65]

Moreover, in the process of privileging medical texts, Laqueur seems to assume that his medical sources were universally accessible and of particularly high currency in the ancient world. While medical texts were undoubtedly important for those privileged enough to access them, Laqueur's assumption blinds him to the worldview-shaping power of myth and folklore, as evidenced earlier in Hesiod's *Theogony*. Indeed, Lloyd has maintained that Greek scientific writings are less concerned with what we might identify as an empirical method. Rather, "Much of Greek science consists in the rationalization of popular belief. . . . [T]he literate representation of Greek folklore."[66] In short, premodern medical texts are very different in character and genre to modern medical texts. In addition, Laqueur's synchronic presentation fails to account for how over time medical texts could merge with other genres, such as myth, and so have different impacts on different audiences at different times.[67] As advanced here, perhaps Laqueur's privileging of static, medical data ironically reflects a more modern high valuation of scientific evidence. Consequently, Laqueur's limited sample offers limited insights, weakening his overall claim, and so the value of his thesis for hermeneutical and theological appropriation.

---

61. Brooke Holmes, *Gender: Antiquity and Its Legacy* (Oxford: Oxford University Press, 2012), 18.

62. Ibid., 19.

63. Froma I. Zeitlin, *Playing the Other: Gender and Society in Classical Greek Literature* (Chicago, IL: University of Chicago Press, 1996), 56.

64. Holmes, *Gender*, 21.

65. Nicole Loraux, *The Children of Athena: Athenian Ideas About Citizenship and the Division Between the Sexes* (Princeton, NJ: Princeton University Press, 1994), 72–110.

66. G. E. R. Lloyd, *Science, Folklore, and Ideology: Studies in the Life Sciences in Ancient Greece* (London: Duckworth, 1999), 202, italics original.

67. For the fluidity of genre as it relates to one-sex body evidence, see Helen King, *The One-Sex Body on Trial: The Classical and Early Modern Evidence*, HMC (London: Routledge, 2013).

B. "Patchy" Citations

A further material concern with Laqueur's project is his lack of care with the sources he cites, what Helen King, "as a historian of medicine in the ancient world,"[68] calls "very sketchy" and "patchy."[69] King levels the accusation against Laqueur that not only does he cite central figures selectively, often ignoring the literary context that might conflict with his meta-thesis,[70] but Laqueur also fails to engage with key texts from the figures he references. This is significant because, as historians of ancient medicine have recently demonstrated, the key sources omitted by Laqueur directly challenge his assertion as to the universality of the one-sex model. Since Laqueur gives significant weight to the medical texts of Galen, I assess his treatment of Galen as representative of other cited figures, which in turn reveals a deeper formal issue with Laqueur's project.

While Laqueur considers one-sex homology to be pre-Galenic, he foregrounds Galen's voice because he regards it as especially succinct, even quoting Galen in the epigraph of chapter 2: "Turn outward the woman's, turn inward, so to speak, and fold double the man's [genital organs], and you will find the same in both in every respect."[71] For Laqueur, this quote is one of many examples of Galenic genital isomorphism. However, King has exposed Laqueur's selective use of Galen, noting his failure to include the first clause of Galen's actual quote: "Consider first whichever ones you please . . . ."[72] In light of Galen's introductory invitation, King encourages readers of Galen to heed his authorial intent. From Galen's use of "consider,"[73] King suggests that Galen is setting up a "thought experiment," rather than presenting a descriptive summary of his anatomical studies.[74] While Laqueur does mention Galen offering "a step-by-step thought experiment," Laqueur presents Galen as more descriptive than speculative.[75] However, since human dissection was culturally unacceptable in Galen's world, a genuine thought experiment is the best he can offer. Indeed, classicist Brooke Holmes warns against reading Galenic homology as "identity."[76] Galen relied upon countless homologies between animals and humans to justify his medical recommendations, without suggesting that animals and humans are simply interchangeable. It thus seems strange to read Galen's use of homology as analogical when referring to humans and animals, but univocal when referring to males and females. This has led Patricia Simons to suggest that for Galen the one-sex model functioned as "an

---

68. Ibid., 8.
69. Ibid., xi, 33.
70. Ibid., 11.
71. Galen, *Usefulness of the Parts*, 2:628.
72. King, *One-Sex Body*, 35.
73. The same verb νοέω is repeated three times in the paragraph under review.
74. King, *One-Sex Body*, 35.
75. Laqueur, *Making Sex*, 25.
76. Holmes, *Gender*, 35.

introductory teaching device . . . more an aid to visualization and memorization than the summation of a complex theory of sexual oneness."[77]

Laqueur bases his confident reading of Galen on just three works: *On the Usefulness of the Parts of the Body*, *On the Natural Faculties*, and *On Seed*. Even if we excuse Laqueur's limited sample of Galenic medical texts,[78] King suggests that within these three works there is still much content that complicates Laqueur's thesis, particularly in *On Seed*, a work that Laqueur cites only once.[79] In his single reference, Laqueur reads Galen as giving further evidence of a confident genital homology, in this case the isomorphic mirroring of the scrotum and testes with the womb and ovaries.[80] However, when one reads this section of *On Seed* in context, it proves striking how Galen struggles to fit the womb and female ὄρχεις (testicles) neatly into the kind of one-sex model Laqueur reads from Galen. Instead, Galen offers another thought experiment,[81] where he concludes that there is a puzzling difference between men and women in that the female testes differ in both location and size to their male counterparts.

Moreover, classicist Rebecca Flemming pinpoints a Galenic source omitted by Laqueur that "clearly contradicts Laqueur's vision of the hegemonic, ancient one-sex model, with its privileging of role over body."[82] In his *Doctrines of Hippocrates and Plato*, Galen offers an account of men and women that recognizes both similarities and differences. Men and women are "similar" (ὅμοιαί) in that they are both "rational animals," and yet "dissimilar" (ἀνόμοιαί) in that men are stronger. Indeed, women are "opposite" (ἐναντίως) to men in that they are "female and, on account of this, adapted for childbearing," something for which their body is "prepared by [their] nature" (ἀπὸ τῆς φύσεως παρασκευασμένα). Thus, Galen concludes, "It is correct to say that in one respect women are similar to men, in another they are opposite."[83]

Furthermore, drawing upon Galen's *Commentary on Hippocrates' Aphorisms*, Holmes avers that female weakness is not just a characteristic relative to the male,

77. Patricia Simons, *The Sex of Men in Premodern Europe: A Cultural History* (Cambridge: Cambridge University Press, 2011), 147.

78. According to R. J. Hankinson, Galen wrote "a vast number of works on a wide variety of topics, ranging from medicine, through logic and philosophy, to philology and literary criticism" ("The Man and His Work," in *The Cambridge Companion to Galen*, ed. R. J. Hankinson [Cambridge: Cambridge University Press, 2008], 1).

79. Laqueur, *Making Sex*, 246 n.12.

80. Ibid., 4.

81. "If one should think . . . ." (Galen, *On Seed* II.5,44, trans. Phillip H. De Lacy, CMG V 3,1 [Berlin: Akademie, 1992], 189).

82. Rebecca Flemming, *Medicine and the Making of Roman Women: Gender, Nature, and Authority from Celsus to Galen* (Oxford: Oxford University Press, 2000), 357.

83. Galen, *On the Doctrines of Hippocrates and Plato* IX.3,25–6, trans. Phillip H. De Lacy, 2nd ed., CMG V 4,1,2 (Berlin: Akademie, 1984), 556.

but "it defines the female sex as different in nature from the male."[84] Holmes reads Galen as a "devoted teleologist, committed to the belief that every part of nature has been created for a purpose and that nature always produces the best outcome possible under the conditions of the material world."[85] As such, for Galen sex difference is both real and necessary for the world to flourish.

In summary, Laqueur seems to reference ancient sources only where they may be interpreted to support his one-sex thesis. Such "patchy" citations trouble the universality of Laqueur's argument. A closer reading of Galen's wider corpus illustrates this critique. Indeed, Laqueur appears mistaken to claim Galen as a key one-sex proponent. In truth, Galen seems to hold both one-sex and two-sex views,[86] and even his one-sex intimations are far from straightforward, his arguments and ideas resisting systematization.[87]

C. Formal Concern

A more formal complaint compounds the material critiques submitted earlier. For Laqueur, sex is cultural and gender is natural—gender being grounded in what

---

84. Holmes, *Gender*, 36.
85. Ibid.
86. King, *One-Sex Body*, 40.
87. Holmes, *Gender*, 37. Scrutiny of Laqueur's use of Hippocrates and Aristotle reveals similarly "patchy" citations. On Hippocrates, Laqueur fails to incorporate the significant work *Diseases of Women*, which argues that a woman should be treated differently to men because her body is fundamentally different, particularly at the level of the flesh. For Hippocrates, it is specifically the womb, with its unique function of menstruation (and childbearing), that means female bodies need to be interpreted, and so treated, differently to male bodies. See Hippocrates, *Diseases of Women*, trans. Paul Potter, LCL 538 (Cambridge, MA: Harvard University Press, 2018). For male diseases being different to female diseases in the Hippocratic corpus, see Florence Bourbon, "La Femme Malade, Le Médecin Hippocratique et la Question du Genre," *Lalies* 32 (2012): 181–9. On Aristotle, Laqueur fails to appreciate how biological sex difference is founded upon the metaphysical premise that the "principles" (ἀρχαί) of generation are *male* and *female*, which in turn map onto the binary of "form" and "matter" (Aristotle, *Generation of Animals* II.731b18; II.738b20–27, trans. A. L. Reck, LCL 366 [Cambridge, MA: Harvard University Press, 2000], 129, 185). For sexual generation, the male as the active principle (correlating with formal, final, and efficient cause) provides the "form" and the female as the passive principle (material cause) contributes the "matter." Male and female are certainly of the same species, under the genus of animals, and yet there remains an irreducible difference between them. By ignoring the metaphysical pressure shaping Aristotle's biology, Laqueur selectively slices Aristotle's account of the sexed body to fit into his one-sex Procrustean bed. For the important caveat, via a nuanced account of Aristotelian hylomorphism, that male association with form and female association with matter should not be taken literally, see Sarah Borden Sharkey, *An Aristotelian Feminism*, HASNMA 1 (Switzerland: Springer, 2016), 120.

Laqueur broadly refers to as the metaphysical, sociological, and political.[88] Yet, as Holmes exposes, for Laqueur's inversion narrative to work he has to drive "a wedge between nature in the sense of masculine and feminine principles [i.e., the metaphysical] and nature as it is realized through the fleshy body."[89] But in doing this, "The binary between 'sex' and 'gender' in the ancient world becomes the product of our own model, imposed on classical antiquity from outside."[90] Thus, Laqueur stands guilty of forcing ancient concepts "into modern straitjackets."[91] Indeed, "The conceptual order of the ancient world is so far away from the modern that it is very difficult to cut it up in this way without doing it considerable violence."[92] Perhaps Laqueur's violence upon ancient texts flows from his modern false assumption that anything ontological must be exclusively ontic.[93]

In contrast to Laqueur's "too simple" reading of the ancient world, guilty of projecting "our own rigid contrast between nature and culture," Holmes suggests that there is a far more complex interaction between metaphysical principles and sexed bodies, namely "a continuum within material bodies along which maleness and femaleness is more or less fixed."[94] This accounts for both humoral fluidity within the body, and yet also asserts that there is a fundamental "baseline of maleness or femaleness [that] seems to be determined at the moment the embryo is formed."[95] Indeed, Holmes draws attention to the embryological theory of Hippocrates' *On Regimen*, highlighting how "some people are fixed as gender deviants at the very moment sex is determined."[96] This happens if the mother's male seed defeats the father's female seed, resulting in ἀνδρόγυνοι.[97] Yet, even though an androgyne is marked as congenitally effeminate, Holmes notes that for Hippocrates, the androgyne is still a male, "classed among the three kinds of men."[98] In short, the complexity highlighted by Holmes troubles Laqueur's

---

88. Laqueur, *Making Sex*, 8.

89. Holmes, *Gender*, 51.

90. Ibid.

91. Flemming, *Making of Roman Women*, 14.

92. Ibid., 17.

93. For Laqueur's reductionistic understanding of "ontological," see *Making Sex*, 8, 29. Flemming avers that Laqueur's use is "particularly unfortunate . . . since he is only prepared to see a modern, materialist ontology as properly ontological, and thus fails to understand that it is often when ancient authors are being least materialist that they are, in their own terms, being most ontological" (*Making of Roman Women*, 17 n.32).

94. Holmes, *Gender*, 53, italics original.

95. Ibid.

96. Ibid., 54, italics original.

97. "Men-women" (Hippocrates, "Regimen I," 28.31, trans. W. H. S. Jones, LCL 150 [Cambridge, MA: Harvard University Press, 1998], 268–9).

98. Holmes, *Gender*, 54. The three kinds of *male* Hippocrates describes are (i) men "brilliant in soul and strong in body" (father's male seed + mother's male seed); (ii) the less brilliant man (father's male seed + mother's female seed); (iii) the androgyne (father's

simplistic inversion narrative, which itself problematically relies upon the formal error of anachronistically imposing modern taxonomies upon ancient literature.

D. Concerning Consequences

If Laqueur's one-sex thesis is correct, then within the ancient world, humanity's ontological (even soteriological) telos becomes peak maleness. However, when attending to authorial intent, it seems strange to read Hippocrates this way, as his primary concern, certainly in *Diseases of Women*, appears to be the discrete well-being of women. Additionally, the teleology of Aristotle is positively silent regarding male perfection compared to the more fundamental need to "reproduce in order to continue to exist."[99] It seems that in the ancient world, people were more anxious about disease, disorder, and death than about "gender slippage." As historian of antiquity Peter Brown maintains, "Citizens of the Roman Empire at its height, in the second century AD [N.B. the time of Galen and Soranus], were born into the world with an average life expectancy of less than twenty-five years. . . . Only four out of every hundred men, and fewer women, lived beyond the age of fifty."[100] As such, ancient society was oriented, either through "conscious legislation" or "the unquestioned weight of habit," toward the need "to replace the dead."[101] Laqueur's privileging of the one-sex model fails to see that the ancient solution to the problem of death was not the anxious ascendancy of a slippery slope of maleness, but the relentless pursuit of life through procreation. If this is correct, then "'one-sex' statements that identified women as 'deformed' men could become 'two-sex' claims for each sex having its own specific, and divinely ordained, role in the process of generation."[102]

Further, Park and Nye suggest that not only is Laqueur's one-sex thesis misleading, but it is also subtly dangerous, and sadly ironic for a project that looks to champion gender justice. Laqueur celebrates the premodern period "as a time of somehow greater sexual indeterminacy and freedom," yet his model "assumes a patriarchy so hegemonic that even women speak with a male voice."[103]

---

female seed + mother's male seed) ("Regimen I," 28 [LCL 150:266–9]). For a helpful table representing sexed possibilities in *On Regimen* 1.28–29, see Tara Mulder, "Flabby Flesh and Foetal Formation," in *Bodily Fluids in Antiquity*, ed. Mark Bradley et al. (New York: Routledge, 2021), 149.

99. Monte Ransome Johnson, *Aristotle on Teleology* (Oxford: Oxford University Press, 2005), 175. Note Aristotle's foundational axiom that "being is better than not being, and living is better than not living" (*Generation* II.731b.30–31 [LCL 366:185]).

100. Peter Brown, *The Body and Society: Men, Women, and Sexual Renunciation in Early Christianity*, 2nd ed., CCRel (New York: Columbia University Press, 2008), 6.

101. Ibid. On the ancient world suffering the anxiety attack of fate and death, see Paul Tillich, *The Courage to Be* (New Haven, CT: Yale University Press, 1952), 57–8.

102. King, *One-Sex Body*, 48.

103. Katharine Park and Robert A. Nye, "Destiny is Anatomy," *NewRe* 204 (1991): 56.

If Laqueur's work "reads in some respects like a male fantasy of a womanless world," any appropriation of the one-sex theory for issues of gender justice seems incongruous.[104]

E. Conclusion

In summary, while *Making Sex* has enduring appeal,[105] Laqueur's decision to limit his sample of evidence to medical texts, the omission of key voices who complicate his thesis, the lack of care when citing sources, all compounded by the imposition of a modern sex/gender binary, raise significant concerns about the accuracy of Laqueur's thesis, and so its fittingness for hermeneutical and theological appropriation. Laqueur "consistently imposes a false homogeneity on his sources,"[106] which leaves "no space for historical development or dissonant voices."[107] As such, for Laqueur, everything premodern becomes one-sex, to varying degrees. But again, this flows from Laqueur's tendency to abstract seemingly one-sex statements out of their historical and literary contexts, often ignoring the authorial intent of specific medical texts.

It may be slightly misrepresentative to follow Park in dismissing the one-sex model as simply "a specific idea contained in a couple of paragraphs of a single book of a single work of Galen."[108] Yet it seems evident that the ancient view of the body was certainly not monolithically one-sex. Indeed, rather surprisingly, in a letter to the *London Review of Books* sent shortly after the publication of *Making Sex*, Laqueur admitted that "both one- and two-sex ways of thinking, contrary to what I thought earlier, have always been, and remain, available."[109] A similar admittance is tucked away in the preface of *Making Sex*: "A two-sex and a one-sex model [have] always been available to those who thought about difference."[110] Unfortunately the rest of Laqueur's book, and its reception, ignored these more nuanced caveats. As

---

104. Ibid. Space precludes probing the extent to which the cultural-historical analysis offered by Laqueur is really a masquerade for his philosophical agenda.

105. On the reception of Laqueur's work, see Heinz-Jürgen Voß, *Making Sex Revisited: Dekonstruktion des Geschlechts aus biologisch-medizinischer Perspektive* (Bielefeld: Transcript, 2010), 18–19. King suggests that one of the key factors explaining the enduring appeal of *Making Sex* is that its "message—of difference between 'then' and 'now,' of the primacy of social construction over essentialism, and of the instability of gender—was one that people wanted to hear" (*One-Sex Body*, 6). King also notes the heavy influence of Foucault on Laqueur's work and its reception (ibid., 4).

106. Park and Nye, "Destiny is Anatomy," 54.

107. Flemming, *Making of Roman Women*, 120.

108. Katharine Park, "Cadden, Laqueur, and the 'One-Sex Body,'" *MFF* 46 (2010): 5.

109. Thomas Laqueur, "One Sex or Two," *London Review of Books* (London, December 6, 1990), vol. 12, no. 23, sec. Letters. Cited August 18, 2019. https://www.lrb.co.uk/v12/n23/letters, italics added.

110. Laqueur, *Making Sex*, viii, italics added.

such, it seems that Laqueur's project is ultimately misleading, and so unhelpful for faithful and fruitful hermeneutical and theological appropriation.

IV. Further Problems with One-Sex Appropriation

Even if one were to grant that the ancient view of the sexed body was not monolithically one-sex, one may still look to appropriate Laqueur's thesis for biblical hermeneutics and theological construction on the grounds that it offers a partial (if not total) explanation of the cultural and historical context of the Bible. Nevertheless, such an attempt to adopt Laqueur's model is problematic on two further fronts. First, the suggested one-sex parallel between the world Laqueur narrates and the world of the Bible lacks sufficient propinquity. Second, one-sex hermeneutics based on broader historical and cultural data lacks clear ANE support. In short, as we assess ancient material beyond the GRW, an attempt to justify one-sex biblical readings based upon historical and cultural grounds faces significant challenges.

A. The Problem of Propinquity

Innovationists commonly assume that what Laqueur narrates about the ancient world corresponds seamlessly with the ancient world of the Bible. However, this assumption overlooks the fact that Laqueur's focus is on the GRW, not the ASW, as the subtitle of *Making Sex: Body and Gender from the Greeks to Freud* indicates. Even if Laqueur remains correct about the universality of the one-sex body in the GRW, the question remains as to what extent the one-sex model of the GRW functions as the cultural context for attitudes to the sexed body in the ASW.

In answering this question, I draw upon the comparative method of Lawson Younger, particularly his lens of propinquity. The task of comparative studies is to discern the extent to which a particular parallel operates as the "silhouette" of any biblical text, in our case the GRW's one-sex model on the ASW.[111] To this end, an evaluation is reached through an analysis of the propinquity of the evidence along four axes: linguistic, chronological, geographic, and cultural.[112] A parallel is stronger the closer (more propinquitous) it is to the biblical material in language, in time, in geographical proximity, and in culture.

In assessing the parallel between the GRW and Genesis 1–2, on the linguistic axis (1), the ancient medical texts Laqueur refers to were written in Classical Latin and Ancient Greek, while Genesis was written in West Semitic Biblical Hebrew. The lexical and semantic differences between these languages are significant, problematizing the easy assimilation of ideas. Indeed, the literary genres and

---

111. Younger, "Cultural Context," 86.

112. K. Lawson Younger, "The 'Contextual Method': Some West Semitic Reflections," in *The Context of Scripture: Archival Documents from the Biblical World*, ed. William W. Hallo and K. Lawson Younger (Leiden: Brill, 1997), 3:xxxvii.

authorial intent of these texts are so distinct that it is questionable whether either form of literature would want to assimilate ideas from the other.

On the chronological axis (2), Thatcher identifies Gen. 2:4b–2:25 with the Jahwist source "dated around 850 BCE," commenting that "the J account helped to shape the one-sex tradition as it manifested itself in Judaism and Christianity."[113] If Thatcher wants to use Laqueur's work on the GRW as the provenance of one-sex thinking in Genesis 2, he faces a sizeable chronological challenge. Indeed, even if one follows Thatcher and dates Genesis 1:1–2:4a to the Priestly source of "around 500 BCE,"[114] that is still before Laqueur's earliest Graeco-Roman source of Hippocrates. It may be that Thatcher intends Laqueur simply to be illustrative of generic one-sex thinking in the ancient world, but a chronological chasm still gapes, leaving the question of one-sex provenance still open.

On the geographical axis (3), there is also significant physical distance between the GRW and ASW. If Thatcher's dating of Genesis 1 is correct, then its composition was in exilic Babylon rather than Israel, adding even further mileage to the already considerable distance between Greece and Israel. Moreover, there appears to be no evidence that copies of the Greco-Roman medical texts cited by Laqueur ever found their way to Babylon. Indeed, even if precious Graeco-Roman medical texts had made their way to sixth-century BC Babylon (a little tricky given they had yet to be written), it seems speculative that the exilic community would have had access to them.[115]

On the cultural axis (4), while both the GRW and the ASW considered death to be the greatest existential threat, Greek culture was notably distinct from Roman culture, let alone Hebrew culture. Indeed, a clarion call throughout the Hebrew scriptures and into the intertestamental period was for Israel to remain culturally distinct from surrounding nations, especially in areas of sexuality.[116] In summary, when these four axes are taken together, the propinquity of the GRW to the ASW on this point is exceptionally small. Even if the direction of influence were reversed, and Genesis 1 formed the cognitive environment for Laqueur's medical texts, thereby improving the chronological axis, the overall propinquity is hardly greater. This lack of propinquity between the GRW and the ASW undermines the value of Laqueur's thesis for faithful and fruitful biblical hermeneutics and theological construction.[117]

---

113. Thatcher, *Redeeming Gender*, 96.

114. Ibid.

115. Although it is worth noting that individual Israelites such as Daniel, Shadrach, Meshach, and Abednego were taught "the language and literature of the Babylonians" (Dan. 1:4).

116. E.g., Leviticus 18–20. See also, William R. G. Loader, *Making Sense of Sex: Attitudes towards Sexuality in Early Jewish and Christian Literature* (Grand Rapids: Eerdmans, 2013); idem, *Sexuality and Gender: Collected Essays*, WUNT 458 (Tubingen: Mohr Siebeck, 2021), 167–92.

117. While the parallel between the GRW and the NT is more propinquitous (on all four axes), even if NT texts are imbedded in a GRW whose cultural river is that of the

B. *The Lack of Clear ANE Support*

Given the challenge of moving from the GRW to the ASW, if one-sex advocates wanted to make a strong claim regarding how the ancient world more broadly viewed the sexed body (to justify one-sex hermeneutical and theological appropriation), one could look for more propinquitous parallels among the textual artifacts of the ANE.[118] To what extent is there evidence of one-sex thinking within the ANE, particularly within Mesopotamia?[119] In cuneiform cultures there were a striking number of terms indicating non-gender-binaries, including "kur-ĝara/*kurgarrû*, *assinnu*, saĝ-ursaĝ, gala/*kalû*, pilipili and *kulu'u*."[120] The majority of these were professional titles reserved for cult personnel, particularly in the service of the goddess Inanna/Ištar. Ilan Peled writes: "As Ištar's most prominent followers, the *assinnu* and *kurgarrû* represented her dual character: masculine and feminine, militant and sexual, aggressive and erotic."[121] Hypothetically, the existence of these individuals could suggest that ANE attitudes to the sexed body were fluid, intimating possible resemblances with one-sex fungible homology.

However, since the available ANE sources emphasize the social role of these individuals, rather than their personal lives, it is very difficult to come to any firm conclusion about their sexed embodiment. It is simply not clear whether the priests of the atypical Ištar were chosen because they were (or were made) atypical in their sexed bodies. Although inconclusive, the fact that Ištar remained a female goddess in textual and archaeological artifacts suggests that her liminal atypicality was functional rather than ontological, intimating a similar arrangement for her priests.[122] Indeed, following the work of Westernholz and Zsolnay on Sumerian contexts, maleness and masculinity were "rooted in class distinctions and societally

---

one-sex body, these texts are not necessarily indebted to their cultural context to form their ideas. This claim is strengthened when we supplement Younger's rubric of propinquity with the vital inner-biblical axis of canonical context.

118. One-sex advocates do not appear to engage ANE literature.

119. My focus on one-sex thinking within Mesopotamia reflects Thatcher's claim that Babylon is the setting for Genesis 1–2. If one followed an earlier dating for Genesis, one might need to assess Egyptian attitudes to the sexed body. The argument of this book does not necessitate this additional analysis.

120. Sophus Helle, "'Only in Dress?' Methodological Concerns Regarding Non-Binary Gender," in *Gender and Methodology in the Ancient Near East: Approaches from Assyriology and Beyond*, ed. Stephanie Budin et al., BMO 10 (Barcelona: Universitat de Barcelona, 2018), 41.

121. Ilan Peled, *Masculinities and Third Gender: The Origins and Nature of an Institutionalized Gender Otherness in the Ancient Near East*, AOAT 435 (Münster: Ugarit-Verlag, 2016), 283.

122. On the transgressive potential (but not fungible fluidity) of divine sexed bodies, see Stephanie Lynn Budin, "Gender in the Tale of Aqhat," in *Studying Gender in the Ancient Near East*, ed. Saana Svärd and Agnès Garcia-Ventura (University Park, PA: Eisenbrauns, 2018), 51–72.

understood age parameters. There would seem to have been little practical use for the construction 'man = male mortal.'"[123]

Again, there seems to be no indisputable and clear access to the biological. Babylonian medical texts may offer Thatcher the closest propinquity and so the strongest contextual warrant for one-sex hermeneutics. However, Heeßel provides a methodological warning. If we attempt to map modern biological classifications onto ancient terms, then we risk losing the moral valuations, specific set of connotations, and background beliefs that undergird the ancient understanding of the sexed body.[124] None of this means the ANE held to a clear two-sex theory of bodily sex difference. But the focus on social roles over biological anatomy, combined with the noted methodological caveat, seems to complicate any confident appeal to the ANE for a one-sex body cultural context.[125]

V. Conclusion

Since the Bible is a collection of textual artifacts from the ANE, ASW, and GRW, the call to discern the historical and cultural context of the Bible to explicate scripture's teaching on intersexuality remains ministerially helpful. However, the assessment earlier has indicated that when it comes to discerning bodily sex difference in the Bible, any employment of the one-sex model on cultural and historical grounds remains highly problematic. Not only are there serious material and formal concerns with the accuracy of Laqueur's thesis, but the distance between the

123. Joan Goodnick Westenholz and Ilona Zsolnay, "Categorizing Men and Masculinity in Sumer," in *Being a Man: Negotiating Ancient Constructs of Masculinity*, ed. Ilona Zsolnay, SHANE (London: Routledge, 2017), 30.

124. Nils P. Heeßel, "Rechts oder links–wörtlich oder dem Sinn nach? Zum Problem der kulturellen Gebundenheit bei der Übersetzung von medizinischen Keilschrifttexten," in *Writings of Early Scholars in the Ancient Near East, Egypt, Rome, and Greece: Translating Ancient Scientific Texts*, ed. Annette Imhausen and Tanja Pommerening, BZA 286 (Berlin: de Gruyter, 2010), 175–88. *Contra* the one-sex anxiety of "gender slippage," what does seem to be clear across the ANE, exilic Babylon being no exception, is the commonly expressed wish to perpetuate one's name by having numerous offspring, for death is both inevitable and untimely. Indeed, the only thing that might alleviate the nightmare of the underworld was the possibility of living offspring offering regular libations (Gwendolyn Leick, "Too Young—Too Old? Sex and Age in Mesopotamian Literature," in *Sex in Antiquity: Exploring Gender and Sexuality in the Ancient World*, ed. Mark Masterson, Nancy Sorkin Rabinowitz, and James Robson, RA [London: Routledge, 2015], 89, 93). Thus, in the ANE (as in the GRW), death was a far greater problem than gender slippage.

125. In favor of sexual polymorphism, Julia M. Asher-Greve has proposed that Sumerian culture knew of, and so allocated, discrete categories for the atypically sexed ("From La Femme to Multiple Sex/Gender," in *Studying Gender in the Ancient Near East*, ed. Saana Svärd and Agnès Garcia-Ventura [University Park, PA: Eisenbrauns, 2018], 15–50).

GRW and the ASW of the Bible seems insufficiently propinquitous for legitimate Graeco-Roman one-sex influence. Even if one looks for more propinquitous parallels within the ANE, clear evidence for the one-sex body model is lacking. Most of the available material focuses more on the function or socially prescribed roles of gender than on precise statements about anatomy and physiology. Indeed, Thatcher's redefinition (horizontalizing and de-sexing) of Laqueur's one-sex theory seems to admit implicitly that the biblical authors are already radically discontinuous with their cultural context. If this is the case, then what is the value of appealing to Laqueur's vertical single male sex spectrum for support?[126] Further, if the biblical authors are so different to the surrounding culture, then is the case for a horizontal, sexless spectrum stronger (on historical and cultural grounds) than the case for the two-sex theory?

Consequently, the strong claim that the ancient view of the sexed body was monolithically one-sex remains unjustified. This is not to make the equally strong counterclaim that the ancient world (both GRW and ASW) only thought in terms of two-sex bodies. Rather, it seems more judicious to make the weaker claim that in the ancient world both one-sex and two-sex views were held, with the one-sex model never being dominant. In short, the historical and cultural background for bodily sex difference in the Bible is multifaceted and complex rather than monolithically one-sex. It therefore seems unwarranted and undesirable to appropriate Laqueur's thesis for faithful and fruitful biblical hermeneutics and theological construction. Nonetheless, the claim for a one-sex "human continuum," whether understood hierarchically or horizontally, may still be a legitimate interpretive option for explicitly exegetical and theological reasons. As such, we must reengage the biblical and theological material to discern the nature and nuances of the sexed body in the Bible, and its import for constructing a dogmatic account of intersexuality.

126. Interestingly, at a colloquium in 2017, Laqueur found fault with Thatcher's appropriation of the one-sex model, highlighting Thatcher's tendency to ahistoricize a theory that is necessarily bound in a particular history. See Adrian Thatcher and Thomas Laqueur, *God, Sex and Gender: A Conversation on Adrian Thatcher's Redeeming Gender*, Berkeley Center for the Study of Religion Colloquium (Berkeley, CA, 2017), 1hr.14mins. Cited 12 August 2019. https://bcsr.berkeley.edu/events/god-sex-and-gender-a-conversation-on-adrian-thatchers-redeeming-gender-2.

Chapter 3

CREATION

INTERSEX IN THE BEGINNING?

The previous chapter argued that the historical and cultural background for bodily sex difference in the Bible is multifaceted and complex rather than monolithically one-sex. Yet a one-sex "human continuum" may be a legitimate interpretive option for exegetical and theological reasons internal to scripture, to which we now turn. While a theology of intersexuality could begin in several places,[1] the proposed theo-dramatic approach follows the example of the canon and Christ (e.g., Matt. 19:4–6) by starting with the doctrine of creation. Commencing with creation affords close engagement with several important innovationist arguments, and by clarifying the creation event and God's creational intent, I preamble the discussion in Chapters 5 and 6 about the nature of redemptive newness in Christ.[2]

The term "creation event" refers to the theo-dramatic act (*creatio*) recorded in Genesis 1–2 that produced a prelapsarian cosmos (*creatura*).[3] The term "creational intent" refers to God's intended order within the cosmos, that is, those things that are intrinsic and characteristic of the universe even if no fall had taken place.[4] For instance, art and technology do not explicitly appear in the creation narratives of Genesis 1–2, but nonetheless could be considered "creational" if it is the case that

---

1. E.g., we could commence with our embodied desire (for others and God) grounded in God's desire for us. See Rowan Williams, "The Body's Grace," in *Theology and Sexuality: Classic and Contemporary Readings*, ed. Eugene F. Rogers, BRMT (Oxford: Blackwell, 2002), 309–21.

2. In the NT redemption is sometimes depicted as a new creation or an act of recreation, both in reference to individuals and the renewal of the cosmos. E.g., 2 Cor. 4:6; 5:17; Rev. 21:1, 5; 22:1–5.

3. For the distinction between *creatio* and *creatura*, see Brian Brock, *Christian Ethics in a Technological Age* (Grand Rapids: Eerdmans, 2010), 325.

4. My focus on "creational order" remains distinct from the related Lutheran conversation about "orders of creation." See Hartmut Rosenau, "Schöpfungsordnung," *TRE* 30:356–8.

they are grounded in and exhibit God's purposes for creation.[5] As Pannenberg explains, the event of creation is "finished" (Gen. 2:1), after which God "does not bring forth any new creatures. But his work needs continuation."[6] There is a sense in which creation's inner reality "unfolds in time,"[7] which contributes "directly to the fulfilment of this [creation] project."[8]

These antecedent terms cohere in God, who in his goodness is the sole author of both *creatio primitiva* (the original *event* of creation) and *creatio continuata* (the conservation of creational *intent* or order).[9] As will become evident here, employment of the term "creational" serves two purposes. First, it provides linguistic nuance, allowing for the possibility that even if intersex conditions do not exist pre-fall, they are a historically subsequent example of "God's plan for a diverse and wondrous creation."[10] Second, the term "creational" connotes a key motif within the book, namely the dynamics of God's wise created order and the dogmatic function of *creatura*.

Consequently, the aim in this chapter is not only to explicate the nature and nuances of bodily sex in the creation event but also to discern God's creational intent for the sexed body. In short, echoing Cornwall's description, is sexual dimorphism (SD) "not just indicative but also imperative: this is the way things were *meant* to be, ordained by God," such that "any attempt to deny or transcend the binary model" is an attempt "to reject God's blueprint for humanity?"[11] Or, does a biblical doctrine of creation have sufficient space to "understand intersex as a specific and positive gift from God?"[12] Further, with an eye toward Chapter 4, given creedal orthodoxy's commitment to the fall, to what extent is intersexuality an example of creational diversity or cursed disorder? At stake for advocates of sexual polymorphism (SP) is the very humanity of intersex persons.[13] Motivating the SD camp is the worry that intersexuality naturalizes apparent postlapsarian disorder.

To explore these kinds of questions, I privilege the biblical story before clarifying its ontological staging. First, I examine the event of creation, outlining and

---

5. "In the broadest terms humans cannot actually create; they can only creatively configure materiality" (Brock, *Christian Ethics*, 325).

6. Wolfhart Pannenberg, *Systematic Theology* (London: T&T Clark, 2004), 2:36.

7. Rowan Williams, *Grace and Necessity: Reflections on Art and Love* (Harrisburg, PA: Morehouse, 2005), 139.

8. Trevor A. Hart, *Making Good: Creation, Creativity, and Artistry* (Waco, TX: Baylor University Press, 2014), 8.

9. *DLGTT*, 84.

10. Sabia-Tanis, "Holy Creation," 195.

11. Susannah Cornwall, "Troubling Bodies?" in *Intersex, Theology, and the Bible: Troubling Bodies in Church, Text, and Society* (New York: Palgrave Macmillan, 2015), 6, italics original.

12. Ibid.

13. Marchal, *Appalling Bodies*, 69.

responding to several arguments for SP in Genesis 1–2.[14] Second, I assess the case for intersex in God's creational intent. Third, I supplement biblical engagement with a Thomistically inflected account of human ontology, our "staging." Finally, the organizing principle of both the literary-canonical and theological material is the leitmotif of God's good, wise, ordered peace of creation. Within the unity of God's created *shalom* (שָׁלוֹם), creational diversity is gloriously abundant without fragmenting into disparate disorganization. Thus, diversity within the unity of ordered peace offers a framework for understanding sexed embodiment in the event and intent of creation. In short, while aware of the epistemic challenges of accessing the protological dispensation,[15] a theological reading of the canon suggests that God's creational intent, revealed in the event of creation, is that human sexed embodiment was likely *either* male *or* female. This conclusion intimates that a fuller theological explanation for intersex embodiment needs to look beyond the locus of creation.

I. Scene 1: Intersex in the Creation Event

A. Primal Androgyny

The case for primal androgyny maintains that in the creation event, the first human was neither male nor female but an androgynous being, be it a "sexually undifferentiated" earth-creature (typically argued from Genesis 1),[16] or a "masculofeminine" combination (typically argued from Genesis 2).[17]

---

14. Genesis 1–2 presents two creation accounts (1:1–2:3; 2:4–25). For the sake of simplicity, I refer to these two accounts as "Genesis 1" and "Genesis 2." While appreciating the insights of historical-critical scholarship, this study approaches the biblical canon *theologically*, by which I mean that it is a communicative whole with internal referentiality and internal coherence. For a defense of this approach, see C. John Collins, *Reading Genesis Well: Navigating History, Poetry, Science, and Truth in Genesis 1–11* (Grand Rapids: Zondervan Academic, 2018), 17–106.

15. See Chapter 4.

16. E.g., Jennifer Wright Knust, *Unprotected Texts: The Bible's Surprising Contradictions about Sex and Desire* (New York: HarperOne, 2011), 51; Paul Evdokimov, *Woman and the Salvation of the World: A Christian Anthropology of the Charisms of Women*, trans. Anthony P. Gythiel (Crestwood, NY: St Vladimir's, 1994), 139.

17. E.g., Wayne A. Meeks, "Image of the Androgyne: Some Uses of a Symbol in Earliest Christianity," *HR* 13 (1974): 185. The concept of an original androgynous ideal is ancient and may be found in Plato's *Symposium* (written between *c.* 385 and 370 BC), Rabbinic literature (*c.* third century AD), and Patristic sources, notably (for some) Gregory of Nyssa's *On the Making of Man* (*c.* fourth century AD). See Plato, *Symposium* 189e, trans. Alexander Nehamas and Paul Woodruff, ed. John M. Cooper (Indianapolis: Hackett, 1997), 473; Jacob Neusner, ed., *Genesis Rabbah: The Judaic Commentary to the*

1. Primal Androgyny in Genesis 1 The case for primal androgyny in Genesis 1 is mounted on three grammatical pillars. First, against the weaponization of Gen. 1:27 as definitive evidence for SD,[18] Sally Gross submits that it is a text "perhaps more 'herm-friendly' than many biblical literalists realise or translations suggest."[19] Gross highlights the "odd" shift from the masculine singular pronominal suffix in 1:27b (אתו) to the masculine plural pronominal suffix in 1:27c (אתם), both referring to האדם.[20] This "syntactical ambiguity" prompts Gross to follow some "Jewish commentators . . . that our species was originally created androgynous."[21] "Hermaphroditism predated Adam's sin," causing Gross to suggest that "it is the birth of people who are *not* hermaphrodites which might be 'the consequence of Adam's sin.'"[22]

A second grammatical pillar for primal androgyny is proposed by Justin Tanis. "The earth-being (*ādām*) created originally is both male and female," for the term *ādām* is not a name but a "description of this being created from the earth."[23] Since "the word *ādām* is a play upon the Hebrew word for earth, *'adamah*," Tanis suggests that "a more accurate rendering of the word would be 'earthling' or 'Earth-being.' Originally, this earthling was one, without gender differentiation, encompassing both female and male."[24] In support of this interpretation, Tanis cites the Jewish commentator Nahum Sarna, that "*ādām* is a singular noun used with plural verb forms, and includes both male and female."[25] Thus, Tanis discerns a scriptural warrant for primal androgyny in the grammatical observation that since the singular noun האדם is collocated with plural verb forms it must be because the singular noun includes male and female—ontologically not just grammatically.[26]

Third, Michelle O'Brien makes a further grammatical observation by highlighting the *waw* coordinating conjunction of זכר ונקבה: "We were created

Book of Genesis: A New American Translation, BJS 104 (Atlanta, GA: Scholars, 1985), 1:73–5; Gregory of Nyssa, *On the Making of Man* 16, trans. H. A. Wilson, *NPNF²* 5 (Buffalo: Christian Literature, 1893; reprint, Peabody, MA: Hendrickson, 2004), 406–7.

18. On the weaponization of Gen. 1:27 for SD, see Michael G. Lawler and Todd A. Salzman, "Sex, Gender, and Intersex: Anthropological, Medical, and Ethical Critiques and Proposals," *ThS* 25 (2019): 205–26.

19. Gross, "Intersexuality," 70.

20. Ibid., 71.

21. Ibid., 73. Gross cites the third-century AD Palestinian haggadist Rabbi Jeremiah ben Eleazar. See Neusner, *Genesis Rabbah*, 1:73.

22. Gross, "Intersexuality," 74.

23. Tanis, *Trans-Gendered*, 58.

24. Ibid.

25. Ibid., 58 n.8, citing Nahum M. Sarna, *Genesis* בראשית, JPSTCP (Philadelphia: Jewish Publication Society, 1989), 12.

26. See also Calum M. Carmichael, *Sex and Religion in the Bible* (New Haven, CT: Yale University Press, 2010), 8.

male *and* female, not male *or* female; there is no disjunction there, only a conjunction."[27] Male and female should not be thought of as discrete categories of embodied sex. Rather, since "the image we were created in is male *and* female, reflecting a G*d who is both male *and* female," humans presently "exist between male and female . . . reflective of the God who is both male *and* female."[28] Putting aside O'Brien's broader theological claim for now, it is sufficient to note O'Brien's endorsement of primal (and universally present) androgyny. Everyone is androgynous, being male *and* female to a greater or lesser degree.

2. Primal Androgyny in Genesis 2 The case for primal androgyny in Genesis 2 begins by asserting that האדם in Gen. 2:7 is "precisely and only the human being, so far sexually undifferentiated."[29] Sexual undifferentiation is usually interpreted either as being truly sexless, "Neither male nor female nor a combination of both,"[30] or as an "earth-being . . . [who] in fact 'contains' both the man and the woman—they make up one body."[31] The earthling evolves to the point of needing to be split surgically into איש and אשה in Gen. 2:21. Thus, "Only after surgery does this creature, for the very first time, identify itself as male."[32]

In summary, whether the primal androgyne was a sexless being or a male-female composite, the various arguments for primal androgyny are significant for a theology of intersexuality because they challenge the *Ur*-status of male and female as sexually dimorphic complements. However one is bodily sexed in the present, we are all derivative of the primal androgyne. Mollenkott extends this logic, opining that since intersex bodies are a combination of both male and female, "Intersexuals are not only part of God's original plan, they are *primarily* so

27. Michelle O'Brien, "Intersex, Medicine, Diversity, Identity and Spirituality," in *This Is My Body: Hearing the Theology of Transgender Christians*, ed. Christina Beardsley and Michelle O'Brien (London: Darton, Longman & Todd, 2016), 48, italics original. Similarly, Vincent E. Gil presses the "conjunctive conjunction" in Gen. 1:27 to extend the claim that all embryonic life begins as sexually undifferentiated (*A Christian's Guide through the Gender Revolution: Gender, Cisgender, Transgender, and Intersex* [Eugene, OR: Cascade, 2021], 67–8).

28. O'Brien, "Intersex," 48, asterisk and italics original.

29. Phyllis Trible, *God and the Rhetoric of Sexuality*, OBT (Philadelphia: Fortress, 1978), 80. Although Trible's interpretation of Genesis 2 grates against her understanding of Genesis 1 (evidenced below), Trible does not appear to offer a reconciling explanation. Presumably for Trible, such an explanation is unwarranted because the Priestly and Yahwist sources for Genesis 1 and 2 respectively are not intended to be reconciled.

30. Ibid., 98.

31. Iain W. Provan, *Seriously Dangerous Religion: What the Old Testament Really Says and Why It Matters* (Waco, TX: Baylor University Press, 2014), 81.

32. Trible, *Rhetoric of Sexuality*, 98.

.... From this angle, hermaphrodites or intersexuals could be viewed as reminders of Original Perfection."[33]

B. Against Primal Androgyny

1. Against Primal Androgyny in Genesis 1 The case for primal androgyny in Genesis 1 is primarily built upon three grammatical arguments. In response to Gross's claim that the shift from a singular to a plural pronominal suffix in Gen. 1:27bc suggests an original androgyne containing male and female, Trible counters that "a sensitivity to poetic language is basic to an interpretation of Genesis 1:27," intimating that humanity's unity is metaphorical rather than literal.[34] As such, "The shift from singular to plural pronouns shows clearly that *hā-ʾādām* is not one single creature who is both male and female but rather two creatures, one male and one female."[35] Indeed, "The plural form reinforces sexual differentiation within the unity of humanity."[36] This point is strengthened by attending to the immediately preceding verse, where a plural verb form ירדו refers to the singular word אדם. Given that verses 26 and 27 should be read together, Trible concludes that "from the beginning humankind exists as two creatures, not as one creature with double sex."[37]

Trible's observations also address Tanis's claim that primal androgyny may be detected from the fact that the singular noun אדם is used with plural verb forms. For Tanis, אדם refers to a single "earthling . . . without gender differentiation, encompassing both female and male," a view that is "strongly supported by the Hebrew text."[38] Implicit yet central for Tanis's interpretation is reading אדם as a nominal representing a single item, in support of which he references the Jewish scholar Nahum Sarna. While Sarna's explanation of אדם as "a generic term for humankind" could possibly be read as a singular nominal referring to a single item,[39] on the very next page of his commentary Sarna clearly indicates that אדם should be read as a singular for a collective.[40] Indeed, the context conveys אדם as

---

33. Mollenkott, *Omnigender*, 98–9, italics original. This claim will become increasingly important when we reach the theo-dramatic act of redemption, and assess if Christ himself is intersex, along with whether the negation of "male and female" in Christ (Gal. 3:28) inaugurates the erasure of SD and a return to primal androgyny.

34. Trible, *Rhetoric of Sexuality*, 15.

35. Ibid., 18.

36. Ibid., 17.

37. Ibid., 18.

38. Tanis, *Trans-Gendered*, 58.

39. Sarna, *Genesis*, 12.

40. For Sarna, the singular noun refers to "one human species," within which there is an "infinite diversity of human culture[s]" (*Genesis*, 13). Cf. BHRG §35.3; JM §135b.

a "collective concept."[41] In Hebrew syntax "a collective singular subject often takes a plural verb,"[42] in this case, the indicative ירדו in v.26 and the string of volitives in v.28. As such, the agreement between subject and verb is *ad sensum* rather than strictly morphological.[43] Thus, Tanis's reading of אדם as a singular noun that refers to a single being inclusive of male and female (due to the singular noun collocation with plural verbs) is not "supported by the Hebrew text," as Tanis claims, let alone "strongly."

While O'Brien claims that the *waw* coordinating conjunction between "male" and "female" endorses primal and enduring androgyny (imaging an androgynous God), this proposal seems guilty of overinterpreting such a polyvalent conjunction without due consideration of the immediate literary context. Even attending to the lexeme itself, it is important to note that the conjunctive *waw* ("male *and* female") could legitimately be understood as implying "male *or* female," depending on the context or content, that is, as two options, each of which is in view (e.g., I am looking to the right and the left).[44] Regardless of this lexical point, the strength of O'Brien's case relies upon the legitimacy of her preceding theological claim. For O'Brien, given that Gen. 1:27ab declares humanity to be in the "image of God," which for O'Brien is epexegetically explicated by the syntactical parallel in 1:27c of "male and female," humanity images something fundamental about God, namely that the one God is both male *and* female.

Although deducing sex "in" God is not unheard of among contemporary theologians and biblical scholars,[45] such a move is unwarranted, whether made univocally or analogically. Concerning 1:27 itself, Thomas Gudbergsen argues that the syntactical parallelism between the two cola of 27b and 27c forms a synonymous "piasm," such that "these parallels semantically throw light upon each other."[46] The interpretative implications of Gudbergsen's claim is that just as the "referent (*hāʾādām*)" of God's image is male and female, "it is natural to conclude that also the object (*ʾĕlōhîm*) must be male and female."[47]

41. Jan Christian Gertz, *Das erste Buch Mose (Genesis): Die Urgeschichte Gen 1–11*, ATD 1 (Göttingen: Vandenhoeck & Ruprecht, 2018), 62.

42. WHS §229.

43. WHS §229. Compare the inverse, when abstract plural subjects may take a singular verb (WHS §233; BHRG §35.5). Further, reading אדם as a collective singular coheres syntactically with the terms used to describe the other classes in Genesis 1, all of which are singular collectives. The exception is התנינם (Gen. 1:21), which is a plural specifying the class of "living creature" (נפש חיה) that teems in the sea (Gen. 1:20).

44. WHS §433; JM §175a–b.

45. Among theologians, see Tanis, *Trans-Gendered*, 57. In biblical studies, see Thomas Gudbergsen, "God Consists of Both the Male and the Female Genders: A Short Note on Gen 1:27," *VT* 62 (2012): 450–3; Francesca Stavrakopoulou, *God: An Anatomy* (London: Picador, 2021), 91–163.

46. Gudbergsen, "Both Male and Female," 451.

47. Ibid., 452.

However, Gudbergsen's univocal interpretation ignores how Genesis 1 as a whole "carefully guards the mystery, singularity and distance of God from creatures, [such that] the thought of such a correspondence, albeit [even] analogical, is neither tolerable nor conceivable."[48] Informed by the infinite qualitative distinction between Creator and creation in Genesis 1, Peter Gentry interprets the syntactical coordination between vv.27–28 as chiastic. Starting with v.27, while the first verb (ויברא) advances the *wayyiqtol* narrative sequence, the shift to two *qatal* verbs, both Qal perfects (ברא), causes the reader to dwell on the climactic event of humanity's creation.[49] Indeed, the clause pattern shifts from the normal Verb-Subject-Object in v27a to a Modifier-Verb-Object pattern in 27bc, both clauses also being asyndetic. As Gentry avers, "This is a clear macrosyntactical signal with pragmatic significance: these clauses do not advance the narrative but digress and pause to comment on the first clause in the verse."[50] With both subclauses being grammatically marked as offering parenthetical asides, the author digresses from the narrative flow in order to emphasize two key points: (i) humanity in some way resembles God (v.27b),[51] and (ii) humankind entails male and female (v.27c).

Pausing to stress these parenthetical points prepares the reader for the five volitives in v.28, which Gentry argues are chiastically arranged to illuminate the meaning of the subclauses in v.27: be fruitful (פרו ורבו ומלאו) reflecting "male and female," and rule over the creatures (וכבשה ורדו) reflecting "in the image of God." I expand on the significance of this chiasm below, but here it is important to note that "the duality of gender is the basis for being fruitful, while the divine image is correlated with the command to rule as God's viceroy. . . . The divine image is *not* to be explained by or located in terms of duality of gender in humanity."[52] Therefore, discerning sex within God is syntactically illegitimate because the parallelism between the two cola of 27b and 27c is "progressive, not synonymous,"[53] anticipating and preparing for the volitives of v.28.

Moreover, the proposal that God is sexed has been rejected historically by orthodox Christians on the grounds that since sex pertains to the body, and God

---

48. Phyllis A. Bird, "'Male and Female He Created Them': Gen. 1:27b in the Context of the Priestly Account of Creation," *HTR* 74 (1981): 156.

49. For the significance of the interruption of a *wayyiqtol* chain, see Alviero Niccacci, *The Syntax of the Verb in Classical Hebrew Prose*, trans. W. G. E. Watson, JSOTSup 86 (Sheffield: Sheffield Academic Press, 1990), 62–72.

50. Peter J. Gentry, "Kingdom Through Covenant: Humanity as the Divine Image," *SBJT* 12 (2008): 25.

51. For a thorough survey of the prepositions כ and ב, see W. Randall Garr, *In His Own Image and Likeness: Humanity, Divinity, and Monotheism*, CHANE 15 (Leiden: Brill, 2003), 95–115.

52. Gentry, "Kingdom Through Covenant," 26. Gentry's use of the term "gender" corresponds with my use of "sex."

53. Bird, "Male and Female," 150. Similarly, Victor P. Hamilton, *The Book of Genesis: Chapters 1–17*, NICOT (Grand Rapids: Eerdmans, 1990), 139.

is a simple incorporeal spirit (John 4:24), God cannot be sexed. As Gregory of Nazianzus excoriated, it is a "joke" like the "trashy myths of old" to think that God is male because of "the masculine nouns 'God' and 'Father.'"[54] "God" is not a noun but a name, with "Father," "Son," and Holy Spirit" as God's proper names. Further, O'Brien employs language for God that is overly univocal, failing to appreciate the ontological distinction between Creator and creature that has been historically acknowledged with anthropomorphic language. In naming God, all language, whatever the genre, is ectypal and analogical.[55] To summarize, the grammatical and theological foundations upon which the case for primal androgyny in Genesis 1 stands remain unstable.

2. Against Primal Androgyny in Genesis 2 Primal androgyny in Genesis 2 asserts that the first human was a sexless or sexed composite earth-creature (2:7) who was subsequently split into male and female (2:21) to remedy its incompleteness (2:18). This reading of Genesis 2 is problematic on two accounts. First, there is no lexical or grammatical indication that the pre-operative הָאָדָם is different from הָאָדָם in vv. 22–25 (other than the loss of a rib/side).[56] Rather, the consistent articular use of הָאָדָם suggests that the same individual is in view.

Second, form-critical identifications strengthen the grammatical point. If we take Genesis 1–5 as a textual unit, Richard Hess notes how the lexeme אָדָם moves from vagueness to specificity.[57] At one end, the report form of Genesis 1 indicates that the text teaches universal truths about origins, suggesting that אָדָם in Gen. 1:26–28 represents all generic humanity.[58] At the other end, Genesis 4–5 is composed of "a mixture of story and list genres within the framework of genealogies," whose intention is to establish relationships between the preceding and subsequent narratives.[59] While the generic use of אָדָם appears (e.g., Gen. 5:1–2), the wider textual unit's focus on genealogies signals that אָדָם is introduced as a personal name (Gen. 4:1, 25; 5:3–5). In between אָדָם as generic (Genesis 1) and specific (Genesis 4–5), Genesis 2–3 consistently employs אָדָם as articular and

54. Gregory of Nazianzus, "Oration 31," 7, in *On God and Christ: The Five Theological Orations and Two Letters to Cledonius*, trans. Frederick Williams and Lionel R. Wickham, PPS 23 (Yonkers, NY: St. Vladimir's, 2002), 122.

55. On the legitimacy and value of analogical and anthropomorphic language for God, see Herman Bavinck, *Reformed Dogmatics*, ed. John Bolt, trans. John Vriend (Grand Rapids: Baker Academic, 2004), 2:95–147, esp. 97–110; hereafter, *RD* followed by volume: page.

56. Davidson, *Flame of Yahweh*, 20.

57. Richard S. Hess, "Splitting the Adam: The Usage of 'Ādām in Genesis I–V," in *Studies in the Pentateuch*, ed. J. A. Emerton, VTSup 41 (Leiden: Brill, 1990), 9–10.

58. For Genesis 1's form as "report," see George W. Coats, *Genesis, with an Introduction to Narrative Literature*, FOTL 1 (Grand Rapids: Eerdmans, 1983), 47.

59. Hess, "Splitting the Adam," 12.

titular.[60] The pericope of Genesis 2–3 has a narratival form, presenting a single plot with limited characters. The temporal context of Genesis 2 suggests that האדם refers to a particular individual who is given a specific responsibility for the garden (Gen. 2:15). Within the single plot, האדם refers to the same character. Since this pericope "intends to explain or teach concerning the present status of humanity in relation to God and the world, it is appropriate that the usage of *'dm* be more general than a personal name, that is, that it be potentially capable of application to all humanity. A title, such as 'The [Hu]Man,' suits these requirements."[61] If האדם has titular significance for readers of Genesis 2–3, and given we have no examples of post-Genesis 3 readers *not* being sexed, attending to the literary function of Genesis 2–3 implies that for האדם to remain relevant for a sexed readership, האדם must be sexed. As such, האדם cannot refer to a primal androgyne without falling outside the literary function of the pericope and its archetypal relevance for a sexed audience, whether Israel or the church.[62]

Further, Gen. 2:21–24 presents pre-operative האדם as already male. The case for primal androgyny would expect the woman to come out of the androgynous earth-creature (האדם), but in Gen. 2:23 the woman comes "from a man" (מאיש), suggesting that the first האדם is "*already* male (*ish*) *before* the woman is taken from his side."[63] Here, Brownson helpfully notes that "the words *ish* and *ishah* are not generic terms; they are specifically *gendered* terms for man and woman."[64] As such, the shift for האדם is not ontological but epistemic or relational. Conversely, if androgyny were the original ideal, then the solitude of האדם in Gen. 2:18 is actually good, and Adam's poem of Gen. 2:23 is not a song of delight, but a lament. Such an inversion of what God calls good sounds proleptically familiar. In sum, as an explanation of intersexuality in the creation event (and sexed embodiment more broadly), the case for primal androgyny remains inadequate biblically, theologically, and ethically. Indeed, while primal androgyny is prevalent within gnostic texts, it cannot be found elsewhere in the biblical canon.[65] The case for primal androgyny is "to read into the text what is not there."[66]

---

60. Gen. 2:5 is the exception in reference to the earth (אדמה) needing to be cultivated by a human (אדם).

61. Hess, "Splitting the Adam," 12. Hess offers further ANE support for the titular use of אדם.

62. More theologically, if *sexless* androgyny is the primordial ideal, then it indicates that there is an essential, asexual human nature that is more fundamental to being human than merely superficial maleness, femaleness, or intersexness. Yet this both ignores the reality that historical humanity is only ever sexed and denigrates the inherent goodness of humanity's sexed embodiment.

63. James V. Brownson, *Bible, Gender, Sexuality: Reframing the Church's Debate on Same-Sex Relationships* (Grand Rapids: Eerdmans, 2013), 28, italics original.

64. Ibid., 28, italics original.

65. Jonathan Cahana, "Androgyne or Undrogyne? Queering the Gnostic Myth," *Numen* 61 (2014): 509–24.

66. Hamilton, *Genesis 1–17*, 178.

C. The Hybrid Argument

If primal androgyny challenges SD by emphasizing humanity's single, androgynous sex, the hybrid argument queers SD by opening space for original SP. For Justin Sabia-Tanis, "The creation story in Genesis sets the broad parameters of the world, stating the poles of a series of continuums: day and night; earth and sky; land and sea; plant, animal, and human; male and female."[67] Reading the creation categories of Genesis 1 as poles on a spectrum enables one to recognize the "liminal spaces in which the elements of creation overlap and merge,"[68] for example, dusk, dawn, the shore, marshes, and amphibians.[69] Given that Genesis 1 paints creation "in broad brush strokes," its failure to mention the mixed forms of dusk and shore does not entail that they are a result of the fall, nor that they stray from God's good creational intent.[70] As such, the mention of "male and female" does not exclude the existence of "others" or "hybrids," such as intersex persons, who instead are "naturally occurring variations [of humanity] . . . which God has declared to be good."[71] Indeed, some see the linear spectrum as too restrictive altogether, arguing instead that "we should be looking up and seeing that the multitude of sexualities and gender identities exist in 3D, sprinkled through space like the stars."[72]

Whether favoring a spectrum or a skyscape, advocates of the hybrid argument all agree that intersex embodiment is an example of good and natural variation in creation. As Tanis concludes, "How people express those spaces, those differences, is part of the beauty that makes up the human family, part of the goodness of God's creation."[73] Thus, intersexuality manifests "the genius and playfulness of the Creator, whose creations push the boundaries of our imaginations."[74] "To deny the value and beauty of these differences may disrespect and devalue the imagination and intention of the Creator,"[75] Sabia-Tanis warns. If we "condemn or attempt to

---

67. Sabia-Tanis, "Holy Creation," 203.

68. Tanis, *Trans-Gendered*, 58.

69. Examples from ibid.; DeFranza, *Sex Difference*, 177.

70. Ibid.

71. Sabia-Tanis, "Holy Creation," 201. For a recent example of the hybrid argument's influence, see Church of England, *Living in Love & Faith: Christian Teaching and Learning About Identity, Sexuality, Relationships, and Marriage* (London: Church House, 2020), 403.

72. Austen Hartke, "God's Unclassified World: Nonbinary Gender and the Beauty of Creation," *ChrCent* 135:9 (2018): 28; idem, *Transforming: The Bible and the Lives of Transgender Christians* (Louisville, KY: Westminster John Knox, 2018), 54.

73. Sabia-Tanis, "Holy Creation," 196.

74. Megan K. DeFranza, "Response to Justin Sabia-Tanis," in *Understanding Transgender Identities: Four Views*, ed. James K. Beilby and Paul Rhodes Eddy (Grand Rapids: Baker Academic, 2019), 234. For a similar appeal to "nature's 'playfulness,'" see Cornwall, "Troubling Bodies?" 12.

75. Sabia-Tanis, "Holy Creation," 195.

eradicate these naturally occurring variations, we are working counter to the will of God for creation, which God has declared to be good."[76] Indeed, "Blessed."[77]

D. Against the Hybrid Argument

Positively, the hybrid argument's encouragement for readers of Genesis 1 to exult in God's "wholly creative" goodness should be endorsed.[78] Following Aquinas, the manifold diversity in creation is an expression of God's infinite and self-communicative goodness (cf. Pss. 119:68; 145:7–9).[79] As Thomas opines, "What belongs to the essence of goodness befits God. But it belongs to the essence of goodness to communicate itself to others."[80] "You created," Augustine exults in God, "not out of need (*non ex indigentia*), but out of the plenitude of your own goodness (*ex plenitudine bonitatis*)."[81] Further, the argument correctly observes that Genesis 1 does not list "an exhaustive inventory of all God's good creatures."[82] It also helpfully reflects some of the literary and rhetorical features of the creation story that suggest created "kinds" (מין) need not be "understood narrowly in terms of the modern scientific concept of species."[83] Finally, as the hybrid hypothesis rightly submits—just because "other forms and mixed forms regularly seen in creation" are not listed in Genesis 1, it does not follow that they are automatically a "result of the Fall."[84]

Nevertheless, in considering the persuasiveness of the hybrid argument, the first thing to notice is that it is an interpretation from silence. Genesis 1 does not deal with "the question of whether one kind can turn into another: It simply notes that, according to God's plan, the different plants produce their seeds, each according to its kind, and that God made the animals, each by its kind."[85]

---

76. Ibid., 201.

77. Ibid., 204.

78. Ibid., 195.

79. Aquinas, *ST* 1.47.1 resp.

80. Aquinas, *ST* 3.1.1 resp.

81. Augustine, *Confessionum libri XIII* 13.4.5, ed. Martin Skutella and Luc Verheijen, CCSL 28 (Turnholti: Brepols, 1981), 244.

82. Megan K. DeFranza, "Good News for Gender Minorities," in *Understanding Transgender Identities: Four Views*, ed. James K. Beilby and Paul Rhodes Eddy (Grand Rapids: Baker Academic, 2019), 173. Although this observation is often made as an implicit critique against more traditional readings, it remains difficult to find anyone who fits DeFranza's strawman of thinking the descriptions of Genesis 1 are exhaustive.

83. Andrew Steinmann, *Genesis: An Introduction and Commentary* (Downers Grove, IL: IVP Academic, 2019), 54. *Contra* Claus Westermann, *Genesis 1–11: A Continental Commentary*, trans. John J. Scullion (Minneapolis: Fortress, 1994), 126.

84. DeFranza, *Sex Difference*, 177. Again, I have yet to find anyone who argues that "rivers, asteroids, planets, amphibians, dusk, dawn, etc." are a result of the fall (ibid.).

85. Collins, *Reading Genesis Well*, 278.

Admittedly, Collins's observation does not disqualify the hybrid argument as an interpretative possibility. Indeed, Genesis 1 says nothing explicit about putative hybrid categories of creation. Yet the hybrid argument remains an unpersuasive proposal because (i) the suggested parallels between non-human and human creation are problematic both philosophically and literarily, and (ii) its emphasis on divine creativity is dislocated from the predominant literary motif of divine ordering.

1. Moving from Non-Human to Human Creation The hybrid argument understands intersex embodiment as part of the diversity of creation, offering parallels with non-human examples. At one level, the proposed link between human and non-human hybrids may merely function to illustrate that mentioning two extremes does not preclude the existence of something in-between. Yet such a weak version of the hybrid argument does not appear to be articulated among innovationists. Rather, strong parallels are seemingly assumed between human and non-human hybrids. This raises certain philosophical and literary concerns.

i. Philosophical Concern A strong version of the hybrid argument confuses distinct categories and misapplies its confusion to humanity, with unfortunate theological consequences. I begin with Tanis's suggested "shore" parallel, a mixed hybrid of sea and land. For any example of diversity to count as a unique particular within a specific spectrum, the whole spectrum must presumably be metaphysically continuous, including the extremes.[86] However, it remains unclear in what way land and sea are metaphysically continuous with each other, for sea and land are distinct metaphysical categories. Rather, it seems more fitting to think of the shore as the name given to the place where the distinct substances of land and sea meet, that is, it is a *name* rather than a distinct *thing* at the edge of two actual things.[87]

Further, even if we assume that the land and the sea are metaphysically distinct things, but we insist that the mud of the shore is still a legitimate hybrid as a *thing* and not just as a *name*, then the very mixing of land and sea would create a *tertium quid*. If the shore really is a third thing, then its application to humanity remains problematic. This is because the application's logic not only requires "intersexuality as hybrid" to mirror "shore as hybrid," but it also assumes "male and female" mirror "land and sea" as poles on the spectrum. Given that land and sea are metaphysically distinct, the same presumably applies to male and female. Thus, in the application of "shore as hybrid" to intersexuality, it seems that intersex embodiment become a third thing (raising the worry of whether intersex persons

---

86. For concrete things to be metaphysically continuous they must share the same universal-essential properties.

87. For a similar objection, see Martin Davie, *Glorify God in Your Body: Human Identity and Flourishing in Marriage, Singleness and Friendship* (London: Lost Coin, 2018), 49 n.68.

are truly human),[88] and a metaphysical wedge is driven between maleness and femaleness (questioning the soteriological extent of the incarnation).

Given these undesirable implications, for a strong version of the "intersexuality as hybrid" argument to work it requires metaphysical continuity along the male/female spectrum, such that intersex embodiment is an example of sexed diversity *within* the single human species. But now we're dealing with a different question, to which the example of the shore becomes irrelevant. Genesis 1 simply does not specify diversity within a particular species, except in the case of humanity. This is not to make the unnecessarily strong counterclaim that the shore did not exist in creation. Nor does this prove that intersexuality does not participate in the diversity of creation. Rather, the objection is that a strong version of the hybrid argument seems to rest upon a philosophically problematic confusion of categories, whose application to humanity is illegitimate, problematized further by unwelcome anthropological and soteriological ramifications.

Second, although Tanis never appears to parse out any qualitative distinction between his hybrid examples, there is a sense in which dusk and dawn suggest a different kind of example that could offer a legitimate parallel with intersexuality. While the shore is the *place* between two metaphysically distinct *things*, dusk and dawn are on a genuine metaphysical spectrum, the operative metric being the existence of light. Thus, as dusk is situated on a light continuum inbetween night and day, so intersexuality is on a sexed continuum inbetween maleness and femaleness.

Nevertheless, if Tanis were to press such logic, a seamless move from "dusk as hybrid" to "intersexuality as hybrid" remains problematic. If night is the absence of natural light, then accurately naming dusk requires identifying the *degree* of light exhibited at a specific time. Dusk "has" more "light" than night. On this logic, regardless of whether femaleness or maleness map onto day or night, whichever gets identified with day "has" more of the essential ingredient required for movement along the continuum. If the metaphysical ingredient paralleling "light" is "sexuality," then it seems that for "intersexuality as hybrid" to work, it must assume something like the hierarchical one-sex theory discussed in the previous chapter—with all its sexist pitfalls.

Alternatively, we could horizontalize the continuum *qua* Thatcher, such that "humankind" rather than "sexuality" becomes the operative metric. But again, because location on the spectrum is determined by the *degree* of the metaphysical metric possessed (i.e., light), if we accept the "dusk to intersexuality" parallel, it must then be the case that some people are more human than others—the very conclusion that revisionists ardently oppose. Thus, the dusk/dawn parallel, while different from the "shore as hybrid" example, appears equally inadequate due to its sexist or dehumanizing implications. In short, if hybrid advocates were to articulate the underpinning logic of their speculative analogies (about which the biblical text is silent), then philosophical concerns remain. To be fair, innovationists do not vocalize the strong claim, but their failure to clarify the nature and function

---

88. Recall the anxiety of Gross, "Intersexuality," 70.

of their putative "hybrid" parallels leaves the strong claim (and its philosophical concerns) open.

ii. Literary Concern Supplementing the philosophical challenge is a literary critique that attends to Genesis 1's emphasis on human uniqueness. While Genesis 1 indicates humanity's commonality with non-human creation—for example, similar food (1:29–30); same means of reproduction with the same blessing (1:22, 28); created on the same day on the same land as the animals (1:24–26)—there are several important literary features that emphasize human uniqueness, thereby problematizing innovationist appeals to other aspects of creation to justify SP.

For example, the narrative of day 6 is longer than that of any other day (1:26–31), marking it out as "the zone of maximum linguistic turbulence,"[89] and causing the reader to slow down and focus attention.[90] Second, in Gen. 1:26, for humanity's creation alone God deliberates before acting ("let us make"), the clause-initial position cohortative deviating from the literary pattern of jussives ("let there be") evidenced in other events (1:3, 6, 9, 14, 20, 24).[91] Whatever is indicated by divine plurality,[92] God creates humanity in a distinctly personal way, literarily marked by "a notable change in style."[93] Third, the creation account peaks in 1:27 with its poetic threefold and repetitive structure (note also the triple use of ברא rather than the regular עשה).[94] As argued earlier, the circumstantial information offered in the subcola of 27b and 27c—grammatically marked as asyndetic with a different verbal pattern—arrests the reader's attention upon this climactic event.

Consequently, while "the human creation is deeply involved with the nonhuman," the literary features presented earlier mark out "humanity as distinct within the whole picture."[95] "Clearly, in form, content, and context," Trible concludes, "this report of the creation of male and female is unique."[96] Humanity's uniqueness does not pass a verdict on the existence or non-existence of intersexuality as an example of good diversity within creation. Rather, Genesis 1's literary emphasis on human uniqueness questions the ease with which the hybrid argument moves from contemporary observations about nonhuman creation to definitive judgments

89. Collins, *Reading Genesis Well*, 163.

90. Stephen G. Dempster presents a column chart showing the number of words allotted to each day of creation. Day 6 has more than twice as many words than the next closest day (*Dominion and Dynasty: A Biblical Theology of the Hebrew Bible*, NSBT 15 [Leicester, UK: Apollos, 2003], 57).

91. Garr, *Image and Likeness*, 85.

92. For a survey of the major positions, see David J. A. Clines, "The Image of God in Man," *TynBul* 19 (1968): 62–9.

93. Gentry, "Kingdom Through Covenant," 22.

94. J. G. McConville, *Being Human in God's World: An Old Testament Theology of Humanity* (Grand Rapids: Baker Academic, 2016), 15.

95. Ibid., 17.

96. Trible, *Rhetoric of Sexuality*, 15.

regarding the sexed embodiment of humanity in the creation account of Genesis 1. Humanity's uniqueness suggests that what *may* be true of non-human creation is not necessarily and equally applicable to humanity.

2. The Primacy of Divine Ordering While hybrid advocates place a healthy emphasis upon God's imaginative creativity expressed in the abundance of biodiversity,[97] they fail to locate divine creativity under the more literarily prominent banner of God's ordering wisdom. This omission need not entail that the hybrid argument lacks an account of divine order in creation. Hybrids are presumably divinely determined. Yet by highlighting how Genesis 1 depicts divine creativity *through* the predominant motif of divine order, I question the suitability of the hybrid hypothesis for interpreting intersex embodiment.

Several reasons exist for privileging the primacy of divine order in Genesis 1. First, note how the chapter is introduced. Gen. 1:2 portrays the earth as תהו ("formless") and בהו ("empty"). תהו speaks of a "lack of order—the absence of the necessary conditions for fruitfulness."[98] בהו refers to "the barrenness that results from that lack of order."[99] Combined, the narrative presents the problem of a "world that is unfruitful because it is disordered,"[100] what Ben Ollenburger calls "an indiscriminate mess."[101] Into such "amorphous chaos" God dictates ordered "definition and identity and differentiation."[102]

Second, we see such divinely determined distinction at the rhetorical-structural level of the text, with the realms formed in days one to three being filled with suitable residents in days four to six.[103] Each day itself is then carefully ordered, being "marked by a repetitive structure of announcement and execution report (*Wortbericht* and *Tatbericht*),"[104] with corresponding "status updates" at the end of days three and six.[105]

---

97. Note the parallelism between the glory of God and the works of God in Ps. 104:31. Cf. Ps. 24:1.

98. Michael LeFebvre, *The Liturgy of Creation: Understanding Calendars in Old Testament Context* (Downers Grove, IL: IVP Academic, 2019), 139.

99. Ibid.

100. Ibid.

101. Ben C. Ollenburger, "Creation and Peace: Creator and Creature in Genesis 1–11," in *The Old Testament in the Life of God's People: Essays in Honor of Elmer A. Martens*, ed. Jon M. Isaak (Winona Lake, IN: Eisenbrauns, 2009), 148.

102. Gregory Mobley, *The Return of the Chaos Monsters and Other Backstories of the Bible* (Grand Rapids: Eerdmans, 2012), 20. Divine fiat rules out any suggestion of conflict in Genesis 1, whether in the form of theomachy or *Chaoskampf*.

103. E.g., Kenneth A. Mathews, *Genesis 1–11:26*, NAC 1A (Nashville, TN: Broadman & Holman, 1996), 115–16; Gordon J. Wenham, *Genesis 1–15*, WBC 1 (Nashville, TN: Thomas Nelson, 1987), 6–7.

104. Bird, "Male and Female," 135.

105. LeFebvre, *Liturgy of Creation*, 142.

Third, zooming in on two specific lexemes, Genesis 1 emphasizes God's ordering wisdom through "separation," the repeated hiphil of בדל connoting intentional causation (Gen. 1:4, 6, 7, 14, 18).[106] Further, divine ordering is evident in God's work of distinguishing plants and animals "according to their kinds" (למין in Gen. 1:11, 12 [x2], 21 [x2], 24 [x2], 25 [x3]). The adjectival use of מין emphasizes God as the Total Creator, who has made everything "in all their varieties."[107] Putting בדל and למין together suggests that creation's manifold abundance is rightly ordered. As Beauchamp submits, God brings order to his "immutable works" through separation and his "mutable ones" through distinction.[108] In all this, the primacy of divine ordering is evident in God *forming* what was תהו and *filling* what was בהו. The rhetorical implication is that without clear separation and differentiation, chaos remains.

The reversing of תהו *and* בהו suggests that instilling order has a particular purpose: "To make the land fruitful, and in that fruitfulness to enable all creation to feast (that is, to thrive)."[109] Striking for its agrarian audience, Genesis 1 depicts God as the "Model Farmer" who orders his world for fruitfulness (Gen. 1:11–12, 15, 17–18, 20, 22, 24).[110] As humanity's prototype, God blesses his image bearers to imitate his wise ordering by keeping "everything in balance and in its proper boundaries for the fruitfulness God ordained."[111] As I develop subsequently, creation being "ordered for fruitfulness" will be significant for interpreting humanity's sexed embodiment, for human procreative fruitfulness requires dimorphic correspondence.[112] Indeed, there may be literary clues that creation at large is ordered along dimorphic lines, Clines evincing that "in Genesis 2, as in Genesis 1, reality has a binary structure . . . by the forging of bonds: between humans and the soil, humans and the animals, the man and the woman, humanity and God."[113] Whether one is persuaded or not of creation's "binary structure," the main point from Genesis 1 is that God reverses תהו ובהו by dividing creation into specific form(s) for the purpose of specific function(s), namely, the function of fruitfulness.

---

106. WHS §147; BHRG §16.7.2.

107. Richard Neville, "Differentiation in Genesis 1: An Exegetical Creation Ex Nihilo," *JBL* 130 (2011): 226. See also Paul H. Seely, "The Meaning of Mîn, 'Kind,'" *SCB* 9 (1997): 47–56.

108. Paul Beauchamp, "מין," *TDOT* 8:289. See also idem, *Création et Séparation: Étude Exégétique du Chapitre Premier de la Genèse*, LD (Paris: Cerf, 2005).

109. LeFebvre, *Liturgy of Creation*, 144.

110. Ibid., 165.

111. Ibid., 178.

112. Ibid., 149–66.

113. David J. A. Clines, *The Theme of the Pentateuch*, 2nd ed., JSOTSup 10 (Sheffield: JSOT, 1997), 81. Clines goes on to demonstrate how the "binary structure" of creation experiences "uncreation" in the fall and through the flood, before being "re-created" in Genesis 8: "Seedtime and harvest, cold and heat, summer and winter, day and night are re-established (8:22)."

These literary observations remain overlooked by the hybrid argument. Again, I am not saying that hybrid advocates have no account of God instilling order in creation. It is simply that no account of order is proposed. Innovationist emphasis is laid upon God being "wholly creative." Yet when we explore the rhetorical-structural and lexical-semantic features of Genesis 1, an account of order emerges from the text that emphasizes God's concern to separate and distinguish for the purpose of creation's fruitfulness. As creatures, humans are ordered for fruitfulness, and as royal image bearers participate in God's work of ordering creation for fruitfulness.

Tanis opines that "to deny the value and beauty of these [hybrid] differences may disrespect and devalue the imagination and intention of the Creator."[114] Undoubtedly, the creativity and imagination of God are lavish (cf. Ps. 139:6, 17–18). But Genesis 1 indicates that God is a God of ordered creativity. As Bavinck puts it, there is a "splendid harmony" in the universe—a unity that is "not a uniformity but an infinitely varied diversity."[115] Diversity in creation is good and beautiful, glorifying God, with each diverse particular intentionally ordered within the whole *universe*.

Contra Tanis, failing to appreciate how creation is divinely ordered for fruitfulness may ironically devalue and disrespect God's intent to inscribe order in creation. Indeed, given Tanis's suggestion that all things participate in the good diversity of creation, it remains unclear how Tanis accounts for disease, disorder, and dysfunction, other than by insisting that all is good and blessed.[116] As such, when considering a condition like barrenness, it seems that Tanis's logic could imply that he labels "good" what the Bible laments as "bad" (e.g., Isa. 54:1–5), and "blessed" what the Bible calls "cursed" (e.g., Deut. 28:18). Further, it remains equally unclear how God is not directly responsible for the pain and suffering that results from bodily dysfunction. If cancer counts as part of the good diversity of creation, then on Tanis's logic, it appears to come straight from God's hand. Ironically, for all Tanis's emphasis on the need for a theology of the sexed body to be pastorally sensitive, Tanis's proposal seemingly lacks the resources to provide Christian compassion.

To conclude, the hybrid argument typically gets presented in the form of broad rhetorical questions. If we resist classifying the hybrids of dusk or dawn as postlapsarian defects, why should we not celebrate another hybrid like intersexuality as a good of the creation event? Some may intend the argument merely to operate as a weak speculative analogy. Yet such a caveat remains unarticulated, suggesting a stronger intention for the argument. However, when the stronger form of the argument is scrutinized, not only does it fail to account for the literary-rhetorical emphasis of God bringing fruitful order out of chaos, but it

114. Sabia-Tanis, "Holy Creation," 195.

115. Bavinck, *RD*, 2:437.

116. I press this observation when considering the sexed body in the fall (Chapter 4) and in the consummation (Chapter 6).

also appears to rely upon spectrum thinking that ends up blurring the distinctions Genesis 1 aims to establish. Indeed, the blurring of ordered distinction appears to promote a return to chaos—a de-creative act. In sum, the hybrid argument fails to provide an adequate theological explanation for intersexuality.

E. *"Male and Female" in the Creation Event*

So far, engagement with arguments for SP in the creation event has been largely deconstructive. Before assessing the trajectory argument, which moves beyond the theo-dramatic event of creation to focus on God's creational intent for sexed embodiment, I shall briefly propose an account of the meaning and significance of "male and female" in Gen. 1:27, drawing on the immediate and wider literary context of Genesis.

As argued earlier, within the chiasm of Gen. 1:27–28, the syntactical relationship between בצלם אלהים (27ba) and זכר ונקבה (27ca) is one of progressive rather than synonymous parallelism. "Male and female" does not explicate "in the image of God" but adds to it by identifying its scope. However exactly one should define the *imago Dei*,[117] "male and female" *denotes* its scope,[118] as well as *connotes* reproductive function, anticipating the reflective colon in the chiastic mirror—the subsequent creational volitives of פרו ורבו ומלאו (28).

Concerning the scope of the image, whether "male and female" are read as a binary pair or poles on a spectrum, the text teaches that all humans are created בצלם אלהים (27ba). This is an important point to stress for any theology of intersexuality. Humanity bears God's image not just collectively but also individually. As Kilner maintains, in Gen. 1:26–28 there is an intriguing "tension between the singularity and plurality of humankind."[119] In v.26, the divine deliberation refers to an anarthrous אדם, and then in v.27 God creates the collective noun האדם, before flitting from the singular pronoun "him" to the plural pronoun "them." Kilner argues from this grammatical tension that the image refers to "the totality of humanity and yet immediately also suggest[s] the plurality of individuals who make up that totality."[120] Thus, all individual humans bear the dignity of being created as divine image bearers, regardless of their bodily sex, as well as humanity as a whole serving as God's

---

117. For an overview of how the *imago* has been interpreted by both ancients and moderns, see Stephen L. Herring, *Divine Substitution: Humanity as the Manifestation of Deity in the Hebrew Bible and the Ancient Near East*, FRLANT 247 (Göttingen: Vandenhoeck & Ruprecht, 2013), 88–9.

118. Barry L. Bandstra, *Genesis 1–11: A Handbook on the Hebrew Text*, BHHB (Waco, TX: Baylor University Press, 2008), 96.

119. John F. Kilner, *Dignity and Destiny: Humanity in the Image of God* (Grand Rapids: Eerdmans, 2015), 86.

120. Ibid., 88.

representational presence.[121] As Kutzer concludes, "Both sexes are images of God, honored with the same dignity."[122] Yet, if "male and female" denotes the scope of the *imago Dei*, and "male and female" minimally signifies a merism for all humanity, intersexuality could implicitly fit within the "male and female" of the creation event.

Nevertheless, the way the phrase "male and female" gets employed elsewhere in Genesis suggests that "male and female" in the creation event connotes the capacity to reproduce. As such, "male and female" should be interpreted along sexually dimorphic lines—one male and one female being the individually necessary and jointly sufficient conditions for the proper functioning of procreation.

The first of the five other uses of the collocation זכר ונקבה is found in Gen. 5:2: "Male and female he created them. And he blessed them."[123] Following Bandstra, v.2 is an appositive paratactic expansion of v.1 ("when God created humankind"), with "male and female" at minimum indicating the scope of God's creative action in making אדם.[124] Further, the wider context of Genesis 5, with its genealogy and repeated refrain of "and he died" after eight of the ten figures,[125] suggests that a key reason why God made humankind "male and female" was so that humankind would continue to multiply. Admittedly, an immediate motivation for multiplication in Genesis 5 is the universal reality of death, seemingly absent in Genesis 1.[126] Nonetheless, whether one affirms or denies prelapsarian human death,[127] at minimum the phrase "male and female" in Gen. 5:2 appears to denote

121. Accordingly, humans are created "as" rather than "in" the image of God, taking the כ as a "כ of essence" (GBHS §4.1.5.h [119]). On the nature and function of the image's democratization within the ANE and its representational presence of the divine, see Catherine L. McDowell, *The Image of God in the Garden of Eden: The Creation of Humankind in Genesis 2:5–3:24 in Light of the Mīs Pî Pīt Pî and Wpt-R Rituals of Mesopotamia and Ancient Egypt*, Siphrut 15 (Winona Lake, IN: Eisenbrauns, 2015), 137.

122. Kutzer, "Mann/Frau," 75.

123. For further parallels between Gen. 1:26–28 and Gen. 5:1–3, see Gary Edward Schnittjer, *Old Testament Use of Old Testament: A Book-by-Book Guide* (Grand Rapids: Zondervan Academic, 2021), 5–6.

124. Bandstra, *Genesis 1–11*, 288.

125. The remaining two are Enoch, who was mysteriously "taken" by God (Gen. 5:24), and Noah, who did eventually die (Gen. 9:29).

126. This observation does not necessarily mean that humanity was only sexually differentiated in logical anticipation of the fall and death, *pace* the common interpretation of Nyssa, *On the Making of Man* 16–17 (NPNF[2] 5:404–7). For Nyssen's sexual morphology, highlighting Nyssen's resistance to systematization, see Raphael A. Cadenhead, *The Body and Desire: Gregory of Nyssa's Ascetical Theology*, CLA 4 (Oakland, CA: University of California Press, 2018), 96–104.

127. See Chapter 4.

the scope of humankind and connote the capacity (and increased necessity) for reproduction.[128]

The remaining four uses of "male and female" occur in the Flood narrative. In Gen. 6:19–20, God commands Noah to bring into the ark two of every living thing, "according to its kind" (למינהו), specifically "male and female" for the explicit purpose of keeping them alive (להחיות).[129] In Gen. 7:2–3, God commands Noah to take seven pairs of all clean animals, one pair of all unclean animals (v.2), and birds by sevens that are "male and female" (v.3), the animal classification of "man and his woman" (איש ואשתו) being synonymous with the avian "male and female" (זכר ונקבה). Again, the ל prepositional prefix indicates that God delineates "male and female" for the express purpose of animal and avian offspring living upon the face of the earth, after he has annihilated/blotted out every living thing (v.4). Finally, since Gen. 7:6–16 is the narratival execution of God's command in the preceding pericope, the meaning of "male and female" in Gen. 7:9 and 7:16 is identical to 7:3.

Thus, in all five occurrences of the phrase "male and female" outside Gen. 1:27, reproduction is consistently a central aspect of its meaning (even if death provides a differing motivation). The two terms זכר and נקבה are collocated in other places within different constructions,[130] thereby not necessarily conveying any reproductive connotations. Yet the precise phrase "male and female" only occurs in Genesis, where it is always associated with reproduction.

1. "Male and Female" in Genesis 1 In returning to the "male and female" of Gen. 1:27, the reproductive connotations indicated from other uses of the phrase are seen when we attend to the juxtaposition of v.27 with v.28, both syntactically and conceptually. First, syntactically, as I advanced earlier, a chiasm exists between vv. 27–28, such that the *imago* (27a–b) conceptually parallels ruling and subduing (28b), with "male and female" (27c) paralleling the volitives to "be fruitful and multiply and fill the earth" (28a). In the outer couplet, the relationship between the *imago* and ruling has already been outlined in Gen. 1:26. God stamps human beings as images of his representational presence for the *purpose* of ruling (וירדו).[131] The motif of ruling as God's representatives is rearticulated at the end of the string of five volitives in v.28 (רדה, collocated with כבש). As Clines clarifies, ruling is not

---

128. Chris H. Smith offers a further reason for the necessity to procreate, highlighting how "the lineage of godly offspring" must participate in propagating the messianic seed ("Singles in the Family of God: An Ecclesial Account of Unmarried Devotion" [PhD diss., Wheaton College, 2021], 241–53).

129. The preposition ל modifies the *hiphil* infinitive construct indicating purpose (WHS §277; BHRG §39.11.6.d). This remains true even if the force is weak (JM §168c).

130. E.g., Lev. 3:1, 6; 12:7; Num. 5:3; Deut. 4:16.

131. The opening cohortative of 1:26 requires the subsequent *waw*-consecutive imperfect to denote purpose or result (WHS §181a). Thus, following Gentry, "The ruling is not the essence of the divine image, but rather a result of being made as the divine image" ("Kingdom Through Covenant," 25).

"definitive of the image itself," but dominion "is so immediate and necessary a consequence of the image, it loses the character of a mere derivative of the image and eventually becomes a constitutive part of the image itself."[132] The function of ruling does not exhaust the *imago*, but it is inseparably connected.[133]

If the syntactical relationship of the outer couplet informs the inner couplet of "male and female" (27c) and "be fruitful and multiply and fill the earth" (28a), then there is a syntactical case for asserting that reproduction is a key connotation of "male and female." Thus, according to Fischer, "The division of the two sexes arises from God's will and prepares for the upcoming blessing and multiplication in v.28."[134] Like the link between the *imago* and ruling, procreation does not exhaust "male and female," but it is inseparably connected.

Moreover, this syntactical point may be supported by a more conceptual observation about the five volitives of v.28. If ruling creation is a consequence of being created in the *imago Dei*, then the implication from the logical connection between the five volitives in v.28 is that ruling (רדה) requires subduing (כבשׁ). But to subdue creation (presumably by bringing order for fruitfulness *qua* the archetype in Genesis 1), ectypal and finite images (limited in space and place),[135] need to be spatially present throughout creation, hence the requirement to fill the earth. However, whether one posits an original pair or a community of c.10,000 *hominins*,[136] the text implies that much of the earth remains unpopulated by humans, a point emphasized in the aloneness of האדם in the second creation account (Gen. 2:18). Filling the earth with other finite images requires multiplying in number (רבה). And to multiply numbers requires being fruitful (פרה), that is, jointly exercising procreative capacity. As Gagnon summarizes, "The pinnacle of God's creative work is . . . human beings as creatures capable of receiving and carrying out commands from God in relation to the rest of creation. Filling or populating the earth with humans is a precondition for ruling it, and procreation is a precondition for filling the earth."[137]

Therefore, God's gift of being made in his image to govern creation secures the likelihood of "male and female" being interpreted as sexually dimorphic

---

132. Clines, "Image of God," 96. Cf. Psalm 8.

133. If the function of ruling did exhaust the *imago*, then those who cannot rule (e.g., coma patients) would presumably no longer be divine image bearers (at least on an individualist reading of the *imago*). Yet even for the collectivist interpretation of the *imago*, the coma patient would only qualify as ruling in a derivative sense, suggesting their second-class status.

134. Georg Fischer, *Genesis 1–11*, HThKAT (Freiburg: Herder, 2018), 154.

135. As Gen. 2:7–8 will indicate, האדם is limited by being embodied and placed in a garden.

136. On the historicity of Adam and the question of human origins, see, e.g., Matthew Barrett, ed., *Four Views on the Historical Adam*, Counterpoints (Grand Rapids: Zondervan Academic, 2013); William Lane Craig, *In Quest of the Historical Adam: A Biblical and Scientific Exploration* (Grand Rapids: Eerdmans, 2021).

137. Robert A. J. Gagnon, *The Bible and Homosexual Practice: Texts and Hermeneutics* (Nashville, TN: Abingdon, 2001), 57.

correspondents. Cohering with the rest of Genesis 1, humanity is ordered as male and female for fruitfulness. While Adam and Eve did not *need* to procreate in order to qualify as God's representatives themselves,[138] it is fitting that the eternally generative God, whose rule is total in extent, should bless and commission his finite representatives to share analogically in the extension of his total rule through creaturely generation.[139] Thus, ruling is secured and extended through procreating.[140] The juxtaposition of vv.27–28 suggests that procreation is the expected and intended functional outworking of a particular ontological configuration—the "sexuate correspondence" of humanity as "male and female."[141]

2. "Male and Female" in Genesis 2 In considering the contribution of Genesis 2 toward an accurate understanding of sexed embodiment in creation, it is noteworthy that most pro-SP arguments concentrate on Genesis 1. This is probably because Genesis 1 focuses more on the biological essence of humanity, whereas Genesis 2 spotlights "psycho-social" relations.[142] Nonetheless, if we see the second creation account as complementing the first,[143] specifically unpacking what dominion looks like for Adam in relation to the animals, creation, God, and the

---

138. This observation severs any necessary link between the *imago Dei* and procreation, guarding against the unwarranted and damaging suggestion that humans only image God when they procreate. Indeed, note how other creatures who are not image bearers also procreate (Gen. 1:22). Admittedly, if one reads the *imago* in a collective sense, then one could argue that SD need not be the exclusive norm. That is, the text only mentions "male and female" because of a sociological concern about procreation. However, as I develop below, such an argument appears to conflict with how the rest of the OT read Gen. 1:28. In addition, although it is important to note the socio-historical situatedness of Genesis 1–2, such that cultural realities are expressed in the text (i.e., in the ANE, one needed many children to survive), the paradigmatic nature of Genesis 1–2 suggests that the text should not be restricted merely to an ANE description of historical and cultural pressures.

139. On the image of God being made manifest through the presence of children in Genesis, see Julie F. Parker, "God as a Child in the Hebrew Bible? Playing with the Possibilities," in *T&T Clark Handbook of Children in the Bible and the Biblical World*, ed. Sharon Betsworth and Julie F. Parker, TTCH (London: T&T Clark, 2019), 160–7.

140. For examples of ancient and modern Jewish agreement with this point, see Yair Lorberbaum, *In God's Image: Myth, Theology, and Law in Classical Judaism* (New York: Cambridge University Press, 2015), 224.

141. Belousek, *Marriage*, 36. See also Julián Marías, *Metaphysical Anthropology: The Empirical Structure of Human Life*, trans. Frances M. López-Morillas (University Park, PA: Pennsylvania State University Press, 1971), 133–42.

142. Bird, "Male and Female," 158.

143. Collins, *Reading Genesis Well*, 169. Collins also identifies several lexical links between Genesis 1 and Genesis 2–3, as well as presenting passages from the OT (Ps. 104:14; Isa. 43:1, 7) and the NT (Matt. 19:4–5; 1 Cor. 15:45, 49) that suggest Genesis 1 and 2 should be read together (ibid., 225).

woman, several features are instructive for discerning the nature and parameters of sexed embodiment in the creation event.

In Gen. 2:18, the emphatically fronted "not good" (לֹא־טוֹב) of Adam being "alone" refers not just to his need for "companionship and friendship,"[144] nor simply to his need for a colleague in working (עבד) and watching (שׁמר) the garden (Gen. 2:15). Relational companionship and material assistance may well be in the literary foreground, expanding our understanding of humanity ordered for fruitfulness beyond mere procreation (Gen. 1:28) to include existential, social, and relational dimensions, climactically encapsulated in the heterosexual, monogamous, covenantal marriage of Gen. 2:22–25 (the right context for procreation).[145] Yet given the theological cohesion between Genesis 1 and 2, Adam's "helper" (2:18) needs to be at minimum a procreative partner so that together they can multiply other divine image-bearing gardeners, and so extend the boundaries of God's ordered garden, thereby extending God's rule. The reasonable deduction is that the required and fitting helper for Adam and his representative task should not be an animal, nor another male, nor an infertile female, but specifically a fertile female with whom he can co-create more gardeners. Thus, as Collins maintains, "The complementarity of 'male and female' (1:27), where together they are in God's image and after his likeness, finds explanation in a wordplay: 'she shall be called Woman (Heb. אשׁה, *'ishah*), because she was taken out of Man (Heb. אישׁ, *'ish*).'"[146] As gendered terms, אישׁ and אשׁה foreground relationality over ontology, but such relational correspondence is grounded in biological realities that are inherently complementary for the purpose of procreation.

Therefore, given the procreative connotations of "male and female" in Gen. 1:27, evidenced in the immediate (v.28) and wider (Genesis 5 and 7) literary context, combined with the deduction from Genesis 2 that a fitting helper for Adam was necessarily a fertile female, it seems reasonable to conclude that humanity's sexed embodiment in the creation event was likely the exclusive norm of male or female. SD does not strictly explicate the *imago Dei* but denotes its scope with a focus on reproduction.

---

144. Sabia-Tanis, "Holy Creation," 198.

145. A defense of a traditional view of marriage is beyond the scope of this book. Genesis 2's more expansive understanding of fruitfulness is ultimately fulfilled theologically in the spiritually fruitful union of Christ and his church (Rev. 21:2). "Fruitfulness" expanding beyond procreation will become significant in Chapter 5, when I consider whether procreation and marriage exhaust SD. As I discuss in Chapter 5, SD relates to humanity's creational structure (pertaining to humanity's *natural* kinds and ends), whereas marriage is a creational ordinance related to a moral and *historical* dimension. Creational ordinances are not arbitrarily related to creational structures. Rather, in loving goodness God gifts humanity with creational ordinances to evoke and historically unfold the God-given goodness natural to creational structures, for the good of human flourishing, and ultimately toward richer communion with God.

146. Collins, *Reading Genesis Well*, 172.

Nonetheless, even if one recognizes the necessary link between procreation and SD, the question remains as to what extent the call to procreate is universally relevant for all humanity without exception or simply pertains to the species in general. As Thatcher muses, "Could not complementarity be affirmed as a general or species-rule while allowing for different individuals within the species to be different, and to opt out of what I call the 'procreative imperative'? Why this all-or-nothing stance?"[147]

An initial response could insist that the imperatival mood of פרו ורבו dictates a universal command for "every individual without exception."[148] If procreation is a "God-given duty" of creation,[149] then we should expect a good God to provide the requisite embodiment of SD. And such sexuate correspondence would be the exclusive norm; otherwise, God would be capricious, good to some and not others, contradicting the tenor of Genesis 1. However, while the imperatival mood often functions as a command,[150] such a hasty conclusion in this case is syntactically and contextually unnuanced (and so unwarranted).[151] As Jamie Viands outlines, the collocation in Gen. 1:28 of the volitive mood with the divine speech-act of blessing suggests that the procreative "imperative" expresses God's permission, intention, and empowerment for humanity to experience the blessing of fruitfulness.[152] To illustrate via another speech-act in the creation event, Gen. 1:28 appears to operate in a different category to something like the speech-act of "you shall not eat" (לא תאכל) in Gen. 2:17. The former functions as an invitation to be lived into. The latter emphasizes agential responsibility as a command to be volitionally obeyed, with dire consequences for disobedience. Given Gen. 1:28's collocation with "blessing," it is thus perhaps better to read it as a blessed commission rather than a command proper.[153]

While interpreting the procreative imperative as a blessed commission highlights God's purposeful intention for humanity, the question remains as to whether such an intent is universal for all without exception or a generic blessing for all without distinction. Drawing in Genesis 2, is the idyllic picture of Adam and Eve descriptive of the statistical majority or normative and prototypical? A fuller

---

147. Thatcher, *God, Sex, and Gender*, 42.

148. Smith, "Singles in the Family of God," 217. For Gen. 1:28 as a command, see also Wenham, *Genesis 1–15*, 33; John Goldingay, *Old Testament Theology: Israel's Gospel* (Downers Grove, IL: IVP Academic, 2003), 379.

149. Sarna, *Genesis*, 41.

150. WHS §188.

151. It also raises the pastorally pressing question of whether someone who does not (or perhaps cannot) procreate disobeys God.

152. Jamie Viands, *I Will Surely Multiply Your Offspring: An Old Testament Theology of the Blessing of Progeny with Special Attention to the Latter Prophets* (Eugene, OR: Pickwick, 2014), 26–30. For imperatives functioning as permission or promise, see GBHS §3.3.2.b,c.

153. This will become significant for thinking through the interplay between covenant faithfulness and fruitfulness, childlessness and curse, in Chapter 4.

answer requires examining the canonical context beyond Genesis 1–2, assessing how God's people read the procreative commission of Gen. 1:28.

II. Scene 2: Intersex in Creational Intent

A. The Trajectory Argument

While primal androgyny and the hybrid argument question SD from the perspective of Genesis 1–2, a further argument looks beyond the event of creation, discerning a trajectory of othering initiated in creation and realized in subsequent history, that suggests the inclusion of intersexuality as a creational good. Intersex embodiment may not have existed in the creation event, but like art or technology, intersexuality is the flowering of seeds intentionally sown in creation—creational diversity rather than disordered curse.

Assuming the validity of the hybrid argument, Megan DeFranza argues that "understanding Adam and Eve as prototypes for all men or women misreads the scope and intention of the creation narratives and overlooks the place of these two characters in the story of revelation and redemption."[154] Instead, reading Genesis 1–2 in its narratival and canonical context reveals a fecund trajectory of othering.[155] A male Adam and a female Eve are simply mentioned in the creation accounts because their "literal fruitfulness was necessary to the divine project" of othering to begin.[156] Thus, Adam and Eve should not be read as prototypes of fixity but as parents of fecundity—a "fountainhead of others who may become more 'other' than their parents could have ever conceived."[157] They are our "first *parents*" rather than "the *pattern* that God established for all people"; the "*beginning* of the story" rather than "God's *best*"; the "statistical *majority*" and not the "exclusive *model* for all humans."[158]

Thus begins a trajectory of othering, which starts with children (Genesis 4), and widens out in the OT to "family, kin, clan, and nation," before extending further in the NT to the church, and even enemies (Matt. 5:43–48).[159] "The love between two is expanded," DeFranza exults: "Love grows. The binary-sex other multiplies to include ever more others."[160] Indeed, from this "expansive notion of otherness . . . other others are born from these parents [Adam and Eve]: other ages, other languages, other cultures, and even others whose sex does not match either

---

154. DeFranza, *Sex Difference*, 178.

155. The use of "othering" is non-pejorative. "Othering" conveys diversification.

156. DeFranza, *Sex Difference*, 178.

157. Ibid.

158. DeFranza, "Gender Minorities," 173, italics original.

159. DeFranza, *Sex Difference*, 179.

160. Ibid.

parent."[161] This trajectory of othering finds its culmination in an eschatological community that is "comprised of more than males and females," promised in Isa. 56:3–7 and fulfilled in Rev. 7:9.[162] Indeed, Revelation 7 "describes human identities that had no place in the garden of Eden. There was no diversity of nations, tribes, peoples, and languages in the garden, yet these differences are preserved at the End. Eunuchs are promised a place in God's house *as they are*, not after some kind of restoration to an Edenic pattern (Isa. 56:5)."[163] Thus, racial and ethnic diversity offers an instructive parallel for diversity of bodily sex.

In summary, "Reading the Genesis account in light of the larger biblical narrative, we are able to affirm the goodness of sex difference as the fountainhead of human difference without requiring the male-female pattern to become the paradigmatic form of the other."[164] SD may well have existed in the creation event, but Genesis 1's emphasis on fecundity indicates that SD is not God's paradigmatic, creational intent. Indeed, a normative SD chafes against the canonical context, which witnesses to a trajectory of othering.

B. Against the Trajectory Argument

The chief methodological contribution of the trajectory argument is to push an examination of sexed embodiment beyond the locus of the creation event, and into the wider canonical context to discern God's creational intent. This is helpful for two reasons. First, while Genesis 1–2 is certainly the place to start for a theology of intersexuality developed from the perspective of creation, it offers few explicit statements about sexed embodiment, and even these are embedded within a larger rhetorical-theological framework. Second, the trajectory argument appreciates our limited access to the state of original integrity, both epistemologically and historically.[165] As such, the encouragement to draw resources from the canonical context promises firmer ground in terms of closer parallels with our lived experience.

The trajectory argument's thesis is that the unfolding narrative of scripture reveals God's creational intent for othering. Even if "male and female" were the exclusive norm in the creation event, intersexuality may be interpreted as part of God's unfolding creational intent. The trajectory thesis rests on two claims: (i) creation is about fecundity, not fixity; (ii) the canonical context indicates a trajectory of othering that demands intersex embodiment as a creational good.

---

161. Ibid., 182.

162. Ibid., 184.

163. DeFranza, "Gender Minorities," 174, italics original. In this 2019 essay, DeFranza transposes her creational "trajectory of othering" argument in Christological and eschatological key. I measure its melody in Chapter 5.

164. DeFranza, *Sex Difference*, 179–80.

165. See Chapter 4.

In response to the first claim, DeFranza's assertion as to the predominance of fecundity in Genesis 1 parallels Tanis's proposal within the hybrid argument for the primacy of divine creativity. Like the rebuttal to Tanis, while both creativity and fecundity are important motifs in the text, both are subsumed under the organizing principle of divine order. Just as God's creativity is a divinely ordered creativity, fecundity is not indiscriminate—at least not from God's perspective. Rather, God purposefully orders creaturely development according to the nature of each creature, a point no doubt obvious to Genesis' agrarian audience. In his ordered creativity, God has ordered biological boundaries *for* fecundity.[166] Thus, rather than pitting parental fecundity against prototypical fixity, perhaps it is more consistent with the literary-theological thrust of Genesis 1 to interpret Adam and Eve as representatives of a prototypical fixity that demands parental fecundity. Adam and Eve are not simply the beginning of the trajectory of othering, but are paradigmatic for sexed embodiment, as the canonical context demonstrates.[167]

This brings us to DeFranza's second claim. While creation may well initiate a trajectory of othering when it comes to language, ethnicity, and culture, all of which are to be celebrated (Rev. 7:9), the "male and female" pattern established in Eden was consistently interpreted by the OT as the universal and creational norm.[168] We see this by attending to the perceived intention for sexed embodiment, which in turn reveals the expected and creational ontology of sexed embodiment. In short, the recurring commission to "be fruitful and multiply," combined with the centrality of children for one's individual covenant identity (*qua* the blessing of faithfulness), suggests that God's creational intent for sexed embodiment was the exclusive rather than the statistical norm of male and female.

1. "Be Fruitful and Multiply" in Canonical Context The collocation "be fruitful" (פרה) and "multiply" (רבה) occurs twelve times in the OT, typically in the context

---

166. This specific counter to the trajectory argument rests upon a certain reading of human evolutionary history, for by privileging the biblical emphasis upon a divinely ordered creativity, it interprets the modern category of species as an ontological rather than a mere historical category. As such, while welcoming microevolutionary changes, my position remains less open to the macro-evolutionary process of one species crossing "biological boundaries" to become another species. Admittedly, a different view of evolutionary history will find the present rejoinder to the trajectory argument less persuasive. As I note in Chapter 4, this does not mean that macro-evolution and divinely ordered creativity are necessarily contradictory claims. I minimally make the weaker observation that privileging the scriptural emphasis on divine order will be more or less persuasive depending on one's view of evolutionary history.

167. At this point, Adam and Eve could simply be paradigmatic for the majority, allowing sexed variation for the minority. Yet, as I argue below, attending carefully to the canonical use of "be fruitful and multiply" forestalls this possibility.

168. I restrict my analysis to the OT because I consider the NT witness to redemptive newness in Christ for sexed embodiment in Chapters 5 and 6.

of God's blessing, with five of these occurrences as volitives addressed to humans and creatures.[169] While the first occurrence of the phrase is given to the sea creatures and the birds (Gen. 1:22), the subsequent four occurrences are for Adam and Eve (Gen. 1:28), Noah (Gen. 9:1, 7), and Jacob (Gen. 35:11).[170] The promise of progeny—through whom God will crush the serpent (3:15) and bless the nations (12:1–3)—is a recurring motif in Genesis.[171] Indeed, Genesis accentuates the central concern for children at both national and individual levels.[172]

If the "be fruitful and multiply" of Gen. 1:28 commissioned an expected pattern for humanity in general, the likelihood that faithful individual Israelites will be procreating (and parenting) Israelites (and so sexed dimorphically) may be seen most clearly in Deut. 7:13–14. In the immediate context, Moses reminds Israel of God's gracious covenant election and redemption, so that Israel will obey (שמר ... לעשה) God's commandments (7:6–11). The result of keeping God's judgments is that God will keep his patriarchal covenant (v.12), and here we witness a striking oscillation between second-person plurals and second-person singulars.[173] The fruit of corporate "listening ... keeping and doing" is individual blessing (v.12). Moses goes on in 7:13–14 to specify the individual covenant blessing:

He [YHWH] will love *you*, and bless *you*, and multiply *you*, and bless *your* fruit of the body and *your* fruit of the ground; *your* grain and *your* wine and *your* oil, the offspring of *your* cattle and the young ones of *your* flock, upon the earth that I swore to *your* ancestors to give to *you*. Blessed will *you* be more than all peoples: there shall not be among *you* a barren man or a barren woman, nor among *your* livestock.[174]

As Moses outlines the contours of individual covenant blessing, the emphasis is on abundant fruitfulness and prosperity in every area of life in the land. Indeed, Moses

169. The imperatival occurrences are Gen. 1:22, 28; 9:1, 7; 35:11. The indicative occurrences are Gen. 8:17; 17:20; 28:3; 48:4; Lev. 26:9; Jer. 23:3; Ezek. 36:11. פרה and רבה are separated by שרץ in Exod. 1:7 and inverted in Jer. 3:16 and Ezek. 36:11. I do not address the occurrences of מלא because it typically expresses the result rather than the act of population increase.

170. Barry Danylak suggests that the progenitorial status of these individuals establishes an expected "pattern" for faithful Israelites (*Redeeming Singleness: How the Storyline of Scripture Affirms the Single Life* [Wheaton, IL: Crossway, 2010], 27).

171. For example, in the Abraham narrative see Gen. 13:14–18; 15:1–21; 17:1–14; 22:15–19. See further Viands, *Multiply Your Offspring*, 21–60.

172. Beyond Abraham, see the matriarchal narratives of Sarah, Rebekah, Leah and Rachel, as well as the example of Lot's daughters (Gen. 19:30–38) and Tamar (Genesis 38).

173. This is a common technique in Deuteronomy to intensify the illocutionary act and heighten its perlocutionary effect for all present.

174. Italics added to illustrate Moses' emphasis on individual blessing, the second person singular being repeated fifteen times in just two verses.

emphasizes the blessing of fruitfulness by both articulating the positive (v.13) and ruling out the negative: "barrenness" (עָקָר, v.14) and "sickness" (חֲלִי, v.15). As this relates to human procreation, the allusion to Gen. 1:28 in the collocation of "bless you and multiply you" is expanded upon in the positive description of God blessing "your fruit of the body,"[175] and in the negation of any barrenness, male or female. The general implication of all this is that God will bless and multiply each faithful Israelite just as he blessed and multiplied the patriarchs. But more specifically, as Danylak demonstrates, "The primary marker of God's blessing instantiated to the individual Israelites is given here as the 'blessing of the womb'; that is, neither they nor their livestock will suffer barrenness of offspring."[176]

This point is reiterated (with cattle and crops) in the key phrase of ברך פרי־בטנך being repeated almost verbatim in the blessings and curses section of Deuteronomy 28. Following obedience, "Blessed shall be your fruit of the body" (Deut. 28:4); "And the LORD will cause you to abound in goodness, in your fruit of the body" (Deut. 28:11). Following disobedience, "Cursed shall be your fruit of the body" (Deut. 28:18). Indeed, as the curses continue, the allusions to childlessness become increasingly horrific.[177] Finally, Deut. 29:18–21 indicates that even though the covenant was given to the nation as a whole, "Every individual was subject to the terms and conditions of the covenant such that if anyone violated the terms of the covenant, he or she *individually* was subject to the full weight of the covenant curses."[178] This culminated in having one's name "blotted out from under heaven" (Deut. 29:20), which referred not just to each individual, but the endurance of one's name or legacy through offspring. As Danylak demands, "No surviving children in ancient Israel meant the loss of one's inheritance, name, and covenant blessings. Conversely, marriage and offspring were fundamentally necessary for the reception of all the covenantal blessings."[179]

At times Danylak may overstate his case, perhaps reading the relationship between covenant faithfulness and fertility back-to-front. As a caveat, there is an important difference between saying that the faithful are fertile and that the fertile are faithful. If the latter logic is pushed, then it could imply that all OT

---

175. Most English translations render פרי־בטנך as "fruit of your womb" (e.g., ESV; NIV; NAB), implying that the blessing or curse is an exclusively female concern. Conversely, Joüon and Muraoka highlight how the pronominal suffix logically affects the block of accusative complements in the noun phrase, such that פרי־בטנך is better rendered as "your fruit of the body" (JM §140b). Thus, my translation "your fruit of the body" clarifies (albeit woodenly) that the blessing or curse is directly relevant for both sexes. Here I offer "body" as a dynamic equivalent for בטן (more commonly, "belly").

176. Danylak, *Redeeming Singleness*, 58–9.

177. E.g., rape (Deut. 28:30) and cannibalism (Deut. 28:54–57).

178. Danylak, *Redeeming Singleness*, 61, italics original.

179. Ibid., 69. For more on the pivotal status and role of children in Israel, see Daniel I. Block, "Marriage and Family in Ancient Israel," in *Marriage and Family in the Biblical World*, ed. Ken M. Campbell (Downers Grove, IL: IVP, 2003), 78–94.

individuals *should* procreate, even if they do not marry.[180] Equally, if one did not marry or married without having children, for all practical purposes one looks to be living under God's direct curse.[181] In contrast, by spotlighting the OT link between faithfulness and fertility, I am minimally claiming that the blessing of children is a reliable but not exclusive indicator of covenant faithfulness.[182] Gen. 1:28 may not have established a procreative command that demanded volitional obedience *qua* the Sinaitic law mentioned in Deuteronomy. Yet inner-biblical interpretation of Gen. 1:28 suggests that it operated as a divine commission, establishing an expected pattern for individual Israelites to follow faithfully.[183] If the OT read procreation as the expected norm for humanity from creation, then the implication is that the requisite sexed form of one male and one female would also be the creational norm.

In short, although the canonical interpretation of "be fruitful and multiply" does not establish beyond doubt that "male and female" is an exclusive norm in creational intent, the cumulative weight of the evidence remains significant. As such, it seems legitimate to infer that Genesis 1–2 provides the rest of the OT with the ontological grounds for fulfilling the commission to "be fruitful and multiply." Read canonically, Adam and Eve *are* prototypical parents, which in turn explains why any hindrance in sexed function (e.g., infertility) or form (e.g., eunuch) is spoken of negatively.[184] While the Bible may point to a trajectory of othering for various anthropological constants (e.g., ethnicity and language), the same cannot be said for bodily sex. Therefore, not only does SD seem to be the

---

180. Lot's daughters would presumably set an exemplary pattern (Gen. 19:30–38).

181. In Chapter 4 I develop the concept of "curse." Here, it is pastorally prescient to note the important distinction between a concrete "curse" for volitional covenantal disobedience (e.g., Deuteronomy 28–29) and the abstract concept of "cursed" that represents the universal experience of living in a postlapsarian world. While Deuteronomy witnesses to a retribution theology at the national level, the OT (especially examples throughout narrative and wisdom literature) resist a strict correlation between disobedience and curse at the individual level.

182. I address the way the NT transforms the faithfulness-fertility nexus in Chapter 5.

183. Again, recalling from above, the universally expected pattern to procreate could be strengthened further by noting how faithful Israelites would presumably want to participate in propagating the messianic seed. See Augustine, "The Excellence of Marriage," 16.18, in *Marriage and Virginity*, ed. David G. Hunter, trans. Ray Kearney, WSA I/9 (Hyde Park, NY: New City, 1999), 47. The only potentially positive example of lifelong, celibate childlessness in the OT is Jeremiah (Jer. 16:2). Yet, as Jer. 16:3–13 explains, YHWH commands Jeremiah's singleness as a sign that judgment is about to fall on Israel. Three other possible categories of celibacy exist in the OT: priests before a sacrifice (Lev. 22:4); fighters before battle (Josh 3:5); Israel before receiving the Ten Commandments (Exod. 19:15). Yet, importantly, all of these are temporary. See Timothy C. Tennent, *For the Body: Recovering a Theology of Gender, Sexuality, and the Human Body* (Zondervan, 2020), 78.

184. See Chapter 4.

best way to read sexed embodiment in the creation event, but, from following DeFranza's charge to read Genesis 1–2 in its canonical context, SD also appears to be God's creational intent, thus obviating any creational trajectory toward SP.

Indeed, in thinking how to read Genesis 1–2 well, it is fitting to conclude with the contribution of Jesus, the OT exegete *par excellence* (Luke 24:27). In Matt. 19:4–6 (cf. Mark 10:6–9), Jesus combines Gen. 1:27 and Gen. 2:24 to affirm that God the Creator made humanity "from the beginning male and female" for the purpose of uniting the two in the "one flesh" of marriage.[185] While the text does not explicitly state whether "male and female" is the exclusive rather than the statistical norm for sexed embodiment, Gagnon helpfully summarizes: "Jesus understood the stories about the creation of humans in Genesis 1 and 2 not merely as descriptive but also as texts that supplied a prescriptive model for subsequent human sexual behaviour."[186] Thus, the emphasis in Deuteronomy on faithful Israelites marrying, procreating, and parenting, plus the cohesion Jesus articulates between Genesis 1 and 2 (reaffirming its theological message), indicates that SD is likely the prototypical pattern in both the creation event and creational intent. As such, the literary-canonical evidence pushes a theological explanation for intersex embodiment beyond the event or intent of creation.

III. Staging: Thomistic Clarification on the Sexed Body in Creation

Having explored the nature of sexed embodiment in creation from the perspective of the literary-canonical context of Genesis 1–2—deducing that SD was likely God's design in the event and intent of creation—I turn now to demonstrate how the same conclusion is supported (and sharpened) by biblically informed theological reflection of a more metaphysical bent.[187] To this end, I retrieve the insights of Thomas Aquinas. Not only is Thomas utilized by innovational scholars,[188] but

---

185. Note the repetition of ἀπ ἀρχῆς in Matt. 19:4 and 8.

186. Robert A. J. Gagnon, "Sexuality," in *Dictionary for Theological Interpretation of the Bible*, ed. Kevin J. Vanhoozer et al. (Grand Rapids: Baker Academic, 2005), 740.

187. Metaphysics, most broadly, is "the philosophical investigation of the nature, constitution, and structure of [created] reality" (Panayot Butchvarov, "Metaphysics," in *The Cambridge Dictionary of Philosophy*, ed. Robert Audi, 3rd ed. [New York: Cambridge University Press, 2015], 661). Metaphysical exposition should take place within the context of God's gracious initiative in revelation, thus becoming "the study of created order under the particular aspect of its revelation of God the Creator" (Duby, *God in Himself*, 209). This book uses the terms "metaphysics" and "ontology" (and their cognates) synonymously. Importantly, metaphysical terms are not evaluative terms pertaining to human dignity. Positively, following Terrence Ehrman, "Knowing the essence or nature of a kind of being enables one to identify when some injury or limitation or defect is present" ("Disability and Resurrection Identity," *NBf* 96 [2015]: 731).

188. E.g., Raby, "You Knit Me Together."

his strong affirmation on the goodness of the body,[189] as well as his metaphysical insights regarding human ontology and sexuality, confirm Thomas as a promising resource for developing a theology of intersexuality.

The *locus classicus* of Aquinas' theological anthropology is found in *Summa Theologiae* 1.75–102. Here, *sacra doctrina* reflects upon *sacra pagina*,[190] in conversation with the catholic tradition, principally Augustine.[191] In short, the human person is a rational body-soul composite, a hylemorphic *minor mundus*,[192] uniquely made in the image of the Triune God to know and love him (John 17:3). Concerning the pre-fall sexed body, Aquinas argues that the material accidents of one's body are necessarily arranged in such a way as to be formally ordered with vegetative powers and natural inclinations toward procreation. Thus, sexed *form* founds procreative *function*, and *function* fits *form*. Accordingly, the prelapsarian sexed body in the event and intent of creation will be either male or female, buttressing the conclusion reached from the biblical assessment earlier. I explicate this claim by retrieving Thomistic insights into the materiality of the body, the forming function of the soul, and the ordered peace of the sexed-body composite preserved in Edenic Original Justice.

189. Note Aquinas' opposition to the Cathars. See David Albert Jones, *Approaching the End: A Theological Exploration of Death and Dying*, OSTE (Oxford: Oxford University Press, 2007), 91.

190. *Sacra doctrina* is graced *scientia*, regulating and ordering other sciences ("handmaidens" [*ancillae*]) such that "dogmatic theology is not only science but wisdom as well" (*sapientia*) (Duby, *God in Himself*, 87)

191. For an account of Augustine's influence on Aquinas, see Michael Dauphinais, Barry David, and Matthew Levering, eds., *Aquinas the Augustinian* (Washington, DC: Catholic University of America Press, 2007).

192. Thomas Aquinas, *ST* 1.91.1 resp. Unless otherwise stated, all Latin citations and English translations are from Thomas Aquinas, *Summa Theologiae*, ed. John Mortensen and Enrique Alarcón, trans. Laurence Shapcote, L/E 13–22 (Lander, WY: Aquinas Institute, 2012). While I recognize that there is a distinction in modern dualist systems between substance dualists (e.g., Joshua Ryan Farris, *The Soul of Theological Anthropology: A Cartesian Exploration*, RNCTRTBS [Abingdon, UK: Routledge, 2017]), Thomistic dualists (e.g., J. P. Moreland, *Body & Soul: Human Nature & the Crisis in Ethics* [Downers Grove, IL: IVP, 2000]), and holistic dualists (e.g., John W. Cooper, *Body, Soul, and Life Everlasting: Biblical Anthropology and the Monism-Dualism Debate* [Grand Rapids: Eerdmans, 2000]), my appropriation of Aquinas is to propose a Thomistically inflected holistic dualism, that affirms the soul as the informing principle of the body, as well as the necessity of body and soul being "fully integrated and interdependent such that the organism as a whole functions properly only when both are working in intimate union" (Marc Cortez, *Theological Anthropology: A Guide for the Perplexed* [London: T&T Clark, 2010], 73). My preference for a soft, holistic dualism need not prohibit a non-reductive physicalist from accepting the book's broader thesis that the sexed body in the creation event and intent was likely sexed dimorphically.

A. *The Body*

When thinking about the body, key biblical texts for Thomas include Gen. 3:19; Eccles. 3:19, 12:7, and particularly Gen. 2:7, "God formed man from the slime [*de limo*] of the earth."[193] The repetition of "dust" (or "slime") in these biblical texts emphasizes the body's composition from contraries,[194] which themselves are formed from matter. Drawing from Aristotle, although importantly reinterpreted through biblical revelation (via Augustine),[195] Aquinas holds that matter has no concrete existence per se; rather, it is metaphysical potency longing to be formed or actualized: "Matter desires form, just as potency desires act."[196] "Without its form," Gondreau explains, "matter remains in pure potency."[197] Since the body is composed of matter, and matter is subject to change and variation, "The human body is intrinsically subject to the contingencies of causality."[198] As Thomas illustrates, like a hard and flexible iron saw, all bodies are good. And yet like the saw is "breakable and inclined to rust" (due to "the natural disposition of iron"),[199] so a material body, Thomas reasons from 2 Cor. 5:4, is also "corruptible of its very nature."[200]

B. *The Soul*

For matter to take on substantial, concrete existence, it requires informing by a "form," that dynamic configurer of prime matter. When matter is informed by a rational soul it becomes a human person.[201] Again, Gen. 2:7 is crucial for Aquinas: "Then the LORD God formed a man from the dust of the ground and breathed

---

193. Aquinas, *ST* 1.91.1 sc. Translation from the Vulgate. Thomas also makes much of Ecclesiasticus 17:1, "God created man out of the earth" (*ST* 1.91.2 sc).

194. The contraries are the four cardinal humors of earth, water, fire, and air. Humans are made from earth and water, hence "slime" (*ST* 1.91.1 ad 4).

195. For an account of Thomas "adapt[ing] the insights of philosophical science to the truths of revelation," see Thomas Joseph White, *Wisdom in the Face of Modernity: A Study in Thomistic Natural Theology*, FR (Ave Maria, FL: Sapientia, 2009), 76.

196. Adam G. Cooper, *Life in the Flesh: An Anti-Gnostic Spiritual Philosophy* (Oxford: Oxford University Press, 2008), 88.

197. Paul Gondreau, "The 'Inseparable Connection' Between Procreation and Unitive Love (Humanae Vitae, §12) and Thomistic Hylemorphic Anthropology," *NV* 6 (2008): 732.

198. Miguel J. Romero, "Aquinas on the Corporis Infirmitas," in *Disability in the Christian Tradition: A Reader*, ed. Brian Brock and John Swinton (Grand Rapids: Eerdmans, 2012), 106.

199. *ST* 1-2.85.6 resp.

200. Thomas Aquinas, *Commentary on the Letters of Saint Paul to the Corinthians*, C.5 L.1 §159, trans. Fabian R. Larcher, L/E 38 (Lander, WY: Aquinas Institute, 2012), 468. The mutability of matter and its tendency toward decay will become significant as I consider the impact of the fall upon the body in Chapter 4.

201. Aquinas, *ST* 1.76.1 resp.

into his nostrils the breath of life, and *the man became a living being.*[202] As its immaterial form, the soul is the "configuring or determining principle" that gives life to all the body.[203] Since "the body is compared to the soul as matter to form,"[204] matter exists for the sake of form. As such, without a rational soul, "A body would not be, and would not be human."[205] Thus, the rational soul is ontologically constitutive for the human person.

Furthermore, in every human person, the soul contains various powers to inform the proper function of the body to reach its proximate and ultimate ends that are importantly appropriate to the kind of being a human is. Appropriating the language of causality, the soul is the formal cause that, in God's wise order, points to the final cause of the human person (a final cause that perfects human nature as graciously created). As articulated in *ST* 1.78, the human is the kind of creature whose rational form contains five powers: the vegetative, the sensitive, the appetitive, the locomotive, and the intellective. For our purposes regarding the nature of sexed embodiment in the creation event and creational intent, the vegetative power of a single human soul preserves life by ordering the body toward three ends: nutrition, growth, and generation, with generation being "more important and more perfect."[206] Thus, part of being human is to possess a soul whose proper function is to order the body toward actualizing procreative potential.[207] This is not to make the strong (and unnecessary) claim that if someone is not reproducing then their soul is malfunctioning. Rather, it makes the weaker claim that a properly functioning soul-body composite has the necessary *capacity* to reproduce. One is not human because she possesses the power of generation; she possesses the power of generation because she is human.

A similar conclusion may be reached when we consider the relationship between human ends and divine law. For Thomas, God providentially governs the universe through the *ratio* of his eternal law, imprinting upon all creatures "their respective inclinations to their proper acts and ends."[208] Shaped by biblical

---

202. Italics added.

203. Cooper, *Life in the Flesh*, 88. For the soul as "configured configurer," see Eleonore Stump, *Aquinas* (London: Routledge, 2003), 6.

204. Aquinas, *ST* 1-2.83.2 ad 3.

205. Joseph P. Wawrykow, *The Westminster Handbook to Thomas Aquinas* (Louisville: Westminster John Knox, 2005), 6.

206. Aquinas, *ST* 1.78.2 resp.

207. For a similar account within Augustine of the "vegetative aspects" of the soul ordering the body toward the goals of "nutrition, metabolism, growth, maturation, and sexuality," see Christoph Horn, "Anthropologie," in *Augustin Handbuch*, ed. Volker Henning Drecoll, 2nd ed., HT (Tübingen: Mohr Siebeck, 2014), 479.

208. Aquinas, *ST* 1-2.91.2 resp. Aquinas fittingly parallels the gift of natural law (and its participation in eternal law) with "light" in Psalm 4:6. See further Reinhard Hütter, *Bound for Beatitude: A Thomistic Study in Eschatology and Ethics*, TRS 12 (Washington, DC: Catholic University of America Press, 2019), 158–60.

passages such as 1 John 3:2 and John 17:3, Thomas maintains that the ultimate *telos* of human existence is to enjoy beatific knowledge of God.[209] To guide us in history to our ultimate end, God sews into the ontological fabric of humans five main natural inclinations toward certain proximate ends: to live (in common with all substances), to propagate and care for offspring (in common with all animals), to live in ordered society and know the truth about God (in common with all rational creatures).[210] Again, in thinking about the sexed body in the creation event and creational intent, part of what it *is* to be human (as opposed to a rock) is to be ordered by God's *ratio*, via the imprinting of natural, rational inclinations, to the natural, rational end of propagating the species.

Thus, on account of possessing a soul with vegetative powers ordered toward generation and imprinted with the natural inclination to propagate, part of the proper function of being human is to be ordered toward actualizing the proximate end of procreative potential. This is necessarily true for all creatures who qualify as metaphysical humans. For Aquinas, it does not appear to be the case that God made humans but then left them to figure out how to live rightly. Rather, Aquinas discerns within *sacra pagina* warrant to affirm a strong account of gracious generic and teleological ordering, particularly for theological anthropology. Indeed, as Messer reflects upon Aquinas, since "form is final cause," there is an inseparable

209. Aquinas, *ST* 1.65.2 resp. For the purposes of this project, it is sufficient to note how, for Aquinas, human nature does not appear to be self-enclosed but is always graciously "ontologically oriented" to God (Reinhard Hütter, *Dust Bound for Heaven: Explorations in the Theology of Thomas Aquinas* [Grand Rapids: Eerdmans, 2012], 243). The extent to which Thomas aligns more readily with an "intrinsicist"/"continuationist" or "extrinsicist"/ "discontinuationist" account of the dynamic between nature and grace remains beyond my scope. For the debate's contours, concerns, and chief contributors, see Edward T. Oakes, *A Theology of Grace in Six Controversies*, Interventions (Grand Rapids: Eerdmans, 2016), 1–46. For an attempt at reconciliation, see Jacob W. Wood, *To Stir a Restless Heart: Thomas Aquinas and Henri De Lubac on Nature, Grace, and the Desire for God*, TRS 14 (Washington, DC: Catholic University of America Press, 2019), 429–31. In tracing the sexed body from creation to consummation, my argument may at times parallel nature/grace debates. For instance, both conversations seek to explicate the "natural" in its theo-dramatic context, and both acknowledge the "natural" as distinct yet inseparable from its gracious fulfilment (i.e., grace presupposes and perfects nature). However, I shall resist developing the conceptual parallels, for nature/grace discussions typically explore epistemic and moral questions (e.g., the intelligibility of human nature *sans* grace; the natural desire for God; the gratuity of grace) that do not directly inform my argument. For a recent reframing of the nature/grace debate that treats nature as "substance" and grace as "activity" (a conceptually closer parallel to my use of "creation" and "redemption"), see Ian A. McFarland, "Rethinking Nature and Grace: The Logic of Creation's Consummation," *IJST* 24 (2022): 56–79.

210. For a Thomistic account of natural inclinations as "the source of freedom and morality," see Servais Pinckaers, *The Sources of Christian Ethics* (Washington, DC: Catholic University of America Press, 1995), 400–56, esp. 437–52, on the "inclination to sexuality."

connection between "kinds" and "ends."[211] Thus, as sexed body-soul composites, human "kind" necessarily includes the inextricable "ends" of certain vegetative powers to generate (imprinted via natural inclinations).[212] Indeed, all "kinds" and "ends" find their unity in Christ, "The principle of cohesion of the universe."[213] All things are "created" (ἐκτίσθη) and "held together" (συνέστηκεν) "in him" (ἐν αὐτῷ)—generic ordering—and "for him" (εἰς αὐτόν)—teleological ordering (Col. 1:16–17).[214] Thus, following Wirzba, "What things *are*, what they mean and signify, and what their value and purpose are—these ought to be understood in terms of the *archē* that Jesus Christ is."[215]

C. The Sexed Body-Soul Composite

Thomas' theological anthropology is motivated by biblical texts, especially the first three volitives of Gen. 1:28, "Be fruitful and multiply and fill the earth."[216] For Aquinas, part of human nature before the fall was to be rightly ordered (generically and teleologically) toward procreative fruitfulness. It is a creational good for both the particular natures of Adam and Eve, as well as universal nature more generally, that human nature (and sex organs in particular) be ordered toward procreation. Thus, sexed *form* founds procreative *function*. Given Thomas is making claims about humanity *qua* species, all humans in the creation event and intent will fall into either male or female categories.

To reach their proximate, procreative end, humanity is necessarily sexed dimorphically as male and female. This is demonstrable on two counts. First, considered empirically, the generation of the human species requires exclusively one male and one female. Human beings are not like the self-pollinating flower *Capsella Rubella*, nor like sequential or simultaneous hermaphroditic clown fish,

---

211. Neil Messer, *Flourishing: Health, Disease, and Bioethics in Theological Perspective* (Grand Rapids: Eerdmans, 2013), 148. As I amplify in Chapters 5 and 6, while "ends" fit "kinds," proximate "ends" (e.g., procreation) do not exhaust "kinds."

212. For a similar immanent teleology of "kinds" and "ends," see Oliver O'Donovan, *Resurrection and Moral Order: An Outline for Evangelical Ethics* (Leicester, UK: IVP, 1986), 31–3.

213. A. Feuillet, *Le Christ, sagesse de Dieu, d'après les épîtres pauliniennes*, EBib (Paris: J. Gabalda, 1966), 213.

214. For a defense of reading "in him" as the sphere of creation (and not simply as the instrumental means of creation), as well as reading the passive "ἐκτίσθη" as including the participatory agency of the Son in creation (alongside God/Father), see Scot McKnight, *The Letter to the Colossians*, NICNT (Grand Rapids: Eerdmans, 2018), 150–1.

215. Norman Wirzba, "Creation *through* Christ," in *Christ and the Created Order: Perspectives from Theology, Philosophy, and Science*, ed. Andrew B. Torrance and Thomas H. McCall (Grand Rapids: Zondervan, 2018), 2:38. Given the centrality of Christ for creation, further comment on *how* creation relates to redemption will be taken up in Chapters 5 and 6.

216. E.g., Aquinas, *ST* 1.98.1 sc; idem, *SCG* 3.136; 4.83.

contra the suggestion of Sabia-Tanis.[217] For Aquinas, although humans share with all creation the same basic matter, humans are fundamentally unique as *rational animals*. The procreative behavior of flowers and fish are therefore irrelevant for human procreation. Further, scientific research has yet to discover a third sex organ alongside the male penis and the female vagina, nor an alternative way to reproduce naturally.[218]

Second, considered biblically, Gen. 1:28 gives the procreative commission to the male and the female, a point readily admitted by advocates of sexual polymorphism.[219] There is no indication in the biblical text of alternative ways for human beings to be generative.[220] Further, if part of what it means to be human is to be ordered toward generation (via the vegetative soul and natural inclinations), and the ability for humans to generate is through one man and one woman, then it is impossible in the creation event and intent for more than two distinct, yet complementary, sexes to exist. As such, it cannot be the case that Adam and Eve are merely parents of fecundity (but other sexes could subsequently exist pre-fall), *pace* DeFranza. To be human before the fall is to be bodily inscribed with unambiguous procreative potential, and this potential is actualized only through a male sexed body and a female sexed body.

Therefore, drawing various threads together, not only does sexed form found procreative function, but function necessarily fits form. Importantly, to avoid needless reductionism, while procreative potential is the *biological* foundation of sex difference, Aquinas is clear in *ST* 1.92.2 that it must be interpreted *spiritually*, where "marriage, nuptiality, marks the intrinsic teleological meaning of human sexuality."[221] As mentioned earlier, the creational ordinance of marriage is not arbitrarily related to humanity's sexed creational structure, but draws out its intended ends by being rightly ordered to the individually necessary and jointly sufficient goods of *proles* (offspring), *fides* (fidelity), and *sacramentum* (indissolubility),[222] where the semiotic significance of the "mystery" (μυστήριον)

---

217. Sabia-Tanis, "Holy Creation," 199.

218. Here, "natural" refers to "without medical intervention." A thorough assessment of reproductive technologies is beyond the purview of this book. For an account that commends the givenness of created order as it relates to sexual ethics, particularly when considering medical intervention, see Oliver O'Donovan, *Begotten or Made?* (Oxford: Clarendon, 1984). In short, that which is begotten should be afforded the same rights as the begetter.

219. DeFranza, "Gender Minorities," 159.

220. Again, without medical intervention.

221. Gondreau, "Inseparable Connection," 746.

222. On the logic of the three goods of *proles, fides,* and *sacramentum* in marriage, see Augustine, "Excellence of Marriage," 3.3 (WSA I/9:34–35). On their necessary integration, see Steven Schafer, *Marriage, Sex, and Procreation: Contemporary Revisions to Augustine's Theology of Marriage*, PrinTMS (Eugene, OR: Pickwick, 2019), 22–51.

described in Eph. 5:32 is fully revealed in Christ and his church.[223] This spiritual interpretation of grace perfecting nature explains the biblical prohibition of incest, fornication, adultery, and other forms of sexual immorality, and enables individuals to meet moral obligations to oneself, one's neighbor, and one's offspring.[224] As such, the human power of generation implies "cascading levels of generativity" that extend beyond procreation.[225] Thus, there is a richer theological meaning to bodily sex than the merely biological.

D. Objection: Two Sexes Equals Two Species

Following Thomistic form, it is fitting to raise an objection. One possible pitfall of the theological-philosophical case for SD articulated earlier is that male and female are differentiated to such an extent that they sound like two different species.[226] As previously mentioned, this would be problematic for several reasons. First, such a position would undermine the basic unity and equality emphasized in Gen. 1:27, legitimizing androcentric powerplays.[227] Second, following Gregory of Nazianzus' logic that "the unassumed is the unhealed,"[228] since Jesus is male, those without a "male nature" would remain outside the salvific extent of the person and work of Christ.[229] Third, if male and female designate two different natures, it remains unclear why this would not result in two different moralities, with two distinct ends. Again, attending to Thomas' careful metaphysical distinctions potentially circumvents these criticisms.

In *ST* 1.29.2, Aquinas clarifies the difference between concrete substances (a subsisting rock or man) and the concept of essence ("substance" in its basic sense

---

223. Aquinas, *ST* 1.92.2 resp; idem, *ST* Supp. 41–68. I develop in Chapter 6 the relationship between the creational ordinance of marriage and humanity's creational sexed structure. One way to explicate this dynamic could be to stress the "spousal" meaning of the sexed body. For example, see John Paul II, *Man and Woman He Created Them: A Theology of the Body* (Boston, MA: Pauline, 2006). In sum: "The body, in fact, and only the body, is capable of making visible what is invisible: the spiritual and divine. It has been created to transfer into the visible reality of the world the mystery hidden from eternity in God, and thus to be a sign of it" (ibid., 19:4). While my argument shares notable similarities with John Paul II's *Theology of the Body*, I remain unpersuaded by his confidence in an unchastened natural theology and the resulting gender essentialist claims.

224. For the link between our sexuate correspondence and moral excellence, see Paul Gondreau, "Thomas Aquinas on Sexual Difference: The Metaphysical Biology and Moral Significance of Human Sexuality," *ProEccl* 30 (2021): 177–215.

225. Timothy Fortin, "Finding Form: Defining Human Sexual Difference," *NV* 15 (2017): 430.

226. Thatcher, *Redeeming Gender*, 161.

227. Ibid., 4.

228. Nazianzus, "Letter 101," 5 (PPS 23:158).

229. I explore this further when considering the maleness of Christ in Chapter 5.

as "the quiddity of a thing").[230] The essence of human nature is to be a rational body-soul composite. When the universal-essential properties (or *principia*) of body-soul are actualized in concrete human persons, individuation is presented in accidental-particular properties. As Petri clarifies, drawing upon *ST* 3.77.1, "An accident is an essence which is apt to exist in a subject. Whiteness does not exist in the abstract in white things; whiteness is an accidental quality."[231] While "the principles constitutive of [human] nature" are body (matter) and soul (form),[232] in chapter 6 of *On Being and Essence*, Aquinas asserts that every concrete human being accrues certain accidents that "follow immediately upon our animality (expressive of the body or of our matter) and upon our rationality (expressive of the soul or of our form)."[233] Accidents derived from form are "properties belonging to the genus or species, and consequently they are found in everything sharing the nature of the genus or species."[234] Here, Aquinas offers the example of risibility: "For laughter occurs because of some perception on the part of the human soul"; that is, it is an act of knowledge.[235] In contrast, accidents derived from matter are "the individualizing attributes of material difference,"[236] Aquinas explicitly offering the example of male and female. Thus, accidents from form pertain to the whole human species, while accidents from matter account for what individualizes particular human beings. As Gondreau summarizes, "Maleness and femaleness are thus to the individual what risibility is to the human species."[237] Consequently, it seems that every human must possess the accidents that flow from their rational form (e.g., the ability to laugh) and from their animal matter (e.g., either maleness *or* femaleness). Here, we see that for Thomas, both formal and material accidents are far from incidental (as Aristotle might define "accidental") but closer to "proto-essential,"[238] equally "constitutive of personhood."[239]

Nevertheless, even if one's sexed body is a material, "proto-essential" accident "constitutive of personhood," in what way, if at all, does sexed embodiment differ

---

230. Aquinas, *ST* 1.29.2 resp.

231. Thomas Petri, *Aquinas and the Theology of the Body: The Thomistic Foundations of John Paul II's Anthropology*, TRS 7 (Washington, DC: Catholic University of America Press, 2016), 215.

232. Aquinas, *ST* 1-2.85.1 resp.

233. Gondreau, "Inseparable Connection," 738.

234. Thomas Aquinas, *On Being and Essence*, trans. Armand Maurer, 2nd rev. ed. (Toronto: Pontifical Institute of Mediaeval Studies, 1968), 69.

235. Ibid.

236. Petri, *Theology of the Body*, 216.

237. Gondreau, "Inseparable Connection," 738 n.21.

238. Ibid., 738.

239. John S. Grabowski, *Sex and Virtue: An Introduction to Sexual Ethics* (Washington, DC: Catholic University of America Press, 2003), 111.

from something like eye color?[240] In thinking about eye color, one could argue *that* my eyes have color (indicating I have eyes) is more essential that *what* my eyes are colored. *Mutatis mutandis*, what matters is *that* I'm sexed (whether male, female, or intersex), not *what* I'm sexed.[241]

In response, on the one hand, the *what* of one's sexed body *is* no different from the *what* of one's eye color—there is bodily diversity. Indeed, Aquinas opines, "Diversity in sex belongs to the perfection of human nature."[242] Yet for Thomistic logic, there remains an important distinction between bodily sex and eye color, clarified by the dynamic between the informing soul and the material body. Given that the soul has a desire to propagate (informed by its vegetative powers and natural inclinations), the soul requires a body that is an appropriate fit, that is, one that provides the material accidents necessary for the soul to actualize its procreative potential. Without the appropriate mode of expression, the generative powers of the soul risk being reduced to vanity,[243] turning the blessed commission of Gen. 1:28 into a cruel joke.[244] In humanity, the power of generation is divided, such that successful procreation requires the complementary combination of a female mode of generativity and a male mode of generativity. Thus, the *what* of sexed diversity is necessarily limited to either male or female. In contrast, the *what* of eye color diversity is a true spectrum, differences of pigmentation determined by the quantity and quality of melanin in the front layers of the iris.[245]

There is a further difference between bodily sex and eye color. While eye color does not affect the proper function of the eye (seeing),[246] not being sexed as either male or female hinders the proper function of bodily sex (procreation). That is, if one is genuinely intersex (as defined in the introduction) then one remains unable to procreate.[247] This distinction between eye color and bodily sex suggests that while both categories might be considered materially accidental for being human,

240. Pastoral conversations inform the choice of this comparison. The argument runs: "If my eye color is incidental, then so is my bodily sex and [by extension] my sexual orientation."

241. Thatcher, *Redeeming Gender*, 157.

242. Aquinas, *ST* 1.99.2. resp.

243. On the reduction of generative power to vanity, see Aquinas on "fornication," *SCG* 3.122.

244. Tying form and function together raises a question about embodiment and procreative potential in the heaven. If procreative function ends (Matt. 22:30), what are the implications for eschatological form? I explore this question in Chapter 6.

245. Richard A. Sturm and Mats Larsson, "Genetics of Human Iris Colour and Patterns," *PCMR* 22 (2009): 544–62.

246. This hypothetical comparison is from the perspective of prelapsarian creation, precluding the objection that some eye colors indicate certain dysfunctions, e.g., orange suggests jaundice, cloudy suggests cataracts, multicolored suggests Waardenburg syndrome.

247. Charlotte Jones, "Intersex, Infertility and the Future: Early Diagnoses and the Imagined Life Course," *SHI* 42 (2020): 143–56.

"Not all accidents are created equal."[248] Thus, given that bodily sex is "inexorably bound to the essential power of generation," it is less accidental than eye color, and so can be rightly classified as a proper or "essential accident,"[249] in contrast to eye color, which is a "pure or contingent accident."[250]

All this indicates that Thatcher's accusation of SD risking two species is unwarranted.[251] There is one human species, essentially identified as rational body-soul composites. Individual diversity comes about through various material configurations that are designed to enable the soul to actualize its potential. In thinking about the sexed body in creation (event and intent), since the soul desires to propagate—reflecting the self-communicative goodness of God—there are only two bodily sexed configurations (or modes of generativity) that can make this achievable—male or female. Thus, sexed form founds procreative function, and procreative function necessarily depends upon sexed form. Hence the rubric: "form founds function—function fits form." The story in creation suggests a sexuate staging.

IV. Leitmotif: The Ordered Peace of Creation

This extended theological reflection on the nature of sexed embodiment as it pertains to the event and intent of creation reveals a similar conclusion to the preceding literary-canonical investigation. In short, both approaches affirm that God's original and enduring design for the sexed body is likely one of sexual dimorphism. The cumulative case for SD from the literary perspective asserted that "male and female" (Gen. 1:27) denoted the scope of the *imago Dei* and connoted procreative potential (Gen. 1:28). All creation, including humanity, was ordered for the function of fruitfulness. Taking Genesis 2 alongside Genesis

---

248. Fortin, "Finding Form," 428.

249. Ibid., 419.

250. Gondreau, "Aquinas on Sexual Difference," 210. The distinction between bodily sex as "essential accident" and eye color as "contingent accident" is also relevant for DeFranza's claim that a biblical trajectory of racial or ethnic diversification offers an instructive parallel for a trajectory of othering regarding sexed embodiment. In short, like eye color, it is not obvious that skin color is a necessary mode of expression for a particular power of the soul. Without denying the important sociological reality of "race" and "ethnicity," nor the biblically good trajectory of ethnic and racial diversification (e.g., Acts 2; Rev. 7:9), DeFranza's proposed parallel between race and sexed embodiment suffers the same philosophical challenges leveled against the "bodily sex" and "eye color" parallel. Nonetheless, DeFranza's claim that the Bible testifies to a trajectory of sexed othering (highlighting the eunuch) could still be true (see Chapter 5).

251. There may well be an historical correlation between SD and treating women as a different species, but this is not strictly causative given the Thomistic account of SD proposed here.

I confirmed this reading of "male and female," deducing a key (but not sole) aspect of the woman as "helper" for the man in her procreative capacity. Reading Genesis 1–2 together, the consequence of being made in the image of God involved the authority to rule creation, which required producing more co-rulers in the image of God to work and watch the garden (Gen. 2:15). The covenantal marriage union of male and female (Gen. 2:22–25) may be a creational ordinance, but their sexuate structuring pertains to creation order.[252] As such, in the event of creation it seems more likely that sexed embodiment was exclusively male and female, excluding primal androgyny and hypothetical hybrids. This conclusion is upheld when we draw in the canonical context, especially noting how the phrases "male and female" and "be fruitful and multiply" were interpreted by faithful Israelites. In short, the expected pattern from the blessed commission of Gen. 1:28 was for the faithful Israelite to be a procreating and parenting Israelite (within marriage). Such parental fecundity requires the prototypical fixity of SD. Thus, the literary-canonical case suggests that the sexed body was likely exclusively male and female in the creation event and creational intent.

Theological reflection on sexed embodiment sustained the literary-canonical conclusion, sharpening its point with metaphysical insights to insist that SD in the event and intent of creation was likely the exclusive norm and not just for the statistical majority. Attractive (but not exclusive) to those sympathetic to holistic dualism, a Thomistically inflected account of human ontology indicated that for the person's procreative potential to be actualized, the body's mode of generativity must be either male or female, both bodily expressions being necessary for successful procreation. The tight connection between the soul's potency and the body providing the means of actualization intimates that one's bodily sex is an "essential accident." Thus, the Thomistically informed rubric of "form founds function—function fits form" submits that sexed embodiment is either male or female in the event and intent of creation. "Male and female" form an irreducible "sexuate correspondence" that is universal-essential for all metaphysical humans.[253] Indeed, "Universal nature . . . requires both sexes for the perfection of the human species."[254]

The organizing principle that gives coherence and cohesion to the literary-canonical and theological accounts submitted earlier is the leitmotif of ordered peace—captured well by the biblical concept of *shalom* (שלום).[255] Although the lexeme שלום does not appear in Genesis 1–2, it is a "profoundly positive concept

---

252. I clarify this distinction and its claim in Chapter 5.

253. Belousek, *Marriage*, 36.

254. Aquinas, *ST* Supp. 81.3 ad 3.

255. The privileging of "order" as an organizing leitmotif is not ignorant of the accusation that any appeal to order is inherently oppressive, order being not "found" in creation but insidiously "placed" there. Nevertheless, while this concern is right to highlight the dangers of imposing social norms on "created order," Genesis 1–2 does appear to witness to a good and non-oppressive order. As I develop in the next chapter, the historic doctrine of the

associated with the notions of intactness, wholeness, and well-being, of the world and of humanity."[256] As I develop in Chapter 4, God sews into the structural fabric of creation an ordered peace, so "that they [all creatures] might all keep their right order and rest in their right places."[257] Augustine clarifies further that "the peace of all things is the tranquility of order."[258] Here, Augustine articulates a totally ordered peace that helpfully summarizes *shalom* in the event and intent of creation,[259] what Aquinas glosses as Edenic Original Justice.[260] Part of creation's *shalom* is its metaphysical "structure," which Albert Wolters explicates as "the creational decree of God that constitutes the nature of different kinds of creatures."[261] Humanity's universal-essential property of *being* sexed conveys an aspect of creation's "structure." And in this chapter, I have argued that *what* one is sexed in the event and intent of creation is the essential accident of either maleness or femaleness. In sum, the sexuate correspondence of SD participates in the ordered peace of creation. As we live according to God's ordered, creational *shalom*, we flourish.[262] "Life within the order and peace of God is life that is blessed."[263]

In contrast, if intersexuality represents a sexed *form* distinct from male and female, then it remains strange that God's first act of relating to his new image

---

fall gives Christian theology resources to account for both the existence and goodness of created order, as well as its distortion and misdirection.

256. F. J. Stendebach, "שָׁלוֹם," *TDOT* 15:19. See also H. H. Schmid who notes from wisdom literature that *shalom* designates existence according to "the ideal order of the world" (*Šālôm: Frieden im Alten Orient und im Alten Testament*, SBS 51 [Stuttgart: KBW, 1971], 54–6).

257. Augustine, *The Trinity*, 6.10.11, ed. John E. Rotelle, trans. Edmund Hill, 2nd ed., WSA I/5 (Hyde Park, NY: New City, 2015), 215.

258. Augustine, *Civ.* 19.13 (CCSL 48:679; WSA I/7:368). Cf. Aquinas, *ST* 2-2.29.1. The basis for all ordered peace in creation is thoroughly theological: "God is not a God of disorder, but peace" (1 Cor. 14:33), ontologically and ethically. As the source of peace (e.g., Judg. 6:24), God gives peace (e.g., Num. 6:26). Creaturely peace is God-given nature, fulfilled "over the course of their histories" in relation to others and God, thus constituting a harmonious and tranquil economy (Webster, *Domain of the Word*, 155).

259. That Augustine's understanding of peace is informed by the biblical concept of *shalom*, see Margaret Atkins, "Pax," *A-L* 4:567–9.

260. Aquinas, *ST* 1.95.1 resp. Daniel W. Houck succinctly summarizes: "Original justice is a state of moral righteousness by which a human being is submitted to God, has rightly ordered concupiscence, and is conditionally immortal" ("Natura Humana Relicta est Christo: Thomas Aquinas on the Effects of Original Sin," *ArV* 13 [2016]: 74).

261. Albert M. Wolters, *Creation Regained: Biblical Basics for a Reformational Worldview*, 2nd ed. (Grand Rapids: Eerdmans, 2005), 59.

262. Matthew Levering, *Aquinas's Eschatological Ethics and the Virtue of Temperance* (Notre Dame, IN: University of Notre Dame Press, 2019), 26.

263. John Webster, *Christ Our Salvation: Expositions and Proclamations* (Bellingham, WA: Lexham, 2020), 77.

bearers is to single out the male and female, invite them into his work of reflecting his rule as vice-regents, and bless them with the noble task of being life-givers like God. If intersex bodies are examples of creational diversity, the fact that they are not mentioned, addressed, commissioned, and blessed, suggests that either they are marginalized from the start of creation, and by God (raising serious questions about God's goodness and justice), or such polymorphic diversity simply does not exist pre-fall. Even if intersex embodiment is a mix of male and female form, the dissonance between sexed form and procreative function remains problematic.[264] Intersex persons may be included as hybrids in v.27, but they simply cannot participate in v.28 (at least not fully). They remain second-class citizens of Eden—a dehumanizing consequence innovationists want to avoid. In short, the argument for intersexuality as creational diversity commits one to their perpetual marginalization by God—a far cry from the sevenfold "good" of Genesis 1. Given these problems, it seems more likely that the God's design in the creation event and intent was for humanity to be sexed as either male or female. As such, without denying the dignity and value of every sexed body, a fuller theological interpretation of intersex conditions needs to supplement the perspective of creation. One such theo-dramatic locus is the fall.

264. One could object that hypothetical Edenic children would also experience a disconnect between sexed form and protective function, for children cannot procreate. However, crucially, for such children the potential to procreate remains open, given the right conditions (e.g., maturing and marrying). This is not the case for intersexuality.

Chapter 4

FALL

DEATH'S DISORDERING DECAY

The previous section marshaled evidence from both literary-canonical and theological perspectives to claim that sexed embodiment in the creation event and intent was most likely dimorphic. The sexed body was intentionally formed as either male or female to provide the individually necessary and jointly sufficient conditions to fulfill the function of fruitfulness, that is, procreation (Gen. 1:28). Such divinely intended sexuate correspondence suggests that "male and female" (Gen. 1:27) should be read as the exclusive creational norm rather than the statistical majority. Accordingly, a fuller theological interpretation for intersexuality needs to look beyond the perspective of creation. One such theological locus is the fall. In this chapter I first explain why a theologically thick account of intersexuality retains a traditional understanding of the fall. I then offer a biblical and theological account of the fall. Finally, I articulate the advantages of interpreting intersexuality from the perspectives of both creation and fall.

I. Why the Fall?

A. Historic Acceptance of the Fall

"Reflection on the fall is a constant preoccupation of *homo religiosus*," and Christianity is no different.[1] While fall narratives vary,[2] within orthodox Christianity there appears to be a consensus over the basic shape: "From original goodness in fellowship with God, humans fell into willful rebellion, to which God responded by placing the cosmos under a curse."[3] Putting aside debate over the

---

1. Julien Ries, "The Fall," *ER* 5:2969.
2. For examples, see Zohar Hadromi-Allouche and Áine Larkin, eds., *Fall Narratives: An Interdisciplinary Perspective* (London: Routledge, 2017).
3. Daniel J. Treier, *Introducing Evangelical Theology* (Grand Rapids: Baker Academic, 2019), 139.

various mechanisms of how Adam's primal sin is transmitted to his progeny,[4] Christian theological traditions have predominantly affirmed the historicity of Adam and Eve,[5] and so an historical fall "in" rather than "into" time.[6] Genesis 3, typically refracted through Rom. 5:12–21,[7] was frequently read as recording the primal act of human disobedience (eating forbidden fruit). This "original sin" exposed humanity to "death and divine judgment,"[8] with "tragic physical, social, and spiritual consequences for the entire human race."[9] These core commitments are both widespread, spanning theological traditions,[10] and deeply rooted, the early and influential Council of Carthage (417 AD) anathematizing anyone who denied that death is the result of sin.[11] In short, the fall remains a theological locus that has been historically affirmed by "all parts of the 'Vincentian Canon'; it is one that has been believed by all Christians, at all times, in all places."[12]

Given the enduring importance afforded to the fall *ubique, semper, et ab omnibus*, it is unsurprising that theological reflection over the significance of intersex embodiment is quick to attribute "these conditions as results of the fallen

---

4. E.g., "federalist," "realist," "mediate," and "corruption-only." The privileging of Adam is not to ignore the agency and guilt of Eve. I follow Rom. 5:12–21 in using Adam as a representative placeholder.

5. David L. Smith, *With Willful Intent: A Theology of Sin* (Wheaton, IL: BridgePoint, 1994), 339.

6. Marguerite Shuster, *The Fall and Sin: What We Have Become as Sinners* (Grand Rapids: Eerdmans, 2004), 5.

7. Rom 5:12–21 is regularly cited or alluded to throughout the historic confessions, particularly those that are evangelical and Protestant. See Philip Schaff, *The Creeds of Christendom: With a History and Critical Notes: The Evangelical Protestant Creeds with Translations*, vol. 3, 6th ed. (Grand Rapids: Baker Academic, 1983).

8. Thomas H. McCall, *Against God and Nature: The Doctrine of Sin*, FET (Wheaton, IL: Crossway, 2019), 384. Concerning humans, death has historically been understood as both physical and spiritual, see e.g., Belgic Confession, Art. XIV in Schaff, *Creeds of Christendom*, 3:398.

9. J. B. Stump and Chad Meister, eds., *Original Sin and the Fall: Five Views*, SMB (Downers Grove, IL: IVP Academic, 2020), 1. Space precludes assessing any prior angelic fall. For a thorough history of the doctrine of original sin, see Julius Gross, *Geschichte des Erbsündendogmas: Ein Beitrag zur Geschichte des Problems vom Ursprung des Übels*, 4 vols (München: Ernst Reinhardt, 1960).

10. For the relevant texts, see the Comparative Creedal Syndogmaticon in Jaroslav Pelikan, *Credo: Historical and Theological Guide to Creeds and Confessions of Faith in the Christian Tradition* (New Haven, CT: Yale University Press, 2003), 549C.

11. Henry Bettenson and Chris Maunder, eds., *Documents of the Christian Church*, 4th ed. (Oxford: Oxford University Press, 2011), 62.

12. McCall, *Against God*, 149. Here McCall refers explicitly to the doctrine of original sin, a necessary subset of the fall.

condition of our world."[13] Intersexuality is an "anomaly that we find in fallen creation";[14] "Disorders of nature";[15] "While acknowledging that this is indeed a painful reality of our fallen world . . . the anomaly doesn't alter the norm."[16]

B. Recent Rejection of the Fall

Advocates for sexual polymorphism (SP) typically find appeals to the fall both pastorally devastating and academically unwarranted. On the pastoral front, "fall explanations" are frequently heard as dehumanizing rhetoric that "stigmatizes intersex bodies, rendering them 'fallen' in a way that other, male and female bodies are not."[17] Teaching that sexual dimorphism (SD) is "not just indicative but also imperative" relegates intersex embodiment to the category of "more fallen," and suggests that "intersex persons are somehow nonhuman or nonpersons," whose only hope is to be "fixed" through corrective surgery.[18] Such a perspective "contaminates intersex persons with a deep sense of personal shame."[19]

Aware of these pastoral caveats, some revisionists still want to retain a modified account of the fall, appreciating its power to explain how "life is not just finite but fractured and faulted . . . full of diminishment, distortion, disability, defect, disease, and death."[20] This revised account de-historicizes our primal parents, emphasizing their "theological" freight,[21] for example, as symbolic parents of fecundity.[22] As such, the dogmatic function of the fall may illumine some conditions but not intersexuality (it being an example of creational diversity).

Advancing beyond a reworked fall, others reject the category outright. Any decline or degradation narrative is academically unwarranted because of recent advances in scientific knowledge, especially in paleoanthropology and genetics. Among advocates for SP, Susannah Cornwall champions this position, drawing upon the work of Christopher Southgate to argue that "evolutionary biology

---

13. Hollinger, *Meaning of Sex*, 84.

14. Denny Burk, *What Is the Meaning of Sex?* (Wheaton, IL: Crossway, 2013), 180.

15. Margaret H. McCarthy, "Gender Ideology and the Humanum," *Comm* 43 (2016): 288.

16. Christopher West, *Our Bodies Tell God's Story: Discovering the Divine Plan for Love, Sex, and Gender* (Grand Rapids: Brazos, 2020), 28–9.

17. Susannah Cornwall, *Theology and Sexuality*, SCMCT (London: SCM, 2013), 54. See the painful testimony of Gross, "Intersexuality."

18. Cornwall, "Troubling Bodies?" 6, 9.

19. Jung, "Intersex on Earth," 178.

20. Ibid., 177.

21. DeFranza, *Sex Difference*, 175 n.75. Also, note the preference for a supposedly "Irenaean" (in contrast to "Augustinian") account of the fall, with its perceived "maturation" trajectory that turns the fall into an "ascent." See e.g., Tina Beattie, "Gendering Genesis, Engendering Difference: A Catholic Theological Quest," *STK* 92 (2016): 108.

22. Recall the trajectory argument in Chapter 3.

suggests that predation and cruelty existed on earth well before *homo sapiens* did."[23] More recently, Southgate has argued that the traditional narrative "is so much at variance with the chronology offered by evolutionary science that alternative ways of reading that Genesis text must be found."[24]

Given this, Cornwall emphasizes an important place for variation in nature. Extending the argumentation of Timothy Gorringe,[25] Cornwall opines that "to eradicate all sickness and suffering would compromise the free nature of the universe in a way that would preclude free will—so God could not eradicate all mutation without erasing that which works for good as well as ill."[26] As such, "Congenital disability, for example, is part and parcel of the random mutations which have led to the rise of all life: God did not specifically intend disability, but disability is a result of the way in which God's world functions freely."[27] "This means a freedom for things to go 'wrong,'" Cornwall concludes. "Mutation is necessary for the way the process has unfolded."[28]

Similarly, Elyse Raby develops a Thomistic account of primary and secondary causality to argue in light of evolutionary biology that creation "retains its autonomy, creativity, and freedom."[29] Creaturely causality is secondary, which includes "chance and randomness,"[30] where chance is not merely "epistemic" but "ontological."[31] Thus, Raby contends, "God, as primary cause, wills and creates intersex persons by willing, creating, and giving freedom to the various secondary causes which give rise to human sexual embodiment in all its diversity."[32] In Raby's schema, "Intersex is not a deviation from a divinely intended norm because genetic variation and diversity are constitutive aspects of how God formed creation and enables its freedom."[33]

As such, Cornwall surmises, one cannot "unproblematically argue that any deviation from male-and-female is also a deviation from a pre-Fall state."[34] Any appeal to the fall to explain intersexuality amounts to a naïve failure to recognize

---

23. Cornwall, *Sex and Uncertainty*, 52. Cornwall cites Christopher Southgate, *The Groaning of Creation: God, Evolution, and the Problem of Evil* (Louisville, KY: Westminster John Knox, 2008).

24. Christopher Southgate, *Theology in a Suffering World: Glory and Longing* (Cambridge: Cambridge University Press, 2018), 112.

25. Timothy Gorringe, *The Education of Desire: Towards a Theology of the Senses*, JAHLS (Harrisburg, PA: Trinity Press International, 2002).

26. Cornwall, *Sex and Uncertainty*, 52.

27. Ibid., 52–3.

28. Ibid., 234.

29. Raby, "You Knit Me Together," 103.

30. Ibid., 104.

31. Ibid., 108 n.44.

32. Ibid., 105.

33. Ibid.

34. Cornwall, *Sex and Uncertainty*, 53.

that random variation and mutation in sexed embodiment is both natural and necessary.[35] As Karen Keen concludes, "Wisdom invites us to be cautious about automatically assuming that a person's physical realities, including atypical sexual development, are fallen."[36]

For Keen, disassociating intersexuality from the fall is not a recent phenomenon, but finds support, perhaps surprisingly, in Augustine.[37] In reflecting upon *De civitate Dei* (hereafter *Civ.*) 16.8, Keen asserts that "in the case of intersex people, he [Augustine] concluded they are not a product of the fall."[38] While "our discomfort with difference can lead us to misdiagnose and mistreat human variation as illness or fallenness," Keen encourages her readers to appreciate with Augustine that "God intentionally created a sexual minority outside the binary."[39] Similarly, Teri Merrick draws upon the same passage of *Civ.* to propose a "Neo-Augustinian theology of nature" that recognizes intersexuality as the manifestation of nature's "playful originality."[40] Such an account "allows us to see atypically sexed bodies as [Augustine] saw them: wonderfully rare and unique creatures intentionally designed by their Creator to have whatever properties they do."[41] Indeed, seeing intersex persons as "deliberate iconic gifts of God can help call into question the gesture of control that results in surgically reshaping the bodies of intersexed children in an effort to 'naturalize' them."[42] Intersexuality should not be stigmatized as "fallen" but lauded as "diversity within the whole."[43]

In summary, while advocates for SP do not appear to expend significant effort developing and defending their own accounts of the fall, two broad approaches may be discerned. Motivated by legitimate pastoral concerns, the fall is either (i) de-historicized and reworked along purely symbolic lines, retained for its "theological" significance, or (ii) rejected *in toto*, given the seemingly contradictory claims of evolutionary biology. Either way, the fall is judged as offering little (if anything) for a theology of intersexuality.

C. Retention of the Fall

It is important to condemn dehumanizing abuses of the fall doctrine. Yet the historical correlation between pastoral abuses and the fall need not entail direct

---

35. A denial of the fall need not mean a denial of sin. For Cornwall, sin seems primarily social (ibid., 234).

36. Keen, *Scripture, Ethics*, 88.

37. Ibid., 98.

38. Ibid.

39. Ibid.

40. Merrick, "Welcome Intersexed?" 195, 193.

41. Ibid., 195.

42. Ibid., 192. In Chapter 6 I develop the "iconic" role of intersexuality in a different direction.

43. Keen, *Scripture, Ethics*, 99.

causation, such that the fall as a theological locus should be rejected in a theology of intersexuality. While certainly salutary, *abusus non tollit usum*. Further, concerning the defeater of human evolution, the fall need only be rejected if its claims and conditions are necessarily contrary or contradictory to those of human evolution. McCall carefully demonstrates that "neither contrariness nor contradictoriness follows from the conjunction of the scientific consensus and traditional Christian belief."[44] Both claims *could* be true because they are not mutually exclusive or mutually exhaustive.[45]

More constructively, given a methodological commitment to a thick theological interpretation of intersex embodiment that emphasizes theo-dramatic coherence, the fall doctrine provides an essential "emplotment" from which to interpret sexed atypicality.[46] Rehearsing comments from the introduction, a theologically thick approach rests upon the evangelical announcement of *Deus dixit* (Heb. 1:2). The Triune God has spoken in his theo-dramatic economy of grace. Indeed, *Deus dicet*—God continues to speak, supremely in scripture (Heb. 3:7). And scripture testifies to the import of the fall, at both the pericopal level and for how the Bible fits together as a coherent narrative.[47] Thus, the denial of the fall and its import within scripture is "untrue to the very logic of the biblical story."[48]

If biblical pressure at the micro and macro-levels requires us to have *some* account of the fall, challenging Cornwall's blanket rejection, further theological reflection suggests that an *adequate* fall doctrine demands two things: (i) that it is "historical," taking place "in time,"[49] and (ii) that it introduced human sin and death.[50] These desiderata rebut the claim of other revisionists that the fall may be

---

44. McCall, *Against God*, 388.

45. McCall outlines three proposals (Refurbishment; Hyper-Adam; Genealogical-Adam), all of which attempt to account for the claims of both sides (to varying degrees). I mention McCall's contribution not to make the strong claim of *how* exactly human evolution and the fall could cohere. Rather, to counter the critique that science and religion are irreconcilable—with the fall being rejected—it is sufficient to make the weaker claim that several accounts exist where reconciliation *remains* a possibility.

46. James K. A. Smith, "What Stands on the Fall?" in *Evolution and the Fall*, ed. William T. Cavanaugh and James K. A. Smith (Grand Rapids: Eerdmans, 2017), 51.

47. E.g., Darrell L. Bock, "Thinking Backwards About Adam and History," *TJ* 40 (2019): 131–43; C. John Collins, "The Place of the 'Fall' in the Overall Vision of the Hebrew Bible," *TJ* 40 (2019): 165–84.

48. Collins, *Reading Genesis Well*, 233.

49. While "history" can be an ambiguous term, the claim that the fall is historical is to make the weak claim that it occurred "in time." An historical fall does not commit one to make the stronger claim that the event was necessarily punctiliar. On the elastic nature of episodic time (especially time recorded within protohistory) as a means of answering challenges from evolutionary history, see Smith, "What Stands," 63.

50. Following Matthew Levering, there is an important distinction between human death and death per se (*Engaging the Doctrine of Creation: Cosmos, Creatures, and the Wise*

retained, so long as it is reworked along exclusively symbolic lines. This becomes evident when we consider the dogmatic function of the fall for other theological loci, particularly the doctrines of God, creation, humanity, Christology, soteriology, and eschatology.[51]

While advances in palaeoanthropology have introduced new concepts for Christian theology, such concepts should be used faithfully, according to "canonical sense" and "catholic sensibility," to clarify accepted biblical judgments for the edification of the church. This means not overextending the concept of evolution such that it distorts the foundational biblical judgments that "God is not the author of evil, that the suffering and evil in the world is not covertly good, and that God is a God who is faithful to his creation and who redeems it (instead of us *from* it)."[52] More positively, the fall provides Christian theology with the language of "dysfunction," "disability," and "defect" as meaningful categories when examining the theological significance of various atypical physical conditions. Without the fall, it appears difficult to avoid the conclusion that all aspects of diversity must be creational, and so celebrated as such.[53] But by including the fall within our process of theological assessment, we have the resources to parse out a distinction between the creational and the dysfunctional or defective, without necessarily attributing moral guilt for certain sexed conditions. This is no easy endeavor, requiring careful attention to the biblical material to work out the precise impact of the fall upon the sexed body.

II. An Account of the Fall

For a theologically thick reading of intersexuality the fall is formally essential. I turn now to consider its material content. First, I offer an exegesis of Genesis 3,

---

and Good Creator [Grand Rapids: Baker Academic, 2017], 234 n.22). Concerning human death, some theologians limit biblical references to human "death" to the spiritual, with a natural "good death" giving way to spiritual angst and the fear of annihilation (R. J. Berry, "This Cursed Earth: Is 'the Fall' Credible?" *SCB* 11 [1999]: 34). However, this interpretation conflicts with the sin-death nexus evident in Rom. 5:12 and 1 Cor. 15:21. As such, human "death" in the Bible has both a spiritual and physical aspect in view. To avoid undermining the (meta)physical continuity of creation through the fall, it is possible to have an account of prelapsarian animal but not human death. See Ingrid Faro, "The Question of Evil and Animal Death Before the Fall," *TJ* 36 (2015): 193–213; Gavin Ortlund, "Augustine on Animal Death," in *Evil and Creation: Historical and Constructive Essays in Christian Dogmatics*, ed. David Luy et al., SHST (Bellingham, WA: Lexham, 2020), 84–110.

51. Michael Reeves and Hans Madueme, "Threads in a Seamless Garment: Original Sin in Systematic Theology," in *Adam, the Fall, and Original Sin: Theological, Biblical, and Scientific Perspectives*, ed. Hans Madueme and Michael Reeves (Grand Rapids: Baker Academic, 2014), 209–24.

52. Ibid., 224, italics original.

53. Even if some mutations are celebrated more than others.

focusing particularly upon the impact of the fall, namely, death, on the human body, briefly noting its canonical development. Second, given the innovationist appeal to Augustine and Aquinas, I explore their theological contribution for interpreting postlapsarian sexed embodiment. *In nuce*, from Genesis 3, sin shatters *shalom*, leading to death. Following a thicker description of death, where "death" is not merely the temporal cessation of biological life but also a power that disorders the wholeness of *shalom*, the fall impacts the sexed body by undermining its structural integrity. Death disorders the sexed body's proper function and form, resulting in sexual dysfunction and defect respectively. Running through my assessment of the biblical and theological material is a core concern: To what extent should intersex embodiment be classified as either creational diversity or postlapsarian disorder, and are these options mutually exclusive?

A. Biblical Material

1. Genesis 3 Genesis 1–2 pictures *shalom*: "*Universal flourishing, wholeness, and delight.*"[54] There was no place for "shame" in Eden (Gen. 2:25), because humanity was preserved in Original Justice (OJ).[55] Since the sexed body participated in the ordered *shalom* of the creation event and intent, bodily form founded function and function fit form to fulfil the blessed commission of Gen. 1:28. Such ordered sexuate correspondence is from the God whose word is utterly effective (Gen. 1:7, 9, 11, 15, 24, 30) and wholly good (Gen. 1:10, 12, 18, 21, 25, 31). As such, the conditional threat of certain death as the punishment of disobedience—emphasized grammatically by the infinitive absolute מוֹת תָּמוּת (Gen. 2:17)—is completely trustworthy.[56]

When Adam and Eve disobey God it is no surprise that God arrives to execute his just judgment, the switch from prose to poetry giving the pericope "formal solemnity" (Gen. 3:14–24).[57] Given how their "disbelieving disobedience is a decreating act" (reversing and undoing the ordered network of relationships created by God),[58] the nature of God's judgment is fittingly and ironically decreational.[59] The "rupture" between God and humanity is seen supremely in

---

54. Cornelius Plantinga, *Not the Way It's Supposed to Be: A Breviary of Sin* (Grand Rapids: Eerdmans, 1995), 10, italics original.

55. Aquinas, *ST* 1.95.1 resp.

56. WHS §205; BHRG §20.2.2.2; JM §123d–q.

57. Kathleen M. O'Connor, *Genesis 1–25A*, SHBC 1 (Macon, GA: Smyth & Helwys, 2018), 65.

58. Steve Jeffery, Mike Ovey, and Andrew Sach, *Pierced for Our Transgressions: Rediscovering the Glory of Penal Substitution* (Nottingham: IVP, 2007), 112.

59. For a table charting how Genesis 3 tragically reverses Genesis 1–2, see Jay Sklar, "Sin," in *The Oxford Encyclopedia of the Bible and Theology*, ed. Samuel E. Balentine, OEB (Oxford: Oxford University Press, 2015), 2:299.

Adam and Eve's banishment from Eden,[60] the act of sending them out (שׁלח) in v.23 being accentuated by the "harsher and more explicit" use of the "stronger verb" גרשׁ in v.24.[61] Cut off from the tree of life, the inference is that they are now exposed to death (Gen. 3:22–24).[62] Thus, sin shatters *shalom*, leading to death. When humanity falls away from God, life falls apart, and "humanity falls back to its point of origin."[63]

"Once the constitutive bond between God and man is broken," laments Torrance, "every other relation suffers irreparable damage."[64] There is a relational rupture between humanity and creation (e.g., thorns and thistles, 3:17–18); between man and woman (e.g., blame shifting and domination, 3:12, 15–16); and even within the human psyche (e.g., fear and shame, 3:10). Indeed, the rupture of the fall appears to be more than merely relational, but pervasively constitutional, particularly for humans. As the climax of the discourse, God declares in Gen. 3:19 the sentence of death over Adam—he will "return to the earth (אדמה), for from it you were taken. Indeed, dust (עפר) you are, and to dust (עפר) you will return."[65]

Genesis 3 depicts physical death as that of structural disintegration. Alluding to Gen. 2:7, Gen. 3:19 portrays Adam's death with a "dreadful wordplay" between "dust" (עפר) and "earth" (אדמה).[66] In Gen. 2:7, God gave the "human of dust from the earth" (האדם עפר מן־האדמה) "the breath of life" (נשׁמת חיים) such that he became a "living being" (לנפשׁ חיה). But in Gen. 3:19, with the conspicuous absence of the "breath of life," אדם "returns" once again to אדמה. As David Kelsey observes, the "breath of life" is a "borrowed breath."[67] It is "loaned to him for a time, but it

---

60. For the fall as "rupture," see Jacques Ellul, *The Humiliation of the Word* (Grand Rapids: Eerdmans, 1985), 229.

61. Sarna, *Genesis*, 30. שׁלח in v.23 also forms an ironic wordplay with Adam "sending out" (שׁלח) his hand in v.22.

62. Christopher Heard, "The Tree of Life in Genesis," in *The Tree of Life*, ed. Douglas Estes, TBN 27 (Leiden: Brill, 2020), 96. On the tree of life conferring "immortality," such that excommunication from Eden entailed both physical and spiritual death, see Wenham, *Genesis 1–15*, 87, 90. Space precludes an assessment of whether Adam and Eve had already eaten from this tree, or if access to the tree was a reward for obedience (Collins, *Reading Genesis Well*, 178).

63. Fischer, *Genesis 1–11*, 258. For a vivid portrayal of how God's indignation (זעם) and David's sin (חטאת) precipitate the disintegration of his body's peace (שׁלום) and wholeness/soundness (מתם), see Ps. 38:3[4].

64. Thomas F. Torrance, *Incarnation: The Person and Life of Christ*, ed. Robert T. Walker, rev. ed. (Downers Grove, IL: IVP Academic, 2008), 39.

65. On 3:19 functioning as a "summary conclusion," giving "marked prominence to the affirmation of the death sentence," see Stephen Kempf, "Genesis 3:14–19: Climax of the Discourse?" *JOTT* 6 (1993): 366–8.

66. Mathews, *Genesis*, 253.

67. Kelsey, *Eccentric Existence*, 1:157.

remains God's possession, something that the man does not have at his command."[68] Thus, in its absence the body deteriorates. Indeed, the chiastic structure of verse 19 highlights Adam's "dust" nature, and while the parallel כי clauses are typically rendered as causal,[69] indicating logical dependency, Kempf makes a persuasive case that the second כי should be taken as an emphatic particle,[70] such that "the death sentence functions as a summary conclusion to the judgement of the man. . . . 'Yes, you are dust and to dust you shall return!'"[71]

2. Toward a Thicker Description of Death While the literary context indicates that Adam's life does not end immediately (Gen. 5:5), raising a concern as to whether the snake was correct in denying human death (Gen. 3:4), the death sentence delivered in Gen. 3:19 should be interpreted as contributing to a concept of death that is thicker than the mere punctiliar cessation of biological life.[72] Biblical death is (i) a disintegrating process, whose (ii) tendrils are total in extent and depth, and (iii) whose personified power is devastating.

First, as Augustine observed, while the death threatened in Gen. 2:17 is comprehensive,[73] the process of dying began "immediately after the first human beings disobeyed the commandment."[74] However our connection with Adam is understood, Augustine's concluding remark is *apropos*: "Once this [Adam's] nature was vitiated on account of sin, and bound by the chain of death, and justly condemned, man could not be born of man in any other condition."[75] A "corrupt root" produces corrupt fruit,[76] a corruption that is evident *before* "the death of the whole man," that is, the separation of body and soul.[77] Thus, the concept of death includes both an historically punctiliar moment *and* a process of dying that begins from day one—a "cancer that is present in us from our conception," Bavinck bemoans.[78]

---

68. Markus Mühling, *T&T Clark Handbook of Christian Eschatology*, trans. Jennifer Adams-Maßmann and David Andrew Gilland (London: Bloomsbury, 2015), 183.

69. E.g., NIV, NASB, NAB, NJPS, NJB.

70. E.g., NRSV, NEB, REB.

71. Kempf, "Climax of the Discourse?" 367–8.

72. For some of the philosophical challenges of defining death, see John Martin Fischer, *Death, Immortality, and Meaning in Life*, FPS (New York: Oxford University Press, 2020), 29–48.

73. Augustine discerns four meanings of death: "The death of the soul, the death of the body, the death of the whole man, or the death that is called the second death" (*Civ.* 13.12 [CCSL 48:394; WSA I/7:78]).

74. Ibid., 13.13 (CCSL 48:395; WSA I/7:78).

75. Ibid., 13.14 (CCSL 48:395; WSA I/7:79).

76. Ibid.

77. Ibid., 13.15 (CCSL 48:396; WSA I/7:80).

78. Herman Bavinck, *Reformed Ethics: Created, Fallen, and Converted Humanity*, ed. John Bolt (Grand Rapids: Baker Academic, 2019), 1:98. For the contemporary medical

Second, the tendrils of death are total in extent and depth. Much of the OT narrates and expands upon all of humanity laboring east of Eden under the dual threat of death as both final moment and disintegrating process,[79] evidenced principally in the close association between "dust" and "death."[80] As Feldmeier observed, "Adam's life is now chained to the cursed *'ădāmâ* 'earth' that transforms into the dust of transience," a recurring motif throughout the Psalms.[81] Indeed, in Ps. 39:4–6, the poetic interplay between חדל ("fleeting"), חלד ("lifespan"), and הבל ("breath") indicates paradoxically that "human transience becomes the ontological definition of humanity."[82] Furthermore, in a less immediately distressed key but with somber reflection, Ecclesiastes teaches the same truth—human life labors under the "dominion of death" (Eccles. 1:2; 3:20; 12:7–8, etc.),[83] a commentary on Genesis 3.[84]

Third, death's collocation with *dominion* suggests a further aspect contributing to a thicker concept of death. Death is an active, personified, "destroying power,"[85] vividly characterized in the OT as an insidious child snatcher "in its relentless pursuit of the living" (Jer. 9:21);[86] a destructive and powerful enslaver (Hosea 13:14); an insatiably greedy gobbler (Hab. 2:5).[87] The motif of death terrorizing creation culminates in the NT *locus classicus* of Romans 8. There Paul clarifies that even for those who are both "in Christ Jesus" (v.1) and indwelt by Christ (v.10), their bodies are still presently subject to "death because of sin" (v.10; cf. 7:24), and their "mortal bodies" still await resurrection life (v.11).[88] Indeed, Paul draws a parallel

---

consensus that biological death is a process whose *terminus a quo* is impossible to identify, see Mühling, *Eschatology*, 173–7.

79. For the extensive and intensive nature of sin and its effects in the Old Testament, see Mark J. Boda, *A Severe Mercy: Sin and Its Remedy in the Old Testament*, Siphrut 1 (Winona Lake, IN: Eisenbrauns, 2009).

80. See *HALOT* 2:862. Appropriate intertexts include: Job 4:19; 7:21; 10:9; 17:16; 20:11; 21:26; Pss. 22:30; 22:16; 103:14; Eccles. 3:20; 12:7; Isa. 26:5, 19; Dan. 12:2.

81. Reinhard Feldmeier, *God of the Living: A Biblical Theology*, trans. Mark E. Biddle (Waco, TX: Baylor University Press, 2011), 388.

82. Ibid., 390.

83. Ibid., 391.

84. David M. Clemens, "The Law of Sin and Death: Ecclesiastes and Genesis 1–3," *Them* 19 (1994): 5–8.

85. Rudolf Bultmann, "θάνατος," *TDNT* 3:18.

86. Eugene H. Merrill, "מות," *NIDOTTE* 2:887.

87. For other examples of death's personification in the OT, see *HALOT* 2:563.

88. Whether σῶμα refers simply to the human body or to the human as a whole person, both positions affirm the dominion of death. Perhaps as a mediating voice, Augustine perceptively notes that as sinners we were under a double death: "Dead in both body and soul—in soul because of sin, in body because of sin's punishment; and thus in *body* too *because of sin* (Rom. 8:10)" (*The Trinity* 4.3.5 [WSA I/5:156], italics original).

between creation being "subjected to frustration" (ματαιότης, v.20),[89] groaning (v.22) for liberation from its "bondage to decay" (φθορά, v.21),[90] and humanity's inward groaning "as we wait eagerly for our adoption to sonship, the redemption of our bodies" (v.23). Death truly is the "last enemy" (1 Cor. 15:26) who powerfully disorders the body, causing it to disintegrate toward decaying decreation.[91]

Thus, a thicker description of death highlights not merely the punctiliar moment, but also death as a decaying process, whose reach is total and whose power is devastating. The originating sin introduces death, which as an active power perennially and terroristically disorders humanity, offering a theological explanation for bodily dysfunction and defect. The advantage of privileging "death" rather than "sin" as the agent that disorders the body is that death verbiage emphasizes how bodily dysfunction and defect are due to external assault, whereas sin language often implies that bodily impairment results from personal culpability.[92] Sickness can be explained via personal sin (e.g., Exod. 15:26), but this is not always correct (e.g., John 9:3).

In summary, the archetypal passage of "Genesis 3 outlines a double problem: the sin we commit is de-creational, and the judgement sin calls forth after Genesis 2:17 also sees a destabilization of the original created order."[93] This destabilization includes the decaying slide toward bodily dissolution and decreation, culminating in the universal return to dust—a return to the formless and fruitless תהו ובהו (Gen. 1:2). While Genesis 3 does not explicitly address the impact of fall on the sexed body per se, its disordering and deteriorating slide toward death may be witnessed as the biblical canon develops, affecting both sexed function and form.

3. Death Disordering the Sexed Body

i. Function Scripture testifies to the disordering effects of death upon both the sexed body's proper function and form. Taking function first, disordered sexual function exhibits itself chiefly in the theme of barrenness,[94] which, as Rebecca

---

89. BDAG, 621, connoting the idea of "emptiness, futility, purposelessness, transitoriness." Douglas J. Moo suggests a "probable allusion" to the fall in Genesis 3 (*The Letter to the Romans*, 2nd ed., NICNT [Grand Rapids: Eerdmans, 2018], 537).

90. BDAG, 1054, connoting the sense of organic matter breaking down, dissolving, deteriorating, corrupting.

91. For death as the instrumental means of the devil's dominion, see, e.g., Heb. 2:14–15.

92. This distinction becomes significant for considering the pastorally pressing question of whether intersex people are more fallen.

93. Michael Ovey, "The Cross, Creation and the Human Predicament," in *Where Wrath and Mercy Meet: Proclaiming the Atonement Today*, ed. David Peterson (Carlisle: Paternoster, 2001), 117.

94. Here, I define barrenness/infertility/childlessness as the frustration of biological procreative abilities. The definition assumes a couple's intent to procreate (following Gen. 1:28) and focuses specifically on "abnormal" biological infertility, as opposed to "natural" biological infertility (e.g., childhood).

Raphael notes, is "the defining female disability in the Hebrew Bible."[95] While space prevents an assessment of the complex social and gendered experiences of infertility,[96] the OT portrays barrenness as a negative state (e.g., Gen. 11:30; 16:2; 20:18; 25:21; 29:31; Judg. 13:2–3; 1 Sam. 1:5; 2 Sam. 6:23; 2 Kings 4:14).[97] Again, the instances of infertility experienced by a community, whether real or threatened, juxtapose barrenness with sickness (חלה, Exod. 23:25–26) or healing (רפא, Gen. 20:17–18).[98] Infertility as an adverse condition is accentuated further by noting the negative corollary in Hosea 9:14, where a "miscarrying womb" is evoked as "a symbol and signal of divine wrath."[99] Ephraim, the fruitful one (Gen. 41:52), will ironically no longer bear fruit (Hosea 9:16), tragically reversing Jacob's blessing on their father Joseph (Gen. 49:25).

Considering its cause, childlessness can appear as a direct judgment for sin in legal (e.g., Deut. 28:18), cultic (Lev. 20:20–21; Num. 5:11–31), wisdom (e.g., Job 18:19), and prophetic (e.g., Hosea 2:8, 16; 9:10–18; 13:1; 14:8) literature. Yet the narrative experiences of some women (e.g., Sarah [Gen. 11:30], Rebekah [Gen. 25:21], Rachel [Gen. 29:31]) suggest that barrenness can also occur through no direct personal fault. "Childlessness was viewed as a curse," Block notes,[100] but while the cause could be identified as personal sin ("curse" proper), it could also simply be the result of impersonal misfortune ("cursed" experience). Whatever the cause, given the negative understanding of childlessness in the Bible, as well as its conceptual association with death, it seems reasonable to infer that there is an indirect link via the fall between sin producing death and the disordering disruption of the proper function of procreation. Thus, while deeply tragic, intersex infertility may be classified as a dysfunction.[101]

95. Rebecca Raphael, *Biblical Corpora: Representations of Disability in Hebrew Biblical Literature*, LHBOTS 445 (London: T&T Clark, 2008), 57–8.

96. E.g., Janice Pearl Ewurama De-Whyte, *Wom(b)an: A Cultural-Narrative Reading of the Hebrew Bible Barrenness Narratives*, BIS 162 (Leiden: Brill, 2018).

97. Indeed, in Luke 1:5–25, Elizabeth perhaps exemplifies the OT lament over childlessness, seeing it as a "disgrace among the people" (v.25). Luke's use of ὄνειδος forms a lexical intertext with Gen. 30:23 in LXX. Conversely, the more children one had, the greater one's sense of divine favor or "reward" (שכר, Pss. 127:3–5; 128:3–4).

98. See further Jeremy Schipper, "Disabling Israelite Leadership: 2 Samuel 6:23 and Other Images of Disability in the Deuteronomistic History," in *This Abled Body: Rethinking Disabilities in Biblical Studies*, ed. Hector Avalos, Sarah J. Melcher, and Jeremy Schipper, SemeiaSt 55 (Leiden: Brill, 2007), 105.

99. Candida R. Moss and Joel S. Baden, *Reconceiving Infertility: Biblical Perspectives on Procreation and Childlessness* (Princeton, NJ: Princeton University Press, 2015), 13.

100. Block, "Marriage and Family," 80.

101. While recognizing the constant need for immense pastoral sensitivity, I reserve the pastoral implications of my theology of intersexuality for the final chapter. Here, note how matriarchal barrenness in Genesis often highlights YHWH's power in fulfilling his promise

ii. Form Second, the biblical text occasionally mentions undesirable forms of the sexed body. In Lev. 21:17–23, priests with bodily defects (מומים) are banned from their service, including those with a "crushed testicle" (מרוח אשך, v.20). This prohibition is expanded in Deut. 23:1 to include *anyone* who has been emasculated, either by "crushing or cutting off" (דכא וכרות),[102] and bars them from entering the "assembly of YHWH." Later Judaism came to differentiate between two kinds of eunuch: the *"saris hamma"* (congenital eunuchism) and the *"saris adam"* (acquired eunuchism).[103]

While one could dispute the link between bodily "defect" (מום) and intersexuality, arguing that "defects" result from injuries (e.g., Lev. 24:19–20) and so exclude congenital conditions, Saul Olyan observes that the semantic domain of מום includes bodily conditions that exhibit a "lack of symmetry and blurring of physical boundaries."[104] The biblical discussion of "defects" appears to be more concerned with *what* the condition is, rather than *when* it first occurred. Thus, Olyan concludes: "'Defect' is a technical term in biblical usage, referring to a specific set of negatively constructed physical characteristics inconsistent with biblical notions of beauty."[105] Even if the "congenitally castrated person" is not foregrounded in the biblical examples, their sexed body remains atypical, epistemically ambiguous for adjudicating Israel, and so they presumably would still be barred from the assembly.[106]

In sum, according to David Tabb Stewart, the reason why sexual impairments (whether as dysfunction or defect) are so problematic is that "they are impediments or full obstacles to fulfilling the prime directive, the first commandment in the Hebrew Bible . . . 'Be fruitful and increase' (Gen. 1:28; 9:1, 7)."[107] If the ordered peace of the creation event required that sexed form is the foundation for procreative function, then anything that disrupts either element of the "form

(often bigger than the matriarchs imagine). Further, YHWH "sees" and "remembers" Hannah (1 Sam. 1:11, 19). Whatever one's "cursed" experience, God is not absent.

102. Interestingly, given the use of תמים in Gen. 17:1, circumcision could be the one form of cutting that "makes a male body whole or complete" (David Tabb Stewart, "Sexual Disabilities in the Hebrew Bible," in *Disability Studies and Biblical Literature*, ed. Candida R. Moss and Jeremy Schipper [New York: Palgrave Macmillan, 2011], 72).

103. Francois P. Retief and Louise Cilliers, "Eunuchs in the Bible," *AcTSup* 7 (2005): 248.

104. Saul M. Olyan, *Disability in the Hebrew Bible: Interpreting Mental and Physical Differences* (Cambridge: Cambridge University Press, 2008), 18.

105. Ibid., 19. Similarly, Wenham comments in reference to Lev. 21:17–24: "The idea emerges clearly that holiness finds physical expression in wholeness and normality" (*The Book of Leviticus*, NICOT 3 [Grand Rapids: Eerdmans, 1979], 292).

106. David Tabb Stewart, "Leviticus–Deuteronomy," in *The Bible and Disability: A Commentary*, ed. Sarah J. Melcher, Mikeal C. Parsons, and Amos Yong, SRTD (Waco, TX: Baylor University Press, 2017), 77. How such a prohibition might have been enforced remains opaque.

107. Stewart, "Sexual Disabilities," 75–6.

founds function—function fits form" rubric cannot be part of God's creational intent. In Genesis 3, the eruption of sin resulted in a death that is not merely the historical and punctiliar cessation of biological life, but also a universal decaying power that disorders both sexed function and form, producing the tragically negative conditions of barrenness, miscarriage, and physical impairment.[108]

B. Augustinian Reflection

While innovationist scholars occasionally appeal to Augustine to argue that intersexuality is not a result of the fall, a closer examination of Augustine's *oeuvre* demands the opposite conclusion. In short, Augustine illumines the preceding biblical argument by pressing the logic of privative evil as a decreational death that disorders the creational form and function of the sexed body.

1. Privative Evil Disorders the Sexed Body Due to the original righteousness enjoyed in the state of integrity, Augustine remarks that humanity "had supreme health in his flesh."[109] Although made from dust, and so "mortal according to the nature of his body," humanity was "immortal by grace."[110] In explicating the impact of the fall, namely, death, upon the whole human, Augustine notes how the soul's departure from God is logically prior to, and consequently disastrous for, the body.[111] God made the world a place of ordered peace,[112] and yet sin has caused

---

108. The classification of intersexuality as impairment is not a simplistic perpetuation of a monolithic "medical" model of disability. I appreciate that the concept of disability is "not a stable category nor is it universally recognized across cultures or over historical periods" (Sarah J. Melcher, "Disability and the Hebrew Bible: A Survey and Appraisal," *CBR* 18 [2019]: 18). Rather, disability is a "complex byproduct of historical, social, environmental, and biological forces" (Jeremy Schipper, *Disability Studies and the Hebrew Bible: Figuring Mephibosheth in the David Story*, LHBOTS 441 [New York: T&T Clark, 2006], 19). Yet, while there is much to learn from more socially or culturally oriented models of disability, the "form founds function—function fits form" argument suggests that from the perspectives of creation and fall there is an unavoidably "medical" aspect to intersexuality (hence, impairment).

109. Augustine, *Civ.* 14.26 (CCSL 48:449; WSA I/7:134). On the importance of bodily "wholeness" for Augustine, see Margaret R. Miles, *Augustine on the Body*, AARDS 31 (Missoula, MT: Scholars, 1979), 128.

110. Augustine, "The Literal Meaning of Genesis," 6.25, in *On Genesis: A Refutation of the Manichees, Unfinished Literal Commentary on Genesis, the Literal Meaning of Genesis*, ed. John E. Rotelle, trans. Edmund Hill, WSA I/13 (Hyde Park, NY: New City, 2002), 321. See also, Jesse Couenhoven, *Stricken by Sin, Cured by Christ: Agency, Necessity, and Culpability in Augustinian Theology* (Oxford: Oxford University Press, 2013), 24.

111. Augustine, *Civ.* 13.15 (CCSL 48:396; WSA I/7:79–80).

112. Ibid., 19.13 (CCSL 48:679; WSA I/7:368).

"a disordering of this order."[113] The result of sin and the fall is that "this order has been shaken."[114]

The precise impact of the fall on the body may be illuminated by attending to Augustine's account of evil. *Contra* his Manichean past,[115] Augustine's commitment to the Christian doctrine of *creatio ex nihilo* affirms that there is only one "immutably good" (*incommutabile bonum*): God, who being the Total Creator, made all things good.[116] All matter is "mortal" and "mutable,"[117] and yet, "whatever is natural [i.e., created] is good."[118] In contrast, evil is essentially privative, in that it is always ontologically derivative. It is a parasitic twisting and absence of what is good and natural (*privation boni*).[119] Augustine clarifies that not all things that lack goodness may be classified as "evil" (*malum*). For example, the night lacks light, but it is not evil.[120] If every form of lack is evil, then anything that is not God is necessarily evil. As Couenhoven summarizes, while "all evils are privations, not all privations are evil."[121] Instead, when something is "*not* exactly as it was supposed to be," it is by definition an evil "defect,"[122] because it lacks "a kind of goodness

113. Winrich Löhr, "Sündenlehre," in *Augustin Handbuch*, ed. Volker Henning Drecoll, 2nd ed., HT (Tübingen: Mohr Siebeck, 2014), 498.

114. Marie-Anne Vannier, *"Creatio," "Conversio," "Formatio": Chez S. Augustin*, Paradosis 31 (Freibourg, Suisse: Éditions Universitaires, 1991), 132.

115. See, for example, *Conf.* IV.

116. Augustine, "The Nature of the Good," 1, in *The Manichean Debate*, ed. Boniface Ramsey, trans. Roland J. Teske, WSA I/19 (Hyde Park, NY: New City, 2006), 325. Parenthetical Latin comes from *Corpus Augustinianum Gissense*. https://cag3.net. For the significance of *creatio ex nihilo* for Augustine, see *Conf.* 12.7.7 (CCSL 28:219).

117. Horn, "Anthropologie," 479.

118. Jesse Couenhoven, "Augustine," in *T&T Clark Companion to the Doctrine of Sin*, ed. Keith L. Johnson and David Lauber (London: Bloomsbury, 2016), 182.

119. The motivation for a privative account of evil is to distance a holy God from becoming the author of evil, as well as ensuring that evil is always parasitic, being ontologically nonessential. Although privation accounts of evil have come under attack (e.g., Todd C. Calder, "Is the Privation Theory of Evil Dead?" *AphQ* 44 [2007]: 371–81), Augustine's account of evil is more sophisticated than mere metaphysical privation. Seamus O'Neill interprets "evil" in Augustine as not only parasitic on being but also as a perversion of the will ("Privation, parasite et perversion de la volonté: Une étude ontologique et psychologique de la doctrine augustinienne du mal," *LTP* 73 [2017]: 31–52). Likewise, Hermann Häring helpfully notes that "with the formula *privatio boni* Augustine never downplayed evil as pure absence, but rather as an extremely effective opposition to God and goodness" ("Malum," *A-L* 3:1112). For Augustine, evil is not only a metaphysical mystery, but also a moral, and supremely theological, problem.

120. Augustine, "Nature of Good," 16 (WSA I/19:328–9).

121. Couenhoven, "Augustine," 183.

122. Augustine, "On the Free Choice of the Will," 3.15.42.145, in *On the Free Choice of the Will, on Grace and Free Choice, and Other Writings*, ed. Peter King, CTHP (Cambridge: Cambridge University Press, 2010), 102, italics original.

natural to it, which God designed it to have."[123] Indeed, Augustine suggests that the dissatisfaction one feels at a "defect" implicitly indicates that "you are really praising something whose completeness you desire."[124]

Couenhoven interprets Augustine's definition of evil as "a privation of a particular sort, one that violates the proper functioning of the thing that is corrupted."[125] Evil is that which inhibits a being from achieving the sort of good that is natural for that particular being. This frustration of natural function could come about not only from a lack of good but also by having too much of a good thing. For example, cancer is evil because it impedes the well-being of the body through excessive cell growth. In short, something is evil if it conflicts with God's creational design for it, causing it to miss out on its natural and proper goods, whether through lack or excess.

Supplementing Couenhoven's comments about evil's teleological frustration of function, in *De natura boni* Augustine explores evil's privative impact on the form that undergirds proper function. For Augustine, God has given every nature the "universal goods" of a particular "limit, form, and order" (*modus, species, ordo*),[126] these terms respectively mirroring Augustine's alternative use of "measure, number, and weight" (*mensura, numerus, pondus*).[127] Evil is "nothing but the corruption of either a natural limit or form or order."[128] While the frustration of proper function may correspond with "bad order" (*ordo malus*), that is, a nature is thwarted from functioning such that it cannot reach its natural telos—Augustine suggests that evil can also privatively corrupt "limit" and "form."[129] Either through lack or excess, a nature's "limit" or "form" can become "strange and unsuitable" (*aliena et incongrua*) because the *malum* does "not fit with the particular thing to which it is applied."[130] Thus, evil can private both form and function.

Augustine applies these insights primarily to the soul. Yet in thinking specifically about the body, the impact of the fall is such that not only is proper function hindered (order), but the structural integrity of the body (limit and form) that grounds proper function is also disordered. The body was made for peace, "the properly ordered arrangement of its parts."[131] Yet death fragments the body's "tranquility of order," disordering both its creational form *and* function.[132] In sum, Augustine seems to have a clear account of human perfection "marked by

---

123. Couenhoven, "Augustine," 183.

124. Augustine, "Free Choice," 3.14.41.143 (102).

125. Couenhoven, "Augustine," 183.

126. Augustine, "Nature of Good," 3 (WSA I/19:325).

127. Ibid., 21 (WSA I/19:330). Appropriated from Wis. 11:20. See Cornelius Mayer, "Creatio, creator, creatura," *A-L* 2:84–5.

128. Ibid., 4 (WSA I/19:326).

129. Ibid., 23 (WSA I/19:331).

130. Ibid.

131. Augustine, *Civ.* 19.13 (CCSL 48:679; WSA I/7:368).

132. Ibid.

harmony, a unification of beauty and utility, of form, shape, and colour."[133] The fall has ruptured this harmony, the evil of death privatively disordering bodily form and function.

2. Objection: The "Beauty" of Intersexuality While one could broadly agree with Augustine's account of disrupted harmony, it is still possible to argue that intersexuality need not be considered a postlapsarian impairment. In *Civ.* 22.24, Augustine exults at how God's goodness and wisdom are manifest in the intricate harmony of the human body, suggesting a distinction between "beauty" and "use." Although all things of "use" in the human body are beautiful, there are other bodily features (e.g., male nipples) that "have only beauty but no use."[134] Indeed, given the eschatologically provisional nature of certain bodily functions,[135] beauty takes "precedence over the necessities of use."[136] As such, while male and female sex organs have a particular "use" in the current dispensation, perhaps intersex embodiment possesses the greater "dignity" of being an additional example of "beauty" outside the statistical norm.[137] If intersexuality presently qualifies as "beauty" *sans* "use," then, by definition, the category of dysfunction or defect is inappropriate.

Further, the affirmation that intersexuality is an expression of "beauty" need not commit one to locating intersexuality as a pre-fall reality. Such a proposal could come in two forms. First, as a *felix culpa*-esque argument, one could view intersexuality as an example of creational beauty, which only becomes a possible reality in the 'better world' *post-lapsum*.[138] Alternatively, and perhaps in a more Augustinian key, one could argue that intersex embodiment is the historical flowering of certain seminal reasons (*rationes seminales*) sown into human nature as "the dynamic principles" of development at the *ictus* of creation event.[139] Just as

---

133. Brian Brock, "Augustine's Hierarchies of Human Wholeness and Their Healing," in *Disability in the Christian Tradition: A Reader*, ed. Brian Brock and John Swinton (Grand Rapids: Eerdmans, 2012), 68.

134. Augustine, *Civ.* 22.24 (CCSL 48:850; WSA I/7:540).

135. E.g., procreation and sexual activity will cease in the Eschaton because there will be no more human marriage (Matt. 22:30).

136. Augustine, *Civ.* 22.24 (CCSL 48:850; WSA I/7:541).

137. Ibid. (CCSL 48:851; WSA I/7:541).

138. Admittedly, such *felix culpa* logic raises other theological concerns over the necessity of sin and evil (implicating God quite directly) that might ultimately discourage its full acceptance. See Kevin Diller, "Are Sin and Evil Necessary for a Really Good World? Questions for Alvin Plantinga's Felix Culpa Theodicy," *FP* 25 (2008): 87–101.

139. Larissa Carina Seelbach, "Schöpfungslehre," in *Augustin Handbuch*, ed. Volker Henning Drecoll, 2nd ed., HT (Tübingen: Mohr Siebeck, 2014), 471. For Augustine, a programmatic verse for thinking through the development of creation is Sir 18:1: "He created all things simultaneously" (*creavit omnia simul*). See, e.g., Augustine, "Literal Meaning of

different plants "extrude through the periods of time proper to each kind,"[140] so too could intersex embodiment be a similarly subsequent development of sexed diversity. Indeed, given the rare and surprising nature of intersexuality, perhaps a more propinquitous parallel may be seen in the blossoming of Aaron's rod (Num. 17:8) and the speaking of Balaam's donkey (Num. 22:28). For Augustine, such miracles were possible because *rationes seminales* were "inserted by him [God] in created things and set fermenting in them."[141] Thus, humanity's *rationes seminales*, expressed in its unique measure, number, and weight, need not necessarily restrict humanity to SD. To my knowledge, no revisionists have appropriated Augustine's use/beauty distinction, nor in its adapted argumentation of *felix culpa* or *rationes seminales*. Yet such a proposal potentially offers a Patristic spin to the "trajectory of othering" argument mentioned in the previous chapter.

Moreover, supplementing the classification of intersexuality as "beauty," some advocates for SP explicitly argue that in *Civ.* 16.8, where Augustine discusses "*androgyni*" in a section more broadly concerned with "certain monstrous races of men,"[142] Augustine offers resources for categorizing intersexuality as a creational good, "contributing to the overall beauty of creation."[143] Adapting the thesis of Lorraine Daston and Katherine Park,[144] Merrick argues that the reason why we do not see atypical bodies as "wondrous variations, but as repugnant deviations," is because Augustinian natural philosophy was hijacked by a rigid Aristotelianism in the Middle Ages.[145] Constructively, Merrick proposes a "neo-Augustinian theology of nature" that recognizes the import of God's supreme sovereignty, such that "what actually occurs is just as God willed that it should be."[146] For Merrick, *Civ.* 16.8 reveals an approach to nature that was "inclined to delight in 'hermaphrodites' as specially created by God."[147]

Merrick's proposal could be strengthened by noting Augustine's assertion in *Civ.* 16.8: "God is the creator of all things; and he himself knows where and when it is right or was right for anything to be created. He knows how to weave together the beauty of the whole in the similarity and diversity of its parts."[148] Similarly in *Civ.* 21.8: "Just as it was not impossible for God to institute the natures that he willed, neither is it impossible for God to change the natures that he instituted into

Genesis," 4.33.52 (WSA I/13:273). See further, Gerald P. Boersma, "The Rationes Seminales in Augustine's Theology of Creation," *NV* 18 (2020): 427.

140. Augustine, "Literal Meaning of Genesis," 5.5.14 (WSA I/13:283).

141. Ibid., 9.17.32 (WSA I/13:395).

142. Augustine, *Civ.* 16.8 (CCSL 48:508; WSA I/7:195).

143. Merrick, "Welcome Intersexed?" 192. See also, Keen, *Scripture, Ethics*, 98.

144. Lorraine Daston and Katharine Park, *Wonders and the Order of Nature, 1150–1750* (New York: Zone, 2012).

145. Merrick, "Welcome Intersexed?" 193.

146. Ibid., 194.

147. Ibid., 193.

148. Augustine, *Civ.* 16.8 (CCSL 48:509; WSA I/7:196).

whatever he wills."[149] Augustine goes on to draw upon Rom. 11:17–24, arguing that while some things might seem contrary to nature, these "marvels" are rightly called "monsters."[150]

For Merrick, Augustine "does not judge the form, function or fittedness of a particular creature in reference to some general kind or nature."[151] Rather, rare individuals should be seen as "specially chosen by God to display his improvisational artistry."[152] Indeed, Merrick could have noted further Augustine's caveat: "The person who is unable to see the whole is offended at what appears to be the deformity of a part, for he does not know how it fits in or how it is connected with the whole."[153] Thus, Brock opines, "What may look to us like a deformity may actually be an artifact of a sinful inability to see God's working in all people to create a beautiful whole."[154]

3. Response: Attending to Literary Context and Common Grace While this reading of Augustine rightly emphasizes the good of human embodiment, the claim that intersexuality should be categorized as part of the "beauty" of the creation event and intent may be queried when we attend to the wider literary context of *Civ.* 22.24 and 16.8, buttressed by the dogmatic function of common grace. First, in *Civ.* 22.24, Augustine demonstrates how God's goodness endures to humanity despite the fall, highlighting the continued gifts of "propagation" (*propagatio*) and "conformation" (*conformatio*). Even though humans have been "vitiated by sin and condemned to punishment," God intends for his commission in Gen. 1:28 to be fulfilled through the function of propagation.[155] As such, God has graciously produced in humanity "the same possibility—but not necessity—of propagating others."[156] Augustine notes that while God has made some sterile, the "power of propagation was not taken away by sin," so that humans might indeed fulfil God's commission in Gen. 1:28.[157] Further, arguing from 1 Cor. 3:7, Augustine opines that propagation succeeds due to God's gift of "conformation," his fatherly providence that "forms and modes of each species" remain as God intends.[158] In short, Augustine subsumes his discussion of "beauty" and "use" underneath the more prominent concern to highlight God's goodness through the fall, evidenced

---

149. Merrick rightly notes that Augustine uses 'nature' in terms of 'properties' ("Welcome Intersexed?" 198 n.34).

150. Augustine, *Civ.* 21.8 (CCSL 48:773; WSA I/7:462). Augustine highlights how *monstrosus* ("monster") is derived from *monstrare* ("to show").

151. Merrick, "Welcome Intersexed?" 194.

152. Ibid.

153. Augustine, *Civ.* 16.8 (CCSL 48:509; WSA I/7:196).

154. Brock, "Augustine's Hierarchies," 76.

155. Augustine, *Civ.* 22.24 (CCSL 48:847; WSA I/7:537).

156. Ibid.

157. Ibid.

158. Ibid.

in the grace of propagation and conformation. Although implicit, the suggestion seems to be that if one is human, then one should expect to possess the "possibility" of fertility to propagate.[159] Such a function requires the form of either maleness or femaleness, intimating that for Augustine, intersexuality would be an impairment of form that frustrates the function of propagation, an example of someone from whom "God has, at his will, taken this fertility . . . leaving them sterile."[160]

Further, situating the *androgyni* comments of *Civ.* 16.8 in their wider literary context illumines Augustine's own understanding. In Books 15–18, Augustine aims "to trace the course that each [city] has followed from the point at which the first two human beings began to have children down to the point at which human beings will cease to have children."[161] Accordingly, the "monsters" or "marvels" Augustine describes in *Civ.* 16.8 are those that appear post-fall and pre-eschaton. Although anachronistic, this observation does not deny that Augustine possibly *could* account for intersexuality as creational diversity pre-fall, nor does it deny that God *could* do a new work of intersex inclusion in the eschaton (as Merrick opines). Rather, the literary context suggests more minimally that for Augustine, intersex embodiment aligns with post-fall disorder rather than creational diversity.[162]

Second, while it is certainly important to affirm the sovereign freedom of God's artistic license, as well as heed the warning about prejudging bodily conditions as divine "mistake[s],"[163] Merrick nevertheless fails to appreciate the theological distinction between God's common grace and his creational intent.[164] While the phrase "common grace" may be anachronistic for Augustine, it captures something intrinsic to his theology. Common grace is part of a doctrinal nexus that enables Christians to affirm the goodness of God and his creation in a fallen world, evidenced particularly in the grace of existence.[165] Although the quantum of grace varies per individual according to God's good pleasure, this grace is called

---

159. Steven Schafer reads *Civ.* 13.14 as "identifying procreative intercourse as part of human nature" (*Marriage, Sex, and Procreation*, 36).

160. Augustine, *Civ.* 22.24 (CCSL 48:847; WSA I/7:537).

161. Ibid., 15.1 (CCSL 48:453; WSA I/7:139).

162. Indeed, Augustine's comments on *androgyni* do not attribute them to a third sex, arguing that "prevailing usage" aligns them with the male sex (*Civ.* 16.8).

163. Augustine, *Civ.* 16.8 (CCSL 48:509; WSA I/7:196).

164. This distinction is clear in ibid., 22.24.

165. E.g., Athanasius, *Contra Gentes* 41, in *Contra Gentes and De Incarnatione*, trans. Robert W. Thomson, OECT (Oxford: Clarendon, 1971), 115. For the relationship between common grace and special grace, see Herman Bavinck, "Common Grace," trans. Raymond Van Leeuwen, *CTJ* 24 (1989): 35–65. For an account of common grace being "established and sustained by the Noahic covenant," see Miles V. Van Pelt, "The Noahic Covenant of the Covenant of Grace," in *Covenant Theology: Biblical, Theological, and Historical Perspectives*, ed. Guy Prentiss Waters, J. Nicholas Reid, and John R. Muether (Wheaton, IL: Crossway, 2020), 111–32.

common because all participate in the good of existence, and all receive some good to some degree (Matt. 20:15).

The doctrine of common grace equips Christians to celebrate the goodness of God's sovereign creativity and providence, happily agreeing with Cornwall that "God *intended* them [surveyed participants] to be intersex," and insist upon the "goodness of their specific embodiment."[166] Yet, *contra* Cornwall, common grace resists automatically attributing every particular of creation to God's pre-fall creational intent.[167] As Todd Daly notes, the "mere observation that a phenomenon exists in nature does not by definition mean that it is part of God's intended good creation order. It may well reflect the consequences of the fall into sin."[168] Indeed, without the distinction between common grace and creational intent, it remains unclear how innovationists can classify any embodied condition as objectively negative.[169] Importantly, the appeal to common grace is not a strong claim to discern *which* embodied phenomena are a manifestation of beauty and *which* are a result of the fall. More minimally, the category of common grace offers helpful resources to follow Augustine in affirming creaturely goodness without necessarily celebrating all diversity as God's creational intent.

Nonetheless, this conclusion should not distract from Augustine's primary intent—that Christians read the "appearance of the unexpected not as freakish or repulsive but a special *communicative act* of God."[170] Given the immutable goodness of God,[171] all postlapsarian creation remains metaphysically good.[172] The sovereign purposes of God (evidenced in his common grace) mean that physical impairment can still be a "divinely communicative 'wonder' of a loving Creator."[173] Thus, *contra* the depressingly contemporary Graeco-Roman worldview, it is an injustice against God to reduce anomalous bodies exclusively to the brokenness

---

166. Susannah Cornwall, "Asking About What Is Better: Intersex, Disability, and Inaugurated Eschatology," *JRDH* 17 (2013): 380, italics original.

167. See, for example, Cornwall, "What Is Better," 380–1.

168. Todd T. W. Daly, "Gender Dysphoria and the Ethics of Transsexual (i.e., Gender Reassignment) Surgery," *E&M* 32 (2016): 50 n.23.

169. This distinction between common grace and creational intent goes some way in responding to Raby's proposal above. A Thomistic account of non-competitive divine agency and causality may well be helpful in discerning the development of human origins. However, abstracted from the insights of common grace (and a Thomistic understanding of natures), Raby's argument seems unable to distinguish between positive and negative embodiment.

170. Brian Brock, *Wondrously Wounded: Theology, Disability, and the Body of Christ,* SRTD (Waco, TX: Baylor University Press, 2019), 17, italics original.

171. Augustine, *Civ.* 11.10 (CCSL 48:330; WSA I/7:11).

172. Ibid., 12.5 (CCSL 48:359; WSA I/7:41).

173. Brock, *Wondrously Wounded,* 17.

of creation.[174] Rather, as Brock contends, we need redeemed minds to "discern these 'strange vocations' in their true light, without pity and fear."[175] What God may be communicating through the "strange vocation" of intersexuality will be expanded upon when the whole divine drama is in view. Here, it is sufficient to conclude that, *pace* revisionist readings of Augustine regarding intersexuality as the "beauty" of creational intent, by attending to Augustine's wider literary context and the contribution of common grace, we can affirm both fallenness *and* creaturely goodness.

4. Remaining Questions From a brief survey of Augustine, it seems evident that prior to the fall the structural integrity of the human body-soul composite, although made from mutable matter, was sustained in original righteousness. In turning away from God, the source of all life, humanity turned toward death. From the historical moment of the fall, the disordering decay of death starts in the soul and spreads to the body, such that the body begins to deteriorate and eventually die. While advocates for SP appeal to Augustine to advance intersexuality as a creational good, a closer look at Augustine's account of privative evil undermines revisionist appropriation.

Nevertheless, further clarification is required from Augustine. While death as the fruit of the fall exhibits itself privatively in disordering both the creational form and function of the sexed body, it remains unclear whether these insights refer to humanity *qua* species or simply at the individual human level. This is important because if Augustine refers exclusively to distinct individuals, then the teleological frustration experienced because of the fall could be interpreted on a case-by-case basis. As such, an advocate for SP could agree that evil privatively corrupts an individual's limit, form, and order, but this admittance need not require that intersex embodiment be an example of privative limit or form for anyone who qualifies as the species "human." Intersex embodiment could be the creational starting point of good nature for some individuals, from which evil subsequently privates, attacking limit, form, and order. If this is the case, then lacking the *form* or *function* to reproduce (so vital in Gen. 1:27–28) would only be privative for the statistical majority of humanity. As such, being male or female would simply be a *common* rather than *universal* property of human nature. Given the historical and literary context of Augustine's comments, it may well be that Augustine intends to

---

174. See Aristotle's demand that "there be a law against nourishing [infants] that are deformed" (*Politics*, trans. H. Rackham, LCL 264 [Cambridge, MA: Harvard University Press, 1932], 7.14.10).

175. Brock, *Wondrously Wounded*, 28. "Strange" or "marvelous vocations" (*miris vocationibus*) is Augustine's label for individuals who are impaired yet exemplary Christians. See Augustine, "The Punishment and Forgiveness of Sins and the Baptism of Little Ones," 1.22.32, in *Answer to the Pelagians*, ed. John E. Rotelle, trans. Roland J. Teske, WSA I/23 (Hyde Park, NY: New City, 1997), 52.

make a universal species claim.[176] However, there does not appear to be anything that strictly necessitates a "species" interpretation that would undermine a sexually polymorphic reading.

This judgment also applies to the proposal that intersexuality is the beautiful flowering of *rationes seminales*. While the examples of Aaron's rod and Balaam's donkey are suggestive, miraculous events do not offend *contra naturam*.[177] Further, as Augustine asserts in the wider context, God's freedom "is almighty, for sure, but with the strength of wisdom, not unprincipled might."[178] This comment implies that if intersexuality is to be a legitimate seminal reason, not only will it not transgress the integrity of created order, but it will also reveal something about God's wisdom distinct from maleness and femaleness, or perhaps further God's redemptive purposes *qua* Aaron's rod and Balaam's donkey. What exactly that unique contribution *could be* for Augustine remains unclear and undeveloped, intimating that reading Augustine in context may cast doubt upon the "intersexuality as *rationes seminales*" proposal. Nevertheless, if we accept Augustine's account of seminal reasons and divine freedom as a helpful way of conceiving the maturation of creation in general, the possibility of intersexuality as a subsequent development of what was "hidden away in God" remains open, at least in theory.[179]

Thus, a question lingers from Augustine: "Can we attribute proper form and function to human nature universally and not just to the statistical majority?" Put differently: "When is embodied particularity simply a manifestation of 'beauty' and when is it a result of the fall?" To help answer these questions, particularly as they relate to intersexuality, I turn to the medieval Augustinian, Thomas Aquinas.

---

176. Mariusz Tabaczek highlights Augustine's "neo-Platonic" preference for "forms as fixed ideas" ("The Metaphysics of Evolution: From Aquinas's Interpretation of Augustine's Concept of Rationes Seminales to the Contemporary Thomistic Account of Species Transformism," *NV* 18:3 [2020]: 946). See also Augustine's intimation that since God "completed all his works" (*consummauerit omnia opera sua*) on the sixth day, God "inserted" (*inseruerit*) every creature's "kind" (*genus*). God may make "new things" (*nova*) in history, but these will never contradict the "kinds of things he set up at first" (*genera rerum quae primo condidit*) (Augustine, "Literal Meaning of Genesis," 5.20.41 [WSA I/13:297]).

177. Gavin Ortlund, *Retrieving Augustine's Doctrine of Creation: Ancient Wisdom for Current Controversy* (Downers Grove, IL: IVP Academic, 2020), 193.

178. Augustine, "Literal Meaning of Genesis," 9.17.32 (WSA I/13:395). Note Augustine's commitment to divine simplicity (cf. *Civ.* 11.10).

179. Augustine, "Literal Meaning of Genesis," 9.17.31 (WSA I/13:394). One potential avenue could be to suggest that intersex performs the same theological function as singleness, but in a more biological key. Just as redemption in Christ opens the vocation of singleness (Matt. 19:12), so too could Christ expand sexed bodily possibilities toward SP. I engage this potential parallel in Chapters 5 and 6.

C. Thomistic Clarification

1. The Fall Like Augustine, Aquinas pictures the state of integrity as one of original justice (OJ),[180] such that human bodies were preserved by grace from dysfunction, decay, and death.[181] To extend the illustration employed above, the iron saw is no longer susceptible to rust because it has been coated with a protective layer of WD-40. However, through a proud and inordinate "coveting of God's likeness," death entered the world.[182] Indeed, a programmatic verse for Thomas, found throughout his corpus, is Rom. 5:12, "Wherefore as by one man sin entered into this world and by sin death: and so death passed upon all men, in whom all have sinned."[183] Aquinas is consistent with the biblical emphasis that death, the "last enemy" (1 Cor. 15:26), is not natural for the human person but an "extremely hostile" and devastatingly destructive punishment for sin.[184]

2. The Effects of the Fall The effects of sin, originated in the fall, are outlined most clearly in *ST* 1-2.85. In Article 1, Aquinas explicates the impact of sin by considering three goods enjoyed by human nature before the fall. The first good is human nature per se, which is not strictly impacted by sin. Thomas mentions this first because he is adamant that "the principles of which nature is constituted, and the properties that flow from them," are "neither destroyed nor diminished by sin."[185] "The reason," Houck notes, "is that these principles [and some properties] are necessary for human existence."[186] Postlapsarian humans remain composed of the universal-essential principles/properties of form (soul) and matter (body), from which flow certain powers (e.g., vegetative, sensitive, appetitive, locomotive, and intellective). As rational body-soul composites, humans are still human, even if fallen.

The second impact of sin that Thomas highlights is how the fall has diminished (*diminuitur*) the "natural inclination to virtue."[187] As stated in *ST* 1-2.85.1 ad 2, the will as something necessary to human nature remains, but its inclination "is changed in so far as it is directed to its term." By paralleling "virtue" with "term" (*ad terminum*—end), Thomas is making the broad case that although the human still has a will, it is teleologically twisted, curved in on itself, such that we become a "slave to sin" (John 8:34), and even the basic acts of the vegetative powers are

---

180. Aquinas, *ST* 1.95.1 resp.

181. Aquinas, *ST* 1.97.1 resp.

182. Aquinas, *ST* 2-2.163.2.

183. Thomas Aquinas, *Commentary on Romans*, trans. Fabian R. Larcher (Green Bay, WI: Aquinas Institute, 2020), 164. Thomas dedicates a whole lecture to this one verse (ibid., 164–70).

184. Aquinas, *Corinthians*, C.15 L.3 §944 (L/E 38: 356).

185. Aquinas, *ST* 1-2.85.1 resp.

186. Daniel W. Houck, *Aquinas, Original Sin, and the Challenge of Evolution* (Cambridge: Cambridge University Press, 2020), 103.

187. Aquinas, *ST* 1-2.85.1 resp.

disordered. Thus, original sin is not merely the privative removal of OJ, where the will remains intact and free, *pace* O'Brien,[188] but also seems to entail a positive corruption (*habitus corruptus*).[189]

Importantly, the positive corruption of sin (point 2) does not cause human nature to mutate metaphysically (point 1), such that human nature is destroyed. Principally, what motivates Thomas' emphasis on the pre- and post-fall continuity of human nature per se seems to be Rom. 5:12–21. Human nature must remain the same to explain how (i) all die because all are "in Adam," and how (ii) all may benefit from Christ, the "second Adam." In the fall, nature is wounded but not destroyed. If sin destroyed the very substance of human nature, there would be no essential (and so soteriological) connection between Adam, Christ, and the rest of humanity.

3. The Effects of the Fall on the Body The third good of nature impacted by sin is that OJ is "entirely (*totaliter*) destroyed through the sin of our first parent."[190] Recalling comments in Chapter 3, although matter is mutable such that death is natural for universal nature, Thomas is firm that since God made whatever is natural in humanity, and "God made not death" (Wisdom 1:13), "death is not natural for man."[191] Aquinas clarifies his claim by emphasizing that humans are body-*soul* composites. Axiomatic here for Aquinas is the principle that "matter is proportionate to form," where form guides matter to its proper end.[192] Since the human person is a body-soul, hylemorphic composite, and the immaterial, incorruptible, rational soul's ultimate end is everlasting happiness (*beatudio perpetua*), when the rational soul perfectly governs the body, it ensures the body stays "naturally incorruptible."[193] In short, "Man is naturally corruptible as regards the nature of his matter left to itself, but not as regards the nature of his form."[194] Being composed of mutable matter, humans are inherently decomposable. And yet, "Our personal, bodily existence is rendered actual by a form whose nature it is not to share the loss of existence suffered by the body at death."[195] Thus, in OJ, God preserved "the body itself in a state of incorruption so that it might match the soul's perpetual existence."[196]

---

188. T. C. O'Brien, "Appendix 8: Original Justice," in *Summa Theologiae: Original Sin (1-2.81–85)* (London: Eyre & Spottiswoode, 1965), 26:144. Such a position would leave the door open to a form of Pelagianism. Whether Thomas satisfies certain "semi-Pelagian" conditions, see Houck, *Aquinas, Original Sin*, 244–7.

189. Aquinas, *ST* 1-2.85.2.1 ad 1.

190. Aquinas, *ST* 1-2.85.1 resp.

191. Aquinas, *ST* 1-2.85.6 sc.

192. Ibid.

193. Ibid.

194. Aquinas, *ST* 1-2.85.6 resp.

195. Cooper, *Life in the Flesh*, 101.

196. Thomas Aquinas, *Light of Faith: The Compendium of Theology*, trans. Cyril Vollert, 3rd ed. (Manchester, NH: Sophia Institute, 1993), §152.

Nevertheless, as Aquinas continues, "When man's soul turned from God in sin, the human body deservedly lost that supernatural disposition whereby it was unrebelliously subservient to the soul. And hence man incurred the necessity of dying."[197] With the loss of OJ, and the "wounding of nature" (*ST* 1-2.85.3 sc), the soul no longer governs the body rightly toward the actualization of its proximate and ultimate ends,[198] resulting in "death, sickness, and all defects of the body."[199] As Romero comments, for Aquinas, "The breach of this immaterial relationship led to a material disorder, insofar as the soul lost the supernatural means to govern the body toward the actualization of both the natural and the ultimate good of the human creature."[200] When the body can no longer do what it is intended to do, it experiences what Cross calls a "teleological failure."[201] As indicated above, in Aquinas' teleological universe certain goods belong to particular creatures, with everything ordered to ends appropriate to its form. But in *ST* 1.48.5 resp., we see that failure to reach appropriate ends can occur for two reasons: either (i) because something has lost its structural integrity, or (ii) because its ordering powers have become disordered—or both. This important passage is worth quoting at length:

> I answer that, Evil, as was said above (Article 3) is the privation of good, which chiefly and of itself consists in perfection and act. Act, however, is twofold. . . . The first act is the form and integrity of a thing; the second act is its operation. Therefore evil also is twofold. In one way it occurs by the subtraction of the form, or of any part required for the integrity of the thing, as blindness is an evil, as also it is an evil to be wanting in any member of the body. In another way evil exists by the withdrawal of the due operation, either because it does not exist, or because it has not its due mode and order.

For Thomas, something is "evil" (*malum*) when it fails "either in maintaining appropriate structural integrity, or in acting in ways that are appropriate to the relevant structure."[202] Similar to Augustine, not every privation of good is necessarily evil, but "only the privation of a good which is naturally due."[203]

The initial cause of every evil parasitic privation in the human person is the loss of OJ, which instigates a disordering of the soul-body relation in the human person, and thus "the loss of the organism's teleologically-appropriate

---

197. Ibid.

198. See also, Thomas Aquinas, *On Evil*, trans. Richard Regan (Oxford: Oxford University Press, 2003), 5.1.

199. Aquinas, *ST* 2-2.164.1 resp.

200. Romero, "Corporis Infirmitas," 113.

201. Richard Cross, "Aquinas on Physical Impairment: Human Nature and Original Sin," *HTR* 110 (2017): 319.

202. Ibid.

203. Romero, "Corporis Infirmitas," 107.

self-control."[204] Here, Aquinas' privative account of evil parallels Augustine's proposal outlined above. For both, since form founds function and function fits form, where form is disordered, function will also be disordered. Inversely, where function is disordered, it may be because form is deformed.

4. *The Effects of the Fall on the Sexed Body* Aquinas' insights regarding the loss of OJ offer an instructive framework for exploring the impact of the fall on the sexed body. In the creation event and intent God created two different sexed bodily configurations that enjoyed "integrity" and "due operation" (from the vegetative powers of the soul and natural inclination) to fulfill the procreative commission of Gen. 1:28. From day one of the fall, sin brings decay toward death.[205] Applying Aquinas' account of privative evil in *ST* 1.48.5 to sexed embodiment, postlapsarian death produces both defects that disorder the sexed body's structural integrity— whether damaging gametes, gonads, genitalia, hormones, secondary sex characteristics, brain sex, or even genes and chromosomes—and defects that result in a disconnect between the volitional operating powers and the sexed body (e.g., impotence and infertility). Thus, privative evil affects both sexed bodily form and function, preventing the vegetative powers and natural inclinations from fulfilling Gen. 1:28.

Moreover, by highlighting the loss of OJ, Thomistic logic clarifies from Augustine that the "form founds function—function fits form" rubric applies to human nature universally and not just to the statistical majority. As Cross confirms, "Since the gift [of OJ] is universal, its loss is too. So once the gift is lost, it is lost to the whole species."[206] Given intersex *persons* are fully human, they too share in the loss of OJ. Since the form of intersex *conditions* prevents procreative function, a correct classification of intersexuality should lean toward postlapsarian disorder rather than creational diversity.[207] Yet, following Augustine's insights from *Civ.* 16.8, the recognition of disorder should not neglect the inherent goodness of intersex bodies. Thus, to capture both the body's enduring goodness alongside the tragic defect of intersex conditions, perhaps we should adjust the original dialectic of intersexuality as *either* creational diversity *or* postlapsarian disorder toward a more nuanced lens of "disordered diversity." Here, the nominal "diversity" emphasizes enduring goodness, with the adjectival "disordered" offering a fall-inflected modifier.[208]

---

204. Cross, "Aquinas on Physical Impairment," 329.

205. Aquinas, *ST* 2-2.164.1 ad 8.

206. Cross, "Aquinas on Physical Impairment," 327.

207. Crucially, for Aquinas, our disorder is principally spiritual, overflowing into the moral and corporeal. While the focus of this project is on the sexed body per se, it is important not to reduce human sexuality to our physicality, ignoring vital spiritual, psychological, and social aspects.

208. In many ways the "disordered diversity" lens parallels Mark A. Yarhouse's "disability" lens, a mediating position between the "integrity" lens and the "diversity" lens

Thus far I have argued that alongside lessons learnt from the creation event and intent, the theological locus of the fall offers valuable insights for developing a fuller theology of intersexuality. However, one may object that if we take the impact of the fall seriously, then appealing to the perspective of creation is simply futile. As Jones contends, traditionalists may affirm the fall doctrine as indispensable but too often assume easy epistemic access to the protological dispensation, especially regarding sexed embodiment.[209]

D. Objection: The Fall Undermines Appealing to Creation

Since we all share in Adam's nature, we all share in the disordering effects of his original sin,[210] devastating bodies and minds. Concerning bodies, Cross applies Thomas' logic to propose that "all humans, after the Fall, are defective in various ways."[211] Thus, Cross continues: "Impairment is not something particular, or unusual; it is just another of the set of defects that are realized disjunctively by all human beings."[212] In a post-fall world, "There are no 'normal' bodies—and thus no 'abnormal' bodies—but just bodies as such, in all their great variety."[213] Positively, for Cross, Thomas' strong account of the extent of the fall normalizes, and so de-stigmatizes, physical defects. Consequently, if everyone is "impaired," there is no "normal" against which to adjudicate bodies, and so no basis to claim that intersex conditions have deviated from the "norm" in a way that the unambiguously sexed have not.

Moreover, the noetic effects of the fall compound and confound any attempt to discern "normal" sexed embodiment. Not only is every body disordered by the fall, but every mind is hindered from reading the body rightly, our fallenness exacerbating our finitude. As Stephen Holmes observes: "Our biological sex . . . is

(*Understanding Gender Dysphoria: Navigating Transgender Issues in a Changing Culture* [Downers Grove: IVP Academic, 2015], 46–60). Yarhouse's three proposed frameworks for understanding gender dysphoria are instructive for thinking about intersexuality. However, I try to avoid the language of disability due to its broader social and cultural interpretation in disability studies. I also resist labeling my position as an "impairment" lens. While I commented above that intersexuality qualifies as a postlapsarian impairment, overuse of impairment language can fail to capture adequately the enduring goodness of embodiment.

209. Beth Felker Jones, "Embodied from Creation Through Redemption," in *Beauty, Order, and Mystery: A Christian Vision of Human Sexuality*, ed. Gerald Hiestand and Todd A. Wilson (Downers Grove, IL: IVP Academic, 2017), 22.

210. Aquinas, *ST* 1-2.85.2 resp.

211. Cross, "Aquinas on Physical Impairment," 330.

212. Ibid., 329.

213. Ibid. On the perils and pitfalls of defining "normal," see Jonathan Heaps and Neil Ormerod, "Statistically Ordered: Gender, Sexual Identity, and the Metaphysics of 'Normal,'" *TS* 80 (2019): 346–69.

bent out of shape and nothing like what it should be."[214] "We cannot specify with any exactness what it is to be male or female, theologically speaking," Holmes laments. "We have almost no access to what it is to be properly human."[215] Consequently, if we take universal fallenness in body and mind seriously, then appealing to creation to establish a sexed norm such as SD remains impossible. This objection comes with pastoral freight when we also note the historical instances "where creation theology has been used to underwrite violence against the body."[216]

1. Response: Biblical The aforementioned methodological caveat rightly stresses the catastrophic somatic and noetic effects of the fall, both in extent and intensity. It also rightly questions the common assumption that we *know* what "normal" prelapsarian bodies were like. Yet such extreme agnosticism regarding the dogmatic function of creation is unwarranted (and unwanted) for biblical and theological reasons. Biblically, both Jesus (Matt. 19:4–6) and Paul (1 Tim. 2:13–14; 1 Cor. 11:7–12; 15:45) explicitly appeal to prelapsarian creation categories to advance their theological ethics.[217] While future chapters explore *how* Jesus and Paul discern, develop, and deploy the dogmatic function of creation, sufficient for our purposes here is to note *that* they both use creation positively to ground their teaching. Thus, Yarbrough asserts: "Paul's references to Adam and Eve . . . confirm his conviction that their creation and fall were in many respects determinative for all people everywhere."[218] Admittedly, it may be that Jesus and Paul interpret creation through the lens of redemption in Christ.[219] Nonetheless, appealing to creation based *solely* upon redemption raises a question over the validity of OT attempts at creation theology, which seem to assume some inherent integrity and intelligibility to created order (e.g., Pss. 19; 104). In light of redemption in Christ, OT reflection may be incomplete, but it is not inadequate.

Furthermore, at the canonical level, Hollinger identifies certain prelapsarian creation categories that are reaffirmed or developed later in scripture, suggesting

---

214. Stephen R. Holmes, "'Shadows and Broken Images': Thinking Theologically about Femaleness and Maleness," *Shored Fragments* (August 19, 2015). Cited February 26, 2019. http://steverholmes.org.uk/blog/?p=7538.

215. Ibid. Holmes qualifies "almost" by stating: "We have 1. the pre-fall creation accounts; 2. the prophetic and apocalyptic visions of the coming Kingdom; 3. the example of Jesus." However, Holmes suggests that the noetic effects of the fall make the data unreadable, especially if we want to move from the descriptive to the prescriptive. The life of Jesus is particularly "difficult data."

216. Jones, *Marks of His Wounds*, 14.

217. Interestingly, in 1 Tim. 2:13–14 Paul simultaneously appeals to creation and fall.

218. Robert W. Yarbrough, "Adam in the New Testament," in *Adam, the Fall, and Original Sin: Theological, Biblical, and Scientific Perspectives*, ed. Hans Madueme and Michael Reeves (Grand Rapids: Baker Academic, 2014), 50.

219. For such an approach, see Jones, *Marks of His Wounds*, 14–15. I address how creation relates to redemption in Chapters 5 and 6.

not only their endurance through the fall, but also their theological import prior to any fulfillment in redemption. For example, first, God created the world as good (Gen. 1:31), and its fundamental goodness remains through the fall (1 Tim. 4:4). Second, God created humanity in his image (Gen. 1:26), which, though marred by sin, endures (Gen. 9:6; James 3:9). Third, God created humanity for the divine vocation of work (Gen. 1:28), which though subject to frustration in the fall (Gen. 3:17–19), remains a God-honoring form of worship (Col. 3:23–24).[220] Indeed, the voice of God's creative wisdom still "calls" (Prov. 8:1, 22), thereby connecting creatures with their Creator, both epistemically (by evoking praise [Ps. 8:1]) and ethically (by revealing accountability [Rom. 1:20]). Thus, biblical evidence indicates that categories established in creation are not completely frustrated and inaccessible due to the fall. This is not to make the stronger claim as to *how* one should read creation wisely *post-lapsum*. Rather, I simply make the weaker claim from the biblical material *that* it is both possible and desirable, warranting the partial voice of creation (pre-redemption in Christ) in a theology of intersexuality.

2. Response: Theological A theological foundation stone grounding the biblical material surveyed above is the conviction that since sin is not a metaphysical substance, it can only privatively disorder rather than destroy nature. As Bavinck illumines, while "the form of things was changed by sin, the essence remained the same. Sin, after all, is not a substance and can neither increase nor decrease the substance of things of which God alone is the author."[221] After the fall, "human beings essentially remained human," even if they "began to function in another direction."[222]

Albert Wolters expands upon Bavinck's proposal, highlighting the important distinction between the "order of creation" and the "order of sin and redemption."[223] Creation order refers to the very God-given "structure" of the cosmos, which "before and apart from sin is wholly and unambiguously *good*."[224] While the "corrosive effects of the fall" touch all of creation,[225] "sin neither abolishes nor becomes identified with creation."[226] This is because parasitic "evil does not have the power of bringing to naught God's steadfast faithfulness to the works of his hands."[227] The "order of creation" and the "order of sin and redemption"

---

220. Dennis P. Hollinger, "Creation: The Starting Point of an Ecclesial Ethic," in *Ecclesia and Ethics: Moral Formation and the Church*, ed. E. Allen Jones III et al., TTCBS (London: T&T Clark, 2016), 15. Hollinger also highlights the creation ordinances of marriage and Sabbath rest enduring through the fall.

221. Bavinck, *RD*, 3:180.

222. Ibid., 3:180, 181.

223. Wolters, *Creation Regained*, 58.

224. Ibid., 48, italics original.

225. Ibid., 53.

226. Ibid., 57.

227. Ibid.

are fundamentally distinct categories, with the fall introducing a sin "axis [that] attaches itself to creation like a parasite."[228]

What sin does is misdirect creation from being rightly ordered to God, leading Wolters to categorize sin in terms of "direction" rather than "structure." Accordingly, Wolters opines that the degree to which something fails to live up to God's creational design for it, indicates the extent to which that thing is "misdirected, abnormal, distorted."[229] To illustrate the interplay between "structure" and "(mis) direction," consider a child, who in one sense is "very good," and yet she still needs to mature to adulthood.[230] While an infant, she contracts a bone-wasting disease from which there is no known cure. As the child grows up, two dynamics are at work: the good process of maturation, and the bad deterioration of her bones, hindering their healthy function. When a teenager, a cure is found, introducing a third dynamic of healing, with the purpose of bringing the youth to sound health and adulthood.

Although far from perfect,[231] this analogy illustrates how "the ravages of sin do not annihilate the normative creational development" of the structure of creation, "but rather are parasitical upon it."[232] Indeed, if sin did destroy nature, then God's goodness as a competent and faithful creator is undermined.[233] Does creation fall into such decay because God *cannot* stop it? Or perhaps God does not *want* to stop it? If the Creator intended such a change, concerns remain over the future stability (and goodness) of creation, and, by extension, the future faithfulness of the Creator.[234] Yet mercifully, sin does not destroy nature. Thus, following O'Donovan, "The universe, though fractured and broken, displays the fact that its brokenness is the brokenness of order and not merely unordered chaos."[235] Although sin has cast an "opacity and obscurity" over created order (including sexed embodiment),[236] post-fall we can nevertheless rejoice with the Psalmist that the stability of created order (אַף־תִּכּוֹן תֵּבֵל) depends exclusively upon the fact that "YHWH reigns"

228. Ibid.

229. Ibid., 59.

230. Illustration adapted from Wolters (ibid., 46).

231. E.g., the unfolding of creation in history is not necessarily as regulative as biological growth.

232. Wolters, *Creation Regained*, 46.

233. For the weight of this worry, see Athanasius, *On the Incarnation* 6, trans. John Behr, PPS 44b (Yonkers, NY: St Vladimir's, 2011), 55–6.

234. In addition, if there is an ontological difference between pre- and postlapsarian humanity, a further problem follows concerning theological anthropology—is a fallen human truly human? Extending the soteriological implications of this point, if human nature mutates metaphysically, then Jesus as the "Last Adam" (1 Cor. 15:45) becomes irrelevant for fallen humanity. Alternatively, if Jesus is the representative of fallen humanity, then scripture's insistence on him being the "Last Adam" is misinformed and untrue.

235. O'Donovan, *Resurrection and Moral Order*, 88.

236. Ibid., 19.

(יְהוָה מָלָךְ) (Pss. 93:1; 96:10).[237] God sustains the "structure" of created order by his wisdom, a wisdom that is "*in* creation" because it is "*of* creation" (Prov. 8:22),[238] a wisdom that still calls out (Prov. 8:1).

Since God's covenant name of YHWH is repeatedly mentioned in the purple passages that extol natural revelation (e.g., Pss. 8; 19), wisdom's clarion call may be heard most clearly within the covenant community. Thus, rather than an optimistic, bottom-up natural theology (creation without fall), or a pessimistic disregard of creation's "structure" and revelatory power (fall without creation), we may appreciate how creation and fall cohere within the divine drama by following the approach of "unveiled continuity."[239] The structure of creation endures through the fall, revealed by God through natural revelation. And yet, given the noetic (and moral) effects of the fall, we can only discern "creational normativity best in the light of Scripture."[240] Via a renewing and illuminating of God's Spirit (1 Cor. 2:13–16), we may read God's word as a "verbal commentary on the dimly perceived sign language of creation."[241] Thus, the goodness of God and his creation ensure that the structure of creation endures through the fall, the book of nature being read through the corrective spectacles of scripture.[242]

In response to Cross's critique that the fall nullifies the "normal," we can readily admit that sin scars all creation, and yet insist that because sin does not destroy nature, creation "structure" endures. The "normal" does still exist, even if we cannot read it naturally, that is, without God's illumination. As such, we return to Spirit-led scripture reading, rehearsing the exegesis in Chapter 3 and the resultant theological rubric of "form founds function—function fits form." Conclusions from creation about sexed "norms" may not be complete (pre-redemption), but they are not inadequate.

In response to the concern raised by Holmes, scripture cautions us to avoid extreme epistemic agnosticism that effectively allows sin to silence the call of creation, making OT and NT appeals to creation categories seem strange and misguided. If creation is silent, why does Jesus reference Genesis 1 and 2 in Matt. 19:4–5? If pushed, Holmes's wariness fails to do justice to "the constancy of God's

---

237. Note the emphatic use of the adverb אַף modifying the verb כּוּן.

238. Oliver O'Donovan, *Self, World, and Time: An Induction*, ET 1 (Grand Rapids: Eerdmans, 2013), 113. O'Donovan cautions against "too hasty a movement from the wisdom in creation to the divine Word" that ends up neglecting the "ordered beauty" of creation.

239. Beth Felker Jones, *Practicing Christian Doctrine: An Introduction to Thinking and Living Theologically* (Grand Rapids: Baker Academic, 2014), 38. While Jones may not agree with this approach, her description is apt.

240. Wolters, *Creation Regained*, 38.

241. Ibid., 39.

242. See John Calvin, *Institutes of the Christian Religion*, trans. Henry Beveridge (Peabody, MA: Hendrickson, 2008), I.6.1. This judgment sharpens my introductory comments about reading nontheological and theological sources.

will for creation" and "the renewing power of Jesus Christ in restoring our faculty of discernment";[243] a renewed discernment to read creation order via scripture (rather than through a regenerative natural theology).

Therefore, on the one hand, the objection rightly recognizes scripture's verdict that, as those darkened and depraved in mind and manner (Rom. 1:28; Eph. 4:18), we have no automatic access to the protological dispensation. Yet, since sin only privatively disorders rather than destroys nature, the "structure" of creation endures. At present we may only see the "shadows and broken images" of our true sexed embodiment.[244] But by grace we still see something rather than nothing—not-knowing is not knowing-not. Scripture provides the spectacles to start reading rightly. Thus, we have cautious confidence to comment on intersexuality in creation *and* fall.

III. Intersexuality in Light of Creation and Fall

Thus far I have mentioned various approaches or lenses used to examine intersex embodiment from the perspectives of creation and fall. I now turn to evaluate these alternative lenses to clarify my own position. First, the "diversity lens" (e.g., Cornwall and DeFranza) reads intersexuality as a creational good. However, it remains unclear how this perspective can draw a distinction between variation and defect, which in turn queries the goodness of both creation and Creator. So, barrenness is simply an alternative way of existing. Indeed, if the "diversity" perspective is being consistent, even something as destructive as cancer should presumably be celebrated. Ironically, a "diversity lens" that fails to take seriously the effects of the fall on the sexed body is itself pastorally blunt, as it is unable to validate the sense of some with intersex conditions that "their deep pain and suffering is not intended by God."[245]

Second, the "integrity lens" (e.g., Gagnon and Burk) emphasizes "the sacred integrity of maleness and femaleness stamped on one's body,"[246] such

---

243. Wolters, *Creation Regained*, 34.

244. Holmes' heading references Ransom's statement upon seeing the King and Queen of *Perelandra*. See C. S. Lewis, *Perelandra*, Scribner Classics ed. (New York: Scribner, 1996), 176.

245. Mark A. Yarhouse and Julia Sadusky, "Response to Megan K. DeFranza," in *Understanding Transgender Identities: Four Views*, ed. James K. Beilby and Paul Rhodes Eddy (Grand Rapids: Baker Academic, 2019), 188. Yarhouse and Sadusky refer to transgender identities, but their observation remains apt for intersexuality. Admittedly, one could respond that this existential pain is simply a result of oppressive social factors, rather than a rupture in creation order. Fix the social and religious issues, and the psychological pain should disappear (e.g., Raby, "'You Knit Me Together,'" 106 n.11).

246. Robert A. J. Gagnon, "Transexuality and Ordination," 2007. Cited November 19, 2020. http://www.robgagnon.net/articles/TranssexualityOrdination.pdf.

that intersexuality is wholly a postlapsarian disorder. While such an approach recognizes the impact of the fall, it insists that there is "an underlying dimorphism encoded in our cells," evidenced in the combination of X and Y chromosomes.[247] So, with the right laboratory test, maleness or femaleness can *always* be read off the body. Burk grounds his articulation of the "integrity" position upon the work of endocrinologist Paul Gard, explicitly citing Gard's comment that "even in the presence of multiple X chromosomes, the presence of a Y chromosome will result in the development of a male."[248]

However, an unnuanced appeal to chromosomal essentialism to determine one's sex may ironically exhibit parallels with the "diversity lens" in failing to account sufficiently for the impact of the fall. For example, someone with complete androgen insensitivity syndrome (CAIS) has a chromosomal makeup that is XY, and yet a variant SRY gene on the Y chromosome results in external genitalia that appear female.[249] The firmness upon chromosomes as *the* determiner for true sex seems arbitrarily reductionistic, as well as historically and culturally naïve. Why chromosomes and not hormones? And why chromosomes at the exclusion of other sex characteristics? Such an approach appears to privilege an unchastened natural theology that fails to account adequately for how the fall could have disordered chromosomes.

The third perspective is the "shadows and broken images" lens (suggested by Holmes), which resigns itself to an extreme agnosticism over the question of intersexuality. While open to the possibility of a protological and eschatological "true binary," it nevertheless insists that the fall makes our sexed body unreadable. However, as argued above, such extreme agnosticism effectively allows sin to silence the voice of creation, inadvertently undermining our assurance in the structure of creation, troubling confidence in the goodness of God and his creation. Even if the full theological meaning of the sexed body far exceeds our present comprehension, this does not mean that we lack genuine apprehension (via illumination) of creational intent in our post-fall experience.

Since the "integrity" lens overplays creation in favor of chromosomal essentialism, and the "diversity" lens underplays the fall in favor of universal diversity,[250] and the "shadows and broken images" lens overplays the fall in favor of an extreme agnosticism, space remains for a final proposal that accounts adequately for both creation and fall, namely the "disordered diversity" lens mentioned above.

247. Burk, *Meaning of Sex?*, 180.

248. Paul R. Gard, *Human Endocrinology* (Bristol, PA: Taylor & Francis, 1998), 133. Gard is referenced in Denny Burk, "Asking the Right Questions about Intersex Athletes: Part 2," *CBMW* (August 23, 2016). Cited November 19, 2020. https://cbmw.org/2016/08/23/asking-the-right-questions-about-intersex-athletes-part-2.

249. Roughgarden, *Evolution's Rainbow*, 291.

250. Both the "integrity" lens and the "diversity" lens seem to exhibit confidence in a variant of natural theology *sans* illumination.

Following the "unveiled continuity" approach, the "disordered diversity" lens intimates that in the creation event and intent, the sexed body was likely either male or female because the procreative function commissioned in Gen. 1:28 required a particular form. Due to the fall, death has touched every sexed body, disordering proper function (e.g., impotence and infertility), which at times may be caused by defective form (e.g., eunuchism). Intersex embodiment is a further example of defective form because it makes proper procreative function impossible. Although bodies with intersex conditions may possess distinct characteristics, they do not represent an additional *form* or third sex beyond male and female. This is because intersex *form* is not ordered to a new and different bodily *function*.

The "form founds function—function fits form" argument offers resources to think through the distinction between diversity and defect. While extensive natural variation abounds within humanity's sexually dimorphic pattern, if the correspondence between form and function is disrupted, then some defect exists. Equally, on this logic, if fertility remains, even certain physical conditions that some might classify as epistemically atypical (e.g., discerning between an extra-large clitoris and a micro-penis)[251] could in fact be interpreted as "male" or "female." While Augustine's "use"/"beauty" distinction may be relevant for other features of the body (e.g., nipples or beards), biblical and theological reflection from the perspectives of the creation event and intent indicates that "sexuate correspondence" was formed (at minimum) for the function of fruitful procreation. As such, if sexed bodily particulars are supposed to have a particular "use," and yet fail in that "use," then that bodily feature falls into the category of dysfunction (potentially due to some defect). In this sense, sexed particulars parallel some bodily features (e.g., ears) but not others (e.g., skin color).

Consequently, we may conclude that while male and female was the exclusive norm prior to the fall, unequivocal maleness and femaleness became the statistical norm post-fall. What was exclusively dimorphic in the creation event and creational intent, became an empirical bipolarity after the fall.[252] The intent of SD remains, but its empirical expression clusters around two poles of "male" and "female." Thus, following O'Donovan, while "the name 'intersex' may suggest to the public mind a kind of rural staging post, situated in the uninhabited countryside half-way between the cities of maleness and femaleness," perhaps "the term 'hermaphrodite,' as offensive as it may be, is conceptually truer, suggesting that the condition is one of both-and, arising from a malfunction in the process of differentiation."[253] From this perspective, speaking of sexed "ambiguity" is more

---

251. Karkazis, *Fixing Sex*, 146–7.

252. Andrew Sloane, "'Male and Female He Created Them'? Theological Reflections on Gender, Biology and Identity," in *Marriage, Family and Relationships: Biblical, Doctrinal and Contemporary Perspectives*, ed. T. A. Noble, Sarah Whittle, and Philip Johnston (London: Apollos, 2017), 233.

253. O'Donovan, *Transsexualism*, 7, 8. "Hermaphrodite" is often characterized as someone possessing a double set of sex organs. Here, O'Donovan offers a thicker conceptual

precise than sexed "atypicality." Nonetheless, even if a theology of intersexuality (where creation and fall are equally axiomatic) concludes that intersex conditions are an example of postlapsarian disordered diversity, a pressing pastoral question remains.

A. Objection: Are Intersex People More Fallen?

If bodily defects are the result of the fall, are intersex persons more fallen (more sinful even, and less human) than individuals with bodies that are unambiguously male and female (and who are still able to actualize procreative potency)?[254] Should this kind of theology be reported as a safeguarding issue for triggering suicidal ideation?[255] If defects are caused by Adam's originating sin, why are the effects more severe for some than others? Is God fair?[256] Here, it is important to note just how dehumanizing the "fall explanation" not only sounds but is painfully heard.[257]

In response, it is prudent to reiterate Augustine's observation that since evil is a metaphysical non-entity, a human may be afflicted by the privative evil of impairment, but human nature itself remains good.[258] In this, "Augustine is unhitching human happiness from human capacity or incapacity."[259] However impaired someone may be, so long as they are alive, they remain truly human. The good of human nature is inviolable against any evil privation of impairment. Further, connecting with the discussion above on *Civ.* 16.8 about the "wonders" of *androgyni*, Augustine makes the point that even if "certain monstrous races of men" exist, "Human beings are creatures born from other humans, and therefore must be affirmed as rational in kind and in possession of a rational soul."[260] Thus, regardless of appearance, "*Every* human being in existence is good because they are *created by God exactly as they are.*"[261]

definition that goes beyond genitalia. While O'Donovan's position is theoretically correct, given how the term "hermaphrodite" is frequently *heard* by intersex persons, a posture of Christian hospitality may discourage its use in personal relationships. The parallel noun "androgyne," as a compound of ἀνήρ and γυνή, could offer an alternative to "hermaphrodite." However, in contemporary discourse, androgyne denotes a non-binary gender identity, rather than a form of sexed embodiment.

254. Note the critique of Cornwall, *Theology and Sexuality*, 54.

255. Jayne Ozanne, "LLF: That Video, Those Principles & a Call for a Public Inquiry," *ViaMedia.News* (November 23, 2020). Cited November 24, 2020. https://viamedia.news /2020/11/23/llf-that-video-those-principles-a-call-for-a-public-inquiry.

256. Cf. Aquinas, *ST* 2-2.164.1 pr 4.

257. E.g., Dee Amy-Chinn, "Is Queer Biology a Useful Tool for Queer Theology?" *ThS* 15 (2009): 59.

258. Augustine, *Civ.* 12.5 (CCSL 48:359; WSA I/7:41).

259. Brock, "Augustine's Hierarchies," 70.

260. Brock, *Wondrously Wounded*, 16.

261. Ibid., italics original.

Similarly, Aquinas draws a careful distinction between the process of "becoming corrupted" (e.g., "deformity") and the state of "being corrupt" ("death").[262] Thus, Romero notes how for Aquinas, "Affliction is the relative privation of a corporeal good, and not the absolute negation of the goodness of corporeality."[263] *Contra* Reinders's claim that a Thomistic account of disability relegates one to an "anthropological minor-league,"[264] Romero helpfully clarifies that for Aquinas, "The evil suffered in corporeal infirmity does not reduce, destroy, or transform the suffering person's essential nature into something subhuman, marginally human, or non-human."[265] As such, intersex persons are no less human than the unambiguously sexed.

Nevertheless, even if intersex persons are not less human, is there a sense in which their bodies are "more fallen" or "more sinful"? In response, Aquinas again takes Rom. 5:12 as foundational, "By one man sin entered into this world, and by sin death."[266] Adam's originating sin caused the loss of OJ and so brought about the punishment of death for all, but in two ways. "One is by way of a punishment appointed by a judge: and such a defect should be equal in those to whom the sin pertains equally."[267] As those ontologically "in Adam,"[268] all of us will equally die at some point (Heb. 9:27).[269] In one sense then, all post-fall bodily defects—"from pimples to plague"—are punishments for original sin.[270] The second way death comes to all is accidentally (*per accidens*), much like when someone displaces a pillar, moving "accidentally the stone resting thereon."[271] The falling stone suffers an "evil punishment" (*malum poena*), but is not directly at "fault" or "blame" (*culpa*) for falling.[272] Under the "accidental" umbrella, Aquinas offers several options to explain why the defects associated with death vary.

First, it may be that bodily defects are caused by someone's direct sin.[273] If a pregnant mother smokes eighty cigarettes a day, there will be a direct effect upon her baby, including the possible impact upon the development of genes, gonads,

---

262. Aquinas, *ST* 1-2.73.2.

263. Romero, "Corporis Infirmitas," 108.

264. Hans S. Reinders, "Life's Goodness: On Disability, Genetics and 'Choice,'" in *Theology, Disability, and the New Genetics: Why Science Needs the Church*, ed. John Swinton and Brian Brock (London: T&T Clark, 2007), 181 n.26.

265. Romero, "Corporis Infirmitas," 108.

266. Aquinas, *ST* 1-2.81.1 sc.

267. Aquinas, *ST* 2-2.164.1 ad 4.

268. Aquinas, *ST* 1-2.81.1 resp.

269. Unless Christ returns beforehand (1 Thess. 4:16–17).

270. Romero, "Corporis Infirmitas," 108.

271. Aquinas, *ST* 1.85.5 resp.

272. For further clarification on *poenae* and *culpae* as they relate to postlapsarian passibility (affective and bodily), see Paul Gondreau, "Disability, the Healing of Infirmity, and the Theological Virtue of Hope: A Thomistic Approach," *JMT* 6 (2017): 77.

273. Aquinas, *ST* 1-2.85.5 ad 3.

gametes, and genitalia. Here, the *malum culpa* rests with the mother, even when the baby suffers the *malum poena* accidentally.[274]

Second, Thomas attempts to explain degrees of suffering and defect by noticing that the concrete substance of each person differs. Returning to the pillar and stone illustration, it is important to note that if someone hits two pillars with equal force, "It does not follow that the movements of the stones resting on them will be equal."[275] If one stone is heavier than the other it will fall faster. The effects depend upon the property of the nature affected. Thus, with OJ "removed, the nature of the human body is left to itself, so that according to diverse natural temperaments, some men's bodies are subject to more defects, some to fewer, although original sin is equal in all."[276] So, regarding intersex, it may be that ambiguous genitalia, or chromosomal variation, or hormonal imbalance are the result of certain genetic defects. Again, this is not the direct result of personal sin where *culpa* may be rightly apportioned, but an accidental result of the fall. It is part of living in a "cursed" world under the shadow of death, where mutable matter is not ordered peacefully by its rational form to its appropriate ends.

Third, Aquinas continues in *ST* 2-2.164.1 ad 4 that since God has complete, instantaneous knowledge of all things, his providence has apportioned the defects of original sin "in different ways to various people." Importantly, following Rom 9:11, this apportioning is "not on account of any merits or demerits previous to this life."[277] Thus, intersex cannot be blamed on supposedly immoral actions committed in a previous life. Christianity is not Karma.

In sum, although death as the punishment for original sin (through the removal of OJ) is universal, the negative consequences of death are not distributed equally, or according to just rewards. Instead, many of the effects of death should be understood as accidental. Thus, as an example of natural rather than moral fallenness, intersex persons should not be considered "more sinful" on account of their sexed impairment. Indeed, wisdom cautions categorizing intersex as "more fallen" than the unambiguously sexed, for it employs an external metric that often runs counter to that of God (e.g., 1 Sam. 16:7). Intersex persons are not "more fallen" than the unambiguously sexed. They are "differently fallen." Thus, even if abstractly conceived, intersexuality qualifies as an example of postlapsarian disordered diversity.

IV. Conclusion

If a theology of intersexuality is to be biblically and theologically faithful it must account for the perspectives of both creation and fall—integral "emplotments"

---

274. Aquinas, *ST* 2-2.164.1 ad 4. Cf. Josh 7:24–26.

275. Aquinas, *ST* 1.85.5 ad 1.

276. Ibid.

277. Aquinas, *ST* 2-2.164.1 ad 4.

within the biblical story. While the creation event and intent suggest that humanity was likely sexually dimorphic, with form founding function and function fitting form, the fall reminds us that death is pervasive, shattering *shalom*, such that both function (e.g., barrenness) and form (e.g., eunuchism) are disordered. Nevertheless, following a privative account of evil, the structure of creation endures through the fall, such that the norm of male and female continues in theological intent, even if at times ambiguous in empirical expression. Thus, the theological explanation for the existence of intersexuality from the perspectives of creation and fall is that of impairment—disordered diversity in a diversely disordered world. Given that sin and death privatively disorder the "direction" rather than the metaphysical "structure" of humanity, this judgment does not make those with intersex conditions any less human than the unambiguously sexed. Every body is subject to "death because of sin" (Rom. 8:10). Every mortal body needs life from the Spirit of Christ (Rom. 8:11). Everybody needs the restoration of *shalom*.

Therefore, while all humans labor east of Eden, the effects of Original Sin exhibit themselves in different ways for different people at different times, according to God's providence, such that some people can serve certain teleological purposes of human nature more readily than others. Importantly, Aquinas' main treatment of sin and its impact upon the body is found in the *Summa*'s *Prima Secundae Pars* and *Secunda Secundae Pars*, where his focus is on the *reditus* movement back to God. In the face of parasitic evil that disorders the sexed body, Aquinas discerns God providentially at work to bring broken sinners back to himself.[278] As such, any theological account of intersexuality must be set within the context of God's redemptive purposes, propelling us forward to consider intersexuality from the perspectives of redemption and eschatology.

278. That the goodness and truthfulness of God necessitates such a move, see Athanasius, *Incarnation* 6-7 (PPS 44b:55–56). Similarly, to let human nature "perish entirely" is "utterly foreign" to God's character (Anselm, "Cur Deus Homo," 2.4, in *Basic Writings*, trans. Thomas Williams [Indianapolis: Hackett, 2007], 291).

Chapter 5

REDEMPTION

NEWNESS IN CHRIST

Chapter 3 submitted that in the creation event and intent the body was likely sexed as exclusively male or female to fulfill the blessed commission of the procreative imperative (Gen. 1:28). Sexual dimorphism (SD) participated in the teleologically ordered peace of creation. Chapter 4 explored the dogmatic locus of the fall, focusing on how the irruption of sin tragically shattered *shalom*, introducing a human death that disorders the sexed body—a death touching both function (e.g., barrenness) and form (e.g., eunuchism). Consequently, while postlapsarian humanity remains in the image of God, the "disordered diversity" lens equips us to interpret intersex conditions as an example of physical impairment.

Given the concern to construct a *Christian* theology of intersex embodiment, I turn to explore the unique contribution of the person and work of our theandric Lord, Jesus Christ, whose arrival inaugurated an anthropological and cosmological "new creation" (Gal. 6:15; cf. 2 Cor. 5:17).[1] In the theo-dramatic act of redemption, Jesus Christ is "the chief heavenly and earthly protagonist,"[2] in whom we find full and final revelation and restoration (Heb. 1:1–4). Indeed, as Marc Cortez advances from Hebrews 1–2, Jesus is not just "*fully* human but also as the one who reveals what it means to be *truly* human";[3] the epistemological and ontological ground and goal for all "ultimate" truth claims about humanity,[4] including sexed embodiment.

Taking Christ as the historical crux of redemption,[5] a distinction may be drawn between the redemption accomplished and applied "now" at Christ's first coming

---

1. On the anthropological and cosmological scope of καινὴ κτίσις in Paul, see Carl B. Hoch, *All Things New: The Significance of Newness for Biblical Theology* (Ada, MI: Baker, 1995), 147–85.

2. Draft material from Daniel J. Treier, *Lord Jesus Christ*, ZNSD (Grand Rapids: Zondervan, forthcoming).

3. Marc Cortez, *ReSourcing Theological Anthropology: A Constructive Account of Humanity in the Light of Christ* (Grand Rapids: Zondervan, 2017), 165.

4. Ibid., 177–9.

5. That redemption is rooted in the distributed doctrine of the Trinity; see John Webster, "'It was the Will of the Lord to Bruise Him': Soteriology and the Doctrine of God," in *God*

(e.g., "redeeming those under the law," Gal. 4:4–5) and the redemption that is "not yet" but will be fully accomplished and applied at Christ's return (e.g., "making all things new," Rev. 21:5). Without ignoring how redemption and eschatology overlap in a "two-ages and two-realms" schema, my use of the term "redemption" refers to redemption "now," whereas language of "eschatology" and "consummation" typically refers to redemption "not yet."[6]

The person and work of Christ is the key to unlocking the meaning and significance of redemptive newness for the sexed body.[7] Assessing the person of Christ first, we are immediately confronted with the maleness of the Messiah, and the resultant soteriological and anthropological concerns. Can a male Messiah save non-males? Does a male Messiah marginalize non-males? One strategy to alleviate anxiety argues that Christ himself is intersex—chromosomally female while phenotypically male. If so, then in the person of Christ SD is overcome. While I argue that the specifics of recent proposals for an intersex Christ are scientifically improbable and theologically implausible, to assuage the soteriological and anthropological objections to Jesus' maleness I develop Nazianzen and Thomistic insights, pressing the distinction between humanity's universal-essential properties and particular-accidental properties.

Second, I continue to examine the nature of redemptive newness in Christ from the perspective of his work, focusing on how redemption relates to creation. While some surmise that redemption expands the creation category of "male and female" toward sexual polymorphism (SP), others discern SD's replacement. In response, I contend that since redemption "now" is the re-directive counterfoil to the mis-"direction" of the fall (and not creation "structure"), Christ's redemptive work restores creational *shalom*, focusing on spiritual and social inclusion rather than any structural expansion of the sexed body. Thus, redemption "now" restores creation, with the possibility of structural transformation left open at its consummation.

I. Person: Jesus' Sexed Body

A. Concerns with a Male Messiah

In constructing an explicitly *Christ*ian theology of intersexuality, it is important to examine the theological significance of Christ's sexed body. While few dispute the biological maleness of Jesus,[8] Mary Elise Lowe represents a broad consensus

of Salvation: Soteriology in Theological Perspective, ed. Ivor J. Davidson and Murray Rae (Farnham, UK: Ashgate, 2011), 15–34.

6. Constantine R. Campbell, *Paul and the Hope of Glory: An Exegetical and Theological Study* (Grand Rapids: Zondervan Academic, 2020), 57.

7. Highlighting Christ's *person* and *work* is a dogmatic distinction rather than a conceptual separation.

8. Although, note Susannah Cornwall's equivocation ("All Things to All? Requeering Stuart's Eucharistic Erasure of Priestly Sex," in *Liturgy with a Difference: Beyond Inclusion*

among revisionist theologians when commenting that "historic claims that Jesus was male . . . have been theologically destructive and physically harmful."[9] All but the unambiguously male are "inevitably repressed and oppressed by his [Jesus'] maleness."[10] As Elizabeth Johnson summarizes via an allusion to Nazianzen: "If maleness is constitutive for the incarnation and redemption, female [and intersex] humanity is not assumed and therefore not saved."[11]

Consequently, two specific fears arise against the maleness of Christ—relevant for a theology of intersexuality that seeks to be good news for all, however sexed.[12] First, if Christ is unambiguously male, are non-males savable? Second, even if non-males are somehow savable, are they second-class? In response, if we want to affirm with Paul that God's desire is for "all people" (πάντας ἀνθρώπους) to be saved, and that the "[hu]man Christ Jesus" (ἄνθρωπος Χριστὸς Ἰησοῦς) is the one true mediator between God and humanity (1 Tim. 2:4–5),[13] then we must answer these soteriological and anthropological concerns by demonstrating how intersex persons are both savable and not second-class.

B. An Androgynous/Intersex Christ?

One strategy that avoids both the soteriological and anthropological worries regarding Jesus' maleness is the proposal that Christ himself was in fact Androgynous/Intersex. According to the biologist Edward Kessel, if one affirms that Jesus received the fullness of his humanity from Mary, then via the natural process of parthenogenesis,[14] "Jesus was conceived as a chromosomal female."[15] Within Christ, "Each cell [is] complete with two X chromosomes, the

---

in the Christian Assembly, ed. Stephen Burns and Bryan Cones [London: SCM, 2019], 59 n. 36).

9. Mary Elise Lowe, "Re-Embracing the Body of Jesus Christ: A Queer, Lutheran Theology of the Body of Christ," in *Lutheran Identity and Political Theology*, ed. Carl-Henric Grenholm and Göran Gunner, CSR 9 (Eugene, OR: Pickwick, 2014), 117.

10. Tyron L. Inbody, *The Many Faces of Christology* (Nashville, TN: Abingdon, 2002), 118.

11. Elizabeth A. Johnson, *She Who Is: The Mystery of God in Feminist Theological Discourse* (New York: Crossroad, 2002), 153.

12. For further, specifically ecclesial, concerns, see Elisabeth Schüssler Fiorenza, *In Memory of Her: A Feminist Theological Reconstruction of Christian Origins* (New York: Crossroad, 1994), 38.

13. Note Paul's repetition of ἄνθρωπος (as opposed to ἀνήρ).

14. Parthenogenesis is reproduction from an egg without fertilization. Edward L. Kessel's preference for parthenogenesis is motivated by a desire to "escape from the docetic model of a supernaturally conceived Christ" (*The Androgynous Christ: A Christian Feminist View* [Portland, OR: Interprint, 1988], 160).

15. Ibid., 77.

cytological badge of femaleness."[16] After approximately eight weeks, the female embryo underwent "*a subsequent sex reversal to the male phenotype.*"[17] "Thus the female embryo Jesus of the Virgin Conception and Incarnation became the two-sexed Infant of the Virgin Birth who was the androgynous Christ, bearing the chromosomal identification of a woman and the phenotypic anatomy of a man."[18] For Kessel, the Androgynous Christ was neither a "hermaphrodite" nor a "pseudohermaphrodite"—"true defectives, possessing mixed up or partially developed organs of both sexes."[19] Rather, given that "Jesus' sex reversal was total,"[20] there was "nothing pathological about Jesus, physiologically, morphologically, or behaviorally. He/She was a perfect human being as well as Perfect God."[21] Thus, for Kessel, the uniquely Androgynous Christ becomes the "great equalizer of the sexes,"[22] thereby alleviating concerns regarding Jesus' phenotypical maleness.

While rejecting Kessel's "pathological or defective" appraisal of intersex persons,[23] thus discerning no significant difference between androgyny and intersexuality,[24] Virginia Mollenkott extends Kessel's case to assert that the virgin birth "introduces an intersexual theme into the heart of the Christian story."[25] Going back to creation, Mollenkott assumes an account of primal androgyny, concluding that "hermaphrodites or intersexuals could be viewed as reminders of Original Perfection."[26] Moving to redemption, Mollenkott argues that "judging from his/her [Jesus'] parthenogenetic birth,"[27] "a chromosomally female, phenotypically male Jesus would come as close as a human body could come to a perfect image of such a God."[28] Thus, "Intersexuals come closer than anybody to a physical resemblance to Jesus."[29] Mollenkott's argument is that if Jesus is intersex,

16. Ibid., iv.

17. Edward L. Kessel, "A Proposed Biological Interpretation of the Virgin Birth," *JASA* 35 (1983): 133, italics original. Kessel suggests that one of Mary's X chromosomes possessed a translocated "histocompatibility-Y" antigen (responsible for determining phenotypic sex).

18. Ibid., 135.

19. Kessel, *Androgynous Christ*, 3–4.

20. Ibid., 82.

21. Ibid., 4.

22. Ibid., iv.

23. Mollenkott, *Omnigender*, 116.

24. Hence the title "Androgynous/Intersex Christ."

25. Mollenkott, *Omnigender*, 114.

26. Ibid., 99.

27. Ibid., 127.

28. Ibid., 116. That is, "a God who is imaged [in Genesis] as male and female and yet is literally neither the one nor the other" (ibid.). To the contrary, since God is incorporeal, he is beyond sexed embodiment. God is not imaged *as* male and female but *in* male and female.

29. Ibid. For similar conjecture, see DeFranza, *Sex Difference*, 248; Susannah Cornwall, "Sex Otherwise: Intersex, Christology, and the Maleness of Jesus," *JFSR* 30 (2014): 26.

then other intersex persons are more like Jesus, and so implicitly superior to the non-intersex. Admittedly, Mollenkott could possibly avoid this ramification by adopting the universal/particular distinction I employ below. However, she does not attempt to nuance her claim, suggesting that she be read with the same "literalness" she advocates for in biblical hermeneutics.[30]

The case for an Androgynous/Intersex Christ, whether advanced via appeals to science (Kessel) or primal androgyny (Mollenkott), is one attempt to alleviate worries about Jesus' maleness. Indeed, the proposal troubles SD in two ways. First, an intersex Christ could reveal that intersexuality was indeed the original plan for sexed embodiment in the creation event and intent (a mystery hidden until the fullness of time).[31] Alternatively, it could be that an intersex Christ embodies a redemptive newness that destabilizes male and female as the exclusive norm of creation intent.[32] Either way, an Androgynous/Intersex Christ favors SP. However, the proposal faces significant scientific and theological challenges.

1. Scientifically Improbable For Kessel's proposal to be viable, two things are required: human parthenogenesis and complete sex reversal. Considering the first, the neonatal biologists Giuseppe Benagiano and Bruno Dallapiccola have argued that while attempts have been made to develop parthenogenetic embryos, it is "highly improbable" that such embryos "may result in term neonates."[33] Viable embryos universally require material from more than one parent.[34]

Considering the second requirement, while female-to-male sex reversal is extremely rare, a recent study has reported on a single family where three adult males were genetic females. "Although these adults suffered from a 46,XX testicular disorder of sex development [manifesting itself with azoospermia, and so infertility], general growth and health, all secondary sexual characteristics, the skeletal system . . . , behavior and intelligence were all those of normal males."[35] However, Jesus' conception is distinct from this case because these three individuals had two parents. Therefore, Benagiano and Dallapiccola conclude that they "could not find any known natural or experimental biological mechanism capable of explaining the conception and birth of Christ."[36] Parthenogenetic

30. Mollenkott, *Omnigender*, xii.

31. Kessel sprinkles the phrase "fullness of time" throughout his work, presumably alluding to Gal. 4:4. Such an approach could complement the "Trajectory of Othering" argument in Chapter 3.

32. Potentially supplementing the "redemption replaces creation" model I outline below.

33. Giuseppe Benagiano and Bruno Dallapiccola, "Can Modern Biology Interpret the Mystery of the Birth of Christ?" *JMFNM* 28 (2015): 242.

34. Given his virgin conception, Jesus is the only exception.

35. Benagiano and Dallapiccola, "Modern Biology," 243. For the recent study, see James J. Cox et al., "A SOX9 Duplication and Familial 46,XX Developmental Testicular Disorder," *NEJM* 364 (2011): 91–3.

36. Benagiano and Dallapiccola, "Modern Biology," 243.

conception followed by complete sex reversal does not occur in the natural world. Thus, any biological debate on the subject is "pure speculation."[37]

Admittedly, Kessel could defend a "parthenogenetic conception + complete sex reversal" model by appealing to the category of "miracle." Yet such a move is precisely what Kessel eschews, advocating instead an explanation of the virgin birth that does not rely upon "the *docetic* model of a supernaturally conceived Christ."[38] But here Kessel's "cavil" seems to reject the plain sense of the biblical story,[39] namely that the virgin birth is necessarily miraculous because Mary becomes pregnant by the "power of the Most High" (δύναμις ὑψίστου, Luke 1:35) for whom nothing is "impossible" (ἀδυνατέω, Luke 1:37), the double use of the δυνα– root emphasizing God's sovereign power. Nevertheless, even if an Androgynous/Intersex Christ is biologically improbable, could such embodiment be theologically fitting?

2. Theologically Implausible From a more theological perspective, Mollenkott advances an Intersex Christ by connecting Christology to primal androgyny. While Mollenkott's proposal does not depend upon the same scientific precision as that of Kessel,[40] the viability of her account hangs upon the protological existence of primal androgyny, as well as the non-existence of the fall.[41] Considering primal androgyny first, the analysis in Chapter 3 indicated that such a suggestion is insufficient on grammatical, contextual, and theological grounds. Second, as argued in Chapter 4, given the evangelical convictions of the book, the fall counts as an essential "emplotment" within the scriptural witness to the divine drama. Remove the fall, and we have a fundamentally different story—at least to the one presented in scripture. Admittedly, sticking to the script of scripture does not appear to be a chief concern for Mollenkott. If it were, she could posit a fall that does not impact the sexed body per se, such that God's people in the OT simply misread the body, but now Christ reeducates his church. However, this solution seems to advocate a quasi-Marcionite disconnect between OT and NT, as well as casting aspersions on God's character, for example, how could a good and truthful God mislead his people for so long, not just implicitly via created order, but with explicit biblical statements? Any insinuation that God might be negligent, or deceitful, or incompetent conflicts with the biblical witness that "the LORD is trustworthy" (Ps. 145:13).

---

37. Ibid.

38. Kessel, *Androgynous Christ*, 160, italics added.

39. For biological parthenogenesis as a "cavil" to the virgin birth producing a male offspring, see Ian A. McFarland, *The Word Made Flesh: A Theology of the Incarnation* (Louisville, KY: Westminster John Knox, 2019), 130 n.7.

40. Mollenkott does not explicitly preclude the category of "miracle."

41. Mollenkott discerns a "great theological-ethical divide" between the "Original Sin" party, who see the fall as "real," and the "Original Blessing" party, who see the fall as "imagined" (*Omnigender*, 91–6).

More parenthetically, one suspects that Mollenkott's linking of primal androgyny and Christology with intersexuality is unlikely to be endorsed by fellow advocates for SP. Innovationists typically emphasize the unique particularity and equality of all people. Mollenkott, however, seems to suggest a hierarchical pyramid of bodily sex. The perfect androgyne sits upon the apex. Others take their positions according to their degree of correspondence to the Androgynous/Intersex Christ. Perhaps unintentionally,[42] this account exhibits striking parallels with the One-Sex theory examined in Chapter 2—universally rejected for being androcentric. Yet, in Mollenkott's case, androgynocentrism replaces androcentrism, ironically reintroducing the same concerns over justice and equality that motivated her initial rejection of orthodox teaching.

Furthermore, it is instructive that there are no explicit biblical texts that teach an intersex Christ. Conversely, there remains considerable biblical material that suggests Jesus was male, whether in terms of OT expectations,[43] the performance of his sexuality,[44] however subversive,[45] or comments about his body itself (e.g., circumcised, Luke 2:21). Therefore, it seems that knowing whether Christ was intersex (whether via science or primal androgyny) is not only highly speculative but also highly improbable.

Nevertheless, the soteriological and anthropological concerns about Jesus' maleness persist. To allay such fears, I extend Thomistic insights developed in Chapter 3 to elucidate the distinction between universals and particulars as they relate to human ontology. In short, the bodily sex of Jesus pertains to his historical particularity and not the universal kind-essence of human nature, meaning that Jesus' maleness (considered metaphysically) does not affect our saveability, nor necessarily denigrate intersex persons as second-class.[46] Jesus is *universally* human, for he assumes a human nature that is a universal kind-essence for all humans— thus all sexes are savable. Jesus is *particularly* male, for the historical instantiation of his humanity is sexed as male, a particularity that need not be universalized— thus no sex is necessarily second-class.

C. Are Intersex Persons Savable?

Elizabeth Johnson correctly notes that "the early Christian aphorism 'What is not assumed is not redeemed, but what is assumed is saved by union with God' sums

---

42. Mollenkott wants "to do away with gender hierarchies altogether" (ibid., 172).

43. E.g., Jesus as the second Adam, the Abrahamic seed, the Davidic king, the prophet like Moses, the man of sorrows, the High Priest, the bridegroom, the Son of God, and the Son of Man. See Bruce A. Ware, *The Man Christ Jesus: Theological Reflections on the Humanity of Christ* (Wheaton, IL: Crossway, 2013), 91–110.

44. E.g., Andrew R. Angel, *Intimate Jesus: The Sexuality of God Incarnate* (London: SPCK, 2017).

45. E.g., Conway, *Behold the Man*.

46. For a similar strategy, see Cortez, *ReSourcing*, 190–211.

up the insight that God's saving solidarity with all of humanity is what is crucial for the birth of the new creation."[47] As the immediately following literary context of Nazianzen's axiom indicates, Gregory's primary concern in his first letter to Cledonius is to defend against Apollinarianism the fullness of Christ's humanity for the sake of offering universal salvation. Accordingly, Gregory maintains: "Had half of Adam fallen, what was assumed and is being saved would have been half too; but if the *whole* fell he is united to the *whole* of what was born and is being saved *wholly*."[48] Thus, Gregory's axiom refers at minimum to Christ's human nature in its completeness, reflecting God's determination that salvation would come through a human (1 Cor. 15:21), who had to become like us "in every respect" (Heb. 2:17) so that "every dimension of human life might be transformed by him."[49] For Nazianzus, since being completely human required possessing human "flesh [i.e., body] . . . soul . . . [and] mind," Christ had to assume all three parts so that like might "hallow" like.[50] Accordingly, Christ meets "the aptness condition" of being wholly human, and so is apt to save anyone else who qualifies as human.[51] If we reverse engineer Nazianzen's logic, given that Christ "assumed" these universal-essential properties,[52] then anyone else who possesses or instantiates the universal-essential properties of body, soul, and mind is also fully human, and so qualifies as being fully savable, however sexed.

Importantly, certain idiosyncrasies of Gregory's position do not preclude one from adopting his core claim that Christ is fully human. For example, one need not commit to his trichotomous account of human ontology to benefit from his logic.[53] Also, even if it is more likely that Gregory's account "presupposes some sort of realism with respect to [essential] *properties*,"[54] a nominalist who can still articulate a vital connection between Christ's vicarious human nature and the

---

47. Johnson, *She Who Is*, 150. Nazianzen's axiom reads: "The unassumed is the unhealed, but what is united with God is also being saved" ("Letter 101," 5 [PPS 23:158]).

48. Ibid. Italics added to highlight Gregory's triple use of ὅλος (cf. Chalcedon's use of τέλειον). Greek text from PG 37:184.

49. McFarland, *Word Made Flesh*, 2.

50. Nazianzus, "Letter 101," 9 (PPS 23:161).

51. Fellipe Do Vale, "Can a Male Savior Save Women? The Metaphysics of Gender and Christ's Ability to Save," *PC* 21:2 (2019): 315, italics original.

52. I retain "assume" minimally to reflect Gregory's language, rather than commit to an abstractist or concretist account of human nature. For a helpful taxonomy of different definitions and contemporary positions, see Timothy Pawl, *In Defense of Extended Conciliar Christology: A Philosophical Essay*, OSAT (Oxford: Oxford University Press, 2019), 22–8.

53. Whether dualist or physicalist.

54. Jay Wesley Richards, "Can a Male Savior Save Women?" in *Unapologetic Apologetics: Meeting the Challenges of Theological Studies*, ed. William A. Dembski and Jay Wesley Richards (Downers Grove, IL: IVP, 2001), 166, italics original.

rest of humanity (e.g., via divine fiat) can also benefit from Gregory's axiom.[55] Therefore, echoing Gregory's rhetorical repetition of ὅλος, since Jesus assumed a *complete* human nature, as *complete* humans intersex persons are *completely* savable.

Nevertheless, while the Theologian may help us affirm that intersex persons are savable, if Christ, the paradigmatic human, is male, and his maleness is part of his completeness, then a possible implication is that all non-males are somehow less complete than males—second-class humans, perhaps in need of *greater redemption* than males.[56] One strategy in response could be to overextend Gregory's contribution, so privileging the universal humanity of Christ that the particularity of Jesus' historical and bodily maleness "has no ultimate significance."[57] Yet the result of such a de-historicizing and de-particularizing of Jesus' sexed body inadvertently minimizes our own historical particularity, which we intuitively feel is significant for our personal identity, and more importantly, significant to God (e.g., Gal. 2:20). Consequently, we need a way to distinguish between human nature's universal-essential properties and its particular-accidental properties in order to clarify how to interpret Jesus' maleness such that intersex persons are not only savable but also not second-class.

D. Are Intersex Persons Second-Class?

In Chapter 3 I advanced Aquinas's metaphysical differentiation between concrete substances (a subsisting rock) and the concept of essence ("substance" in its basic sense as "the quiddity of a thing").[58] The essence of human nature is to be a rational body-soul composite. When the universal-essential properties of rational soul-body are actualized in concrete human persons, individuation is presented in particular-accidental properties. In *On Being and Essence*, Thomas maintains that individual humans express particular accidents derived from their form

---

55. Although there are different versions of nominalism (e.g., class, trope, resemblance), and its history is variegated and complex, at minimum, nominalists deny the existence of universal properties, either by asserting that "everything is particular (i.e., there are no universals)" or by maintaining that "everything is concrete (i.e., there are no abstract objects)" (Michael C. Rea, *Metaphysics: The Basics*, TBas [London: Routledge, 2014], 41).

56. For a similar caveat, see Cornwall, *Sex and Uncertainty*, 184.

57. E.g., Rosemary Radford Ruether, *Sexism and God-Talk: Toward a Feminist Theology* (Boston: Beacon, 1983), 137. A similar criticism could be leveled at Adrian Thatcher's "human continuum" thesis, where Christ's abstract human nature is the "centre around whom all humanity revolves" (*Redeeming Gender*, 140). While Thatcher "allows for sexual difference, among many others . . . accommodat[ing] everyone who does not straightforwardly identify with either of the sexual binaries," it remains opaque what difference concretely sexed particularity really makes, at least theologically (ibid., 140–1).

58. *ST* 1.29.2 resp.

(e.g., risibility) and matter (e.g., bodily sex).[59] To avoid teleological frustration, the vegetative powers of the soul inform the material body to be sexed as either male or female.[60] Thus, *that* I am sexed is a universal condition of being a body. The concrete particular of *what* I am sexed reflects the informing principle of my particular soul.[61]

Applying this Thomistic concretism to Christ's enhypostasized flesh, *that* Jesus is sexed is further evidence that he satisfies one of the "aptness" conditions noted above (i.e., a body). The *what* of Jesus' particular sex (i.e., his maleness) is a result of *his* particular human soul informing *his* particular material body. Consequently, while Jesus' bodily condition of "being sexed" participates in humanity's universal kind-essence (all bodies are sexed), Jesus' "being male" refers specifically to his individual-essential historical particularity. Thus, a male Messiah need not relegate non-males to a second-class status because the individual *whatness* of Jesus' bodily sex strictly pertains to *his* historical particularity.[62]

Indeed, considering the counterfactual, if one shifts Jesus' maleness from the category of individual-essence to the category of kind-essence then one appears open to the charge of arbitrariness. While not a direct defeater, it remains unclear why the historical particular of Jesus' bodily sex should be universalized and not any other concrete particular, for example, Jesus' Jewishness, or even his height. Indeed, if one were to be consistent, then presumably all of Jesus' particulars should be universalized. Yet the logical *reductio ad absurdum* of this account would be "the denial that a genuine human life . . . could never be redemptively significant for any other, let alone for all."[63] Any *real* link between Jesus and the rest of humanity is effectively severed, such that "we are all right back to dying for our own sins—the state of affairs for which the Logos became incarnate in the first place."[64]

More positively, being able to distinguish between the universal-essential properties of Christ's kind-essence and the particular-accidental properties of his individual-essence enables us to appreciate the significance of Christ's concrete maleness. As Harrison warns, any attempt to ignore or explain away Jesus' maleness is to "stumble against the rock of offense which is the 'scandal of

---

59. Aquinas, *On Being and Essence*, 69.

60. At least in the event and intent of creation. On the "vanity" of frustrated generativity, see Aquinas on "fornication," *SCG* 3.122.

61. On whether the soul is sexed, see Gondreau, "Aquinas on Sexual Difference," 212.

62. Appreciating Thomistic logic need not commit one to endorsing the sexist conclusion of Aquinas (or Augustine) that Jesus became male because maleness is the "nobler sex" (*ST* 3.31.4 ad 1). For Thomas' various reasons, see Francis Ruello, *La christologie de Thomas d'Aquin*, ThH 76 (Paris: Beauchesne, 1987), 154–5; Guillaume D'Anselme, "La convenance de l'incarnation masculine," *BLE* 121 (2020): 27.

63. Trevor A. Hart, *In Him Was Life: The Person and Work of Christ* (Waco, TX: Baylor University Press, 2019), 282.

64. Richards, "Male Savior," 172.

particularity' of the incarnation."[65] Given the soteriologically motivated conviction from Nazianzus *that* the incarnation is universally relevant,[66] Jesus "could not have become incarnate as 'humanity-in-general' because human nature exists only in particular persons."[67] As Thomas presses from Heb. 2:17, since "sex is natural to man," Christ "had to assume a sex . . . for the perfection of nature."[68] Thus, the *how* of the incarnation necessitates Jesus having a "historical existence that anchors him in this world,"[69] part of which is his male sexed body. Anything short of this smacks of Docetism.[70]

Furthermore, while Cornwall avers that "Jesus' historic physical maleness might simply have to be something Christians say *less* about in theological terms,"[71] Amy Peeler counters that Jesus' male particularity serves not as a barrier but as a bridge to inclusion. Peeler presses her point by focusing on the unique mode of Jesus' incarnation, noting how the virgin birth has traditionally served as the locus for valorizing both females and males (cf. Gal. 4:4).[72] "The only way it is possible within the system of human procreation for God to involve both sexes in the revelation of divine embodiment is to have the image of God born as a male from the flesh of a female."[73] "Because Jesus is male from a female alone," Peeler continues, "the mode of the incarnation allows a male Savior to embrace all humans."[74] Cornwall rightly desires greater inclusion for non-males in Christ. Yet

65. Nonna Verna Harrison, "The Maleness of Christ," *SVTQ* 42 (1998): 114.

66. Christ "hallowing humanity through himself, by becoming a sort of yeast for the whole lump" (Nazianzus, "Oration 30," 21 [PPS 23:111]).

67. Harrison, "Maleness of Christ," 115.

68. Aquinas, *Commentary on Sentences* 3, d.12, q.3, a.1, qc.1, sc and ad 2. This *quaestio* is infused with the language and logic of Nazianzus. https://aquinas.cc/la/en/~Sent.III.D12 .Q3.A1.qa1.

69. Harrison, "Maleness of Christ," 115.

70. That Aquinas' discussion of Christ's maleness is similarly motivated by anti-docetic concerns, see Paul Gondreau, *The Passions of Christ's Soul in the Theology of St. Thomas Aquinas* (Providence, RI: Cluny Media, 2018), 107–15.

71. Cornwall, "Sex Otherwise," 39.

72. E.g., "The male sex is honored in the flesh of Christ; the female is honored in the mother of Christ" (Augustine, "Sermon 190," 2, in *Sermons 184–229Z: On the Liturgical Seasons*, ed. John E. Rotelle, trans. Edmund Hill, WSA III/6 [New Rochelle, NT: New City, 1993], 39). For the argument that the virgin birth prohibits Christ's full humanity, see Andrew T. Lincoln, *Born of a Virgin? Reconceiving Jesus in the Bible, Tradition, and Theology* (Grand Rapids: Eerdmans, 2013), 258–60. In response, Daniel J. Treier invites Lincoln to demonstrate how he avoids "a sophisticated form of 'adoptionism'" ("Virgin Territory?" *ProEccl* 23 [2014]: 376).

73. Amy Peeler, *Women and the Gender of God* (Grand Rapids: Eerdmans, 2022), 141.

74. Ibid., 142 n.91. Similarly, Nonna Verna Harrison concludes that "both genders are united with God in him, and both, insofar as they differ, are saved" ("The Trinity and

following Peeler's insights on the virgin birth, we achieve inclusion by speaking *more* about Jesus' "historic physical maleness" rather than less.

Admittedly, emphasizing the virgin-born particularity of Jesus' maleness to safeguard the equal inclusion of non-males in the redemptive purposes of God only works if we interpret intersex embodiment within the dimorphic framework of male and female, and not as a third sex. If the preceding account of Jesus' uniquely virgin-born maleness is correct, then a potential implication impinges upon advocates of SP. Either disregard the mode of the Incarnation or ironically *exclude* intersex persons from the salvific work of Christ.

In summation, pressing the distinction between universals and particulars via Aquinas alleviates certain soteriological and anthropological concerns regarding Jesus' maleness. Negatively, arguments proposing that redemption in Christ indicates a shift from SD to SP need to find support beyond Jesus' sexed body. Positively, we can affirm that Jesus is *universally* human, thus all sexes are savable. Also, Jesus is *particularly* male, valorizing both sexes in his virgin birth, such that no sex is necessarily second-class.[75] Consequently, *that* Jesus is sexed means our "being sexed" remains inherently good, however disordered and disorienting. As the wholly "[hu]man Christ Jesus," the one true mediator between God and humanity (1 Tim. 2:4–5), Jesus calls all people, however sexed, to "repent and believe the good news" (Mark 1:15).

II. Work: How Does Redemption Relate to Creation?

If Christ's sexed embodiment does not appear to ground SP, perhaps his redemptive work offers more promising resources for innovationist scholars. Rightly reading a trajectory from Genesis 1–2 to Revelation 21–22,[76] revisionist proposals typically cluster around a central question: "How does redemption relate to creation?" Or more specifically: "How does the redemptive work of Christ relate to the 'male and female' of the creation event?" For Megan DeFranza, Jesus enfolds eunuchs "*as they are*" into the purposes of God (Matt. 19:12; cf. Isa. 56:3–5).[77] Just as Jesus expands the selection on the food menu (Mark 7), so too does Jesus expand divinely intended possibilities for the sexed body. Advancing beyond DeFranza's "redemption expands creation" rubric, Robert Song argues that redemptive newness for the sexed body is not so much a gradual crescendo of creation but

Feminism," in *The Oxford Handbook of the Trinity*, ed. Gilles Emery and Matthew Levering, OH [Oxford: Oxford University Press, 2011], 526).

75. The universal/particular distinction could also be extended to alleviate ecclesial concerns (e.g., *in persona Christi* views of priesthood).

76. For examples of correspondence and heightening between Eden and the eschaton, see G. K. Beale, *A New Testament Biblical Theology: The Unfolding of the Old Testament in the New* (Grand Rapids: Baker Academic, 2011), 29–87.

77. DeFranza, "Gender Minorities," 174, italics original.

a disjunctive step-up, indicated most clearly in the "celebrated formula" of Gal. 3:28.[78] SD was fitting in creation, but "baptism and the new identity in Christ takes us *beyond* the creation categories of male and female in a way that renders them no longer of defining importance."[79] While the models of DeFranza and Song are distinct, both scholars advocate for SP in Christ, arguing from specific biblical texts that are set within a broader theological understanding of how redemption relates to creation. In short, redemption advances beyond creation such that SD in creation becomes SP in Christ.

At the heart of both proposals is a pre-understanding of how the biblical story coheres. Noting the joint appeal to Irenaeus, how we piece together the biblical mosaic reveals different portraits of Christ—whether a "miserable . . . fox" or the "beautiful . . . king."[80] What is at stake is not only a biblically faithful view of the sexed body in redemption "now," but also a clear picture of Christ the Creator, Redeemer, and Exemplar of sexed embodiment, as well as the gospel he heralds. Accordingly, in the section below I begin by explicating the exegetical and theological facets of Song's "replacement" rubric and DeFranza's "expansion" model. In response to Song, I argue that redemptive newness in Christ does not replace but restores creation. *Contra* DeFranza, I explore scripture's trajectory as it pertains to the sexed body, maintaining that redemption's development of creation concerns spiritual and social inclusion, rather than an expansion of sexed bodily structure toward a divinely intended SP. Undergirding each response is the conviction that redemption "now" is primarily restorative, reordering what sin disorders, whereas redemption "not yet" focuses predominantly on the eschatological transformation of creational structure, that is, its glorification. Jesus' healing ministry illustrates this distinction, where individuals are restored but not yet glorified *qua* 1 Cor. 15:42–44. For example, Jesus restores Lazarus' life (John 11:43–44), but Lazarus still lacks the quality of resurrection life Jesus promised moments earlier (John 11:26). This distinction between restoration "now" and transformation "not yet" does not preclude a radical renovation of creation at the consummation. However, as I elucidate from Song and DeFranza,

---

78. Robert Song, *Covenant and Calling: Towards a Theology of Same-Sex Relationships* (London: SCM, 2014), 49.

79. Ibid., italics added. Similarly, Ruth Heß discerns from Gal. 3:28 an "eschatological antithesis" between creation and redemption. This antithesis reveals not a "possible" but "necessary . . . [r]econfiguration of gender" that is both social and also has "a bodily dimension" ("'Es ist noch nicht erschienen, was wir sein werden': Biblisch-(de)konstruktivistische Anstöße zu einer entdualisierten Eschatologie der Geschlechterdifferenz," in *Alles in allem: Eschatologische Anstösse: J. Christine Janowski zum 60. Geburtstag*, ed. Ruth Heß and Martin Leiner [Neukirchen-Vluyn: Neukirchener, 2005], 310).

80. Irenaeus, *Against Heresies* 1.8.1, trans. Alexander Roberts and James Donaldson, *ANF* 1 (Buffalo: Christian Literature, 1885; reprint, Peabody, MA: Hendrickson, 2004), 326.

to overemphasize structural transformation this side of the eschaton falls foul of an over-realized eschatology.[81]

A. Proposal 1: Redemption Replaces Creation

Gal. 3:28 states that "there is no longer male and female; for all of you are one in Christ Jesus."[82] As Brigitte Kahl notes, "Feminist and liberation oriented readings rather commonly have treated the baptismal formula of Gal. 3:26–28 as a kind of *ET*, a lovely lonely alien unhappily trapped in the hostile matter of a Pauline letter."[83] From this free-floating baptismal formula,[84] the claim is advanced that the redemption inaugurated by the coming of Christ results in a "oneness" that overthrows the purportedly creational category of "male and female." Thus, as Twomey opines, Gal. 3:28 "is about the abolition of dimorphic sexuality itself."[85] Gal. 3:28 "could and should be taken literally," Mollenkott champions, legitimizing the imagining and constructing of an omnigendered society.[86] Concerning sexed embodiment, innovationist scholars interpret oneness in Christ as either referring to the reinstatement of primal androgyny,[87] an original continuum,[88] the anticipation of an eschatological androgyny,[89] or to a rainbow of polymorphism in glory.[90] While these proposals are important to consider, they need not detain us here. Protological androgyny and an original continuum were considered in Chapter 3, and eschatological embodiment is explored in Chapter 6. Further, since this section examines the argument that redemption replaces creation, the interpretations listed above do not strictly qualify, either because they discern

---

81. For some problematic ramifications of an over-realized eschatology, see D. A. Carson, "Partakers of the Age to Come," in *These Last Days: A Christian View of History*, ed. Richard D. Phillips and Gabriel N. E. Fluhrer (Phillipsburg, NJ: P&R, 2011), 91–2.

82. I offer the NRSV translation as my later expanded translation reveals my judgment.

83. Brigitte Kahl, "No Longer Male: Masculinity Struggles Behind Galatians 3:28?" *JSNT* 79 (2000): 37.

84. Beverly Roberts Gaventa observes the different ways Gal. 3:28 has been "kicked around like a child's toy" when "taken out of context" ("The Singularity of the Gospel Revisited," in *Galatians and Christian Theology: Justification, the Gospel, and Ethics in Paul's Letter*, ed. M. W. Elliott et al. [Grand Rapids: Baker Academic, 2014], 196).

85. Jay Twomey, "Stranger in a Stranger World: Queering Paul with Michael Faber's *The Book of Strange New Things*," in *Bodies on the Verge: Queering Pauline Epistles*, ed. Joseph A. Marchal, SemeiaSt 93 (Atlanta, GA: SBL, 2019), 273.

86. Mollenkott, *Omnigender*, xi.

87. E.g., Meeks, "Image of the Androgyne."

88. E.g., Thatcher, *Gender and Christian Ethics*, 133–7.

89. E.g., Jeremy Punt, "Power and Liminality, Sex and Gender, and Gal 3:28: A Postcolonial, Queer Reading of an Influential Text," *Neot* 44 (2010): 152.

90. E.g., Jung, "Intersex on Earth," 186.

redemption expanding creation (e.g., eschatological SP), or because they propose a repristination of creation (e.g., primal androgyny).

One reading of Gal. 3:28 that does see redemptive oneness in Christ "take us beyond the creation categories of male and female" is that of Robert Song.[91] Although the focus of Song's project is how the "creation ordinance" of heterosexual marriage has been fulfilled in Christ (opening up the eschatologically oriented vocations of both celibacy and "covenant-partnership"), Song's theological argumentation is suggestive for the continuity/discontinuity question regarding the "creation categories" of bodily sex difference.[92] In contrast to the proposals above, Song offers an account where SD is a necessary good in creation, which is then overcome in redemption. Such a theo-dramatic shift is indicated in Gal. 3:28, buttressed by other more eschatologically oriented NT texts.[93] To clarify Song's "redemption replaces creation" argument, I proceed in three movements: creation, redemption, and the relationship between the two.

1. Creation Stressing the ANE context of Genesis 1, Song argues that to be made in God's image means to "rule" as God's vice-regents (Gen. 1:28).[94] Adam and Eve can only "rule" and "subdue" the earth on God's behalf if they commit to the prior "command" to "fill the earth." As such, if imaging God is about ruling on God's behalf, and to rule over the earth requires people, and people come about through procreation, then SD is a good and necessary category of creation. Put simply, in creation humanity rules through physical procreation, which God commands within the context of heterosexual marriage. Second, commenting on Luke 20:34–36, Song submits that "marriage is instituted to deal with the problem that people die."[95] Combined, Song discerns a *nexus indivulsus* between SD-procreation-marriage that God established as the necessary means to the end of (i) ruling and (ii) overcoming death.

91. Song, *Covenant and Calling*, 49. Song would protest this accusation, stating that "eschatology may be the fulfilment of creation, but it is not its denial" (ibid., xvi). Song's language for redemption's relationship to creation is that of "fulfilment," "transformation," and "resituating." However, as I argue below, I believe the way this verbiage *functions* within the Songian case amounts to redemption *replacing* creation. The use of "replacement" terminology is my attempt to demarcate the implications of Song's position. Nevertheless, given Song's explicit vocabulary, my argument bears the burden of proof.

92. Song employs the terms "creation ordinance" and "creation categories" without articulating any conceptual difference.

93. Song suggests that "the task of interpreting scripture is a dance" that requires "drawing a contrast between the surface meaning of texts and the deeper structure of the biblical story" (*Covenant and Calling*, 63). Part of this interpretive dance means being open to "a trajectory in Scripture that indicates a direction of travel" that may contradict the surface reading (ibid., 73).

94. Ibid., 16.

95. Ibid., 15. Song does not register concern about human death pre-fall.

Romans 1 reveals that the SD-procreation-marriage nexus endures through the fall and remains universally normative as "a creation good."[96] Paul provides "an account of a fall from the created, protological good. . . . Since creation is understood in terms of procreative, sexually differentiated order, a fall from it would be portrayed in terms of a disruption of that order."[97] Thus, combining Genesis 1 with Romans 1, the nexus of SD-procreation-marriage is God's plan in the creation event and intent. SD is part of the goodness of creation both in its "materiality" and intended "form."[98] Any "effort to escape the formed matter of creation, including the form of the body, is one of the characteristics of the various gnostic and spiritualizing movements that pervaded the climate within which the early Church grew up."[99]

2. Redemption In redemption, Christ both defeats death and succeeds in ruling where Adam failed, for God "has subjected everything under his feet" (1 Cor. 15:27).[100] Yet Christ did not accomplish dominion through procreation. As such, in Christ the link between procreation and ruling/defeating death is cut. "Procreation has become redundant, theologically speaking, for those who are in Christ," Song asserts.[101] Consequently, if Christ inaugurates a "resituating" of procreation such that procreation is no longer necessary for ruling and defeating death,[102] then as Schafer helpfully notes in assessing Song's thesis, "marriage loses its telos and reason for existence."[103] Thus, while "the nexus of marriage and procreation, will in the eschatological fulfilment of creation [ultimately] become redundant,"[104] this has begun in the redemptive work of Christ.

Considering Song's *nexus indivulsus* of SD-procreation-marriage, the implication is that under redemptive and eschatological pressure, if the first two elements have been superseded (procreation and marriage), then the third (SD) must follow. So, where there is no marriage, "sexual differentiation is unnecessary."[105] While Song's immediate referent is marriage, his logic applies to sexed embodiment. Noting how the "no longer male *and* female" in Gal. 3:28 "deliberately" echoes Gen. 1:27 (LXX), Song suggests that "baptism and the new identity in Christ take us beyond the creation categories of male and female in a way that renders them no longer of defining importance."[106] "Indeed," Song continues, "we may even find

---

96. Ibid., 67.
97. Ibid.
98. Ibid., 25.
99. Ibid.
100. Ibid., 17.
101. Ibid., 27.
102. Ibid., 16.
103. Schafer, *Marriage, Sex, and Procreation*, 140.
104. Song, *Covenant and Calling*, 15.
105. Ibid., 49.
106. Ibid., italics original.

the creation categories here partly contradicted."[107] All of this is "clearly . . . of decisive significance for thinking about intersex conditions."[108]

3. Replacement Song remains adamant that "creation is not an independent realm" but is "theologically inseparable from an understanding of Christ."[109] From Col. 1:15–18, Christ "makes creation cohere," and "all creation has its being aboriginally in Christ."[110] Alluding to Irenaeus, Song contends that in redemption "Christ 'recapitulates' creation, gathering up in himself the entire history of created being, both human and non-human."[111] Appealing to Oliver O'Donovan's *Resurrection and Moral Order*, Song identifies the resurrection as *the* event that best articulates the relationship between creation and redemption, highlighting "not only its [creation's] repristination, but also its transformation. . . . Creation has a good beyond itself."[112]

Nevertheless, while Christ is indeed the key to creation and redemption, and while much of Song's proposed relationship between creation and redemption is helpful, in considering sexed embodiment per se Song offers a rubric of redemption replacing creation. Creation in general may remain, but SD as a fixed category of creation is rejected and replaced by SP. This is because redemption in Christ fulfils the creation command to rule—defeating death without needing to reproduce—thereby severing the old-order *nexus indivulsus* of SD-procreation-marriage. As Shafer summarizes, for Song "sexual difference is necessary only in its relationship to procreation. If procreation has been fulfilled by Christ and is no longer necessary, then the theological logic requiring relationships to be sexually differentiated no longer holds."[113] And I would push this one step further: SD as a necessary and stable category of creation no longer holds. As Song states, "Sexual differentiation is unnecessary."[114] It is "no longer a theologically all-determining category."[115] In sum, "Sex BC is not the same as sex AD,"[116] for SP in Christ has replaced SD in creation.

Moreover, on Song's reading of Gal. 3:28, since the baptismal corresponds with the eschatological,[117] baptismal renewal in Christ resituates Christians

107. Ibid.
108. Ibid.
109. Ibid., 8.
110. Ibid.
111. Ibid.
112. Ibid., 13.
113. Schafer, *Marriage, Sex, and Procreation*, 172.
114. Song, *Covenant and Calling*, 49.
115. Schafer, *Marriage, Sex, and Procreation*, 172.
116. Song, *Covenant and Calling*, x.
117. Note the present tense blessing of Gal. 3:28.

beyond creation.[118] To ignore this redemptive-historical shift not only undermines eschatological justice but downplays the significance and glory of Christ's advent. The existential force of this argument should prick those committed to a thick theological reading of the divine drama. For if we claim to take the Triune God's revelation in Christ seriously, then we need to appreciate the eschatological scope and significance of his advent. We should implement Christ's eschatological justice by championing how SP in Christ replaces SD in creation.

B. Response: Not Replacement but Restoration

Song's proposal commendably emphasizes the unique "significance of the advent of Christ for sexuality,"[119] correctly recognizing what Witherington glosses as "the primacy of eschatology over protology" in the NT.[120] Yet, in piecing together the biblical mosaic, Song's model does not provide an adequate portrait of how King Jesus in redemption relates to the sexed body of creation. In short, Song's "redemption replaces creation" case is rooted in an overly historicist, and so reductionistic, view of creation that produces unwanted gnostic fruit. In response, I offer a "thicker" account of creation, before arguing principally from 1 Corinthians 15 that redemption restores creation.

1. An Historicist Root Produces Gnostic Fruit While Song maintains that the Christological "fulfilment of creation" is its "repristination," he is equally clear that this does not include SD.[121] Rather, in Christ the cord of SD-marriage-procreation unravels, such that procreation becomes "redundant, theologically speaking,"[122] and "sexual differentiation is unnecessary."[123] While the immediate referent of these negations is marriage, Song's logic extends beyond marriage. Thus, Song can call male and female "creation categories," but only in an historical sense as what was necessary for ruling and thwarting death pre-

---

118. Song, *Covenant and Calling*, 49. See also Wayne Litke, "Beyond Creation: Galatians 3:28, Genesis and the Hermaphrodite Myth," *SR* 24 (1995): 173–8.

119. Song, *Covenant and Calling*, x.

120. Ben Witherington, *New Testament Theology and Ethics* (Downers Grove, IL: IVP Academic, 2016), 2:317.

121. Song, *Covenant and Calling*, 13.

122. Ibid., 27.

123. Ibid., 49. Here, Song's constructive proposal for "covenant-partnerships" sees Christ inaugurating a divergence between the covenantal and the creational. Song is correct that the biblical narrative envisages an eschatological transformation of creation (explored in Chapter 6). However, "across Scripture, we see an eschatological convergence of God's creational purpose and covenantal promise in Christ" (Belousek, *Marriage*, 115). Indeed, God's "plan for the fullness of time to unite all things in him [Christ]" (Eph. 1:10) remains both covenantal and creational.

Christic.[124] By reducing SD to a mere historical moment, "male and female" is important but replaceable. To illustrate from the world of theatre, within the divine drama Song interprets creation as a mere temporal *act*, supplanted by the later historical *act* of redemption.

Nonetheless, while Song draws upon Oliver O'Donovan to buttress his disjunctive argument, a closer reading of O'Donovan undermines Song's proposal. For O'Donovan, much Western theology has been infected by an "all-pervasive" historicism, where "all teleology is historical teleology," and "the natural exists only to be superseded."[125] Since everything serves the supernatural end of history, however that end might be conceived will ultimately triumph over all that precedes. Within such an historicist framework, "Natural order and natural meanings are understood only as moments in the historical process. They are to be dissolved and reconstituted by that process, and their value lies not in any integrity of their own but in being raw material for transformation."[126] Historicism is thus the nihilistic "re-assertion of freedom against nature . . . . [A] totalitarian concept, substituting for nature and de-naturing the world."[127]

Song may avoid the historicist charge in his account of creation's stability in general. But by uncoupling humanity's sexuate correspondence from creation's stability, Song remains open to the criticism that his view of SD is overly historicist, making it replaceable. For Song, SD has a natural order and meaning in the *act* of creation, but there is nothing inherent about SD that necessitates its normative endurance throughout the divine drama. SD is good but only temporarily so. Thus, Song can insist that marriage should remain heterosexual, for it testifies to the goodness of sexual difference given in creation.[128] Yet having "become something new in Christ,"[129] sexual difference evidenced in marriage is no longer exclusive nor exhaustive of humanity *in toto*.

However, such an overly historicist view of SD undermines any assurance in the *enduring* goodness of the sexed body itself. If all teleology is historical, such that purportedly natural structures have no inherent stability, then the true and stable goodness of sexed embodiment can only be defined from the perspective of its fulfillment. Yet, since the sexed body's historical fulfillment is still to come, "good" is at best incomplete and imperfect. Further, since evil is not defined against the standard of a good natural order but the fulfilment of history, evil too has no clear meaning. Both "good" and "evil" are merely "historical imperfection[s] from which we are to advance."[130] In this, historicism has confused "the good with the

---

124. Song, *Covenant and Calling*, 49.

125. O'Donovan, *Resurrection and Moral Order*, 58.

126. Ibid., 59.

127. Oliver O'Donovan, *Finding and Seeking*, ET 2 (Grand Rapids: Eerdmans, 2014), 232.

128. Song, *Covenant and Calling*, 88.

129. Ibid., 91.

130. O'Donovan, *Resurrection and Moral Order*, 63.

future" and induces "a profound loss of nerve over any claim to discern the good hand of God within the order of a good creation."[131]

Admittedly, Song may contest the historicist charge, responding that it is only SD that is replaced in redemption—all other "creation categories" are repristinated. Yet to escape the subsequent charge of arbitrariness (why replace SD and not our physicality, say), Song needs to demonstrate further how SD is inseparably connected to (and exhausted by) marriage and procreation, such that when one element becomes "redundant" all become "redundant." However, Song's proposed *nexus* is not as *indivulsus* as he maintains. While SD is a necessary and sufficient condition for marriage and procreation, neither marriage nor procreation exhausts SD. Indeed, SD remains part of the givenness of created order, a point that may be reaffirmed by rehearsing insights from Genesis 1–2 about humanity's generic and teleological ordering from Chapter 3.

Considering "kinds," to be human is to be embodied, and to be embodied is to be sexed. Informed by Thomistic reflection upon Gen. 1:27–28, our sexed condition is not polymorphic but a "sexuate correspondence" between "male and female."[132] Hence the proposed rubric of "form founds function—function fits form." Considering "ends," while Song correctly identifies from Gen. 1:28 that a central facet of SD is its procreative potential, procreation does not exhaustively define the "end" of SD. Like the rest of creation in Genesis 1, humanity is ordered for fruitfulness. But Genesis 2 expands humanity's fruitfulness from a focus on procreation (Gen. 1:28) to include and foreground themes of unity and bonding.[133] In Genesis 2, the emphasis is on the fitting provision of the woman as the solution to the problem of Adam being alone, both existentially (Gen. 2:18, 23) and in terms of fulfilling the mandate to "work" and "guard" the garden (Gen. 2:15). As I deduced in Chapter 3, reproductive fruitfulness is not absent from Genesis 2— the lone male needs a fertile female to reproduce more divine images to extend God's ordered rule. But fulfilling reproductive fruitfulness does not exhaust God's gift of the woman. As Schafer presses from Genesis 2, "It is not clear that sexual difference is merely a functional distinction that is necessary only for the purpose of procreation."[134] In short, since marriage and procreation do not exhaust SD, creation could make sense structurally even if marriage and procreation did not exist. In contrast, if we were not sexed bodily, we would have a very different kind of creation.

The possibility of a very different kind of creation becomes a reality within Song's framework. While Song could simply be guilty of introducing into the present a possible structural transformation (at least in divine intent) that other

---

131. O'Donovan, *Church in Crisis*, 88.

132. Belousek, *Marriage*, 36.

133. For elaboration on the theme of "fruitfulness" in Genesis 2, see David Albert Jones, "Gender Identity in Scripture: Indissoluble Marriage and Exceptional Eunuchs," *SCE* 34:1 (2021): 8.

134. Schafer, *Marriage, Sex, and Procreation*, 147–8.

scriptures seem to reserve for the eschaton (e.g., 1 Cor. 15:42–55)—an over-realized eschatology—Song's case exhibits a more fundamental problem. Since Song does not attend to Genesis 2 sufficiently, his overly reductionistic and historicist proposal lacks adequate guardrails to protect it from viewing the sexed body as merely temporal, potentially replaceable, perhaps even incidental. Ironically, when considering the sexed body in creation, Song makes a strong case to uphold both its "materiality" and its "form," accusing those who attempt to "escape the formed matter of creation, including the form of the body," of gnosticism.[135] Yet, with SD as a stable good becoming obsolete in redemption, Song seems to be guilty of the very criticism he levelled at those when addressing SD in creation. Thus, channeling O'Donovan, Song's overly historicist case "betrays resemblances . . . to the old gnostic dualism which called creation evil."[136] In sum, while Song appeals to O'Donovan to establish a "redemption replaces creation" argument, a closer examination of O'Donovan ironically critiques Song's case, highlighting its insufficient account of the stability of creation, thereby troubling our assurance in the enduring goodness of the sexed body in the present.

2. *"Creation as Stage" and "Redemption as Act"* More positively, while it is certainly fitting to speak about "*creatio*" in terms of God's historical "act of creating," to do so at the neglect of "*creatura* as the result of that act" is theologically inadequate.[137] Continuing the theatrical illustration, creation cannot be reduced to a mere historical *act* but must also function as the very *stage* upon which the theo-drama of the divine οἰκονομία is enacted (cf. Eph. 1:10). Following Chapter 3, a thicker doctrine of creation asserts that creation proper (*creatura*) is primarily the given and structured order of the cosmos (the *stage*). Part of the created order is the creation category of SD, since being human includes being bodily sexed as either male or female. Humanity's "sexuate correspondence" pertains to created order, rather than minimally serving the creation ordinance of marriage.

Redemption "now" is God's gracious response to the problem of Satan, sin, and death.[138] As noted in Chapter 4, since sin is not a substance it does not destroy nature but can only parasitically disorder it. Similarly, redemption "now" is not a substance but a divine action that reorders and restores nature, "inverting our earlier inversion."[139] As Bavinck comments: "The stuff (*materia*) of all things is and remains the same. However, the form (*forma*), given in creation, was *de*formed by sin in order to be entirely *re*formed again in the sphere of grace."[140]

---

135. Song, *Covenant and Calling*, 25.
136. O'Donovan, *Resurrection and Moral Order*, 63.
137. Brock, *Christian Ethics*, 325.
138. E.g., 1 Tim. 1:15; Heb. 2:14; 1 John 3:8.
139. Telford Work, *Jesus—The End and the Beginning: Tracing the Christ-Shaped Nature of Everything* (Grand Rapids: Baker Academic, 2019), 8.
140. Bavinck, *RD*, 2:574, italics original.

Consequently, while creation can refer to either substantial *stage* or historical *act*, since fall and redemption lack substantial "structure," they are necessarily restricted to the category of *act*—or recalling Wolters's language from Chapter 4, "direction."[141] Put differently in a grammatical metaphor, redemption is a verbal category that acts upon rather than competes with the more nominal category of creation. Thus, in the divine drama, redemption is the historical counterfoil to fall (not substantial creation), both fall and redemption functioning as dramatic *acts* that portray first the "complication" and then its "denouement" through the "peripetitic" work of Christ.[142]

Given its historicist root, resulting in an overly reductionistic view of creation, Song's case fails to attend to the important category distinction between creation as *stage* and redemption as *act*. While such an account might look to defend the gratuity of redemption, it remains unclear how creation can be called good without the help of redemption (hence the charge of incipient gnosticism submitted above). Worse, if creation needs redemption to be good, it implies that sin and the fall are somewhat necessary for creation. Further, it could suggest that creation is fallen by its very nature, for otherwise salvation would not be needed.

However, these implications conflict with the goodness and faithfulness of God, as well as the inherent logic of the divine economy. The divine drama of grace has a restorative character (e.g., Acts 3:21; Rom. 12:2; Eph. 4:24; Col. 3:10), requiring us to confess both creation's original goodness and the contingency of the fall and redemption. Creation as *stage* serves as the "presupposition" and "condition of history's movement, a condition to which, in one form or another, history will always bear witness."[143] Thus, the *act* of redemption does not destroy the *stage* of creation, but in the divine drama, creation endures through redemption, and as we shall see, is restored by redemption. Thus Bavinck: "Christianity does not introduce a single substantial foreign element into the creation. It creates no new cosmos but rather makes the cosmos new. It restores what was corrupted by sin. It atones the guilty and cures what is sick; the wounded it heals."[144] With the category distinction between "creation as *stage*" (structure) and "redemption as *act*" (direction) in mind, I turn to explicate *how* redemption restores creation.

---

141. This claim does not require rejecting structural transformation (e.g., glorification) in the eschatological "not yet," nor the Irenaean idea of the maturation of original creation, both of which are addressed more fully in Chapter 6. Here, I focus on the "direction" of redemption "now." For a clear summary of "structure" and "direction," see Gordon J. Spykman, *Reformational Theology: A New Paradigm for Doing Dogmatics* (Grand Rapids: Eerdmans, 1992), 109–10.

142. Here I appropriate the nomenclature of Aristotle, *Poetics* 18, trans. Stephen Halliwell, LCL 199 (Cambridge, MA: Harvard University Press, 1995), 91.

143. O'Donovan, *Resurrection and Moral Order*, 62, 63.

144. Bavinck, "Common Grace," 61.

3. The "Act" of Redemption upon the "Stage" of Creation Although postlapsarian, unregenerate humans constantly act to uncreate themselves, the redemptive work of Christ indicates that creation is not a lost cause. The stage may be in tatters, with broken actors frantically fumbling around in darkness,[145] but the advent of Christ (as set designer, stage manager, director, and owner) inaugurates not a gnostic redemption *from* creation, but the very redemption *of* creation. For O'Donovan, the NT demonstrates this truth most clearly in the "Easter principle" of the resurrection of Christ.[146] This is not to downplay the other scenes in Christ's *act* of redemption, whether his life, death, or ascension, since they form a "knot of mutual intelligibility."[147] Yet O'Donovan concentrates on the resurrection as his starting point "because it tells us of God's vindication of his creation, and so of our created life."[148]

We see this vindication of creation in the Adam-Christ typology of 1 Corinthians 15. In Christ's resurrection God demonstrates his "reversal of Adam's decision to die" (see 1 Cor. 15:22), and so a restoration of his original affirmation that Adam should live.[149] This is not just good news for humanity, but the whole created order. O'Donovan argues that since Adam was the representative head of creation, in the resurrection of the Last Adam a promise is held open that "all shall be made alive" (1 Cor. 15:22).[150] In the resurrection, God demonstrates that he has "stood by his created order"[151] and promises that at Christ's return humanity's proper place "'in the middle' of the cosmic order" will be fully restored.[152] Thus, redemption ("now" and "not yet") does not void and replace but vindicates and restores creation to its ordered peace. The Last Adam redeems rather than replaces the First Adam. Indeed, O'Donovan argues that the very term 'redemption'

---

145. E.g., Job 5:15; Eccles. 9:3.

146. O'Donovan, *Resurrection and Moral Order*, xvii.

147. Ibid., 14.

148. Ibid., 13.

149. Ibid., 14. As I develop in Chapter 6, the resurrection also indicates creation's eschatological transformation (see 1 Cor. 15:50).

150. Ibid., 15. Although O'Donovan takes the πάντες of v.22 as referring to all creation, it seems more likely that the immediate referent is limited to humanity (Paul J. Brown, *Bodily Resurrection and Ethics in 1 Corinthians 15: Connecting Faith and Morality in the Context of Greco-Roman Mythology*, WUNT 2/360 [Tübingen: Mohr Siebeck, 2014], 146). Specifically, "all *who are in Christ* will be made alive," as v.23 explicates (Gordon D. Fee, *The First Epistle to the Corinthians*, rev. ed., NICNT [Grand Rapids: Eerdmans, 2014], 831). Nevertheless, O'Donovan's larger point about Christ as the Last Adam, and so representative head of created order, can still stand, but if argued from 1 Cor. 15:27–28, where Paul cites Ps. 8:6. Christ "as *man* is thus the representative 'Man' to whom all things are subjected," and through whom death is destroyed, and the whole created order is healed (ibid., 839 n.200), italics original.

151. O'Donovan, *Resurrection and Moral Order*, 15.

152. O'Donovan, *Finding*, 62.

presupposes the created order, since "'redemption' suggests the recovery of something given and lost."[153] While questions still linger regarding the precise character of redemption "now,"[154] at this juncture it remains sufficient to observe from 1 Corinthians 15 redemption's inherently restorative complexion.

Furthermore, given Song's appeal to Irenaean recapitulation,[155] it is worth noting that any redemptive replacement of creation would seriously undermine Irenaeus' argument against the Valentinians and the Marcionites. Irenaeus' whole enterprise was to stress the unity and completeness of God's single economy, in terms of both his work (*contra* the Valentinians) and his word (*contra* the Marcionites). Thus, in *Adversus haereses* 5.1.3, Irenaeus alludes to Paul's typological correlation between Adam and Christ in 1 Cor. 15:22, expanding it into "an all-embracing account of the economy of God, understanding the end in terms of the beginning, with the end in turn shedding light on the beginning,"[156] guided from beginning to end by the "hands of God."[157] As Behr clarifies, Irenaeus' emphasis on the unity and singularity of God's economy suggests that "recapitulation" is a rhetorical device that serves as a "literary summary," helping readers of scripture grasp its "succinct synopsis."[158] Thomas Holsinger-Friesen presses the language of recapitulation to capture well scripture's synopsis: "Humanity, originally 'capitulated' by virtue of its relationship to its 'head,' has found itself 'de-capitulated' (or decapitated). What is needed is a re-capitulation wherein the original connection between creation and Creator is restored, thus replacing death with life."[159] Indeed, when Irenaeus himself considered how redemption relates to creation, he states simply: "Know ye that He brought all novelty, by bringing Himself."[160] In redemption the king has finally come. He brings nothing new but himself, and the joyful fulfilment of what had been announced beforehand. All this suggests that Song's appeal to Irenaean recapitulation to advance a "redemption replaces creation" thesis is mistaken.

---

153. O'Donovan, *Resurrection and Moral Order*, 54. Similarly, Wolters asserts that "virtually all of the basic words describing salvation in the Bible imply a *return* to an originally good state or situation" (*Creation Regained*, 69), italics original. Wolters lists the terms "redemption," "reconciliation," "renewal," "salvation," and "regeneration," concluding that "all these terms suggest a *restoration* of some good thing that was spoiled or lost" (ibid., 70), italics original.

154. Addressed below.

155. The following could well apply to DeFranza's attempt to pit Irenaeus against Augustine, and East against West. See below.

156. John Behr, *Irenaeus of Lyons: Identifying Christianity*, CTC (Oxford: Oxford University Press, 2013), 122.

157. Irenaeus, *Against Heresies* 5.1.3 (*ANF* 1:527). That is, the Son and the Spirit.

158. Behr, *Irenaeus*, 137.

159. Thomas Holsinger-Friesen, *Irenaeus and Genesis: A Study of Competition in Early Christian Hermeneutics*, JTISup 1 (Winona Lake, IN: Eisenbrauns, 2009), 128.

160. Irenaeus, *Against Heresies* 4.34.1 (*ANF* 1:511).

Recapitulation is a succinct synopsis of Christ in redemption restoring creation, all so that we may see Christ, creator and redeemer, more clearly.[161]

In summary, in the *act* of redemption, Christ as set designer, stage manager, director, and owner steps onto the *stage* of his crumbling creation, and in his resurrection inaugurates its restoration through a renovation of the actors, such that the Gen. 1:28 prefigured pattern of imaging God through responsible rule may finally be fulfilled. In contrast to the "redemption replaces creation" model, the relationship between the *stage* of creation and the *act* of redemption is inherently "organic," a unity that coheres ontologically and epistemologically in Christ.[162] By making redemption conflict with creation, Song ultimately offers a conflicted Christ. "If Christ delivers us from creation," Belousek warns, "then the Savior conquers the Creator."[163] Yet, as Hollinger maintains from Col. 1:15–20, "God the Creator and God the Redeemer are one, and thus an ethic of redemption can neither negate nor neglect creation," and *vice versa.*[164] Again, in Irenaean key, our approach in piecing together the biblical mosaic of creation and redemption bears significant Christological implications. What is at stake is an accurate portrayal of both Christ and the gospel drama within which we participate.

4. Implications for Intersexuality Refracting insights from O'Donovan, Song's proposal is inadequate because its historicist root undermines the dogmatic function of creation as *stage.* Such a reduced view of creation fails to account for the "structure" of SD, thereby questioning the stability and goodness of sexed embodiment, as well as introducing an over-realized eschatology. In response, I advanced from 1 Corinthians 15 that the "structure" of creation endures through the mis-"direction" of the fall and the re-"direction" of redemption. Thus, in the redemptive work of Christ creation is not replaced but "regained."[165] Creation structure (including sexed structure) matters to God because it confirms his goodness and faithfulness.

Nonetheless, if SD pertains to the enduring structure of creation, and if redemption restores creation, then does redemption require intersex embodiment to be "restored" to a protological maleness or femaleness? Whatever eschatological transformation may look like, does the focus on restoration in redemption "now" justify "corrective" surgeries? Redemption may restore creation in general, but how is that "gospel" for intersex persons in particular? At first glance the "redemption restores creation" model appears to confirm every revisionist fear that such theology is inherently dehumanizing. In response, we need to clarify the precise character of restored creation. Here, we turn to DeFranza's "redemption expands creation" rubric. While DeFranza's doctrine of creation seems to emphasize evolving systems

---

161. Ibid., 1.8.1 (*ANF* 1:326).
162. Bavinck, *RD*, 1:383.
163. Belousek, *Marriage*, 112.
164. Hollinger, "Creation," 4.
165. Hence Wolters' title, *Creation Regained.*

rather than stable structures, her developmental approach recognizes the inclusive character of redemption in Christ, affording the opportunity to explore whether this inclusion in redemption "now" pertains to sexed structure or something else.

C. Proposal 2: Redemption Expands Creation

1. OT Eunuchs For Megan DeFranza, the modern categorization of intersexuality is evidenced in the ancient world by the term "eunuch," an "umbrella concept" for bodily "in-between-ness."[166] In assessing the biblical material, DeFranza highlights not only the stigma of being a eunuch under the old covenant, but she also offers a rationale for why the eunuch was judged to be "the epitome of 'other,'"[167] namely as a mixed foreigner. Taking "mixed" first, DeFranza (via Mary Douglas) draws from the food laws of Leviticus 11 to claim that unclean "detestable" creatures are those that "mix the categories of animals named in Genesis 1:28."[168] For old covenant Israel, "Separation equaled holiness. Mixing was detestable, an abomination."[169] The food laws reinforced for Israel that "mixed things . . . were unclean."[170] DeFranza extends this insight to "eunuchs, whose bodies blurred the lines between male and female."[171] Second, the eunuch's "outsider status" is inscribed in Deut. 23:1,[172] DeFranza discerning a close association between "castrated eunuchs" and "ancient fertility religions."[173] Thus, there is a sense in which old covenant eunuchs were doubly disadvantaged, considered to be both mixed and foreign.

2. NT Eunuchs Against this OT backdrop DeFranza highlights the shock of Jesus not only *not* healing any eunuch, nor speaking of them as "proof of the fall," but actively heralding eunuchs in Matt. 19:12 as "icons of radical discipleship."[174]

---

166. DeFranza, *Sex Difference*, 68. While Defranza recognizes that the suggested link between intersex and eunuch is anachronistic, she still advances its validity given the experienced liminality of both groups (ibid., 103).

167. Ibid., 78.

168. DeFranza, "Gender Minorities," 167. See Mary Douglas, *Purity and Danger: An Analysis of Concept of Pollution and Taboo*, RC (London: Routledge, 2005), 51–71. For Douglas, "The underlying principle of cleanness in animals is that they should conform fully to their class" (ibid., 69). Unclean animals are those that defy the class boundaries established in Gen. 1:28 (water, air, and earth) through their mode of "locomotion" (ibid.). Note that for Douglas there were no "hybrids" in creation, *contra* DeFranza (ibid., 68).

169. DeFranza, "Gender Minorities," 167.

170. Ibid., 166.

171. Ibid.

172. Ibid., 165.

173. DeFranza, *Sex Difference*, 78. DeFranza refers to the people of Deut. 23:1 as "cut eunuchs," but she seems to assume rather than develop the link with intersex embodiment ("Gender Minorities," 164).

174. DeFranza, "Gender Minorities," 160, 169.

Here, debate focuses on the identity of the third category of eunuch that Jesus mentions. DeFranza insists that while the majority of the Christian tradition has followed Augustine in reading "eunuchs who have made themselves eunuchs for the sake of the kingdom" (Matt. 19:12c) as figurative for voluntary celibacy,[175] such an interpretation is an illegitimate backreading of 1 Corinthians 7 into Matthew 19.[176] Augustine was misled (perhaps unwittingly) by a pagan desire to uphold the "Roman cultural values" of a "hierarchically ordered household, within a hierarchically ordered city, overseen by a hierarchically ordered church."[177] For too long has Augustinian order triumphed over the "freedom of the future kingdom of God."[178]

In contrast, DeFranza argues that this third category of eunuch should be read literally. Noting the juxtaposition of eunuchs in v.12 with "children" (παιδίον) in the immediately following pericope (Matt. 19:13–15), DeFranza offers in the form of a highly suggestive question that children "represent those without gender,"[179] highlighting how "in Greek, the word for child (teknon) is neuter."[180] By privileging the literal eunuch, Jesus "provided an important supplement to the binary model of human sex and gender."[181] In this, Jesus demonstrates that he is the Isaianic Messiah, fulfilling the promise of Isa. 56:3–5 that eunuchs are given "a place in God's house as they are, [and] not after some kind of restoration to an Edenic pattern."[182]

DeFranza supports her exegesis with an appeal to tradition, narrating the early church practice of self-castration, offering the famous example of Origen. Indeed, "There were enough Christians taking Jesus' words literally that the Church Fathers, as early as the Council of Nicaea (325), saw the need to address the issue."[183] What remains subtly implicit for DeFranza, but is made explicit by David Hester (whom DeFranza cites positively), is the "extremely powerful, naturalized and self-evident reading that Jesus was calling his followers to perform ritual castration as

---

175. E.g., Augustine, "The Work of Monks," 32, in *Treatises on Various Subjects*, trans. Mary Sarah Muldowney, FC 16 (New York: Fathers of the Church, 1952), 390–3.

176. DeFranza, *Sex Difference*, 72.

177. DeFranza, "Gender Minorities," 163.

178. Ibid.

179. DeFranza, *Sex Difference*, 81.

180. Ibid., 81 n.63. Although, note that Matthew uses παιδίον not τέκνον in the immediate context.

181. Ibid., 106.

182. DeFranza, "Gender Minorities," 174, italics original.

183. DeFranza, *Sex Difference*, 72. Although, for suggested "loopholes" in canon 1 of Nicaea I, see J. David Hester, "Queers on Account of the Kingdom of Heaven: Rhetorical Constructions of the Eunuch Body," *Scri* 90 (2005): 819 n.66. That Origen may not have been castrated, see Jones, "Gender Identity," 11.

a sign of religious devotion and commitment."[184] Thus, Matt. 19:12's logion about the privileged standing of eunuchs in the new covenant "threatens the sacred boundaries between male and female."[185]

Such a literal interpretation of Matt. 19:12 has "the advantage of a 'plain text' reading."[186] In contrast, the figurative interpretation ends up concluding that the third "eunuch is not a eunuch at all, but a man who chooses celibacy," a conclusion "premised upon a completely ideological misreading of eunicism altogether."[187] Those who "rhetorically invent an allegorical reading"[188] must "confront both the fact of the dominical *rejection* of this [sexually dimorphic] norm and the early Christian practices that embraced this rejection."[189] In summary, Jesus' focus in Matt. 19:12 is not on singleness as an alternative vocation to marriage. Such a reading would neuter the plain intent of the first two kinds of eunuch. Rather, all three categories of eunuch should be read literally. Jesus valorizes all three above marriage, thereby supplementing the old covenant binary of male and female.[190]

3. New Covenant Expansion To support her case that new covenant eunuchs are a "supplement to the binary model,"[191] DeFranza argues that "these changes parallel other biblical movement from the Old to the New Testament—laws about mixing things that should be distinct."[192] DeFranza notes from Mark 7:18–23 that just as "Jesus declared as clean those animals that mixed creational categories . . . [he] also spoke positively about humans who didn't fit the categories of male or female, naturally born eunuchs."[193] OT holiness was about external separation, enforced by laws that acted as "every day reminders that God's people were to remain separate from all others" until the coming of Christ (cf. Gal. 3:14).[194] With Christ's advent, external holiness is now internalized (Mark 7:18–23). Thus, things

184. J. David Hester, "Eunuchs and the Postgender Jesus: Matthew 19.12 and Transgressive Sexualities," *JNST* 28 (2005): 31.

185. Ibid., 37.

186. Hester, "Queers on Account of the Kingdom of Heaven," 820.

187. Ibid., 822. For Hester, the figurative reading is falsely premised on the ideological "naturalness" of "nature" and the "male/female binary" (ibid., 823).

188. Hester, "Eunuchs and the Postgender Jesus," 34.

189. Ibid., 40, italics original.

190. While Hester reads Jesus' words as rejecting the binary model of creation, DeFranza prefers the language of supplementation because she still recognizes the good of heterosexual marriage as "the majority story" (cf. Matt. 19:4–6) ("Journeying from the Bible to Christian Ethics in Search of Common Ground," in *Two Views on Homosexuality, the Bible, and the Church*, ed. Preston Sprinkle, Counterpoints [Grand Rapids: Zondervan, 2016], 90).

191. DeFranza, *Sex Difference*, 106.

192. DeFranza, "Gender Minorities," 165.

193. Ibid., 169.

194. Ibid., 172.

that were previously mixed and unclean now become clean and accepted. Here, "The story of eunuchs parallels the narrative of clean and unclean things."[195] This narrative continues to expand throughout Acts, with the inclusion of the Ethiopian eunuch (Acts 8:26–40), unclean food (Acts 10:15), and Gentiles (Acts 10:34–35). Indeed, DeFranza emphasizes an important "expansive notion of otherness" set within an "eschatological trajectory," where "other others are born . . . other ages, other languages, other cultures, and even others whose sex does not match either parent," climaxing in the "eschatological community" of Rev. 7:9.[196]

DeFranza's juxtaposition of sexed embodiment and food reveals her understanding of how redemption relates to creation. "The Christian story is not circular but linear," DeFranza delineates.[197] "It does not end where it started. As God's revelation unfolds, more and more outsiders are brought in."[198] Thus, Adam and Eve were not prototypes of fixity but progenitors of fecundity. As the trajectory incipient in creation expands in redemption, the task of the church today is to follow the example of the Jerusalem Council in Acts 15 and continue to improvise freely within God's "unfinished drama."[199] DeFranza affirms the approach of Sparks, who beseeches a willingness to "move beyond the written word by listening to God's living voice, which includes not only Scripture but also the voices of creation, tradition, and the Spirit."[200] Indeed, the "only way that conservative Christians will be able to move beyond heteronormativity is by adopting a similar hermeneutic."[201]

D. Response: Not Structural Expansion but Spiritual Inclusion

Although DeFranza expresses a correct intuition that there is a *more* to creation, and her compassion for sexual minorities is laudable, her overall model of "redemption expanding creation" remains problematic, in large part due to key

---

195. Ibid.

196. DeFranza, *Sex Difference*, 182.

197. DeFranza, "Gender Minorities," 174.

198. Ibid.

199. Megan K. DeFranza, "Rejoinder," in *Two Views on Homosexuality, the Bible, and the Church*, ed. Preston Sprinkle, Counterpoints (Grand Rapids: Zondervan, 2016), 122. DeFranza grounds her trajectory hermeneutics in N. T. Wright, "How Can the Bible Be Authoritative," *VE* 21 (1991): 7–32. However, note Wright's caveat that "new improvisation" must fit with the preceding acts of creation, fall, Israel, and Jesus. Further, since the NT forms the first scene in the fifth act of the church, "giving hints . . . of how the play is supposed to end," subsequent scenes must cohere with the first scene (ibid., 19).

200. Kenton L. Sparks, *God's Word in Human Words: An Evangelical Appropriation of Critical Biblical Scholarship* (Grand Rapids: Baker Academic, 2008), 299. See DeFranza, *Sex Difference*, 267.

201. DeFranza, *Sex Difference*, 267.

aspects of her exegesis (as I detail below).[202] Given that the core of DeFranza's argument rests on the propinquity of her proposed parallel between Jesus expanding options on the food menu and Jesus expanding divinely endorsed options for the sexed body, I first examine her claim that in the OT the eunuch was an unclean mixture of male and female. Second, I analyze the intent of Matt. 19:12, before third, exploring whether Jesus' inclusive move with food in Mark 7 indicates a similar expansion toward SP. The cumulative case maintains that the focus of Jesus' work in redemption "now" concerns spiritual and social inclusion rather than structural expansion of the sexed body.

1. OT Eunuchs: A Mix of Male and Female? DeFranza asserts that for old covenant Israel, certain foods were "detestable" because they mixed the clearly defined categories of Gen. 1:28. Similarly, "eunuchs, whose bodies blurred the lines between male and female, were considered foreign,"[203] and so excluded from the assembly of YHWH (Deut. 23:1). However, even if we assume the accuracy of Douglas's "mixed" thesis as it relates to unclean food,[204] it remains opaque how OT eunuchs fit the "mixed" category. First, this is because on closer examination there is only one biblical text that may satisfy the modern definition of an intersex person (genuine sexed body ambiguity because of a congenital condition), and second, the qualifying text employs the descriptor of "blemish" (מום), which does not parallel the concept of "mixed."

i. Intersex as "Eunuchs" The Hebrew word for eunuch (סריס) has a broad semantic range, which depending on the context refers mostly to a high-ranking male official, but can also indicate a castrated male.[205] The rabbinic distinction between congenital "eunuchs of the sun" (סריסי חמה) and "man-made eunuchs" (סריסי אדם) is not explicit in the OT, even if subsequently recognized by Jesus in Matt. 19:12.[206] Where סריס appears in Isa. 56:3, the focus is not directly on biological markers but on religious status. The "eunuch" is placed in parallel with the "foreigner" (בן־הנכר), and both of them are drawn into the covenant community via their faith in YHWH, expressed by religious Sabbath observance (vv.2, 4, 6). While it is not clear what

202. Like Song's proposal, there is also a sense in which DeFranza's preference for evolving creational systems over stable creational structures is overly historicist, resulting in a reductionistic doctrine of creation.

203. DeFranza, "Gender Minorities," 166.

204. For a list of "errors" in Douglas's argument, see Jacob Milgrom, "Ethics and Ritual: The Foundations of the Biblical Dietary Laws," in *Religion and Law: Biblical-Judaic and Islamic Perspectives*, ed. Edwin Brown Firmage, Bernard G. Weiss, and John W. Welch (Winona Lake, IN: Eisenbrauns, 1990), 176–9, 184–5.

205. *HALOT* 2:770. For an overview of סריס in the OT, see Retief and Cilliers, "Eunuchs."

206. On the rabbinic distinction, see Hermann Leberecht Strack and Paul Billerbeck, *Kommentar zum Neuen Testament aus Talmud und Midrasch*, 2nd ed. (München: Beck, 1956), 1:805–7.

kind of eunuch Isa. 56:3 has in mind, Delitzsch makes the insightful suggestion that it refers to those who "had been mutilated against their wills, that they might serve at heathen courts" (cf. Isa. 39:7).[207] For these "unfruitful trees" returning from exile, their fear of exclusion is valid in light of Deut. 23:1 expressly declaring that "no kind of emasculated person is to enter the congregation of Jehovah."[208] In Isa. 56:3, סריס could represent the "ambiguous bodies" of intersex persons,[209] but given the intratext of Isa. 39:7, combined with the explicit concern with infertility, it seems more likely that סריס refers to a castrated male rather than a congenital condition.

DeFranza's other oft-cited biblical text is Deut. 23:1, where the word סריס does not occur, but where DeFranza discerns the concept of intersexuality. However, the juxtaposition of eunuchs and foreigners in Deut. 23:1–8 further implies that those "who are bruised-crushed and have a severed male organ" (23:1[2] פצוע־דכא וכרות שפכה) are in fact castrated individuals, perhaps associated with pagan worship, and not those born with a congenital condition.[210] The phrase "bruised-crushed" does not indicate which part of the body is damaged, and although scholars typically agree that the noun שפכה refers to the penis, it is a *hapax legomenon* in the OT, challenging semantic certainty. The translational test is evidenced further by the LXX rendering the whole phrase as θλαδίας ("eunuch"), likely a euphemism. Indeed, given the three passive participles, it remains unclear whether the damage referred to is inflicted oneself or by others. Either way, as Wang concludes, "The most we can say about this category is that it is a group whose male organs are damaged like a eunuch, voluntarily or not."[211] Thus, the juxtaposition with foreigners intimates that these are likely castrated men, probably excluded due to their association with a pagan cult.[212] Interestingly, DeFranza recognizes the individuals of 23:1 as "castrated eunuchs," noting the literary context of "ritual castration" and its association with foreign religions,[213] and yet insists that these "bodies blurred the lines between male and female."[214] While this latter comment could be correct on a social level, any claim

---

207. Franz Delitzsch, *Biblical Commentary on the Prophecies of Isaiah*, trans. James Martin (Grand Rapids: Eerdmans, 1949), 2:362.

208. Ibid. It is also possible that the reward of a יד (Isa. 56:5) is a poetic reference to a "penis," and not simply a "memorial" (NIV, NASB), "monument" (ESV, NRSV), or "place" (NKJV). This possibility is increased when we appreciate the proclivity for polyvalence in Hebrew poetry, and well as the clear use of יד as "penis" in Isa. 57:8 (plus its more metaphorical employment in Isa. 57:10). See further P. R. Ackroyd, "יד," *TDOT* 5:402–3.

209. DeFranza, "Gender Minorities," 168.

210. The numbering in square brackets refers to the versification of the MT.

211. Franklin Wang, "A Holy People of YHWH: Deuteronomy's Vision of Israelite Identity" (PhD diss., Wheaton College, 2020), 284.

212. Retief and Cilliers, "Eunuchs," 250. Similarly, Jeffrey H. Tigay, *Deuteronomy* דברים, JPSTCP (Philadelphia: Jewish Publication Society, 1996), 210.

213. DeFranza, "Gender Minorities," 165. Cf. DeFranza, *Sex Difference*, 78.

214. DeFranza, "Gender Minorities," 166.

advanced at the sexed structural level remains overdrawn. Consequently, on closer inspection the suggested text of Deut. 23:1 does not qualify as sufficient evidence for intersexuality.

The only text where the concept of intersexuality *may* be in view is Lev. 21:20, which prohibits offspring of Aaron who have the "blemish" (מום) of a "crushed testicle" (מרוח אשך)[215] from offering food as priests. Again, the text does not record how the blemish came about, whether self-inflicted, caused by others, or congenital. But given that some of the other blemishes mentioned could be from birth (e.g., a hunchback, גבן),[216] a "crushed testicle" as a congenital condition remains a possibility.[217] Accordingly, could a "blemish" qualify someone as a "mixed" thing *qua* unclean food?

ii. Intersex as "Mixed" While God banned mixing in some areas (cf. Deut. 22:9–11), DeFranza's claim that eunuchs are also "mixed," and so "unclean," remains unpersuasive. First, the connection DeFranza draws between "mixed" and "blemished" conflicts with the way OT texts use these words. Congenital eunuchs may be described by the adjective of "blemish" but never "mixed." As Douglas details, "Leviticus never uses the word for blemish (מ[א]ום) for the physical characteristics of species forbidden as food."[218] Admittedly, even though the word may be absent, the concept may still obtain.

Second, animals that are mixed and so unclean are prohibited as a whole class. For example, the pig *qua* kind-essence is unclean (Lev. 11:7–8), not individual pigs who might be guilty of specific infringements. In contrast, blemishes are only predicated of individuals. These individuals could be grouped into a set, but the class itself, whether sacrificing people or sacrificed animals, are not "detestable" *qua* kind-essence. If we make the blemished set a mixed (and so detestable) class, then we inadvertently suggest that intersex persons are of a different kind-essence to the unambiguously sexed. Such logic is inherently dehumanizing of intersex persons, the very conclusion revisionists rightly want to avoid.

Third, the important difference between blemished individuals and unclean classes of food may be further clarified by attending to the economy of holiness in Leviticus, which slides from holy to common/clean to unclean.[219] As Thiessen

215. Both words are hapax legomena in the OT.

216. Another hapax legomenon. Some of the twelve blemishes listed in vv.18b–20 are notoriously tricky to translate. That these blemishes represent generic categories that were "arbitrarily chosen" to parallel the "equivalent blemishes of sacrificial animals (22:22–24)," see Jacob Milgrom, *Leviticus 17–22: A New Translation with Introduction and Commentary*, AB 3A (New York: Doubleday, 2008), 1838.

217. Nobuyoshi Kiuchi, *Leviticus*, AOTC 3 (Nottingham, UK: Apollos, 2007), 398.

218. Mary Douglas, "Sacred Contagion," in *Reading Leviticus: A Conversation with Mary Douglas*, ed. John F. A. Sawyer, JSOTSup 227 (Sheffield: Sheffield Academic, 1996), 101.

219. See Wenham, *Leviticus*, 18–25.

notes, some food is "ontologically . . . impure. It [a pig] is born impure, passes on that impurity to any of its offspring, and then dies impure."[220] In contrast, while blemished priests are not holy, they are "not said to be unclean."[221] They may not approach the altar (Lev. 21:23), but they still enjoy the "holy food" (Lev. 21:22) within the covenant community. Indeed, "Even 'blemished' *kōhănîm* have more access to the sacred than ordinary Israelites."[222] Thus, an individually blemished priest remains clean, importantly distinct from a class of unclean food.

Therefore, the single text that could qualify as referring to the concept of intersexuality does not support DeFranza's claim that in the OT eunuchs are "mixed" beings. This conclusion problematizes DeFranza's later move of discerning a propinquitous parallel between Jesus declaring mixed food "clean" and eunuchs as acceptable.[223]

2. NT Eunuchs: Literal or Figurative? From Matt. 19:12, DeFranza claims that Jesus enfolds eunuchs into the purposes of God *"as eunuchs,"*[224] thereby providing "an important supplement to the binary model of human sex."[225] DeFranza is correct in noting that Jesus never explicitly heals a eunuch,[226] and that in Matt. 19:12c Jesus lauds eunuchs διὰ τὴν βασιλείαν as "icons of radical discipleship,"[227] thus demonstrating his "identification with the messianic visions of Isaiah."[228] However, these accurate observations do not necessitate DeFranza's conclusion that Jesus expands the creation category of male and female into SP. This becomes evident when we scrutinize DeFranza's insistence that all three categories of eunuch should be read literally. In short, such a reading is exegetically unwarranted on three levels (contextual, pericopal, and grammatical), as well as being ethically dubious.

First, at the contextual level, DeFranza's literal reading does not sufficiently account for the immediate literary context. Her interpretation of children (19:13–15)

---

220. Matthew Thiessen, *Jesus and the Forces of Death: The Gospels' Portrayal of Ritual Impurity Within First-Century Judaism* (Grand Rapids: Baker Academic, 2020), 188.

221. Wenham, *Leviticus*, 20.

222. Julia Watts Belser, "Priestly Aesthetics: Disability and Bodily Difference in Leviticus 21," *Int* 73 (2019): 357.

223. Perhaps DeFranza is motivated to read OT eunuchs as "mixed" more from a prior commitment to the hybrid argument from Genesis 1 than from a close reading of Leviticus. Somewhat ironically, DeFranza's hermeneutical inclination parallels the Augustinian inclination of reading Matthew 19 alongside 1 Corinthians 7, thus obviating her indictment of the latter.

224. DeFranza, "Gender Minorities," 168, italics original.

225. DeFranza, *Sex Difference*, 106.

226. However, given DeFranza's own "umbrella" definition of eunuch, the hemorrhaging woman of Mark 5:25–34 *may* qualify for DeFranza as someone whose functional barrenness, and so "eunuch" status, was healed.

227. DeFranza, "Gender Minorities," 169.

228. DeFranza, *Sex Difference*, 82.

as representing those "without gender" (because their grammatical gender is neuter),[229] not only fails to heed Jesus' own link between children and humility in Matt. 18:2–4, but also commits the "unwarranted associative" logical fallacy of jumping from an observation about grammatical gender to make a claim about biological reality.[230] Indeed, Matt. 19:3–12 is set within Jesus' fourth teaching discourse that focuses on the relational status and characteristics of those in the new kingdom community (Matthew 18–20). The literary context is about kingdom status rather than bodily structure.

Second, the eunuch logion is located within a pericope whose topic is marriage and divorce, and whose intended speech-act explicates relationship status (married or single) in light of the "kingdom of heaven," rather than sexed bodily structure (SD expanding toward SP). In Matt. 19:3–11, *contra* the Pharisees' leniency, Jesus reemphasizes the indissolubility of marriage via a "creation principle,"[231] combining Gen. 1:27 with Gen. 2:24. Yet, while the gift of marriage is given to some, Jesus surprisingly commends the disciples' "ironical" conclusion by stating that God gives others an alternative gift, namely the relationship status of not being married, that is, singleness.[232] If Jesus' intent is to include singleness as a legitimate vocation within the inaugurated kingdom of heaven, then DeFranza's argument for an expansion toward SP conflicts with the occasion and inherent logic of the passage.

Third, the figurative reading is strengthened by noting how Matt. 19:12 exhibits the grammatical structure of a "climactic tricolon," which as Yaron catalogues is a typical pattern within wisdom literature.[233] As Davies and Allison summarize, "The first two lines relate concrete facts about the everyday world and serve to introduce or illustrate the third line, which proclaims a truth—much less concrete—from the moral or religious sphere."[234] Thus, in response to the disciples' statement in v.10, Jesus employs "two concrete realities of everyday existence (those born eunuchs and those made eunuchs) to support a third spiritual or moral truth (those eunuchs for the kingdom)."[235] If Jesus had moved straight to the spiritual truth, employing "eunuch" as a placeholder for "singleness," then his disciples would have remained confused because "eunuch" most naturally referred to a literal condition. Rather, Jesus uses a wisdom formula, offering the first two categories for conceptual clarity.

---

229. Ibid., 81 n.63.

230. D. A. Carson, *Exegetical Fallacies*, 2nd ed. (Carlisle, UK: Paternoster, 1996), 115. Further, DeFranza's juxtaposition of "eunuch" with "children" seems strained. DeFranza wants "eunuch" to represent a fixed category to supplement the male-female binary, and yet being a child is an inherently fluid state (one grows out of childhood).

231. Grant R. Osborne, *Matthew*, ZECNT 1 (Grand Rapids: Zondervan, 2010), 703.

232. R. T. France, *The Gospel of Matthew*, NICNT (Grand Rapids: Eerdmans, 2007), 722.

233. Reuven Yaron, "The Climactic Tricolon," *JJS* 37 (1986): 153–9. E.g., Prov. 10:26; 17:3; 25:3; 27:3.

234. W. D. Davies and Dale C. Allison, *A Critical and Exegetical Commentary on the Gospel According to Saint Matthew*, ICC (Edinburgh: T&T Clark, 1997), 3:22.

235. Osborne, *Matthew*, 702.

Finally, the literal reading is ethically dubious. If the third category of eunuch is literal, then Jesus calls for self-castration. While DeFranza remains conspicuously silent, Hester lauds this "self-evident" conclusion as a sign of "religious devotion."[236] Yet such extreme self-harm contradicts God's concern for life and wholeness evidenced throughout the Bible.[237] Thus, the literal reading "so expounds one place of Scripture that it be repugnant to another."[238]

Therefore, the literary context, the topic and occasion of the pericope, the syntax of v.12 itself, as well as the ethical implication of the literal reading, all undermine DeFranza's claim that Jesus expands male and female into SP. In contrast, Jesus' focus is not on sexed bodily structure, but on relationship status (married or single) that serves spiritual faithfulness (cf. Isa. 56:3), as recognized throughout church history.[239]

3. New Covenant Expansion DeFranza is correct to discern a trajectory from OT to NT. But again, the intended contrast in Matt. 19:3–12 is not between sexed structure (male, female, or intersex), but between relationship status (married or single) in the inaugurated kingdom community. Recalling the argument advanced in Chapter 3, old covenant adult Israelites were expected to marry, experiencing blessing through progeny. But here, in the new covenant, Jesus expands legitimate relationship options, valorizing the vocation of singleness. "To be blessed in the kingdom of God," Danylak deems, "no longer requires marriage and offspring."[240] Jesus then introduces the concept of volition to categorize singleness further. Some have the gift of singleness involuntarily, either because of a congenital condition or because of human harm,[241] and some have the gift of singleness voluntarily;[242] that is, they choose to live like their involuntarily eunuchized brothers and sisters by ordering their total devotion "on account of" the kingdom of heaven.[243] Thus, the new covenant *more* of Jesus' redemption is about the inclusion of singleness as a legitimate vocation, rather than the expansion of sexed body structure toward SP.

This conclusion accounts more naturally for what is promised in Isaiah 56:3–5 and filled out in Acts 8:26–40 (cf. Acts 10 and 15). In both passages, DeFranza is

---

236. Hester, "Eunuchs and the Postgender Jesus," 31.

237. E.g., Gen. 9:6; Exod. 15:26; Lev. 19:28; Deut. 30:19; Ps. 139:13–16; 1 Cor. 15:54. Although, note Candida R. Moss' claim that Jesus calls for "literal self-amputation" in Mark 9:43–47 (*Divine Bodies*, 57).

238. Article XX in Thomas, *Principles of Theology*, 281.

239. For representative literature, see Ulrich Luz, *Matthew 8–20: A Commentary on the Gospel of Matthew*, trans. James E. Crouch, Hermeneia (Minneapolis: Augsburg, 2001), 2:497.

240. Danylak, *Redeeming Singleness*, 157.

241. The involuntary nature of the respective conditions is emphasized by the choice of passive indicative verbs (ἐγεννήθησαν and εὐνουχίσθησαν).

242. Emphasized grammatically by an active reflexive verb (εὐνούχισαν ἑαυτούς).

243. Taking διὰ in a cause sense (rather than final).

correct to stress that the eunuch is welcomed *as a eunuch*. But again, the focus in both passages is on spiritual inclusion. Neither text explicitly mentions any physical healing for eunuchs because the shock value of both passages is the greater spiritual healing,[244] as former "outcasts are now included in the restored people of God" as priests (cf. Isa. 66:21), thus reversing Deut. 23:1 and Lev. 21:20, and fulfilling the Isaianic New Exodus.[245]

Indeed, Jesus' introduction of involuntary/voluntary, combined with his verbiage of "eunuch," indicates further the character of Jesus' redemptive inclusion of singleness. Again, DeFranza helpfully observes from background sources how Jesus' shocking choice of "eunuch" emphasizes absolute dependence and devotion to God.[246] As such, Jesus' focus is not just on the bare status of singleness (vs. the status of being married), but on the volitional and sacrificial service that the gifted status of singleness calls for in the kingdom of heaven. Singleness is not simply about forsaking marriage, but sacrificing "one's right to marriage, procreation, and sexual relations, for the sake of the kingdom of God."[247] In short, DeFranza is correct to note that the redemptive work of Jesus introduces a trajectory, but it is one that pertains to the inclusion of singleness for the service of spiritual ends, rather than the expansion of sexed bodily structure.

Consequently, if we combine this conclusion from Matt. 19:3–12 (status not structure) with the earlier observation that OT eunuchs do not qualify as "mixed things," then DeFranza's claim that Jesus' expansion of new covenant food options (Mark 7) indicates a similar expansion of sexed embodiment looks increasingly unpersuasive. DeFranza's proposed parallel between food and sex does not obtain. Food and bodily sex exhibit different trajectories from creation to redemption. Concerning food, creation vegetarianism (Gen. 1:29) expands to a postdiluvian carnivorous diet (Gen. 9:3). The Mosaic law then stipulates a narrowing of dietary options (e.g., Leviticus 11), before a further expansion in the new covenant (Mark 7:19). In contrast to food's fluctuating trajectory, there is no textual evidence to support a similar trajectory for bodily sex. Admittedly, this does not mean that the sexed body *cannot* undergo new covenant expansion (especially in the eschaton), but only that DeFranza's appeal to Mark 7 as a propinquitous parallel is unwarranted.

In summary, while DeFranza helpfully notes that there is a *more* to creation, her argument that redemption "now" structurally expands the creation categories of male and female into SP remains unconvincing. DeFranza's central text of Matt. 19:12 is not concerned with expanding bodily structure but with including

244. Although note the restorative and recreative language of 66:22 (cf. 65:17), set within a pericope (66:18–24) that mirrors Isa. 56:1–8. On the chiastic mirroring of these pericopes, see John N. Oswalt, *Book of Isaiah: Chapters 40–66*, NICOT (Grand Rapids: Eerdmans, 1998), 461–5.

245. David W. Pao, *Acts and the Isaianic New Exodus*, WUNT 130 (Tübingen: Mohr Siebeck, 2000), 141.

246. E.g., DeFranza, "Gender Minorities," 162.

247. Danylak, *Redeeming Singleness*, 157.

and valorizing the vocation of singleness for the service of God. By advancing a redemptive expansion toward SP, DeFranza brings future expectations for structural transformation (e.g., 1 Cor. 15:50) into the present—an over-realized eschatology. Conversely, a closer examination of Matt. 19:3–12 indicates that while the sexed bodily structure of creation endures, godly expression of one's sexed body now includes the new covenant vocation of singleness for kingdom service, supplementing the old covenant vocation of marriage. Thus, redemption "now" emphasizes spiritual and social inclusion as opposed to any structural expansion of creation's "male and female."

E. Returning to Galatians 3:28

Informed by a "redemption restores creation" model, and Jesus' emphasis in Matthew 19 on spiritual and social inclusion (rather than sexed expansion), it is fitting to return to Gal. 3:28 to assess whether the chief progressive proof text suggests any redemptive shift toward SP.[248] In Gal. 3:26–29, Paul offers "the pivotal, climactic center of the letter,"[249] arguing that all who are incorporated by faith (26) through baptism (27) into Christ the true Seed (16) are all "sons of God" (26) and "Abraham's seed and heirs" (29), regardless of racial, social, or sexed condition. Indeed, the theological heart of this pericope, and perhaps even the letter, is oneness in Christ,[250] expressed succinctly in πάντες γὰρ ὑμεῖς εἷς ἐστε ἐν Χριστῷ Ἰησοῦ (Gal. 3:28d). To a "humanity obsessed by social rank and ethnic origin," Butticaz avers, "he [Paul] contrasts an eschatological humanity whose unique point of reference is Christological."[251] While oneness refers to incorporation into Christ, debate hinges around whether its collocation with "neither male and female" signifies a change in spiritual/social status or sexed structure.

To discern Paul's intended meaning, it is important to note the wider literary context, especially how the negated couplets of 3:28 are clarified when read alongside the couplet negated in Gal. 5:6 ("For in Christ Jesus neither circumcision nor uncircumcision has any value [τι ἰσχύει], but rather [what has value is] faith working through love") and Gal. 6:15 ("For neither circumcision is anything [τί ἐστιν] nor uncircumcision but [what is something is] a new creation"). It is appropriate to read Gal. 5:6 and 6:15 as a commentary on Gal. 3:28, not only because of the syntactical parallels (the negation of a couplet and something that replaces it) but also because the circumcised of the first century were typically Jewish (not Gentile), free (not enslaved) men (not women), such that circumcision

---

248. E.g., DeFranza, *Sex Difference*, 246; Song, *Covenant and Calling*, 49.

249. A. Andrew Das, *Galatians* (St. Louis, MO: Concordia, 2014), 377.

250. A. Andrew Das, "Oneness in Christ: The Nexus Indivulsus Between Justification and Sanctification in Paul's Letter to the Galatians," *ConJ* 21 (1995): 173–86.

251. Simon Butticaz, *La crise galate ou l'anthropologie en question*, BZNW 229 (Berlin: De Gruyter, 2018), 203.

seems to function as a metonym for the three divisions in 3:28.[252] The implication from Gal. 5:6 and 6:15 is that while the physical difference of circumcision/ uncircumcision may last, in light of the "apocalypse" of Christ (1:12), circumcision or uncircumcision no longer carry any soteriological "validity" or "invalidity" (note the immediately preceding verses of 5:2–5 regarding justification), suggested further in Paul's choice of the verb ἰσχύω.[253] Indeed, Paul's use of ἰσχύω in 5:6 may illuminate the enigmatic negation οὐκ ἔνι in 3:28, Baumert arguing that the "flat" translation of ἔνι as "there is" (*Es ist/gibt*) is an incorrect "product of the twentieth century," and should be translated more accurately as "it is valid/of significance" (*Es gilt*).[254] As such, with the redemptive-historical adiaphorization of circumcision in Christ, so too are the religious privileges of Jewish, free men relativized—privileges formerly afforded under the guardianship of the law (3:23–24).

Applying the same logic to Gal. 3:28, in Christ racial, social, and bodily sex differences have been redemptive-historically adiaphorized rather than structurally abolished. Thus, as Hubing avers, it is "impossible to take Paul's language here in an absolutely literal way."[255] "The emphasis in Gal 3:28–29 . . . is not the obliteration of different human identities," Bird submits, "but the *inclusion* and *transformation* of multiple identities under a single meta-identity marked by Christ and the new creation. But that can only be true if existing identities, which are means of distinction and status, are themselves negated in value and lessened in their ability to cause differentiation."[256]

---

252. See Troy W. Martin, "The Covenant of Circumcision (Genesis 17:9–14) and the Situational Antithesis in Galatians 3:28," *JBL* 122 (2003): 111–25.

253. For the use of ἰσχύω connoting legal validity, see BDAG, 484.

254. Norbert Baumert, *Antifeminismus bei Paulus? Einzelstudien*, FB 68 (Würzburg: Echter, 1992), 328. Similarly, Walden asserts that ἔνι is not a synonym of ἔστιν ("it is"). Rather, ἔνι is a contraction of ἔνειμι, which has a very specific function of "calling attention to the matter in hand," in this case, who belongs to Christ ("Galatians 3:28: Grammar Observations," *ResQ* 51 [2009]: 47).

255. Jeff Hubing, *Crucifixion and New Creation: The Strategic Purpose of Galatians 6.11–17*, LNTS 508 (London: Bloomsbury, 2015), 239–40.

256. Michael F. Bird, "Salvation in Paul's Judaism?" in *Paul and Judaism: Crosscurrents in Pauline Exegesis and the Study of Jewish-Christian Relations*, ed. Reimund Bieringer and Didier Pollefeyt, LNTS 463 (London: T&T Clark, 2012), 28–9, italics original. It remains instructive that in Galatians, Paul does not stop being a Jew (2:15) and Gentiles join the people of God *as Gentiles* (2:3, 11–14), the core of Paul's argument in Galatians 3. Considering the slave/free couplet, in Christ the social distinction is adiaphorized, even if the social positions of "slave" and "free" still exist in the cultural context of the GRW (see Philemon). Importantly, even if Paul's focus is the spiritual and social adiaphorization of prior difference, the creational structure of "male and female" need not dictate a similar fixity for "slave" and "free," especially given the macro-liberationist trajectory of slavery in scripture. See further, Belousek, *Marriage*, 200–4.

Consequently, the couplet "male and female" should be treated like the preceding two—redemptive change is spiritual and social rather than structural. The creation categories of male and female have not been abolished in Christ, but non-males, who were typically marginalized in the first century by Jews and Gentiles, are now afforded with men equal status in Christ's kingdom through baptism. The shock of Gal. 3:28 is only felt if sex differences remain real. Thus, "Paul, without abolishing the differences, integrates them in the unity that 'all' (*pantes*) constitute 'in Christ Jesus.'"[257]

Concerning Paul's allusion to Gen. 1:27 (LXX), if the intertext in its literary context primarily explicates the scope of the *imago* (v.26), thereby delineating the subjects necessary for producing more image-bearers (v.28),[258] then that which is negated in Christ could simply be the need for physical reproduction. If so, then it seems acceptable to follow the "informed assumption" that "male and female" may well have been a first-century idiom for marriage.[259] In light of the Christ event, and being baptized into Christ (v.27), kingdom value and inheritance (v.29) are no longer dependent on getting married and producing children.[260] "For you are all [married or single, fertile or infertile] one in Christ Jesus" (Gal. 3:28). Indeed, Keener insightfully submits that the collocation of the predicate adjective εἷς with a reference to creation suggests that Paul "envisions a restoration of the primeval unity of male and female that flourished before the judgment of Gen. 3:16."[261] Although Paul is not explicit, the use of a masculine numeral could indicate that Christ is the new Adam. By faith, whatever one's racial, social, or sexed status, we form one new humanity in Christ the new Adam.[262] Our "new creation" (6:15) in Christ both "recast[s] the fundamental nature of the world"[263] and introduces a

---

257. Simon Légasse, *L'Épître de Paul aux Galates* (Paris: Cerf, 2000), 284.

258. See Chapter 3.

259. Preston M. Sprinkle, *Embodied: Transgender Identities, the Church & What the Bible Has to Say* (Colorado Springs, CO: David C Cook, 2021), 259 n.25. Note how Jesus quotes Gen. 1:27 in the context of marriage (Matt. 19:4). See also the *Damascus Document* 4:20–5:2, which condemned polygamy by citing "the foundation of creation," which is "male and female he created them" (Gen. 1:27). See James H. Charlesworth, ed., *The Dead Sea Scrolls: Hebrew, Aramaic, and Greek Texts with English Translations: Damascus Document, War Scroll, and Related Documents*, PTSDSSP (Tübingen: Mohr Siebeck, 1994), 2:19–21.

260. Esau McCaulley, *Sharing in the Son's Inheritance: Davidic Messianism and Paul's Worldwide Interpretation of the Abrahamic Land Promise in Galatians*, LNTS 608 (London: T&T Clark, 2019), 162–70.

261. Craig S. Keener, *Galatians: A Commentary* (Grand Rapids: Baker Academic, 2019), 308.

262. Bruce Hansen, *All of You Are One: The Social Vision of Galatians 3:28, 1 Corinthians 12:13 and Colossians 3:11*, LNTS 409 (London: T&T Clark, 2010), 101.

263. Douglas J. Moo, *Galatians*, BECNT (Grand Rapids: Baker Academic, 2013), 254. Keener notes extensively how the literature of Second Temple Judaism frequently believed that the end would recapitulate the beginning (*Galatians*, 308 n.882).

transposition in key as we live out our new humanity in the power of the Spirit, an implication expanded upon in Galatians 5–6. As Witherington notes, if Paul had wanted to assert the "obliteration of sexual distinctions in Christ," he would have used ἄρσεν ἤ θῆλυ, as well as employing the neuter form for "one," not the masculine εἷς.[264]

Therefore, given how "the theology of creation plays a permanently important role" for Paul, oneness in Christ does not signify the "complete elimination" or expansion of bodily sex difference.[265] Rather, οὐκ ἔνι ἄρσεν καὶ θῆλυ refers to the redemptive-historical "*adiaphorization of sexual difference* in the new creation in Christ."[266] While sexed bodily identities remain significant in some sense, they lose their redemptive-historical weight for equal participation in the new covenant people of God. Relocated in Christ, and in the power of his Spirit, humans (however sexed) are set free from "all forms of symbolic capital not derived from 'belonging to Christ,'"[267] liberated to relate to each other as God always intended from creation.[268] In light of this, a fuller translation of Gal. 3:28c could be: "There is no longer [for redemptive-historical significance the status of being] male and female [i.e., married], for you are one [new creation humanity] in Christ Jesus." This re-exegesis of oneness in Christ as it relates to SD fits well with both the theological "redemption restores creation" framework and the figurative reading of Matt. 19:12c.

III. Conclusion

Robert Song rightly emphasizes the "significance of the advent of Christ for sexuality."[269] To discern that significance for the sexed body, I began by exploring the person of Christ. Aware of soteriological and anthropological concerns over Jesus' maleness, I argued that Jesus is universally human—thus all sexes are savable—and particularly male (not intersex), such that no sex is necessarily second-class. In turning to how the redemptive work of Christ relates to creation, I maintained that the biblical mosaic displays Christ more clearly and faithfully

---

264. Ben Witherington, "Rite and Rights for Women-Galatians 3:28," *NTS* 27 (1981): 599–600.

265. Johanna Körner, *Sexualität und Geschlecht bei Paulus: Die Spannung zwischen "Inklusivität" und "Exklusivität" des paulinischen Ethos am Beispiel der Sexual- und Geschlechterrollenethik*, WUNT 2/512 (Tübingen: Mohr Siebeck, 2020), 105.

266. Judith M. Gundry-Volf, "Beyond Difference? Paul's Vision of a New Humanity in Galatians 3:28," in *Gospel and Gender: A Trinitarian Engagement with Being Male and Female in Christ*, ed. Douglas A. Campbell and Alan J. Torrance, STS 7 (London: T&T Clark, 2003), 22, italics original.

267. John M. G. Barclay, *Paul and the Gift* (Grand Rapids: Eerdmans, 2015), 397.

268. Recall the ordered relational peace in Gen. 2:23–25, outlined in Chapter 3.

269. Song, *Covenant and Calling*, x.

when redemption does not replace but restores the *stage* of creation. I then clarified the character of restoration in redemption "now" by re-exegeting Matt. 19:12 and Gal. 3:28 to propose that the *act* of redemption "now" focused on spiritual and social inclusion rather than any sexed expansion toward SP.

Given the emphasis of redemption "now" on spiritual and social status over sexed structure, there is an important pastoral implication to highlight straightaway—God invites all people, however sexed, to become "children of God through faith" (Gal. 3:26). All are savable. None are second-class. Further, since the *act* of redemption pertains to "direction" rather than "structure," it seems inappropriate to justify "corrective" surgeries on intersex bodies based upon what Christ has accomplished in redemption "now." Christ calls his church "to heal intersex people, not physically, but by welcoming them."[270] Nevertheless, while redemption "now" brings spiritual and social transformation, we still groan as our bodies eagerly await their full redemption (Rom. 8:23). In the consummation, all groaning will cease as all tears are wiped away and all things are made new (Rev. 21:4–5). But what might this eschatological newness mean for intersex bodies—a structural "repristination," a "renovation," or a total "remodeling"? What might be the import of eschatological transformation for contemporary ethics?

---

270. Cox, *Intersex in Christ*, 109.

Chapter 6

CONSUMMATION

INTERSEX IN HEAVEN?

I. Intersex in Heaven?

The previous chapter argued that the *act* of redemption "now" does not replace but restores the *stage* of creation. While decaying death disorders the sexed body, the person and work of Christ begins its reordering. In redemption "now," this reordering does not refer to structural expansion, where intersexuality could "supplement" the sexuate correspondence of creation,[1] but pertains to a "re-direction" of "our inner self" (ὁ ἔσω ἡμῶν, 2 Cor. 4:16), signifying the spiritual and social inclusion of all sexed bodies in Christ (Gal. 3:28).[2] All are savable. None are second-class.

Nevertheless, "our outer self" (ὁ ἔξω ἡμῶν, 2 Cor. 4:16), that is, our body, still groans, eagerly awaiting its final redemption (Rom. 8:23), longing to put on its heavenly dwelling (2 Cor. 5:2).[3] God promises such somatic transformation "at the last trumpet" (1 Cor. 15:52), when Christ arrives (v.23) and completes in time and purpose the "eschatological fatherhood of God,"[4] when "all shall be well, and all shall be well, and all manner of things shall be well" because God will be "all in all" (v.28).[5] The public appearing of Christ reveals "the end of believers' suffering

---

1. DeFranza, *Sex Difference*, 106.

2. Depending on one's anthropology, "our inner self" (contrasted with "our outer self") could refer to the "soul," or more minimally, "aspects of the human person that cannot be seen" (affective, cognitive, etc.). Transformation for our "inner being" (Rom. 7:22) in redemption "now" includes a clear conscience that we are fully and finally forgiven (Hebrews 9–10) and the permanent indwelling of God's Spirit for adoption to sonship (Rom. 8:14–17), plus social/ecclesial oneness (Gal. 3:28). The distinction between our "inner" and "outer" self should not be heard as overly dualistic.

3. Note the repetition of στενάζω in both passages.

4. David A. Höhne, *The Last Things*, CCTheo (Downers Grove, IL: IVP Academic, 2019), 38.

5. Julian of Norwich, *Revelations of Divine Love*, trans. Barry Windeatt, OWC (Oxford: Oxford University Press, 2015), 74.

and the end of death."[6] We shall see Christ "just as he is" (καθώς ἐστιν), becoming like him (ὅμοιοι αὐτῷ, 1 John 3:2), Christ transforming "our lowly body [into the] form of his glorious body" (Phil. 3:21). But what might this eschatological newness mean for intersex bodies—elimination via a "repristination" to creational dimorphism or inclusion via some sort of structural "renovation" or "remodeling"?

Apologists for sexual polymorphism (SP) follow the traditional affirmation that the hope of glory is someway redemptive, bodily, sexed, and informs present ethics.[7] Since this set of working assumptions reflects (redemptive and bodily) and legitimately extends (sexed and shapes ethics) conciliar creedal orthodoxy,[8] there is no need to examine alternative proposals outside SP literature (e.g., eschatological androgyny or a disembodied state). Nonetheless, debate rumbles regarding our precise sexed condition in the eschaton. Will we be unambiguously "male and female" or is there space for intersex in heaven?[9] While the Christian tradition has historically read Augustine's claim that "both sexes will rise again" as signaling sexual dimorphism (SD) in the consummation,[10] Susannah Cornwall fears that such logic is "unhelpfully totalizing and may tend to erase difference and diversity."[11] Indeed, where the case for eschatological SD is linked with the eradication of bodily impairments, Candida Moss complains that such "heavenly

---

6. Campbell, *Hope of Glory*, 103.

7. E.g., Jung, "Intersex on Earth," 177; Cornwall, *Sex and Uncertainty*, 182. Susannah Cornwall is typical of intersex theologians in criticizing queer theologians for erasing sexed particularity ("All Things," 49, 48). The emphasis upon sexed bodily particularity explains a preference for Augustine when exploring eschatological embodiment in conversation with Christian tradition (see, e.g., Merrick, "Welcome Intersexed?"). This contrasts with queer theologians, who typically draw upon Gregory of Nyssa as a "Queer Father (see, e.g., Burrus, "Queer Father"). Concerning ethics, Cornwall suggests the neologism "sexchatology" for the "mode of doing theology" where our sexed state in the eschaton informs contemporary body politics (*Theology and Sexuality*, 155).

8. E.g., The Nicaeno-Constantinopolitan creed, read and approved at Chalcedon, looks "for a resurrection of the dead." See Bettenson and Maunder, *Documents of the Christian Church*, 28.

9. Intersex literature offers little definitional clarity regarding "heaven," especially in terms of time, space, and embodiment. At minimum, it is the preferred word to refer to the post-mortem destination of Christians. While the term "heaven" is polyvalent in scripture, for my purposes here I use the language of "heaven," "eschaton," and "consummation" interchangeably to signify the final time and place spoken of in Revelation 21–22. See Peter Toon, *Heaven and Hell: A Biblical and Theological Overview*, NelSBT (Nashville, TN: Thomas Nelson, 1986), 3–11.

10. Augustine, *Civ.* 22.17 (CCSL 48:835; WSA I/7:526). For Augustine's influence on traditional sexual ethics (particularly up to the Reformation), see Roberts, *Creation and Covenant*, 8.

11. Susannah Cornwall, "Intersex and the Rhetorics of Disability and Disorder: Multiple and Provisional Significance in Sexed, Gender, and Disabled Bodies," *JDR* 19 (2015): 111.

healing"[12] amounts to "heavenly eugenics."[13] Consequently, innovationist scholars argue that "sex is polymorphic in the new creation, that is, in some transformed sense there will be male, female, and intersex persons in the life to come";[14] a "rainbow of sex";[15] an "eschatological plurality of gendered bodies and identities" that go "beyond the [previously] given boundaries of the (dualizing) gender matrix."[16]

A. Methodological Caveats

The burden of this chapter is to examine the possibility of intersex in heaven. Such an examination must avoid certain pitfalls. First, given that the eschatological body is reserved strictly for the future, about which we struggle to imagine (1 Cor. 2:9; 13:12), any speculation as to its nature must avoid an illegitimate "hankering to understand in too great detail the forms of resurrected bodies" that amounts to "foolishness" (1 Cor. 15:36).[17] Yet scripture does not leave us at the crossroads in agnosticism. Rather, scripture permits and guides our examination as our *norma normans*. Indeed, scripture demands an investigation into the eschatological body, for eschatology (inaugurated in Christ's resurrection) is "indicative not only of final hopes," Jones adduces, "but also of present attitudes toward the bodies of the living" (e.g., 1 Cor. 6:13–14).[18]

Second, attempting to investigate the eschatological body (just one of the *eschata*) has the potential to distract us from the center of all eschatology, namely Christ "the *eschatos*" (Rev. 22:13).[19] As Christopher Holmes holds, "It is ultimately God, and not ourselves, that will one day 'be all in all' (1 Cor. 15:28). God . . . is not only the one who brings about the end of time but in his very being is our goal, our salvation, and blessedness."[20] Focusing on the sexed body must not distract us from Christ, "the hope of glory" (Col. 1:27).

Third, we must avoid abstracting biblical speech about individual, physical bodies in the eschaton from their primary and "*rightful place in the peaceable communion of the body in Christ*."[21] Brock cautions that overly "anthropologically

---

12. Candida R. Moss, "Heavenly Healing: Eschatological Cleansing and the Resurrection of the Dead in the Early Church," *JAAR* 79 (2011): 991–1017.

13. Moss, *Divine Bodies*, 26.

14. Jung, "Intersex on Earth," 173.

15. John Hare, "Afterword," in *Intersex, Theology, and the Bible: Troubling Bodies in Church, Text, and Society*, ed. Susannah Cornwall (New York: Palgrave Macmillan, 2015), 200.

16. Heß, "Eschatologie der Geschlechterdifferenz," 320.

17. Brock, *Wondrously Wounded*, 184.

18. Jones, *Marks of His Wounds*, 4.

19. Gerhard Sauter, *Eschatological Rationality: Theological Issues in Focus* (Grand Rapids: Baker, 1996), 146, italics original.

20. Christopher R. J. Holmes, "Last Things," in *The Oxford Handbook of Reformed Theology*, ed. Michael Allen and Scott R. Swain, OH (Oxford: Oxford University Press, 2020), 610.

21. Brock, *Wondrously Wounded*, 186, italics original.

ordered eschatological speculations are a temptation, not a solution to the pains of this life,"[22] for such proposals often forget that "individuals are destined to become stones in a living temple."[23] Questions about eschatological bodily configurations are important, but they are subservient to (and find their meaning within) the "redeemed *community*."[24] To summarize the preceding caveats, if we want to avoid Jesus' warning to the Sadducees, "You are wrong because you know neither the Scriptures nor the power of God" (Matt. 22:29), our speculation must be guided by scripture via a posture of prayerful humility.

B. *"Heavenly Healing" as "Heavenly Eugenics"*

Before considering specific biblical and theological arguments for intersex in heaven, it is important to clarify motivating concerns so that any response is apposite. Among advocates for SP there is a strong resistance to "hegemonies of 'goodness' and 'healing' which lead to the marginalization of intersexed."[25] For Cornwall, narratives of heavenly healing are problematic because, first, they "already presume that some configurations of human bodiliness are more perfect than others, but for reasons which are somewhat arbitrary if the 'givenness' of heteronormativity and procreativity are queried."[26] Second, believing that "bodies will be 'fixed' after death sometimes makes it too easy to dismiss the struggles faced currently."[27] Indeed, healing as *fixing* or *curing* haunts intersex persons as an insidious powerplay, "privileging and rationalizing the world as it is now, a world set up for life as unambiguously sexed . . . to be easier all round."[28] Third, undergirding Christian tradition's apotheosizing of "unblemished bodies" is a doctrine of an "aseitic [God], complete in Godself, all-powerful and able to act independently of human activity."[29] This view of God has informed the idea that dependence is "less than perfect," such that "those with certain impairments [are] even more imperfect."[30] In contrast, a God more open to creaturely involvement is more open to diverse bodily configurations.[31]

Consequently, *if* the "rhetorics and strategies of 'healing'" are to be retained at all,[32] heaven is "not 'healing from,' but living comfortably and healthily with

---

22. Ibid., 192.

23. Ibid., 183. Cf. 1 Pet. 2:4–5.

24. Ibid., italics original. See also, Matt O'Reilly, *Paul and the Resurrected Body: Social Identity and Ethical Practice*, ESEC 22 (Atlanta, GA: SBL, 2020).

25. Cornwall, "Kenosis," 181.

26. Cornwall, *Sex and Uncertainty*, 69.

27. Ibid., 183.

28. Ibid., 175.

29. Ibid., 173.

30. Ibid.

31. Ibid., 234.

32. Note that Cornwall does recognize the "need to be 'saved' from physical pain, suffering and death" (ibid.). What exactly Cornwall intends by placing 'saved' in inverted

oneself as intersex."[33] Healing is not the eradication of physical differences, but about "changing a culture, and reframing or resisting a particular narrative in order to claim a body-story as legitimate and good."[34] "Rather than assuming intersexed bodies will be perfected to unambiguity," Cornwall counters that "we ought to ask what eschatologies of perfection suggest about our own body anxieties."[35]

In exploring eschatological embodiment, clarifying such concerns is helpful for two reasons. First, they warn us that since the meaning of terms such as *good*, *normal*, or *healing* are often culturally determined (in part), definitions must be consciously informed by scripture. Second, these concerns indicate that at stake in the debate over heavenly embodiment is the threat of eschatological erasure—what Candida Moss provocatively calls "heavenly eugenics."[36] Thus, any querying of intersex in heaven will need to demonstrate how its proposal is ultimately *good news* for individual intersex persons.

Before any alternative, I assess current arguments for intersex in heaven, focusing first on those that appeal to the Trinity as a blueprint for "polymorphism in glory."[37] Second, I analyze arguments that cluster around the concept of bodily identity in heaven.[38] Having outlined several hurdles that revisionist proposals fail to clear, I third exegete elements of 1 Corinthians 15 to construct an account of sexed embodiment in the new creation that explicates how final redemption in Christ both restores *and* transforms creation.

II. The Trinity and Intersexuality

The Trinity as a blueprint for SP could equally be discussed in the chapter on creation.[39] Yet innovationist scholars who appeal to the Trinity typically do so when examining eschatology. Adrian Thatcher offers the most recent and developed

commas remains unclear, as does the mechanism of such salvation. Throughout her account, the focus is on social rather than physical salvation.

33. J. David Hester, "Intersex and the Rhetorics of Healing," in *Ethics and Intersex*, ed. Sharon E. Sytsma, ILELNM 29 (Dordrecht: Springer, 2006), 48.

34. Cornwall, "What Is Better," 385.

35. Cornwall, *Sex and Uncertainty*, 184.

36. Moss, *Divine Bodies*, 26. She refers to the healing of disability in general.

37. Hare, "Afterword," 200.

38. I employ the language of "identity" at minimum to refer loosely to that which is *me* and not something or someone else. For more detailed definitions of "identity" and "persistence conditions" see John Heil, *Philosophy of Mind: A Contemporary Introduction*, 4th ed., RCIP (New York: Routledge, 2020).

39. Note Susannah Cornwall's comment that "difference in creation is always more than binary, . . . because it echoes the Trinitarian difference which is always at least tri-directional" (*Un/Familiar Theology*, 90).

account for intersex in heaven via an appeal to "divine ontology."[40] I assess the adequacy of Thatcher's appeal by (i) presenting and then (ii) scrutinizing his claim that the Trinity furnishes a blueprint for SP in heaven.

A. Claim: The Trinity as a Blueprint for Intersex in Heaven

While "there are qualifications and disclaimers galore in affirming an analogy between divine and human persons,"[41] the "glorious binary-busting doctrine" of the Trinity "provides a model for sexual difference unique to theology."[42] Since God is Trinity, and humans are created in the image of the Triune God, we should expect humans to image the Trinity in unity and difference, both individually and corporately. Considering sexed embodiment in the present, Thatcher finds it empirically demonstrable that humanity forms a single-sex "continuum," inclusive of the diversity of male, female, and intersex: "a place for everyone."[43] In "the new creation, in which there is 'no longer male and female,' . . . the binary understanding of gender" is finally "overcome."[44] Although Cornwall, DeFranza, and Jung argue similarly (often via an underdeveloped appeal to Trinitarian *perichoresis*),[45] Thatcher reaches this conclusion by actively expositing the doctrine of the Trinity in unique ways.

First, divine threeness disrupts the "conceit of complementarity," including sexual dimorphism.[46] For Thatcher, "If God is One and God is Three, that God is Two is ruled out absolutely."[47] Thus, "The doctrine of the Trinity is itself non-binary, and grounds a non-binary understanding of human being."[48]

Second, Thatcher articulates humanity's non-binary nature by explicating its analogy with divine oneness. "God has a single essence. . . . [Likewise] human beings together have a single common essence."[49] Humans exhibit "myriad

---

40. Thatcher, *Gender and Christian Ethics*, 103. See also (to varying degrees), Cornwall, *Sex and Uncertainty*; Jung, "Intersex on Earth"; DeFranza, *Sex Difference*.

41. Thatcher, *Gender and Christian Ethics*, 103.

42. Ibid., 6, 103. As I shall demonstrate, this "model" extends beyond gendered-relations.

43. Ibid., 142–65.

44. Ibid., 14. For Thatcher, the term "gender" pertains to "relations" (performative and physical [so inclusive of "non-binary and intersex"]), a culturally constructed "symbolic system," and "identity" (ibid., 5–6).

45. I have transliterated περιχώρησις to follow my interlocutors.

46. Thatcher, *Gender and Christian Ethics*, 96–118. Thatcher extends Sarah Coakley's claim that "ontological threeness always challenges and 'ambushes' the stuckness of established 'twoness'" (*God, Sexuality, and the Self: An Essay "On the Trinity"* [Cambridge: Cambridge University Press, 2013], 330).

47. Thatcher, *Gender and Christian Ethics*, 137.

48. Ibid., 14.

49. Ibid., 46.

differences, including sexual difference," but these are subservient to the core fact that humanity comprises "an inclusive continuum."[50] This "human continuum" is not linear, with male and female as extreme poles, but represents a "more circular model,"[51] with Christ "as the centre around whom all humanity revolves."[52] Thus, "Humanity understood as a continuum or spectrum not only overcomes harmful binaries but follows plausibly and directly from doctrinal foundations."[53]

Third, just as divine oneness is not monadic but triune, the human continuum does not swallow up human difference. The "continuum replaces the binary of opposite sexes, but it does not replace sexual difference. It restores sexual difference to being what it always was—a matter, not of kind, but of degree."[54] Here, Thatcher not only speaks of gendered relations, but includes sexed embodiment. Thus, "There is diversity within God and within humanity, and human diversity extends to biological sex."[55]

Consequently, "Just as theology can illuminate human difference by modelling it on divine difference, so theology can illuminate human nature by modelling it on the nature of God."[56] What unites divine/human nature and divine/human difference is the term *perichoresis*. "There are no polarities in God," Thatcher asserts, but "only Persons in living, vibrant, creative, loving, reciprocal relation, sometimes referred to by the (ambivalently derived) term *perichòrèsis*."[57] Likewise, "Human persons, when they are transformed beyond this life, . . . relate to one another in a manner dimly analogous to the relations within God, called in the tradition *perichoresis* or *circumincession* (and sometimes traced back to the Greek root meaning 'dance')."[58] Although Thatcher emphasizes gendered relations, his comments above about the "human continuum" indicate that intersex persons participate *as intersex* in the ever-flowingly perichoretic "circle dance of love."[59]

---

50. Ibid.

51. Ibid., 122

52. Thatcher, *Redeeming Gender*, 140. Recall from Chapter 5 how this model runs the risk of downplaying the significance of concrete particulars.

53. Thatcher, *Gender and Christian Ethics*, 15. For Thatcher, these doctrinal foundations are the Trinity, Christology, and humanity in God's image (ibid.).

54. Ibid., 11.

55. Ibid., 147.

56. Ibid., 104.

57. Ibid., 140. Thatcher's parenthetical comment presumably refers to the terminology of *perichoresis* debuting in Christological debates (via Gregory of Nazianzus and later by Maximus the Confessor), before migrating to Trinitarian discourse (via John of Damascus). See Giulio Maspero, "La perichoresis e la grammatica teologica dei primi sette Concili ecumenici," *Theo* 4 (2020): 161–81.

58. Thatcher, *Gender and Christian Ethics*, 181.

59. Ibid., 197. Thatcher draws upon Richard Rohr, *The Divine Dance: The Trinity and Your Transformation* (New Kensington, PA: Whitaker House, 2016), 27. However, as Daniel Wade McClain rebuts, "There is no evidence whatsoever for linking *perichoresis* with the

B. Response: Problems with a Trinitarian Blueprint

Since Thatcher offers the most sustained proposal, my response focuses on his account. Positively, Thatcher intuits that theology proper informs theological anthropology, and this is via an appropriate appeal to "analogy,"[60] thereby affirming the "absolute binary . . . between uncreated and created being."[61] However, as Katherine Sonderegger advises, while anyone can affirm the difference between the Creator and creatures, the challenge "is the delicate one of *securing* such a primary distinction."[62] On this, Thatcher could strengthen his case by clarifying the *sui generis* nature of God's essence as distinct from created being, emphasizing divine aseity and simplicity,[63] as well as define his use of analogy (both of which would help him avoid collapsing or confusing the Creator/creature distinction).[64]

While these preceding points are important, for my purposes the plausibility of the Trinity functioning as a blueprint for SP hinges upon the theological legitimacy (and mechanism) of moving from the divine life to human life. Yet Thatcher's proposed transition, so vital for his thesis, remains dubious on several fronts, for it (i) lacks sufficient biblical support, (ii) fails to engage objections, (iii) suffers a category misapplication, (iv) remains historically aberrant.

First, Thatcher offers no biblical support for his Trinitarian Blueprint other than the observation that humans are made in the image of God (Gen. 1:26),[65] simply noting that "the very similarity of concepts in the case both of divine and human persons is more than coincidental or serendipitous."[66] But this seems to be an aspirational assertion more than an attuned argument. Humanity *may* mirror

---

activity of dancing, much less group dancing. . . . An adoptionistic, nonpersonal, flow-based Trinity takes us far from the field of anything resembling classical trinitarian discourse" ("What (Not) to Do with the Trinity: Doctrine, Discipline, and Doxology in Contemporary Trinitarian Discourse," *AThR* 100 [2018]: 609–10).

60. Thatcher, *Gender and Christian Ethics*, 103, 181.

61. Ibid., 9.

62. Katherine Sonderegger, *Systematic Theology: Volume 2, The Doctrine of the Holy Trinity: Processions and Persons* (Minneapolis: Fortress, 2020), 81, italics original.

63. Thatcher does not expand upon his assertion that God's essence is "single and indivisible" (*Gender and Christian Ethics*, 46).

64. Thatcher's employment of an undefined "analogy" appears worryingly univocal, thereby threatening the Creator/creature distinction so resolutely upheld by scripture and tradition. E.g., Gen. 1:1; Ps. 115:3; Eccles. 5:2; Rev. 4:11. For a nuanced account of "analogical equivocation," emphasizing the qualitative distinction between God's archetypal theology and humanity's ectypal theology as a "relief image," see Franciscus Junius, *A Treatise on True Theology: With the Life of Franciscus Junius*, trans. David C. Noe (Grand Rapids: Reformation Heritage, 2014), 103–6.

65. Examinations of *perichoresis* typically focus on John's gospel. E.g., Ciril Sorč, *Entwürfe einer perichoretischen Theologie*, TOW 5 (Münster: Lit, 2004), 54–60.

66. Thatcher, *Gender and Christian Ethics*, 139

Trinitarian relations perichoretically, but nothing in Gen. 1:26 necessitates the claim.

Second, while Thatcher recognizes Linn Tonstad's charge of "corrective projectionism,"[67] his hasty dismissal of Tonstad as "overstat[ing] her case" and introducing a "disconnection between the divine and the human" is insufficient.[68] Thatcher does not address Tonstad's specific complaint,[69] nor does he provide an explanation for *how* the infinite Trinity can shape finite sexual difference, including sexed embodiment. Again, the move is assumed.

Third, even if it were legitimate to move seamlessly from the divine life to human life,[70] application to sexed embodiment is harder to obtain. As a single, simple Spirit (John 4:24), God does not have a body.[71] In contrast, humans are inescapably embodied. Even if inner-Trinitarian relations inform human relationships, the analogy would refer at best to human relationality rather than embodiment. Yet, since intersexuality is an embodied condition, it remains unclear how divine ontology "directly" determines a single sexed spectrum, the grounds for SP. Moving from Trinitarian relations to SP suffers from a category misapplication.[72]

Fourth, the common appeal to Trinitarian *perichoresis* as a "silver bullet"[73] to explain the unity and diversity inherent within SP (whether in creation or new creation) must be analogical and not the apparently univocal use often implied. However, even an analogical employment of Trinitarian *perichoresis* is aberrant to its historic use. As Jung recognizes, the concept of *perichoresis* enters Trinitarian discourse via John of Damascus.[74] More precisely, Twombly demonstrates how

---

67. Linn Marie Tonstad, *God and Difference: The Trinity, Sexuality, and the Transformation of Finitude*, GTS 17 (New York: Routledge, 2016), 13.

68. Thatcher, *Gender and Christian Ethics*, 139.

69. Tonstad inveighs against the spatialized, invasive, penetrative logic of classical Trinitarian theology more generally, but her specific complaint that applies against Thatcher is that he seems to identify "certain problems of human existence" and then "generates a trinitarian theology" as the solution (*God and Difference*, 13). As such, idealized human difference is projected onto divine difference to justify his social agenda.

70. Or even make the weaker claim with Sonderegger that the unicity and multiplicity in sex/gender acts as a *vestigium* or echo or "*secular parable* of the Holy Trinity" (*Systematic Theology*, 229, italics original).

71. Thatcher affirms God's incorporeality, noting that "God is beyond sex" (*Gender and Christian Ethics*, 140).

72. Further, the direct line that Thatcher draws from the immanent Trinity to created reality seems to bypass the economy of salvation. In 1 Cor. 11:1, Paul does not exhort Christians to imitate the inner-Trinitarian life of God but the incarnate Christ, i.e., the human person in whom God has fully revealed God's Triune self in salvation history.

73. Christopher Woznicki, "Dancing around the Black Box: The Problem and Metaphysics of Perichoresis," *PC* 22 (2020): 103.

74. Jung, "Intersex on Earth," 185; John of Damascus, "The Orthodox Faith," I.8, in *Writings*, trans. Frederic H. Chase, FC 37 (New York: Fathers of the Church, 1958), 185–8.

Damascene appropriates the language of *perichoresis* from its Christological context to express the four vital adverbs of Chalcedon (without confusion, change, division, separation) in a Trinitarian register so as to provide "increased intelligibility to the notion of union-without-absorption."[75] Where Gregory Nazianzen and Maximus the Confessor had employed *perichorein* with the preposition *eis* + accusative to "signify the communication of idioms" in Christology, John Damascene reemployed *perichorein* with *en* + dative for Trinitarian theology.[76] The former focused on Christological "nature-perichoresis," the latter on Trinitarian "person-perichoresis."[77] It is specifically "person-perichoresis" that the "Trinitarian Blueprint" argument attempts to appropriate for SP in heaven.

However, a closer examination of Damascene indicates that "it is impossible [ἀδύνατον] for this [Trinitarian person-*perichoresis*] to be found in any created nature."[78] In the section of *De fide orthodoxa* that Jung cites, John allows the terms *ousia/physis* and *hypostasis* to operate analogously with humanity, but when it comes to Trinitarian person-*perichoresis* he asserts that any analogy between humanity and God is "quite the contrary" (ἀνάπαλιν).[79] Damascene goes on to propose what Twombly calls a "reversed analogy . . . . [Where] human life is such and such; God's life is just the opposite."[80] Indeed, Damascene doubles down on Trinitarian person-*perichoresis* being the exclusive prerogative of the inner-divine life when he insists that because of the infinite qualitative difference between God and creation,[81] creatures relate to God not by *perichoresis* but through μετέχειν (participating).[82]

In short, *contra* Thatcher (and others who appeal to Trinitarian *perichoresis* to ground SP) proper historical attention to John's use of *perichoresis* (and μετέχειν), negatively avoids the tendency of attaching "quasi-substantial descriptions to the Names,"[83] and positively upholds the Creator/creature distinction, ensuring

75. Charles C. Twombly, *Perichoresis and Personhood: God, Christ, and Salvation in John of Damascus*, PrinTMS 216 (Eugene, OR: Pickwick, 2015), 42.

76. Emmanuel Durand, "Perichoresis: A Key Concept for Balancing Trinitarian Theology," in *Rethinking Trinitarian Theology: Disputed Questions and Contemporary Issues in Trinitarian Theology*, ed. Giulio Maspero and Robert J. Woźniak (London: T&T Clark, 2012), 179.

77. Oliver Crisp, *Divinity and Humanity: The Incarnation Reconsidered*, CIT (Cambridge: Cambridge University Press, 2007), 1–33.

78. John of Damascus, "Orthodox Faith," I.14 (PG 94:859).

79. Ibid., I.8 (PG 94:828).

80. Twombly, *Perichoresis and Personhood*, 43.

81. Note how John brackets his positive doctrine of the Trinity (chapters 5–8) with a strong affirmation of divine transcendence, infinity, and incomprehensibility (chapters 1–4 and 9–14).

82. John of Damascus, "Orthodox Faith," I.8 (PG 94:821).

83. Sonderegger, *Systematic Theology*, 564. Dogmatically, *perichoresis* "must govern the Divine Relata and keep watch over the Radical Unicity of God" (ibid.).

that God retains power to save and is worthy of worship. John reserves person-*perichoresis* exclusively for the mystery of the Trinity, for it necessarily encapsulates the perfect diversity in unity that Trinitarian persons alone enjoy.

Admittedly, narrating historical reservations about employing person-*perichoresis* analogously to humanity in general is not a decisive refutation of its usage. More minimally, if the concept of person-*perichoresis* has any anthropological application,[84] then we must be clear that (i) it is only a weak analogy, and (ii) we should not neglect to delineate fundamental dissimilarities.[85] Thatcher's "Trinitarian Blueprint" remains insufficient on both counts. Significantly, while Thatcher initially claims that humanity as a perichoretically circular continuum, including sexed embodiment, "follows *plausibly* and *directly* from doctrinal foundations,"[86] toward the end of his project, Thatcher accepts the criticism that he finds "in Christian doctrines only what [he] want[s] to find."[87] Thus, Thatcher pares down his original claim to a mere "hope to demonstrate plausibility, no more."[88] As he acknowledges, the "stimulus for reading the tradition differently," and I would submit selectively,[89] is the "anguish of marginalised people" and the authority of contemporary science.[90] While I want to downplay neither the voice of the marginalized nor insights from the book of nature, Thatcher's admission suggests that he ultimately grounds his claims for a sexed continuum in an

---

84. For example, possibly in John 14:20; 17:21–23. For a cautious assessment of the dogmatic function of person-*perichoresis* and its anthropological application, see D. Glenn Butner, *Trinitarian Dogmatics: Exploring the Grammar of the Christian Doctrine of God* (Grand Rapids: Baker Academic, 2022), 133–52. Although, note Twombly's observation of Damascene: "Never is the word [*perichoresis*] used to identify the bond that exists between God and the created world or the saving relationship that unites baptized believers to God (or Christ or eternal life)" (*Perichoresis and Personhood*, 93). That Christological discourse may have adopted the concept of *perichoresis* from Neoplatonist anthropology, see Aloys Grillmeier, *Christ in Christian Tradition: Volume Two: From the Council of Chalcedon (451) to Gregory the Great (590–604): Part Two: The Church of Constantinople in the Sixth Century*, trans. John Cawte and Pauline Allen (London: Mowbray, 1995), 34–40. But again, the "Trinitarian blueprint" argues for person-*perichoresis*, not the parts-*perichoresis* (body-soul) of Neoplatonic anthropology.

85. See the famous maxim of Lateran IV: "Between the Creator and the creature there cannot be a likeness (*similtudo*) so great that the unlikeness (*dissimiltudo*) is not greater" (Henry Joseph Schroeder, ed., "Twelfth Ecumenical Council: Lateran IV 1215," in *Disciplinary Decrees of the General Councils: Text, Translation, and Commentary* [St. Louis, MO: Herder, 1937], Canon 2 [241]).

86. Thatcher, *Gender and Christian Ethics*, 15, italics added.

87. Ibid., 183.

88. Ibid.

89. Note the comment on divine simplicity above, as well as his ambivalence to Creedal relations of origin (ibid., 138). Thatcher refers to the Athanasian Creed.

90. Ibid., 183.

empirically informed natural theology, rather than in divine ontology proper as intended.

Therefore, given the lack of direct biblical support, a failure to engage objections, a category misapplication of relationality to embodiment, an historically aberrant use of Trinitarian person-*perichoresis* compounded by a selective reading of the tradition, and finally, a prioritizing of lived experience for theological exploration, the "Trinitarian Blueprint" argument for intersex in heaven (or equally creation) remains problematic, following neither "plausibly" nor "directly from doctrinal foundations."[91] Nonetheless, intersex in heaven could still be possible on other grounds.

III. Bodily Identity and Intersexuality

A. Claim 1: The Normativity of Jesus' Scars

A further argument for intersex in heaven highlights the scars (τύποι) of Jesus' post-resurrection body in John 20:24–29,[92] arguing that if Jesus' identity-constitutive bodily impairments last, so too will ours, including the impairment of intersexuality. Representatively, Susannah Cornwall draws upon Nancy Eiesland to submit the most sustained appeal to the normativity of Jesus' resurrection scars.[93] Cornwall suggests that "if God has come to inhabit *this, Jesus'* unexpected, non-dominant body, the way is opened for other unexpected, non-dominant bodies to reflect and live God too. The resurrected Jesus, with his impaired hands and feet, *is* God's revelation of a new humanity."[94] Jesus' "wounds" are "not to be vilified, nor to be pitied; they are marks of life experience, and signposts to a new kind of life."[95] Jesus' scars establish his identity, and so mark *his* resurrected body.[96] If the eschaton erases the specificity of my present embodiment, then my identity is eradicated. It

---

91. Ibid., 15.

92. While many render τύπος simply as "wound," Moss has persuasively demonstrated that since τύπος typically refers to the effect of "a blow or pressure" (BDAG, 1019), the marks on Jesus' body are not open holes but "healing or scarred wounds" (Moss, *Divine Bodies*, 29).

93. Nancy L. Eiesland, *The Disabled God: Toward a Liberatory Theology of Disability* (Nashville, TN: Abingdon, 1994), 99–100.

94. Cornwall, "Kenosis," 195, italics original.

95. Ibid.

96. "Scars were the ultimate form of identification in the ancient world" (Moss, *Divine Bodies*, 31). E.g., Odysseus' scar in Homer, *Odyssey: Books 13–24* 19.467–75, trans. A. T. Murray, LCL 105 (Cambridge, MA: Harvard University Press, 1995), 268–9. Thus, Jesus' scars testify that he is not a ghost, for "real bodies heal themselves" (ibid., 36).

is not *me* in heaven—not to me, not to others, nor to God.[97] But as the "firstfruits" of the final resurrection (1 Cor. 15:20; cf. Phil. 3:21; 1 John 3:2), Jesus' identity-constituting scars are normative for our eschatological embodiment. Thus, given the "exemplary" status of "the wounded risen Christ," Jung concludes that "some persons will rise transformed into glory as recognizably intersex."[98]

B. Claim 2: "Body-Story" plus "Eccentric Grounding"

Noting the historical particularity of Jesus' scars, Cornwall argues that the unique specificity of our bodily identity (including its sexed condition) is not metaphysically fixed, but socio-historically fluid. We see this presently at the *individual* level, where the body undergoes an impressive set of changes from conception to coffin. Cornwall continues: "The sexuate nature of a single given individual across their lifespan—is as much shifting, transient and uncertain as it is stable, permanent and irreducible."[99] The fluid meaning of the body is also inscribed *corporately*, since "bodies are made and emblazoned by socio-cultural narratives, and in turn constitute, propagate, appraise and contest such narratives."[100] Thus, bodies are "ecstatic" palimpsests, being both "socially-constructed and self-directing," thereby rejecting "any finality or fixity of meaning for themselves."[101] Cornwall labels the resultant identities as "body-stories."[102]

Given such a strong account of how the body itself (and not purely its interpretation) is fluid, any claim for numerical identity in the eschaton would be hard to substantiate. As such, Cornwall asserts that the meaning (and so identity) of the body is not completely fluid but is grounded eccentrically in God.[103] Here, Cornwall appropriates David Kelsey's proposition that human identity is "centered outside itself in the triune God in regard to its being, value, destiny, identity, and proper existential orientations to its ultimate and proximate contexts."[104] Yes, our

---

97. Recognizability is of central importance within much disability theology. E.g., Frances M. Young, *God's Presence: A Contemporary Recapitulation of Early Christianity*, CIT (Cambridge: Cambridge University Press, 2013), 107.

98. Jung, "Intersex on Earth," 182.

99. Susannah Cornwall, "Faithfulness to Our Sexuate Bodies: The Vocations of Generativity and Sex," in *Thinking Again About Marriage: Key Theological Questions*, ed. John P. Bradbury and Susannah Cornwall (London: SCM, 2016), 114. Although, for Cornwall, what qualifies the body as "stable, permanent and irreducible" seems to be *that* we are embodied rather than any particular bodily configuration or norm.

100. Cornwall, *Sex and Uncertainty*, 233.

101. Ibid.

102. Cornwall, "What Is Better," 385. For a similar account of "nature" being "obviously shapeable and malleable," with creation as a "backdrop" and not a "prison," see idem, *Constructive Theology and Gender Variance*, 214–15.

103. Cornwall, "Rhetorics of Disability," 107.

104. Kelsey, *Eccentric Existence*, 2:893.

bodies participate in "mutual making,"[105] but "the meanings of our embodiment *exceed* the social hegemonies to which we are subject."[106] As such, our "fundamental identity is identity in God."[107] For Cornwall, the primacy of "human existence as grounded outside itself in God means that human ideology (even in areas that have often been unquestioned or theologically sanctioned, like the assumption that to be human is to have a clear binary sex as male or female) is also relativized."[108] The only stable assurance of bodily meaning and identity (both now and in heaven) is grounded extrinsically in God.[109] Such emphasis on our eccentric existence allows Cornwall to uphold an account of radical particularity and embodied diversity.[110]

Consequently, thinking specifically about eschatological embodiment, if I am my body, and the meaning of my body is constructed individually and socially throughout my personal history, then my complete body-story must endure into the new creation if what exists in heaven is truly *me*. Here, Cornwall applies Jürgen Moltmann's "*Gestalt* theology," which emphasizes "wholeness" and "integration," and operates "as shorthand for the way in which we recognize ourselves."[111] "Everything that is bound up with a person's name," Moltmann maintains, "is 'preserved' in the resurrection and transformed: . . . The whole configuration of the person's life, the whole life history, and all the conditions that are meant by his or her name."[112] Thus, "Eschatologies for intersex people," Cornwall opines, must "assert a goodness of the valuing of lived body-stories."[113]

Cornwall appeals to Augustine to support her case for eccentrically grounded whole "body-stories" as constituting numerical identity in heaven. For Augustine, Cornwall surmises, "Physical 'perfection' in the resurrection body is less significant than right relationship and the eradication of inequity in bodies. This applies to

105. Cornwall, *Sex and Uncertainty*, 92.

106. Cornwall, "Rhetorics of Disability," 114.

107. Ibid., 115.

108. Ibid.

109. I use "extrinsic" as a synonym of "eccentric."

110. For a similar emphasis on concrete particularity within a proposal for SP, see Thatcher's employment of Duns Scotus' *haecceitas* in *Gender and Christian Ethics*, 103–7.

111. Cornwall, "What Is Better," 384. Moltmann defines *Gestalt* as "the configuration or total pattern—of the lived life" (*God in Creation: A New Theology of Creation and the Spirit of God* [Minneapolis, MN: Fortress, 1993], 259).

112. Jürgen Moltmann, *The Coming of God: Christian Eschatology*, trans. Margaret Kohl (Minneapolis, MN: Fortress, 1996), 75. For the significance of someone's "name" as their personal "life-history," see Moltmann, *God in Creation*, 262.

113. Cornwall, "What Is Better," 384–5. For a similar stress on "body-stories" determining identity, see Amos Yong, "Disability Theology of the Resurrection: Persisting Questions and Additional Considerations—A Response to Ryan Mullins," *ArsD* 12 (2012): 6. "Infants are thus raised as infants and octogenerians as octogenerians, etc., with each body marked variously according to the person's earthly journey."

variant sex and gender just as much as to impairment."[114] So, for Cornwall, when Augustine insists that nothing "naturally present in the body is going to perish. . . . [For] the substance itself is preserved as an integral whole,"[115] we should expect intersex conditions like CAIS or genetic mosaicism to endure into eternity. Mosaicism simply *is* the individual's biological substance, and an essential part of their body-story.[116] To demand physical perfection is not only arbitrary,[117] but would also turn "distinct individuals" into "indistinguishable items," which would amount to "their destruction."[118] Present intersex conditions endure into the new creation, which, as Augustine suggests, will be a "time . . . when we shall enjoy each other's beauty for itself alone, utterly without lust."[119] As Cornwall construes, we shall be freed from "the patriarchal-capitalist lust to perfect, correct, regulate, manage, dominate and homogenize," and freed to "embrace the fact that scars and stretch marks testify to the processes which have happened in and through bodies."[120]

To conclude, the "Body of Christ is intersexed, because its members (or constituents) include intersexed bodies,"[121] both now and "even in the blossoming of the new creation."[122] The normative particularity of Jesus' scars demands that our body-story, as our essential nature or "essence, *Gestalt*, [must be] carried forward,"[123] being grounded eccentrically in God. Concerning ecclesial and eschatological embodiment, "Differences and particularities in bodies persist: problems and limitations attached to those differences do not."[124]

C. Methodological Implication: Eschatology Trumps Creation

Via an appeal to the normativity of Jesus' scars and an emphasis on "body-stories" constituting the *Gestalt* of our resurrection identity, advocates for intersex in heaven aim to disrupt SD and open space for "'polymorphism in glory,' a rainbow

---

114. Cornwall, *Sex and Uncertainty*, 190.

115. Augustine, *Civ.* 22.19 (CCSL 48:838; WSA I/7:529).

116. Cornwall, *Sex and Uncertainty*, 191.

117. Ibid.

118. David A. Pailin, *A Gentle Touch: From a Theology of Handicap to a Theology of Human Being* (London: SPCK, 1992), 165. Cornwall cites Pailin approvingly.

119. Augustine, *Civ.* 22.24 (CCSL 48:851; WSA I/7:541). For a "neo-Augustinian theology of nature" that emphasizes the beauty of "mysterious mutations," and so a welcome for intersex bodies in heaven, see Merrick, "Welcome Intersexed?" Recall the response to Merrick's thesis in Chapter 4.

120. Cornwall, *Sex and Uncertainty*, 192.

121. Ibid., 108.

122. Ibid., 69.

123. Cornwall, "All Things," 51.

124. Cornwall, "Sex Otherwise," 37.

of sex."[125] Before evaluating these arguments, it is worth noting the shared conviction among revisionists that eschatology exerts immense pressure upon present-day ethics. As Rémy Bethmont observes, there is currently a "stronger eschatological awareness in the Western Church" that "emphasises the new reality of the New Creation, which surpasses rather than restores the perfection of the old."[126] In more truculent tone, Cornwall excoriates the "apotheosizing of origins" by traditionalists.[127] "Originalism," Cornwall criticizes, is "a kind of original sin," owing more to "Plato and Augustine than to the biblical canon itself."[128] Instead, Cornwall proposes the task of "Un/familiar theology" that privileges the "primacy of the eschatological" to queer the familiar of creation.[129] "Theology's rightful orientation to eschatological ends" is not simply a matter of emphasis,[130] for by necessity the eschatological trumps the "cult of originalism"[131] and "insists that whatever is to come colours and shapes what already is."[132]

If the eschatological is sexually polymorphic, then, as DeFranza opines, by "putting off the reordering of sex and gender to an eschatological future, significant harm will continue to be perpetuated in the present."[133] Likewise, Thatcher seeks to liberate our "eschatological imagination," being determined "to give pre-eminence to Jesus and the present and future hope of new life, over forced readings of Genesis and their alleged prescriptions for the social and moral order" that have been responsible for so much "violence against women and LGBTIQ people."[134] Therefore, as Jung concludes, since the church is called to live "in light of the new

---

125. Hare, "Afterword," 200.

126. Rémy Bethmont, "How Queer Can Christian Marriage Be? Eschatological Imagination and the Blessing of Same-Sex Unions in the American Episcopal Church," in *New Approaches in History and Theology to Same-Sex Love and Desire*, ed. Mark D. Chapman and Dominic Janes, GSH (Cham, Switzerland: Palgrave Macmillan, 2018), 212.

127. Cornwall, *Un/Familiar Theology*, 12.

128. Ibid., 12, 11. "Originalism" is not a wooden attempt to return to Eden. The "originalism" Cornwall inveighs against is the theological approach that gives "ontological primacy" to "orders of creation" (ibid., 11).

129. Ibid., 17–18.

130. Ibid., 157.

131. Ibid., 18.

132. Ibid., 167. See further James M. Childs, "Eschatology, Anthropology, and Sexuality: Helmut Thielicke and the Orders of Creation Revisited," *JSCE* 30:1 (2010): 3–20. For the growing appeal of an "'apocalyptic turn' in Christian dogmatics," which looks to develop "patterns of thinking that are fluid and continually open to the unexpected," see Michael Mawson and Samuel Tranter, "Guest Editorial: Apocalyptic Theology and Christian Ethics," *SCE* 34 (2021): 424.

133. DeFranza, *Sex Difference*, 251.

134. Thatcher, *Gender and Christian Ethics*, 112–13, 12. Thatcher goes on to castigate a traditional Christian sexual ethic with "heteronormative and complementarian assumptions" for perpetuating a "rape culture" of "epistemic violence" (ibid., 17–36).

creation," this "could well mean transgressing on earth any normative account of sex and gender that obscures the pluriform nature of the body's grace."[135] Since there will be intersex in heaven, theologies of intersexuality "must continue to query and critique the social and religious norms which curb the multiplicity and possibility of the sexed bodies which make up the Body of Christ."[136]

D. *Response 1: Problems with the Assumed Normativity of Jesus' Scars*

The preceding case for intersex in heaven does well to focus on the biblical particularity of Jesus' resurrection scars and demonstrates a concern for bodily continuity in heaven, laudably motivated by a care for the marginalized. However, at each stage of the hypothesis questions linger. Before offering a constructive account of sexed embodiment in the eschaton, I shall suggest several shortcomings of the innovationist case (chiefly represented by Cornwall), querying first the assumed normativity of Jesus' scars, then the serviceability of "body-story" plus an entirely "eccentric grounding" to ensure our numerical identity in heaven.

The biblical material proffered to justify intersex in heaven focuses on Jesus' resurrection body, particularly his scars mentioned in John 20:24–29 and Luke 24:36–43. As Cornwall evinces, "The resurrected Jesus, with his impaired hands and feet, *is* God's revelation of a new humanity."[137] Since Jesus is the "firstfruits" of the final resurrection (1 Cor. 15:23), his scarred body is paradigmatic. However, while the intuition to focus on the particularity of Jesus commendably recognizes Christology as the ultimate foundation for theological anthropology, the line between Jesus' scars and the expectation that we shall be raised with pre-mortem impairments is not as straightforward as initially assumed. Concerns cluster around (i) a seemingly arbitrary focus on Jesus' scars, and an underestimation of (ii) the uniqueness of Jesus' mission and (iii) the uniqueness of Jesus' two-stage resurrection/ascension.

First, Cornwall privileges Jesus' scars, yet ignores other features of his raised body, for example, instantly appearing in locked rooms (John 20:19, 26), vanishing without a trace (Luke 24:31), and knowing Thomas' thoughts from a week prior (John 20:27). Are these features equally normative or distinct to Jesus? Why focus on physical impairment, yet disregard intangibility? Second, there are hints that Jesus' scars may have a unique function tied to his specific mission, emphasizing his physical integrity (in Luke) and his numerical identity (in John) in order to elicit belief in him as the "Messiah, the Son of God" (John 20:28–31).[138] Even the

---

135. Jung, "Intersex on Earth," 196. Reference to "the body's grace" is an allusion to the seminal essay of Williams, "Body's Grace." Williams emphasizes the transformative grace that comes from knowing oneself as desired by God.

136. Cornwall, *Sex and Uncertainty*, 229.

137. Cornwall, "Kenosis," 195, italics original.

138. For literature on different interpretations of Jesus' scars, including antidocetic polemic, resurrection apologetics, and even as evidence that Jesus never really died, see Moss, *Divine Bodies*, 136 n.6.

intimation of Jesus remaining scarred in the heavenly tabernacle (Heb. 9:12)[139] and the new creation (Rev. 5:6) is explicitly tied to the uniqueness of his atoning work, further problematizing attempts to extend the normativity of Jesus' scars for others into the eschaton. Third, the uniqueness of Jesus' scars may be advanced by noting that Jesus remains the only person in scripture whose movement from earthly death to heavenly life was a two-stage process. Jesus was raised, and then forty days later ascended into heaven (Acts 1:3, 9, 11). If stage two (ascension) introduces bodily transformation, then the normativity of stage one (resurrection) is dubitable.[140]

Turid Karlsen Seim explores this question in Luke-Acts, noting several differences between Jesus' pre- and post-ascension body. In Luke 24, there is "an earthly, sarkic ordinariness about Jesus," who suggests touching and eating to dispel the fear that he is a πνεῦμα (v.39).[141] Yet the record of Jesus' post-ascension appearances in Acts (7:55–59; 9:3–9; 22:6–11; 26:12–18) are "characterised not by Jesus' bodily presence, but by the absence of any bodily form: there are no bodily features which would allow him to be recognised."[142] *Contra* Marcion, this does not mean the risen and ascended Jesus is without a body.[143] Stephen clearly sees Jesus "standing" (Acts 7:55–56) and Paul identifies Jesus with the geographical location of Nazareth (22:8).[144] Yet the "heavenly vision" (26:19) is of a heavenly

---

139. Although, note the recent suggestions that the presentation of Jesus' "blood" need not be literal (thus no need for continuing scars) but functions metonymically for Jesus' humanity (David M. Moffitt, *Atonement and the Logic of Resurrection in the Epistle to the Hebrews*, NovTSup 141 [Leiden: Brill, 2011]) or Jesus' death (R. B. Jamieson, *Jesus' Death and Heavenly Offering in Hebrews*, SNTSMS 172 [Cambridge: Cambridge University Press, 2019]).

140. Yet, note how in the *Martyrdom and Ascension of Isaiah* (c. second century AD), while Jesus transforms in his descent through the seven heavens, in his ascent "he was not transformed" (repeated three times in *Mart. Ascen. Isa.* 11:23–30). See James H. Charlesworth, ed., "Martyrdom and Ascension of Isaiah," in *The Old Testament Pseudepigrapha*, trans. Michael A. Knibb (Peabody, MA: Hendrickson, 2009), 2:175–6.

141. Turid Karlsen Seim, "The Resurrected Body in Luke-Acts: The Significance of Space," in *Metamorphoses: Resurrection, Body and Transformative Practices in Early Christianity*, ed. Turid Karlsen Seim and Jorunn Økland, Ekstasis 1 (Berlin: de Gruyter, 2009), 35.

142. Turid Karlsen Seim, "In Heaven as on Earth? Resurrection, Body, Gender and Heavenly Rehearsals in Luke-Acts," in *Christian and Islamic Gender Models in Formative Traditions*, ed. Kari Elisabeth Børresen, STTA 2 (Roma: Herder, 2004), 38.

143. Tertullian, "Against Marcion," 4.43, trans. Alexander Roberts and James Donaldson, *ANF* 3 (Buffalo: Christian Literature, 1885; reprint Peabody, MA: Hendrickson, 2004), 422. Tertullian records Marcion as referring to Jesus' risen body in Luke 24:39, but his logic applies equally to Jesus' ascended body.

144. That Jesus must be fully human to exercise his role as the ascended prophet, priest, and king, see Patrick Schreiner, *The Ascension of Christ: Recovering a Neglected Doctrine*, Snapshots (Bellingham, WA: Lexham, 2020).

Jesus, who is heard but not seen (v.14), appears as or in "light from heaven" (v.13), and who is identified by name (v.15) not bodily features. Indeed, the prominence of light and glory in the post-ascension appearances reported in Acts recall the transfiguration (Luke 9:28–36), where "the emphasis is on change, not so much on corporeal continuity."[145] As the early church underscored, especially Tertullian, the transfiguration was a revelatory "trailer of the heavenly, immortal Jesus, which entails a transformation of his bodily form different from its earthly physicality."[146]

Admittedly, the fact that the heavenly appearances of Jesus emphasize his name/light/glory, and the earthly appearances accentuate his scars, need not necessitate a sharp discontinuity between Jesus' pre- and post-ascension body per se. The differences in description may simply reflect the physical location of the body or reveal what the author chose to emphasize for various literary and theological purposes. However, Seim ruminates via 1 Cor. 15:38–41 that there is a "qualitative difference between earthly and heavenly" space, such that bodies ought to match their environment.[147] Jesus' resurrected body matches earthly space, and his ascended body fits heavenly space. Following Seim's logic, Jesus' scars pertain to his earthly location and should not necessarily be read as normative for heavenly embodiment. Admittedly, Seim seems to blur the biblical distinction between present heavenly space and future new creation space. Yet, even if new creation space shares qualities more akin to the present terrestrial realm (Rev. 21:1), Seim's observations regarding the differences between Jesus' pre- and post-ascension body (i.e., fit for their distinct environments) problematize the swift assumption that Jesus' post-resurrection scars are normative for eschatological embodiment.[148] As I develop in Augustinian key below, it is possible to affirm the importance of scars for resurrection identity, yet without innovationist implications.

E. Response 2: Problems with "Body-Story" plus "Eccentric Grounding"

The case for SP in heaven poses an important question. To what extent do present bodily configurations constitute essential identity such that they must persist into

---

145. Seim, "In Heaven," 38. For a speculative attempt to justify gender alignment and transitioning from the transfiguration, see Michelle Wolff, "A Diptych Reading of Christ's Transfiguration: Trans and Intersex Aesthetics Reveal Baptismal Identity," *ThS* 25 (2019): 98–110.

146. Seim, "Resurrected Body," 37. On Tertullian, see Caroline Walker Bynum, *Resurrection of the Body in Western Christianity, 200–1336* (New York: Columbia University Press, 1996), 42.

147. Seim, "Resurrected Body," 31.

148. Pushback against the normativity of Jesus' scars need not deny Jesus' paradigmatic significance for humanity. As submitted in Chapter 5, Christ is paradigmatic in assuming universal-essential properties, but his historical particular-accidental properties remain unique. Hence, *that* Jesus is sexed is paradigmatic; *what* Jesus is sexed is historically unique to him.

the new creation for me to be *me*? Here, Susannah Cornwall invokes Augustine to argue that our eschatologically enduring "essential nature" is our complete "body-story." Our present bodies are "ecstatic" palimpsests, continually reinscribed individually and socially. Numerical identity in heaven requires a resurrection of my body-story, which will include present intersex conditions (minus any physical or social pain). All this is possible because the *Gestalt* of my body-story is grounded eccentrically in God.

In her account of eschatological embodiment, Cornwall articulates a right concern for historical and social situatedness. Our stories matter to us, and they matter to the one who calls each of us by name (John 10:3). Further, Cornwall paraphrases Col. 3:3–4 well when commenting that our "fundamental identity is identity in God."[149] Nevertheless, challenges remain as to the logical and theological fittingness of Cornwall's argument for intersex in heaven. Accordingly, I focus first on whether identity is entirely grounded extrinsically, before, second, turning to assess the logic and implications of identity as "body-story." This opens space for my own constructive account of eschatological embodiment as it pertains to intersex, concentrating on bodily transformation in 1 Corinthians 15.

First, if my future resurrection body must be numerically identical with the essential nature of my present body-story, Cornwall's only stated justification for *how* my present diachronic identity can cross the temporal gap of death is her assertion that persistent identity is eccentrically grounded in God.[150] However, while divine freedom and determination is foundational in all good theology (e.g., Ps. 115:3), especially when it comes to embodiment (1 Cor. 15:38), it is not obvious on Cornwall's logic that an intersex person whose identity is entirely grounded extrinsically must be resurrected *as intersex*. If our "fundamental identity is identity in God," could not God resurrect us into a completely different resurrected form, and yet still know us as the distinct individuals we are? Indeed, our present bodies have already undergone an impressive set of changes from conception until now, none of which affects God's ability to know us as discrete people (Ps. 139:1–18).

Consequently, whatever the transformation in the eschaton, God would still know us as people whose bodies have undergone the set of changes associated with the resurrection. If our identity is entirely extrinsic, there does not appear to be sufficient reason to claim that any of the particularities of our present embodied condition *should* persist in heaven. On Cornwall's logic, God could resurrect a

149. Cornwall, "Rhetorics of Disability," 115.

150. Cornwall fails to cite any of the voluminous philosophical literature on identity and immortality, e.g., Kevin Corcoran, ed., *Soul, Body, and Survival: Essays on the Metaphysics of Human Persons* (Ithaca, NY: Cornell University Press, 2001). For an assessment of various strategies that *could* fit with Cornwall's physicalist sympathies, highlighting "replica," "reassembly," "simulacrum," "spatiotemporal gaps," and "constitution" theories, see Omar Fakhri, "Physicalism, Bodily Resurrection, and the Constitution Account," in *The Ashgate Research Companion to Theological Anthropology*, ed. Joshua R. Farris and Charles Taliaferro, ARC (Farnham, UK: Ashgate, 2015), 103–12.

presently intersex person as intersex, but equally he could not, and their true identity would not be affected at all. Indeed, nothing appears to forestall a doctrine of reincarnation, which would have problematic implications both for our recognizability to others (and perhaps ourselves),[151] and our assurance regarding the inherent goodness of our current concrete embodiment.

Cornwall could strengthen her case by supplementing her entirely extrinsic proposal with an account of that which is intrinsically essential for human identity. Admittedly, this would push Cornwall to develop a metaphysically thicker anthropology, forcing her to parse out anthropological essentials and accidentals. However, Cornwall's cumulative case for identity as "body-story" suggests she might resist a move toward metaphysics. Even if her appropriation of Augustine on enduring "substance" sounds metaphysical, she employs the terms to focus on the materially lived constitution of the body. Thus, my "substance" *is* my individual body-story.[152] Yet, since "the link between embodiment and temporality is essential,"[153] everything (not just an intersex condition) appears to be equally important in forming one's identity or "name" (even if I feel some things are more essential than others, e.g., a congenital impairment versus a broken leg).[154]

This raises a second problem. Recalling comments from Chapter 4 on the fall, if everything is essential, then nothing is accidental, and by extension, nothing can be deemed defective or problematic (at least absolutely). This fits with Cornwall's aversion to any physical, heavenly healing. Every impairment is identity constitutive, and so my impairment must last if my identity is to last. Yet, as Mullins notes in conversation with disability theology more broadly, such logic has several striking implications. First, considering medical ethics, if each impairment is identity constitutive, then eliminating disability (through research or surgery) is "eliminating a person."[155] Cornwall may desire better medical access and provision for intersex persons, but her logic appears to eviscerate the ability of medical professionals to diagnose and treat various conditions, a key concern motivating the use of "Differences of Sex Development" (DSD) terminology.[156]

---

151. Recall the concern of Frances Young in the footnote above. Ironically, for all the emphasis Cornwall places upon the social meaning of the body, her account of eschatological embodiment appears strikingly individualistic.

152. Cornwall's metaphysical anti-realism regarding the body relies upon Judith Butler. See Cornwall, *Sex and Uncertainty*, 12. For the perilous "Promethean Protagoreanism" of metaphysical anti-realism, see Nicholas Wolterstorff, *Practices of Belief: Selected Essays, Volume 2* (Cambridge: Cambridge University Press, 2010), 12–40.

153. Ibid., 189.

154. In short, Cornwall reads Augustine through Moltmann.

155. Ryan T. Mullins, "Some Difficulties for Amos Yong's Disability Theology of the Resurrection," *ArsD* 11 (2011): 28. E.g., "Every cochlear implant is a murder" (ibid.).

156. My criticism does not necessitate endorsing an exclusively medical model of disability.

Further, Cornwall's logic prompts us to reevaluate the healing ministry of Jesus. Rather than see Jesus' healing miracles as a "gospel for the body,"[157] evidencing his divinity and the in-breaking of his kingdom (Matt. 4:23; 9:35; John 5:17–30),[158] by healing "Jesus is eliminating people left and right in the gospels,"[159] causing us to question his moral character, and doubt his claim that God works inseparably with him (John 5:19).[160] Interestingly, if the overarching evil of impairment is social, as Cornwall maintains, and bodily healing is unnecessary, then perhaps Jesus' earthly ministry needed rethinking (cf. John 7:3–5). Perhaps Jesus should have left the sick and impaired alone and focused exclusively on changing attitudes within the dominant community. Cornwall's approach forces us to ask a falsely dichotomous question, "Is it the impairment that needs to be changed or the hearts of selfish independence?"[161]

Finally, considering the eschaton, although Cornwall affirms the absence of physical and social pain, if the root cause of pain persists (e.g., a chromosomal disorder resulting in genetic mosaicism), it is unclear why the resultant physical pain should not remain alongside (e.g., "a genetic predisposition to the development of tumors").[162] Social pain may have disappeared as the heavenly community is conformed to Christ in love,[163] but Cornwall does little to explain the removal of one's physical pain. Indeed, if my particularities are necessary for my individual identity, then how can my physical *or* social pain be removed without also obliterating *me*? Within Cornwall's schema, how can pain be a contingent feature of my identity, and yet intersex embodiment remain essential? Cornwall could respond that God simply *will* erase physical pain, but there is nothing intrinsic to the eschatological body that necessitates it.

In summary, Cornwall's case for intersex in heaven relies upon defining the substance of human identity as that which is constituted by my body-story. My eschatological body is my resurrected body-story, made possible because my identity is entirely grounded extrinsically in God, divorced from any intrinsic ordering. While I do not want to lose a strong account of divine determination for eschatological embodiment, an identity grounded entirely in an extreme

---

157. Jan-Olav Henriksen and Karl Olav Sandnes, *Jesus as Healer: A Gospel for the Body* (Grand Rapids: Eerdmans, 2016), 113–30.

158. In this sense, Jesus as "Healer" operates on multiple levels, a nuance Brock captures well in the title "Jesus as Restorer" (*Disability: Living into the Diversity of Christ's Body*, PFL [Grand Rapids: Baker Academic, 2021], 46–8).

159. Mullins, "Some Difficulties," 28.

160. Note the motifs of life and resurrection in John 5.

161. Ehrman, "Resurrection Identity," 737.

162. Ute Moog et al., "Disorders Caused by Genetic Mosaicism," *DAI* 117 (2020): 119–25.

163. Nevertheless, the extent to which a body-story constituted by negative experiences requires such negative experiences to continue into eternal life remains unclear in Cornwall's account.

divine voluntarism does not require that an intersex person be raised intersex for God to know that person as the same pre-resurrection individual. Further, identity as body-story suggests a vision of eschatological embodiment that has troubling implications for medical ethics, our view of Jesus' healing ministry, and the persistence of pain in heaven. Ironically, while Cornwall aims to champion the marginalized, her proposal dismantles hope for those who long for bodily transformation, potentially leading them into the temptation of despair.[164] Further, for all her emphasis on divine determination grounding human identity, Cornwall ironically seems to limit God's freedom to bring transformation (*qua* 1 Cor. 15:51–54). God's eschatological freedom to transform is restricted by my past (fallen) body-story, which makes one wonder in what way God will make everything new (Rev. 21:5)—if he even needs to.

F. Conclusion

I have offered several challenges to the Trinitarian, biblical, and theological arguments for intersex in heaven. Even if Trinitarian person-*perichoresis* somehow informs anthropology, since God is Spirit (John 4:24) any application of the divine life to human embodiment per se appears strained. Considering the biblical material, the normativity of Jesus' scars for eschatological embodiment is troubled when we note the uniqueness of Jesus' mission and resurrection process, as well as draw in other biblical evidence regarding his raised embodiment. Finally, innovationist theological reasoning about eschatologically enduring human identity so prioritizes our present body-story (often neglecting the impact of the fall) that bodily transformation is downplayed (*contra* 1 Cor. 15:50–53). Further, such an account requires persistent identity to be entirely grounded extrinsically in God. Yet this move does not necessitate that a presently intersex person be resurrected as intersex to be known as the same person. Given that the eschaton is a future reality, there may well be other reasons that intersexuality will exist in heaven. However, the principal arguments proposed thus far all face significant challenges, requiring an alternative approach.

IV. Constructive Account

Accounts for intersex in heaven tend to start with present-day identity-constituting impairments before moving to speculate about eschatological embodiment. While such proposals rightly value the historical and social concreteness of individuals, they fail to situate the heavenly body within scripture's grand theo-dramatic metanarrative of creation to eschatological consummation. Following the thick theological approach outlined above, the divine drama of grace furnishes a frame

---

164. For a juxtaposition of disability and the sin of "oppressive sorrow" (*tristitia aggravans*) in Aquinas, see Gondreau, "Healing of Infirmity," 95–6.

for the sexed body at every dramatic *act*, including the final consummation of all things.[165] The *locus classicus* for this strategy as it impinges upon eschatological embodiment is 1 Cor. 15:35–58, a passage conspicuously absent in much intersex literature.[166]

Accordingly, I assess the question of intersex in heaven by first exegeting portions of 1 Corinthians 15, highlighting Paul's emphasis on the necessity of somatic transformation to "inherit the kingdom of God" (v.50). While Paul's account of bodily change involves both continuity and discontinuity, I spotlight the disjunction between present and future embodiment due to its neglect among intersex innovationists. Yet, second, eschatological transformation need not result in agnostic, even apophatic, indeterminacy. Rather, since eschatological redemption both restores and transforms creation to its ordered peace, the sexed body in heaven will likely be unambiguously male or female (as in creation). Third, while the specter of "heavenly eugenics" may haunt my thesis, Augustine offers resources to envision a "heavenly eulogization" of intersex scars. God will heal bodily impairments, and where present impairments have cultivated virtue, God may inscribe former impairments as "marks of honor" to the delight of the City of God.[167]

A. Consummation Redemptively Transforms Creation

1. 1 Corinthians 15 and Bodily Transformation Cornwall's concentration on "body-story" to justify intersex in heaven overlooks the necessity of somatic transformation for eschatological embodiment. In 1 Corinthians 15, Paul tackles the objection of some within the Corinthian church that while they believe that Christ is risen (v.11),[168] they deny a general resurrection of the dead (v.12).[169] In response, for the sake of church unity (1:10) and authentic belief in the gospel

---

165. John Webster, "Eschatology, Anthropology and Postmodernity," *IJST* 2 (2000): 13–28.

166. While other NT passages speak of spiritual/bodily resurrection (e.g., 1 Cor. 6:13–14; 15:12–34; 2 Cor. 4:14; Eph. 2:4–7; Phil. 3:10–11; Col. 1:18; 2:11–13; 3:1–4; 1 Thess. 4:13–18) and somatic transformation in the eschaton (e.g., Rom. 6:4–1; 8:11; 18–25; 2 Cor. 5:1–10; Phil. 3:18–21; 1 John 3:2–3; Rev. 21:5), I focus on 1 Cor. 15:35–58 because Paul's strategy in answering the question of v.35 regarding the nature of eschatological embodiment is instructive for discerning intersex in heaven. For a thorough exegesis of the Pauline texts above, see Campbell, *Hope of Glory*, 167–203.

167. Augustine, *Civ.* 22.19 (CCSL 48:839; WSA I/7:530).

168. That Paul's interlocutors are probably a subgroup within the church, see Jeffrey R. Asher, *Polarity and Change in 1 Corinthians 15: A Study of Metaphysics, Rhetoric, and Resurrection*, HUT 42 (Tübingen: Mohr Siebeck, 2000), 36–48.

169. Dale B. Martin, *The Corinthian Body* (New Haven, CT: Yale University Press, 1995), 105–8. Martin suggests that "popular philosophy to deprecate the body" led the "Strong" to oppose the idea of a resurrected body (ibid., 107).

(15:2), Paul emphasizes "the necessity and plausibility" of the resurrection,[170] particularly of the body per se (vv.12–13, 16, 29–32), first outlining the "*fact*" (vv.1–34) and then the "*how*" of the resurrection (vv.35–58).[171]

To explicate the "kind of body [with which believers] will come" (v.35), Paul concludes that "flesh and blood cannot enter the kingdom of God . . . [thus] we shall all be changed" (vv.50–51).[172] This provides a strong assertion that "somatic transformation is absolutely necessary for resurrection life."[173] Paul twice employs the future passive of ἀλλάσσω (vv.51, 52). Here, Brock and Wannenwetsch discern a stress upon the "*divine* action of transformation, in that the adjective *alla*, 'other,' lays emphasis on our being 'othered' in the resurrection."[174] This revealed "μυστήριον" (v.51) of somatic transformation is an axiom that is universal in scope and indicates that "both the living and the dead will undergo a transformation, which is necessary to obtain the imperishable and glorious body that God created by analogy to the resurrection of the Messiah, who as life-creating Spirit effectuates this transformation."[175]

The bodily change Paul stresses in vv.50–52 hangs from a string of nine antitheses in vv.42–49. These contrasting couplets distinguish between the creational and eschatological body, epitomized respectively by Adam and Christ.[176] The central antithesis is in v.44, where Paul states via his famous seed metaphor (cf. John 12:24) that our somatic transformation involves the sowing in death of our "σῶμα ψυχικόν" ("ensouled earthly body") and the sprouting in life of our "σῶμα

---

170. Victor Paul Furnish, *The Theology of the First Letter to the Corinthians*, NTT (Cambridge: Cambridge University Press, 1999), 109.

171. Douglas J. Moo, *A Theology of Paul and His Letters: The Gift of the New Realm in Christ*, BTNT (Grand Rapids: Zondervan Academic, 2021), 153, italics original.

172. The climax is syntactically marked in v.50 by the emphatic metacomment "τοῦτο δέ φημι" (Timothy A. Brookins and Bruce W. Longenecker, *I Corinthians 10–16: A Handbook on the Greek Text*, BHGNT [Waco, TX: Baylor University Press, 2016], 179–80). Perhaps prompted by the passing of Paul of his generation, some early manuscripts move the negative particle from the first clause to the final clause ("we shall all sleep, but we shall not all be changed," e.g., ℵ, C), while others conflate the two readings (e.g., P46, A). Yet the current wording both explains the variant readings and enjoys strong external support.

173. Sarah Harding, *Paul's Eschatological Anthropology: The Dynamics of Human Transformation*, ES (Minneapolis, MN: Fortress, 2015), 365.

174. Brian Brock and Bernd Wannenwetsch, *The Therapy of the Christian Body: A Theological Exposition of Paul's First Letter to the Corinthians* (Eugene, OR: Cascade, 2018), 2:224, italics original.

175. Eckhard J. Schnabel, *Der erste Brief des Paulus an die Korinther*, HTA (Wuppertal, Germany: R. Brockhaus, 2006), 982–3.

176. That Adam is employed as a prelapsarian parallel is evident in Paul's appropriation (and adaptation) of Gen. 2:7 (LXX).

πνευματικόν" ("enspirited risen body," v.44).[177] This core contrast is illuminated by the surrounding antitheses.

Represented by "the first man Adam" (v.45), our "ensouled earthly body" is characterized by a *constitution* that is physically (and morally) corruptible (φθορά, v.42),[178] a *status* that is dishonorable (ἀτιμία, v.43), and a *capability* that is inherently weak (ἀσθένεια, v.43).[179] In contrast, "the last Adam" (v.45) reveals a body raised with an incorruptible *constitution* (ἀφθαρσία, v.42), a glorious *status* (δόξα, v.43), and a powerful *capability* (δύναμις, v.43). Like the first Adam, creation bodies passively receive life. But the last Adam is an active "life-giving spirit" (πνεῦμα ζῳοποιοῦν, v.45). Like "the first human" was "of the earth, [so] dusty" (ἐκ γῆς χοϊκός, v.47), we too are "the dusty ones" (οἱ χοϊκοί, v.48) bearing the image of "the dusty one" (τοῦ χοϊκοῦ, v.49).[180] But as "the second human" is "of heaven" (ἐξ οὐρανοῦ), so too are "the heavenly ones" (οἱ ἐπουράνιοι, v.48), bearing the image of "the heavenly one" (τοῦ ἐπουρανίου, v.49). Here, Paul employs the multivalent preposition ἐκ to *denote* the source of our existence and *connote* something of the inherent qualities of each source, that is, corruptibility, dishonor, weakness vs. incorruptibility, glory/honor, power.

Thus, Tappenden's rendering of σῶμα ψυχικόν as "ensouled earthly body" and σῶμα πνευματικόν as "enspirited risen body" captures well the cumulative contrast between the bodies of creation and new creation, and hence the need for somatic transformation in the eschaton. While Tappenden probably dismisses too quickly the majority opinion that ψυχικόν and πνευματικόν emphasize ethical agency,[181] Tappenden rightly avers that the "stress is very much upon the somatic exterior: it will be a body that is qualitatively appropriate both for the heavens and the indwelling πνεῦμα (contra the present earthly body of flesh and blood)."[182] Indeed, offering an approach paralleling Seim above, Tappenden concludes that

---

177. Frederick S. Tappenden, *Resurrection in Paul: Cognition, Metaphor, and Transformation*, ECL 19 (Atlanta, GA: SBL, 2016), 118. Translations that capture the intended meaning of σῶμα ψυχικόν and σῶμα πνευματικόν are notoriously challenging. Noting the earlier use of ψυχικός and πνευματικός in 1 Cor. 2:12–15, the scholarly consensus is that the present contrast is not material/immaterial (Harding, *Eschatological Anthropology*, 361–5). However, while the NRSV, NIV, NASB, ESV, and KJV distinguish between the "natural/ physical body" and the "spiritual body," Tappenden queries these translations for implying a Cartesian matter/nonmatter dualism—at least to modern ears, thus "obscuring rather than illuminating the passage" (*Resurrection*, 115 n.71). For a history of interpretation, see Anthony C. Thiselton, *The First Epistle to the Corinthians: A Commentary on the Greek Text*, NIGTC (Grand Rapids: Eerdmans, 2000), 1276–81.

178. Note Paul's use of φθορά in 1 Cor. 9:25 in reference to the crown that does not last.

179. Since Paul has the first prelapsarian Adam in view, these characteristics are not pejorative.

180. BDAG, 1086.

181. Tappenden, *Resurrection*, 20–1.

182. Ibid., 120.

the bodies of creation and resurrection are "qualitatively discontinuous with one another because of their cosmo-somatic locations."[183] For Paul, "Eschatological transformation concerns not only the body but also the body's location within the cosmos."[184] Thus, following Fee, the transformed body is "adapted to the eschatological existence that is under the ultimate domination, and animated by, the Spirit."[185] All of this suggests that given its new environment, somatic transformation is essential for eschatological embodiment.[186]

Paul's emphasis on the necessity of bodily change stands in contrast to Cornwall's presentation of eschatological embodiment. This is not to say that Cornwall disregards the motif of heavenly transformation *in toto*,[187] yet her wider proposal prioritizes a social change that overlooks somatic change.[188] Undoubtedly, as indicated above, social harmony is an eschatological blessing (e.g., Rev. 7:9), the foretaste of which Paul has already illuminated in 1 Corinthians 12–14. Yet social dynamics do not exhaust transformation, as 1 Corinthians 15 demonstrates.

Moreover, adapting the critique of Brock and Wannenwetsch, Cornwall's stress on "body-story" as some "*ens continuum*" inevitably denies "the necessity of the seed really to die . . . [and] thus evacuate[s] [the resurrection] of its transformational potency."[189] Cornwall's account of social *sans* somatic change so stresses continuity that it minimizes the impact of sin and death upon the body, and so the need for actual transformation. Ironically, it seems that death is not swallowed up in victory (1 Cor. 15:54–57) but keeps decaying and devouring bodies that groan for redemption (Rom. 8:23). Nevertheless, by emphasizing somatic transformation, is eschatological embodiment unanchored and discontinuous with the current creation?

2. Creation Contours Consummation In 1 Corinthians 15, Paul privileges divinely determined eschatological transformation, a motif that innovationist accounts

183. Ibid., 132.

184. Ibid., 87.

185. Fee, *First Corinthians*, 869.

186. A fuller examination of the necessity of somatic transformation would include exegeting 2 Cor. 5:1–10 and Phil. 3:21. E.g., note the "swallowing" (καταπίνω) metaphor in 2 Cor. 5:4 (cf. 1 Cor. 15:54), "an image of consumption that implies the terminal end of that which is ingested" (Tappenden, *Resurrection*, 130).

187. Cornwall, *Sex and Uncertainty*, 234.

188. Ibid., 182–4.

189. Brock and Wannenwetsch, *Therapy of the Christian Body*, 2:215, italics original. Brock and Wannenwetsch seem to recognize the incompatibility of "body-story" and an entirely "eccentric grounding" for numerical identity in heaven. However, while they appreciate that there must be some continuity to forestall "a complete undoing and denial of the first creation," they appear to accentuate an extreme account of divine voluntarism, basing all continuity in God's "remembering" (cf. Ps. 8:4, referenced in light of Ps. 8:6. being cited in 1 Cor. 15:27) (ibid., 2:214).

overlook. Yet emphasizing such transformation does not legitimize complete eschatological indeterminacy, where SD and SP (even androgyny) are equally likely.[190] Intriguingly, as Paul develops an answer to the question regarding raised embodiment (v.35), he does not first appeal to the resurrected flesh of Jesus (*qua* revisionists) but draws heavily upon the creation accounts in Genesis 1–2. This is because in Paul's mind, creation contours consummation.[191]

We see this in several places. For example, in 1 Cor. 15:38 Paul emphatically fronts ὁ δὲ θεὸς to accentuate God's prerogative and power to give specific embodiment in creation (and new creation [v.42]). Schnabel identifies "the decisive vocabulary" that links v.38 with Gen. 1:11–12 as δίδωσιν and ἠθέλησεν.[192] Thus, *creatura* circumscribes *creatio*.[193] This stress on divine determination echoes the divine fiat of "God said . . . and it was so" in Gen. 1:9, 11, 14, 15, 24. Second, God not only gives each "seed" a body, but to each one its "own body," ἴδιον σῶμα in v.38b echoing למינ- in Gen. 1:11, 12, 21, 24, 25.[194] Indeed, the strong emphasis on distinctly ordered kinds is marked syntactically by the repetition of ἄλλος (x4 in v.39; x3 in v.41), and the threefold recurrence of δέ in correlation with μέν (v.39).[195] Third, in vv.39–41 Paul catalogues creation days 4–6 in reverse order, perhaps to highlight the subject of concern for the Corinthians. Finally, that Paul has in mind the creation narrative is evident by his direct quotation of Gen. 2:7 (LLX) in v.45, supplemented slightly with the addition of "πρῶτος" and "Ἀδάμ."

While this catena of creation allusions is widely recognized,[196] the rationale for Paul's strategy may be elucidated further. Minimally, it could be that Paul draws upon creation motifs because they provide him with the lexical, idiomatic, and conceptual tools to describe the new creation body. However, if the Corinthians just needed educating about the nature of the resurrection body, then as Brown

---

190. For an historical survey of the church's attitude to eschatological androgyny, see Leah DeVun, "Heavenly Hermaphrodites: Sexual Difference at the Beginning and End of Time," *PostM* 9 (2018): 132–46.

191. The same conclusion may be reached by attending to Revelation 21–22. See Bruce Riley Ashford and Craig G. Bartholomew, *The Doctrine of Creation: A Constructive Kuyperian Approach* (Downers Grove, IL: IVP Academic, 2020), 308–15.

192. Schnabel, *Der erste Brief*, 961.

193. Recall Chapter 4.

194. This is an echo rather than a quotation because the LXX renders למינ- as κατὰ γένος.

195. Bringing points 1 and 2 together, Wolfgang Schrage suggests that the phrase "ἴδιον σῶμα" brings "the entirety of creation into view in its differentiation," and so stresses the scope of God's absolute life-giving power (*Der erste Brief an die Korinther*, EKKNT 7 [Düsseldorf: Benziger, 1991], 4:288).

196. For representative literature, other creation allusions, and a strong case for Paul's dependency upon the creation accounts in Genesis, see Roy E. Ciampa and Brian S. Rosner, *The First Letter to the Corinthians*, PiNTC (Grand Rapids: Eerdmans, 2010), 801–9.

suggests, "Paul could have simply identified Jesus as the exemplar."[197] Ultimately, this is where Paul takes his argument (vv.45–49). But his prior appeal to the edenic narrative suggests that creation necessarily informs eschatology, not just lexically or idiomatically, but more purposively.

Although the Corinthians had believed the gospel (v.11), they had fallen into the "foolish" error of denying the resurrection body (v.36). As Brown suggests, the Corinthians' "working presuppositional narrative was informed primarily by Greek mythology."[198] As such, they lacked an adequate biblical framework to protect them from false thinking. In response, Paul outlines a theo-dramatic metanarrative from creation to consummation (hence the Adam-Christ typology) within which he subsequently locates his presentation of Jesus as the ideal. As Wright writes, "Paul is setting up categories from the created order to provide a template of understanding for the new creation."[199] This "template" of creation contouring new creation operates not merely at the conceptual level but permeates *der Tiefenstruktur* or "deep structure" of the eschaton itself.[200] That our eschatological embodiment has its *Tiefenstruktur* rooted in creation may be explicated by recalling the dynamic between "structure" and "direction."

3. Theological Clarification: "Structure" and "Direction" Summing up the exegetical observations gleaned from 1 Corinthians 15 across Chapters 5 and 6, redemption involves both restoration and transformation. I argued in Chapter 5, from 1 Cor. 15:20–28, that "redemption restores creation." The resurrection of Christ, O'Donovan demands, is "God's final and decisive word on the life of his creature, Adam."[201] In reversing Adam's decision to die (v.22), God restores his original affirmation that Adam should live, vindicating creation. Yet, as expounded so far in this chapter, God's affirmation of life also "goes beyond and transforms the initial gift of life" (v.45).[202] Thus, 1 Corinthians 15 intimates that "in the resurrection of Christ creation is restored *and* the kingdom of God dawns."[203] "The resurrection of Christ . . . vindicates the created order in this double sense: it redeems it and it transforms it."[204] In short, consummation both restores and transforms creation.

---

197. Brown, *Bodily Resurrection*, 180.

198. Ibid., 181.

199. N. T. Wright, *The Resurrection of the Son of God*, COQG 3 (Minneapolis, MN: Fortress, 2003), 341.

200. The use of *Tiefenstruktur* comes from Hermann Häring's analysis of Augustine's eschatology ("Eschatologie," in *Augustin Handbuch*, ed. Volker Henning Drecoll, 2nd ed., HT [Tübingen: Mohr Siebeck, 2014], 546).

201. O'Donovan, *Resurrection and Moral Order*, 13.

202. Ibid., 14.

203. Ibid., 15, italics added.

204. Ibid., 56.

The definition of and dynamic between "restoration" and "transformation" may be clarified when read through the previously employed lenses of "structure" and "direction." As I submitted in Chapter 4, while sin and death misdirect and disorder the sexed body, causing it to disintegrate toward decay, the sexed body's metaphysical structure is not destroyed. Humans remain human, even if we possess accidental impairments, including intersex conditions.[205] In Chapter 5, I argued that redemption "now" inaugurates a restoration (and transformation) of God's creational intent that pertains to "our inner self" (2 Cor. 4:16), that is, restoration "now" is spiritual and social. Whether intersex, female, or male, we become children of God through faith in Christ (Gal. 3:26)—liberated and Spirit-indwelt to relate rightly to God and others. As Bavinck notes, this regeneration does not "introduce any new substance into the existing creation."[206] It is a spiritual and social re-formation, not a structural re-creation.

The claim so far in this chapter is that eschatological redemption "not yet" completes the restoration and transformation of creation, perfecting at the consummation the creational structure of humanity—spiritually, socially, and somatically. Following Bavinck again, "Whereas Jesus came the first time to establish [his] kingdom in a spiritual sense, he returns at the end of history to give *visible* shape to it. Reformation proceeds from the inside to the outside. The rebirth of humans is completed in the rebirth of creation."[207] For our "inner self," restorative transformation finalizes the redemption begun at Christ's first coming, a telos that has been described historically in terms of intellectual Beatific Vision.[208] For our somatic "outer self," restorative transformation is sudden and total (1 Cor. 15:52). We are structurally the same, remaining metaphysically human, and yet we exemplify "heavenly" qualities that go beyond the "dusty" of creational intent (1 Cor. 15:47–49).[209]

To encapsulate the motif of transformation as it relates to human persons *in toto*, Christian tradition has historically employed the language of *theosis* or deification.[210] Importantly, *theosis* is not *apotheosis*, an ontological migration from humanity to divinity.[211] That would be both heretical and impossible. Divinization does not involve "the 'de-hominization' of man or the 'uncreation' of the created world; but

205. Accidental in the metaphysical sense, rather than existentially incidental.

206. Bavinck, *RD*, 4:92.

207. Ibid., 4:718, italics added.

208. For an historical overview see Hans Boersma, *Seeing God: The Beatific Vision in Christian Tradition* (Grand Rapids: Eerdmans, 2018).

209. Thus, the proposal exhibits certain parallels with an Irenaean maturation of creation (in a consummative key).

210. Most famously, "God became man so that man might become God" (Athanasius, *Incarnation* 54 [PPS 44b:107]).

211. James Starr, "Does 2 Peter 1:4 Speak of Deification?" in *Partakers of the Divine Nature: The History and Development of Deification in The Christian Traditions*, ed. Michael J. Christensen and Jeffery A. Wittung (Grand Rapids: Baker Academic, 2008), 81–92.

it does succeed in conveying the truth that man is summoned to a destiny that is not given immediately in his creation."[212] "With the fulfilment of history in Christ behind" and the "peace-giving of God before," at the consummation we enter into "Rest," enjoying "wholeness of form as well as wholeness of accomplished destiny."[213]

Consequently, scripture testifies to both "restoration" and "transformation" motifs, and affirming both is vital for a correct apprehension of eschatological embodiment. The "transformation" rubric reminds us that while creational "flesh and blood cannot inherit the kingdom of God" (1 Cor. 15:50), God graciously "fashions" (2 Cor. 5:5) what we need to be "at home with the Lord" (2 Cor. 5:8). The necessity of transformation signals that we are saved *from* something (death) and saved *for* something (deification). Importantly, this new work of God is *sola gratia* and *solo Christo*.[214] As O'Donovan opines, "The fulfilment of history is not generated immanently from within history . . . [but is] a work 'from outside.'"[215]

The "restoration" rubric reaffirms that God graciously transforms within the structures of creation. As the temporal and telic logic between the first and last Adam in 1 Cor. 15:45–49 indicates, there is a sense in which God sews into the fabric of creation a teleological (properly eschatological) thrust toward consummation.[216] In Augustinian key,[217] the Father gives creation its *mensura* (boundaried existence), the Son determines its *numerus* (essential form), and the Spirit provides individual *pondus* (intrinsic weight), drawing all things to their proper place and Sabbath rest in relation to God.[218] This commitment of God to the goodness of creation rules out "the gnostic possibility that creation is to be repudiated or overcome in the name of some higher good."[219] Adapting Brock and Wannenwetsch's appeal to Ps. 8:4 via Paul's quotation of Ps. 8:6 in 1 Cor. 15:27, God "remembers" humankind (זכר, Ps. 8:4) in the eschaton through his divine determination that creation "structure" should ground continuity.

If the theme of "restoration" captures something of humanity's natural/creational "structure," and the motif of "transformation" maps onto historical "direction," then it remains necessary to clarify the relationship between the two. In Chapter 3, I noted how creation is an expression of God's infinite and self-communicative goodness (e.g., Pss. 119:68; 145:7–9).[220] God creates natural things with discrete kinds and ends that reflect his goodness. The God-given goodness

---

212. O'Donovan, *Resurrection and Moral Order*, 56.

213. Oliver O'Donovan, *Entering into Rest*, ET 3 (Grand Rapids: Eerdmans, 2017), 106.

214. The δεῖ of 1 Cor. 15:53 is "not a necessity of natural order but of divinely ordained eschatology" (Fee, *First Corinthians*, 887 n.387).

215. O'Donovan, *Resurrection and Moral Order*, 64.

216. For an examination of whether this logic suggests the necessity of the incarnation, see Cortez, *ReSourcing*, 68–98.

217. See Chapter 4 on Augustine's *rationes seminales*.

218. Augustine, "Literal Meaning of Genesis," 4.17.29, 18.34 (WSA I/13:258, 260).

219. O'Donovan, *Resurrection and Moral Order*, 55.

220. Aquinas, *ST* 1.47.1 resp.

of natural things is not static, but created for a dynamic unfolding in history, evidenced in scripture by God establishing a history of covenantal fellowship with human creatures. In Barthian key, creation provides the external basis of the covenant, while the covenant operates as the internal basis of creation.[221] Covenant and creation neither compete nor conflict but complement each other, finding their ultimate coherence in Christ—Creator and Redeemer.[222] In sum, the relationship between the historical and the natural—direction and structure—transformation and restoration—is one of "consummation *restoratively transforming* creation." Rendering "restoration" as the adverbial modifier does not lessen the importance of its foundational contribution. I minimally look to reflect the biblical pattern of emphasizing narrative action over its metaphysical underpinnings.

Extending the previously employed theatrical metaphor, we discern the meaning of the sexed body when it is tracked and traced within the divine drama that moves from the *act* of creation (*creatio*) to the *act* of consummation. This theo-dramatic metanarrative is performed upon the structural *stage* of creation (*creatura*), which includes human actors as "part of the furniture." Hence, the structural stage supports the scriptural story. Within the story itself, we see God intrinsically ordering humanity's sexed staging (i.e., its creational structure) as a sexuate correspondence between "male and female" (Gen. 1:27) to fulfill penultimate procreative ends (Gen. 1:28), and so to propel the play forward—multiplying image bearers to represent God's presence throughout his world and enjoy the ultimate end of Sabbath rest with God (Gen. 2:2–3). In the *act* of the fall, our misdirected sexed staging may languish in tatters, but it is not destroyed. In the *act* of redemption, God graciously steps onto the stage and extrinsically redirects our sexed staging toward the consummative double-act of restoration and transformation—all so that we may celebrate at the eschatological denouement of the divine drama the nuptial union of God with his innumerable people (Rev. 7:9; 19:7–9; 21:2–3). Like the National Theatre in London, whose flat stage is primed to spring into life,[223] so humanity's sexed staging is intrinsically primed and

221. Karl Barth, *Church Dogmatics: The Doctrine of Creation*, vol. III/1, ed. G. W. Bromiley and T. F. Torrance (London: T&T Clark, 2010), §41.2–3.

222. Samuel Tranter accuses O'Donovan of privileging creation over covenant, thereby orienting his moral theology to a natural rather than eschatological ethic. For Tranter, O'Donovan's emphasis on creation is (i) "not sufficiently formed by those [biblical] narratives," (ii) causes O'Donovan to "part ways a little with the Reformer" (Calvin [Tranter also lists Barth]), and (iii) risks "dislodging Christology from some of its canonical footing" (*Oliver O'Donovan's Moral Theology: Tensions and Triumphs*, TTCETE [London: T&T Clark, 2020], 80–1). While my task is not to defend O'Donovan, I hope the exposition of 1 Corinthians 15 goes some way to assuage Tranter's concerns.

223. The stage contains a massive revolving drum that can elevate, rotate, and light up at key moments in performances.

extrinsically (re)directed toward its perfection—a Trinitarian act of grace.[224] Thus, consummation restoratively transforms creation in an upward spiral motion, where "the end returns to the beginning and yet is at the same time the apex which is exalted high above the point of origin."[225]

i. Benefit 1: The Macro-Standard of Peace The schema of "consummation restoratively transforms creation" enjoys two notable benefits. First, as Augustine advanced, since the consummation confirms creation as good, it suggests a macro-standard against which to assess bodily defects.[226] Accordingly, because the new creation is a place of "final peace,"[227] the resurrection body enjoys "the properly ordered arrangement of its parts."[228] Thus, the "bodies of the saints will rise again with no defect, no deformity, no corruption, burden, or difficulty, and their facility in living will be equal to their felicity."[229] Like a musical instrument, the "whole body, inside and out," possesses the beauty of proportionality (*numerus*), harmony (*harmonia*), and symmetry (*symmetria*),[230] where the body submits to

224. Webster, "Eschatology, Anthropology and Postmodernity," 28. My use of "extrinsic" should not be confused with a mechanistic account of the *natural* and the *supernatural* often discussed in parallel debates regarding nature and grace. At minimum, "extrinsic" claims that it is God alone who must graciously guide human nature toward its eschatological telos from creation to consummation. My use of "intrinsic" minimally identifies discrete kinds and ends sown into humanity's creational structure. In explicating the logic between creation and consummation, space prevents me from developing further judgments about the intelligibility of creational structure *sans* historical "direction," or the gratuity of grace.

225. Herman Bavinck, *The Wonderful Works of God: Instruction in the Christian Religion According to the Reformed Confession*, trans. Henry Zylstra (Glenside, PA: Westminster Seminary Press, 2019), 127.

226. Augustine, *Civ.* 22.1 (CCSL 48:806; WSA I/7:496).

227. Ibid., 19.27 (CCSL 48:698; WSA I/7:387).

228. Ibid., 19.13 (CCSL 48:679; WSA I/7:368). Space precludes analyzing the relationship between the body, time, and motion in the new creation. While Bynum reads Augustine's eschatological vision as "the crystalline hardness not only of stasis but of the impossibility of non-stasis" (*Resurrection of the Body*, 97), Virginia Burrus rejects such an interpretation, arguing instead that Augustine's eschatological body stretches the boundaries of imagination in an "exceeding beauty of becoming" ("Carnal Excess: Flesh at the Limits of Imagination," *JECS* 17 [2009]: 256).

229. Augustine, "The Enchiridion on Faith, Hope, and Charity," 23.91, in *On Christian Belief*, ed. Boniface Ramsey, trans. Bruce Harbert, WSA I/8 (Hyde Park, NY: New City, 2005), 325.

230. Augustine, *Civ.* 22.24 (CCSL 48:850; WSA I/7:540). Cf. ibid., 5.11; 11.22. Similarly, Aquinas emphasizes the glorified body possessing the qualities of incorruptibility (*impassibilitas*—impassibility), subtlety (*subtilitas*—harmony), agility (*agilitas*—movement), and clarity (*claritas*—light) (e.g., *Compendium of Theology*, §168). Thus, the incorruptible soul is finally and fittingly united with an incorruptible body, "a saw that [will]

the peacefully ordered soul and the soul submits to God.[231] As Beth Felker Jones summarizes, the eschatological body witnesses "to holiness, to right order, and to peace."[232]

Moreover, eschatological peace is not merely individual. Since "we also are made partakers in his peace according to our capacity, we too know supreme peace in ourselves, among ourselves, and with him, insofar as what is supreme is possible for us."[233] The peace of the City of God is our corporate Sabbath rest, for "we ourselves shall become that seventh day,"[234] recapitulating and perfecting the holistic, ordered peace of creation. "Peace and holiness and order join together in the bodies of the faithful to enact praise."[235] As Häring concludes, "It will be the day of divine rest and divine celebration without end."[236]

In contrast, because Cornwall's account of eschatological embodiment is entirely grounded eccentrically in God, and since God has no body, it remains unclear how to adjudicate bodily defects. Admittedly, Cornwall may well dispute the need to adjudicate diverse bodily configurations. Yet, following Cornwall's logic, while an individual may lament a particular bodily condition, Cornwall's proposal does not appear to have the resources to assert more normatively that certain bodily configurations are defective (e.g., tumors)—neither now, nor eternally. Indeed, as noted above, Cornwall may claim that we will "be 'saved' from physical pain [and] suffering," but it remains opaque how the embodiment that causes the pain (e.g., genetic mosaicism) can persist without the concomitant pain persisting too. In short, Cornwall's eschatological vision lacks the means to adjudicate defective embodiment, thereby undermining the rationale to provide medical care in the present, and not adequately preventing the possibility of perpetual pain in the future.

ii. Benefit 2: Confidence in Recognizability A second benefit relates to our recognizability in the new creation. As argued above, Cornwall's entirely extrinsic account does not necessitate numerical bodily identity for eschatological recognizability. Since my identity is grounded in God alone, for my identity to persist it only needs to be recognizable to God. Yet, in theory, God could

---

not rust" (*ST* 2-2.164.1 ad 1). Extending the illustration, the saw that was once susceptible to decaying rust, that lost its protective coating of WD-40, has now been transformed through refining fire, and bonded with carbon and chromium to make a high carbon stainless steel saw, impervious to rust, and fit for its master's use. Importantly, the saw is still a saw, but now it is the saw it was always intended to become.

231. Augustine, *Civ.* 13.20 (CCSL 48:403; WSA I/7:87). See Peter Burnell, *The Augustinian Person* (Washington, DC: Catholic University of America Press, 2005), 41–4.

232. Jones, *Marks of His Wounds*, 109.

233. Augustine, *Civ.* 22.29 (CCSL 48:857; WSA I/7:546).

234. Ibid., 22.30 (CCSL 48:866; WSA I/7:554). "There we shall be still and see, see and love, love and praise."

235. Jones, *Marks of His Wounds*, 110.

236. Häring, "Eschatologie," 546.

reincarnate me as a chicken, and still know me as *me*. In contrast, if we supplement an extrinsic account with the biblical insight that God also determines for creation structure to contour eschatology, then the new creation body will at minimum be human and sexed according to the creational intent for my body. Thus, the double-helix of graced intrinsic ordering perfected extrinsically by grace ensures that the Christian doctrine is one of resurrection, not reincarnation.[237]

B. Methodological Implications

Thus far I have expounded (principally from 1 Corinthians 15) the *that* and the *how* of eschatology's relationship to creation. Before suggesting several *so whats* for the sexed body in the new creation, it is fitting to elucidate briefly an important methodological implication. In short, to read the sexed body rightly, we must appreciate the body's theo-dramatic situatedness. This requires reading the body through canonically "wider" and metaphysically "thicker" lenses.

1. A Canonically "Wider" Lens Considering the hermeneutical contribution of a canonically "wider" lens, while Cornwall concentrates on the dispensation of redemption, she fails to attend to Paul's wider strategy, where he situates Jesus' exemplary body, and our raised bodies, beneath the umbrella of a divine drama that runs from creation to consummation. Given Cornwall's appeal to Augustine, it remains instructive that "if Augustine's view of human sexuality is to be understood properly, it must be represented across the history of creation, fall and redemption."[238] As demonstrated in the structure of *De civitate Dei* 11–22,[239] Augustine views history as "a narrative, crafted by God and portrayed in Scripture, in which one's relation to God is the defining feature of the role one plays in that narrative."[240] My body-story matters, for "selves . . . are located in particular stories."[241] And yet, its meaning is discerned within God's grander story, a point Augustine emphasized to catechumens.[242] Indeed, problematically for Cornwall, Augustine interprets creation as informing eschatology, and especially when thinking about sexed embodiment. "Both sexes will arise again," Augustine

---

237. For "why reincarnation is incompatible with Christianity," highlighting the doctrines of God, humanity, and salvation by and in Christ, see Jean-Pierre Torrell, *Résurrection de Jésus et résurrection des morts: Foi, histoire et théologie*, Épi (Paris: Cerf, 2012), 181–5.

238. Paul Ramsey, "Human Sexuality in the History of Redemption," *JRE* 16 (1988): 56.

239. Books 11–22 attempt to show "the origin, the course, and the due ends of the two cities" (Augustine, *Civ.* 10.32 [CCSL 37:314; WSA I/6:348]).

240. Do Vale, "Cappadocian or Augustinian?" 192.

241. Couenhoven, *Stricken by Sin, Cured by Christ*, 184. Couenhoven goes on to add the helpful caveat that not all parts of our story are equally essential to our identity.

242. Augustine, *The First Catechetical Instruction* 3.5, trans. Joseph P. Christopher, ACW 2 (New York: Newman, 1978), 18–19.

evinces, and "they will evoke praise for the wisdom and compassion of God, who both *created* what was not and freed what he *created* from corruption."[243] As Augustine goes on to explain, God created Adam and Eve to enjoy a "unity" that sacramentally "prefigured" the unity of Christ and the church.[244] Although there will be no human marriage in heaven,[245] "The one who established the two sexes will restore them both,"[246] because their united "sociability" continues to point us to the "storied significance of Christ and the church."[247] Therefore, although Cornwall invokes Augustine, she fails to appreciate how he prioritizes the *whole* divine drama as a wider hermeneutical lens through which to read human identity, particularly the importance of creation contouring consummation.

2. A Metaphysically "Thicker" Lens Furthermore, the wider canonical lens needs to be complemented by a metaphysically thicker lens to guard against a reductionistic reading of creation as mere historical *act*. Extending insights from the argument against Song in Chapter 5, while Cornwall's account rightly reflects Paul's emphasis on divine determination (1 Cor. 15:38), God's freedom is not a matter of raw voluntarism. Rather, in his freedom, God freely covenants to work within the structures of *creatura*, as implied in the "very good" of creation (Gen. 1:31), and reaffirmed post-fall (Gen. 9:15–17) and post-parousia (Rev. 4:3).[248] Indeed, pressing O'Donovarian logic, there is an organic and "irreducible duality between the freedom of God to act particularly in history and the generic ordering of the world."[249] Without creation's stable kind/ends structure, history can "only be uninterpretable movement."[250] Such raw historicism robs us of stable and shareable norms.

However, creation structure is not so mechanically monistic that it locks God out, nor does it prohibit God from acting graciously.[251] Positively, the unchanging one (James 1:17) is "the author, not only of change itself, but of the order which

---

243. Augustine, *Civ.* 22.17 (CCSL 48:835; WSA I/7:526), italics added.

244. Ibid.

245. The historical, proximate end of marriage is complete.

246. Augustine, *Civ.* 22.17 (CCSL 48:836; WSA I/7:527).

247. Do Vale, "Cappadocian or Augustinian?" 195.

248. E.g., the "rainbow" encircling the heavenly throne (Rev. 4:3) alludes back conceptually to the rain-"bow" marking God's covenant commitment to the structures of creation after the flood (Gen. 9:15–17). See Peter J. Leithart, *Revelation 1–11*, ITC (London: Bloomsbury, 2018), 227–8.

249. O'Donovan, *Resurrection and Moral Order*, 45.

250. Ibid.

251. For an account of human identity that is metaphysically thick and narratively rich, seeking to avoid "mechanical monism" and "dynamic diversity" via a teleological, "organic worldview," see Herman Bavinck on "Being and Becoming," in *Christian Worldview*, trans. Nathaniel Gray Sutanto, James Eglinton, and Cory C. Brock (Wheaton, IL: Crossway, 2019), 57–92.

makes that change good."[252] In Pauline key, the organic dynamic between a "thicker" creational structure and a "wider" historical direction from creation to consummation simultaneously testifies to the possibility of a radical somatic transformation in history (vv.50–53), but one necessarily informed and contoured by creational structure (vv.35–49). Conversely, by narrowing her lens to the *act* of redemption, Cornwall's case considers and presents only half the story, which amounts to a different story, on a different stage.

C. *Implications for the Sexed Body in the New Creation*

1. Claim: Sexed Epistemic Clarity I have argued that the theological interpretation of intersex embodiment is illuminated as intersexuality is tracked and traced through scripture's theo-dramatic metanarrative. In thinking specifically about the sexed body in the consummation, God's redirecting work of eschatological redemption restoratively transforms creational structure. Consequently, if the sexed body in creation is unambiguously male or female, and if male or female pertains to creational structure, then when consummation restoratively transforms creation, the new creation sexed body will likely be unambiguously male or female. As I claimed considering creation, given the lavish and self-communicative goodness of God, unambiguous maleness and femaleness still allow for considerable diversity of sexed form. Yet, with death and its disordering decay swallowed up (1 Cor. 15:54), all people, however sexed, will likely be unambiguously male or female. Due to the epistemic and somatic effects of the fall, the creational sex of intersex persons is currently occluded. But the fall did not destroy creational structure, and God knows his creation intimately (Ps. 139:13–16) such that he is able to reveal finally through a restorative transformation our true sexed embodiment.

2. Objection: Epistemic Clarity Serves No Eschatological Purpose One may object to the revelation of an intersex person as truly male or female on the grounds that such epistemic clarity serves no eschatological purpose or benefit. From the perspective of others, that someone is now unambiguously male or female is seemingly irrelevant. On earth, knowing someone's sex is useful for marriage and procreation. But in heaven, there is no marriage among humans (Matt. 22:30), for we shall all be married to the Lamb (Rev. 21:2). Indeed, without marriage (and death) there is no need for reproduction (nor sexual activity).[253] If there is no sexual activity in heaven, why should sexed morphology be restricted to either male or female? More positively, Augustine suggests that while the necessary "use" of certain embodied conditions will "pass away" (e.g., eating),[254] "we shall enjoy

---

252. O'Donovan, *Resurrection and Moral Order*, 45.

253. *Contra* the "holy polyamory" proposed by Patricia Beattie Jung, *Sex on Earth as It Is in Heaven: A Christian Eschatology of Desire* (Albany, NY: State University of New York Press, 2017).

254. Augustine, *Civ.* 13.22 (CCSL 48:405; WSA I/7:89).

each other's beauty for itself alone."[255] As such, why would an intersex person need to become unambiguously male or female for others to enjoy their unique beauty? Moreover, from an individual intersex perspective, becoming unambiguously sexed seems to offer little benefit for one's sense of self, especially given that our primary identity is in Christ, now fully revealed in glory (Col. 3:3–4). As Ian Paul posits, even if sexed "differentiation persists in the resurrection, the New Testament displays a decided indifference to sex identity."[256]

3. Response: The Fittingness of Sexed Epistemic Clarity There are three reasons (biblical, theological, ethical) for the fittingness of sexed epistemic clarity in the consummation.[257] First, considered biblically, even if no scriptural passages exist that explicitly address eschatological sexed embodiment, the overarching biblical pattern is for creational structure to contour consummative transformation. If sexed embodiment was clear in creation (with form founding function and function fitting form), then we should expect clarity regarding our sexuate condition in the new creation (even with the proximate function of procreation having been historically fulfilled). While an appeal to a *felix culpa*-esque argument to make a case for continuing sexed ambiguity may be possible, given the biblical pattern of "consummation restoratively transforming creation" such a proposal would have to account for (i) *how* intersex undergoes necessary transformation, and (ii) *why* some effects of the fall persist and others presumably do not.[258]

Second, considered theologically (in Athanasian key),[259] epistemic clarity communicates something of God's faithfulness—to the structural goodness of his creation (Gen. 1:31) and his promise to redeem (Rom. 8:22–23). As glorified women and men, we can behold our sexed bodies as those freed from the disordering effects of the fall, knowing that God has been faithful to the goodness of our bodies and faithful to his promise to deliver his people from the "cords" and "snares of death" (Ps. 18:4–5; Luke 1:68–75). In a broad sense, the good work God began in creation will indeed be brought to completion at the day of Christ (cf. Phil. 1:6), for the goodness of God ensures that his good work will not go to waste.[260] God's

255. Ibid., 22.24 (CCSL 48:851; WSA I/7:541).

256. Ian Paul, "Are We Sexed in Heaven? Bodily Form, Sex Identity and the Resurrection," in *Marriage, Family and Relationships: Biblical, Doctrinal and Contemporary Perspectives*, ed. Thomas A. Noble, Sarah K. Whittle, and Philip S. Johnston (London: Apollos, 2017), 117.

257. I employ the concept of "fittingness" merely to communicate something of the inner-coherence, intelligibility, wisdom, and beauty of sexed epistemic clarity (rather than its strict biblical or theological "necessity"). "Fittingness" language also acknowledges the inherently speculative character of exploring eschatological embodiment.

258. I attempt to make a similar argument below via Augustine's interpretation of bodily scars as "marks of honour" (*Civ.* 22.19).

259. See Athanasius, *Incarnation* 6 (PPS 44b:55).

260. See Anselm, "Cur Deus Homo," 2.4.

word does not return to him empty (Isa. 55:11). While a new *creatio ex nihilo* may be "simpler," Bavinck evinces, God's good pleasure for an eschatological *creatio ex vetere* demonstrates his absolute power over sin and death (1 Cor. 15:54–57), such that "Christ is a complete Savior."[261] Indeed, "God's honor consists precisely in the fact that he redeems and renews the same humanity, the same world, the same heaven, and the same earth that have been corrupted and polluted by sin."[262] Sexed epistemic clarity attests to God's faithfulness and honor, and so remains a matter of concern both corporately and individually. Clarifying Ian Paul's observation, while the NT certainly gives literary prominence to our fundamental identity in Christ (Col. 3:3–4) over "sex identity," textual "indifference" does not mean sexed indeterminacy.

Third, considered ethically, since eschatology shapes ethics (1 Cor. 6:13–14; 15:58), sexed indeterminacy in heaven (hence SP) would suggest a place for indeterminacy and SP in the present, with all the queering ramifications for a traditional doctrine of marriage, gender identity, and (for some) gender roles. Yet, while SP in glory could pressure the contemporary church to "see" difference more expansively, astonishing eschatological diversity (e.g., Rev. 7:9) need not dictate indeterminacy.[263] The Body of Christ can delight in difference without following the logic of indeterminacy.

Comment on the relationship between marriage and sexed embodiment may reveal further ethical problems (at least for a traditional sexual ethic) with an innovationist push toward eschatological SP. As noted above, God ensures that the God-given goodness of natural "structure" unfolds in historical "direction." If SD pertains to humanity's creational structure, then it seems fitting that the good, prelapsarian, creational ordinance of marriage is God's gift *for* the historical unfolding of the natural goods associated with SD, that is, its sexuate form and procreative function.[264]

In Chapter 5 I noted how the human expression of the creational ordinance of marriage is fulfilled in Christ's first advent, thereby valorizing the vocation of singleness (Matt. 19:12). Further, the human expression of the creational ordinance of marriage will be filled full to completion at Christ's Second Advent, for human marriage will be no more (Matt. 22:30). Yet it is fitting for the semiotic significance of "male and female," as a good of creational structure, to endure into the eschaton, for humanity's sexuate correspondence, that undergirds marriage, continues to

---

261. Bavinck, *RD*, 4:694.

262. Ibid., 4:717.

263. Note how the fourfold formula of "nation, tribe, people, language" appears in varying order seven times in Revelation (5:9; 7:9; 10:11; 11:9; 13:7; 14:6; 17:15), perhaps suggesting "completeness" rather than indeterminate diversity (Richard Bauckham, *The Climax of Prophecy: Studies on the Book of Revelation* [Edinburgh: T&T Clark, 1993], 326).

264. Although, recall from Chapters 3 and 5 how procreation does not exhaust the meaning of marriage, whose ends are not only procreative, but also relational, social, and spiritual.

point to the eternal marriage of Christ and his church (Eph. 5:21–33; Rev. 19:6–9; 21:2). By implication, if we revise the sexuate correspondence of "male and female" in the consummation (whether via androgyny or SP), then we seem to occlude the present and eschatological witness of humanity's creational structure to the "marriage supper of the Lamb" (Rev. 19:9).[265]

Admittedly, advocates for SP could retort that I only "see" what I want to "see." Since I am persuaded by a traditional doctrine of marriage (which requires *being* male and *being* female), I "see" SD in heaven, and then read that back into the present to ossify my prior commitment. Thus, my argument is circular, perhaps viciously so. Now, while I could riposte with *tu quoque* (for all eschatological reflection is speculative), debate perhaps should rest on the strength of one's biblical and theological argumentation. This drives us back to the preceding points about God's faithfulness to the goodness of creation, and his promise to deliver from the effects of sin and death.

Nonetheless, even if the proposed biblical and theological case is cogent, if it effectively involves the elimination of intersex identity, then can it really qualify as faithful, ectypal, life-giving theology? If the proposal lacks love, is it worth anything (1 Cor. 13:2)? As Augustine warns: "If it seems to you that you have understood the divine scriptures, or any part of them, in such a way that by this understanding you do not build up this twin love of God and neighbor, then you have not yet understood them."[266]

D. *"Heavenly Healing" as "Heavenly Eulogization"*

At first glance, sexed epistemic clarity intimates the elimination of intersex identity. Unambiguous SD in heaven seems like a "Hollywood ideal" that "cannot but

---

265. For further development, the juxtaposition of "marriage" and "supper of the Lamb" evokes intriguing resonances, potentially providing a suggestive supplementary argument for sexed epistemic clarity. If the future "supper of the Lamb" includes echoes of the present Lord's Supper, then the future feast could encompass both the eschatological fulfillment *and* the enduring celebration of the present supper. In one sense the semiotic significance of the Lord's Supper is fulfilled (cf. 1 Cor. 11:26), and yet it continues to be filled full with celebratory significance. That is, the "supper of the Lamb" perpetually proclaims the Lamb's victory (Rev. 19:1–2; 11–21). Similarly, the future "marriage . . . of the Lamb" (cf. Rev. 21:9) fulfills the sign-character of human marriage, and yet it could be that, as food undergirds future feasting, so the sexuate correspondence of "male and female" continues to testify to the ultimate correspondence and communion between Christ and his church. In short, while the function of present signs will be fulfilled in the new creation, this does not necessarily mean that *all* their semiotic significance will be lost. Indeed, the retention of the sexed body's semiotic significance accentuates God's faithfulness to both the natural *and* the historical, for, as I develop via Augustine, both creation *and* the marks of history matter to God.

266. Augustine, *Teaching Christianity* 1.36.40, ed. John E. Rotelle, trans. Edmund Hill, WSA I/11 (Hyde Park, NY: New City, 1996), 124.

entrench stereotypes about disability,"[267] confirming Moss's concern of "heavenly eugenics."[268] However, the Christian tradition offers nuanced resources to alleviate such fears. With the help of Augustine, I supplement the case for the fittingness of sexed epistemic clarity with an argument for the fittingness of present intersex conditions being eschatologically valorized as virtuous "marks of honor."[269]

1. The Beauty of Peace In Book 22 of *De civitate Dei*, as Augustine responds to a plethora of objections to the resurrection of human flesh,[270] all his answers exhibit a concern to maintain (i) material identity between the present body and the future body,[271] and (ii) the resurrection body displaying "a beauty fitting the kingdom of God."[272] As such, influenced by Jesus' promises that all our hairs are numbered (Luke 12:7) and that not a hair on our head will perish (Luke 21:18), Augustine suggests an eschatological process of material reassembly and reorganization.[273] The "omnipotent artist" ensures that the congenital "deformity will perish while the substance itself is preserved as an integral whole."[274] The beautifully ordered peace of the City of God requires "unflawed beauty, such that none of its [the body's] substance is lost but only its deformity."[275] As Augustine illustrates with blindness, "Bodily deformities and defects are characterized as malformations in development."[276] God made eyes to see, and "yet a defect in development undermines its created potential."[277] Illustrating further, in the resurrection, God the metal

---

267. Brock, *Wondrously Wounded*, 181.

268. Moss, *Divine Bodies*, 26.

269. Augustine, *Civ*. 22.19 (CCSL 48:839; WSA I/7:530).

270. E.g., what happens to aborted babies (ibid., 22.14), or bodies devoured by wild beasts, or fire, or cannibals (ibid., 22.20).

271. That for Augustine "the body provides the material and formal continuity of a person," see Tarmo Toom, "Totus Homo: Augustine on Resurrection," in *Resurrection and Responsibility: Essays on Theology, Scripture, and Ethics in Honor of Thorwald Lorenzen*, ed. Keith D. Dyer and David J. Neville (Eugene, OR: Pickwick, 2009), 67.

272. Jones, *Marks of His Wounds*, 28. See Augustine, *Civ*. 22.20.

273. For the anti-Manichean motivations behind Augustine's account of reassembly, see Bynum, *Resurrection of the Body*, 95. For several philosophical problems with reassembly, see Peter van Inwagen, "Possibility of Resurrection," *IJPR* 9 (1978): 114–21. The "heavenly eulogization" of intersex does not rest upon Augustine's account of reassembly.

274. Augustine, *Civ*. 22.19 (CCSL 48:838; WSA I/7:529). "The body becomes spiritualized and imperishable, devoid of all defects; bodily deformities disappear" (Häring, "Eschatologie," 545).

275. Augustine, *Civ*. 22.19 (CCSL 48:838; WSA I/7:529).

276. Kristi Upson-Saia, "Resurrecting Deformity: Augustine on Wounded and Scarred Bodies in the Heavenly Realm," in *Disability in Judaism, Christianity, and Islam: Sacred Texts, Historical Traditions, and Social Analysis*, ed. Darla Schumm and Michael Stoltzfus (New York: Palgrave Macmillan, 2011), 103.

277. Ibid.

worker will melt down our mutable matter and recast the statue to fulfil its created potential, indeed, with a heightened spiritual sight to see God.[278] Cornwall may well be correct that for Augustine bodily healing is "less significant than [being in] right relationship."[279] Yet, given the shape of Augustine's argument in *Civ.* 22, "less significant" does not mean insignificant, *contra* Cornwall. Admittedly, thus far Augustine voices tropes that disability scholars find distastefully troubling: Brock accusing Augustine of introducing "Neoplatonic theologies" whose "metaphysical overlay" obscures "the plain sense of Scripture."[280]

2. "Marks of Honor" Nevertheless, when Augustine turns to consider the eschatological embodiment of "the blessed martyrs," although he reads Luke 12:7 and 21:18 as intimating that severed limbs will be reassembled, Augustine ponders whether it is "fitting for the marks of their glorious wounds (*vulnera*) to be visible."[281] "Perhaps" (*fortasse*) we may still "see" the "marks [scars] of the wounds (*vulnera cicatrices*) they suffered for Christ's name."[282] Importantly within Augustine's schema, these will "not be marks of deformity (*deformitas*) but marks of honor (*dignitas*)," shining with a "kind of beauty" that although occurring "in" the body is not strictly a beauty "of" the body.[283] Rather, these are "marks of virtue" (*virtutis indicia*) or "glorious marks" (*indicia gloriosorum*), which God himself will graciously inscribe through heavenly "scars" (*cicatrices*), precisely where limbs were originally hacked off.[284] Thus, the new scars "ensure a continuity of the self as an individual person with an individual history."[285]

For Augustine, the "chief of martyrs" is Christ,[286] whose "*vulnerum cicatrices*" testify to his victory over death and the promise of resurrection life.[287] In a special way, the bodies of martyrs, whose *vulnera* have become virtuous *cicatrices/*

278. Augustine, *Civ.* 22.29 (CCSL 48:861; WSA I/7:550).

279. Cornwall, *Sex and Uncertainty*, 190.

280. Brock, *Disability*, 131. Augustine's dependence on Neoplatonism should not be overstated. While Augustine recognizes (*c.* AD 387) merits in Plato to combat "Academic" skepticism ("Answer to Skeptics," 3.43, in *Writings of Saint Augustine*, trans. Denis J. Kavanagh, FC 5 [New York: Cima, 1948], 220), he later (*c.* AD 426) distances himself from their "great errors" (*The Retractions*, trans. Mary Inez Bogan, FC 60 [Washington, DC: Catholic University of America Press, 1968], 1.1.4 [10]).

281. Augustine, *Civ.* 22.19 (CCSL 48:839; WSA I/7:530)

282. Ibid. *Cicatrix* is a "scar" more than a "mark." For "mark" (as in sign or inscription), Augustine tends to use *indicium*.

283. "*In corpore, non corporis*" (ibid.).

284. Ibid.

285. Susan Ashbrook Harvey, *Scenting Salvation: Ancient Christianity and the Olfactory Imagination*, TCH 42 (Berkeley, CA: University of California Press, 2006), 233.

286. Augustine, "Sermon 316," 2, in Augustine, *Sermons 306–340A: On the Saints*, ed. John E. Rotelle, trans. Edmund Hill, WSA III/9 (Hyde Park, NY: New City, 1994), 138.

287. Augustine, *Civ.* 22.19 (CCSL 48:839; WSA I/7:530).

indicia, also "witness to the victory over death brought about decisively in Christ's resurrection."[288] Therefore, within a wider framework that emphasizes bodily symmetry, Augustine not only interprets the present deformities of martyrs as signs of cruciform holiness, but his heavenly vision includes the asymmetry of God inscribing or imputing some transformed citizens with glorious scars. As Jones distils, "Here beauty and blemish are themselves radically redefined by the Body of Christ, in both the senses of Jesus' body and of the Church that becomes that body. What once meant pain and disfigurement now shines in glory."[289]

Initially, the admittance of scarred martyrs into God's city of perfect proportionality may appear contradictory. Yet, given that Augustine defines personal peace as a rightly ordered body-soul-will,[290] reversing the proud primal sin of *incurvatus in se,*[291] Upson-Saia suggests that "by willingly submitting to and valiantly enduring martyrdom, these saints demonstrated a proper ordering of the body-soul-will, which were rightly calibrated with God's will."[292] Thus, martyrs exemplified a "symmetry of body-soul-will" that Augustine appraises as beautiful, and so fitting within the heavenly city.[293] Indeed, there is a sense in which a martyr radiates an especially beautiful glory, because in the eyes of other heavenly citizens the martyr's divinely marked "identity [is] always *in relation* to God, their master."[294] Unlike unmarked eschatological bodies, the martyr's divinely inscribed scars manifest "not just the *telos*—the perfected, resurrected body—but the history of salvation in the body: from creation to fall to redemption."[295] By embodying a richer redemptive story, martyrs tangibly testify to the scarred and slain Lamb (Rev. 5:6) more clearly than non-scarred bodies.

3. The Possibility of Intersex Scars On the surface, the link between intersex Christians and early church martyrs may not be immediately apparent. However, in Augustine's sermons, especially *Sermones* 314–320 on Stephen's martyrdom, Augustine connected ordinary Christian audiences with the devotion of the martyrs, by both closing the gap between martyrs and laity,[296] and enlarging the

---

288. Jones, *Marks of His Wounds,* 109.

289. Ibid., 29. Augustine's strategy of reading scars as a lens through which to adjudicate spiritual identity finds precedence in Gregory of Nyssa, *The Life of Saint Macrina,* trans. Kevin Corrigan (Eugene, OR: Wipf & Stock, 2001).

290. Augustine, *Civ.* 19.13 (CCSL 48:678; WSA I/7:368).

291. Ibid., 14.11. This leads to "more disobedience," including that of the body and soul (ibid., 14.15).

292. Upson-Saia, "Resurrecting Deformity," 106.

293. Ibid.

294. Ibid., 118 n.52, italics original.

295. Ibid., 109.

296. E.g., Augustine, "Sermon 317," 4 (WSA III/9:144). "Nobody should say, 'It's too much for me.' He was human, you're human."

scope of what counted as martyrdom.[297] As such, if the godly virtue of martyrs will be marked in heaven, and martyrdom is expanded to include daily acts of devotion that cultivate virtue, then it suggests that every resurrection body will be marked up in variegated ways. But on this logic, if all are marked, what makes the marks of martyrs particularly remarkable?

The possibility and scope of being significantly more marked up than perhaps expected demands further clarification. What exactly qualifies as a heavenly "mark of honor"? While there is a sense in which we shall all be marked with God's name on our foreheads (Rev. 22:4), Augustine's close association between virtue and physical impairment suggests that not all virtue per se will be bodily marked, nor for that matter all physical impairment. Rather, "marks of honor" refer specifically to divinely inscribed scars that God elevates because they are a bodily witness to God's work of cultivating godly virtue. Since intersex conditions qualify as bodily impairments, Augustine's logic intimates that where God uses intersexuality to grow individuals in godliness (whether in perseverance, hope, faith, etc.), while the impairments themselves will be eschatologically healed (ordered peace suggests sexed epistemic clarity), God may impute "marks of honor" that testify to the intersex individual's virtue and God's glorious redemption.

Put simply, an intersex individual will likely be unambiguously male or female, but could also display on their body a "mark of honor" for cultivating virtue through their intersex condition. For example, someone presently with CAIS (chromosomally male; phenotypically female) will know themselves in the eschaton to be truly male or female (and presumably recognized as such by others). And yet, God inscribes some record of CAIS on their body, in which the intersex individual can exult. For Augustine, the martyr's "mark of honor" was in the precise place of former impairment. If Augustine is correct, then an intersex Christian could expect God to emblazon his "mark of honor" in a place unlikely to be seen by other heavenly citizens.[298] But a hidden mark is no less honorable, for such a "mark of honor" fittingly reflects God's love for and faithfulness to historical particularity, especially a history that testifies to God's redeeming grace.[299] Extending the earlier connection between intersexuality and "strange vocations," in heaven God continues to communicate through intersex "marks of honor" that an individual's bodily history matters to God. He sees, completely and truly, even when others may not. In sum, Augustinian insights answer the charge of "heavenly eugenics" with a *felix culpa*-esque "heavenly eulogization" of intersex bodies among the citizens of heaven.[300]

---

297. E.g., prayer and forgiveness (§314), endurance through opposition (§316), loving enemies (§317), scorning the world's delights and fighting sin (§318).

298. Also, note the white robes in Rev. 7:9.

299. Christ's scars provide exhibit A.

300. For an example of *felix culpa* thinking in Augustine, see "Enchiridion," 8.27 (WSA I/8:290). If intersexuality qualifies as a *felix culpa*, then present bodily defects cannot be indiscriminately dismissed as results of the fall to be rectified, since some impairments

Admittedly, the proposal thus far is a *"fortasse"* argument.[301] As Jones rightly maintains, echoing the demand for divine determination in 1 Cor. 15:38, ultimately, "only God can name our bodies rightly."[302] Yet my speculative suggestion exhibits advantages over revisionist alternatives. For instance, my proposal counters Cornwall's complaint about hegemonies of healing, for it does not denigrate present struggles but orients them heavenward in hope. In contrast, Cornwall's denial of any physical healing not only downplays the biblical necessity for somatic transformation (1 Cor. 15:50, 53) but also ironically ignores the unique struggles of those who *do* long for change. Nor need the affirmation of an "aseitic [God], complete in Godself" belittle physical dependence.[303] While Augustine sustained a strong account of divine perfection,[304] his proposal for heavenly scars suggests an elevation of the "wondrously wounded."[305] Intersex Christians can entrust themselves to an aseitic God, for only an omniscient God knows us perfectly to know the best for us; only an omnipotent God has the power to give the best to us; and only a perfectly good God always acts for our good.[306] A God who limits himself for the sake of creaturely libertarian freedom and risk can offer no such assurances.[307] In summary, unlike revisionist accounts, my proposal for the possible heavenly eulogization of intersex is not only biblically and theologically coherent, but also good and life-affirming, as it orients ultimate hope toward יהוה רפאך (Exod. 15:26), thereby also satisfying Augustine's caveat regarding the double love command.

V. Conclusion

This chapter explored the possibility of intersex in heaven. The best arguments for SP in glory invoked the normativity of Jesus' scars, the primacy of our "body-story" plus "eccentric grounding" for numerical identity, and the promise of Trinitarian person-*perichoresis*. Having suggested numerous problems with the revisionist case, I emphasized via 1 Cor. 15:35–58 the necessity of somatic transformation for resurrection life, as well as Paul's strategy of situating the meaning of the resurrection body within scripture's theo-dramatic metanarrative.

---

may well be the very places where God is growing virtue that lasts into eternity (and will be marked as such). This point could have far-reaching implications for understanding other impairments, whether physical, mental, or emotional.

301. Cf. Augustine, *Civ.* 22.19.

302. Jones, *Marks of His Wounds*, 110.

303. Cornwall, *Sex and Uncertainty*, 173.

304. E.g., Augustine, *Civ.* 11.10.

305. The phrase is from Brock, *Wondrously Wounded*.

306. Divine aseity coheres with omniscience, omnipotence, and omnibenevolence because God is perfectly simple (*Civ.* 11.10).

307. Cornwall, *Sex and Uncertainty*, 234.

In God's economy of grace, eschatological redemption restoratively transforms creation toward the ordered peace of the City of God. Hence Gaiser's gloss: "To be healed, finally, is to be complete (*šālôm*)."[308]

Heavenly healing is holistic, carrying "a sense of *integration* as well as *completion*."[309] For the sexed body, this entails the epistemic clarification of one's creational sex—transposed in transformative key. Whatever our current sexed embodiment, we shall all be unambiguously male or female. This need not imply heavenly eugenics for intersex persons. Following Augustine's rumination on ordered peace, heavenly healing may be interpreted as heavenly eulogization. Not only is the body "*narratively-indexed* to the great story of what God is doing in Christ,"[310] but where God has cultivated virtue, intersex bodies may also be "virtuously indexed" (*virtutis indicia*) with divinely gifted scars,[311] beauty in which heavenly citizens will delight and praise God.[312] Thus, the legacy of intersexuality may remain in heaven, not in terms of ambiguous embodiment, but as "marks of honor" (*dignitas*): a transformative dignity greater than revisionist arguments currently conceive.

308. Frederick J. Gaiser, *Healing in the Bible: Theological Insight for Christian Ministry* (Grand Rapids: Baker Academic, 2010), 243.

309. O'Donovan, *Entering*, 106, italics original.

310. Do Vale, "Cappadocian or Augustinian?" 193, italics original.

311. Augustine, *Civ.* 22.19 (CCSL 48:839).

312. Ibid., 22.24, 30.

Chapter 7

CONCLUSION

THEOLOGICAL GLASSES

How should Christian theology interpret intersex embodiment? Should we accept the traditional reading and interpret intersexuality as a postlapsarian anomaly set within the exclusive framework of sexual dimorphism (SD)—a case largely built upon the perspectives of creation and fall? Or is it high time to innovate Christian doctrine by recognizing how the phenomenon of intersexuality explodes the male-female binary into sexual polymorphism (SP)—a proposal typically foregrounding redemptive newness in Christ? For traditionalists, the goodness of creation is under assault. For innovationists, the very humanity of intersex persons remains at risk. Into the traditional-innovational impasse I offer a dogmatic account of intersexuality, primarily contributing a set of thick theological glasses through which to read intersex embodiment.

My theologically thick reading moves beyond an ontological commitment to the Christian narrative of creation and redemption *simpliciter*. More maximally, I emphasize the ordered coherence within "God and God's actions," self-disclosed in the coherent scriptural narrative of creation to consummation.[1] A theologically thick interpretation of intersexuality thus demands careful attention to each theo-dramatic act within the grand divine drama. The benefit of this approach is the ability to make synthetic judgments about what remains essential for the "structure" of the sexed body as it travels through history and what may be accidental to the sexed body's "direction" within a particular theo-dramatic act. Having tracked and traced the sexed body through the complete economy, I am now well placed to offer my theological interpretation of intersexuality.

To this end I first rehearse the key argumentative steps I made at each theo-dramatic act. Second, with the whole divine drama in view, I reiterate the descriptive strapline for how the scripturally attested economy coheres, subsequently condensing the strapline into a set of theological glasses that aid the accurate theological reading of intersexuality. Third, I undertake a cost-benefit analysis of the proposed theological glasses, acknowledging potential pastoral problems, yet attempting to alleviate apprehension. Finally, I consider ways to

---

1. Webster, *Confessing God*, 25.

move from the book's relatively abstract dogmatic judgments about intersexuality to the concrete concerns of pastoral theology, briefly thinking about the complex matter of marriage for intersex individuals.

I. Reviewing the Divine Drama

After outlining in Chapter 2 several pitfalls with appropriating the cultural-historical one-sex theory for biblical hermeneutics and theological construction, Chapter 3 explored the theo-dramatic act of creation. Literary-canonical exegesis of the scriptural story (aided by theological reflection) suggested that in the scenes of creation's event and intent the sexed condition of humanity was mostly likely dimorphic. Foregrounding Genesis 1–2, humanity's creational structure was intentionally sexed with a sexuate correspondence between "male and female." At minimum, such sexuate correspondence was designed to meet the proximate goal of procreation (Gen. 1:28). All creation, including humanity, was ordered for fruitfulness. Hence the Thomistically inflected rubric—sexed form founds procreative function, and procreative function fits sexed form—organized around the leitmotif of God's ordered peace (*shalom*) for creation. The cumulative case for SD in the event and intent of creation obviates alternative protologies such as the hybrid argument, primal androgyny, and the trajectory argument. While it remains unlikely that intersexuality existed in creation (whether as a discrete third sex or as a mix of male and female), discerning whether humanity's sexuate correspondence is structurally essential for human nature or simply particular to *that* theo-dramatic act required progressing through the divine drama.

The next theo-dramatic act on display was the fall (Chapter 4). I argued from Genesis 3 that the fall shattered the ordered peace (*shalom*) of the sexed body. The *malum poena* of death privatively disorders the sexed body in its form (e.g., congenital eunuchism) and function (e.g., infertility) to varying degrees east of Eden. Epistemically, the prelapsarian exclusive norm of SD became the statistical majority post-fall. The empirical expression of humanity's sexuate correspondence now clusters around two poles of "male" and "female." Yet, to forestall any potential gnostic denigration of creation, the ontological "structure" of sexed humanity remains dimorphic, even if death disorders the form and function of its "direction." Thus, from the perspectives of creation and fall, intersex conditions may be classified as physical impairments—disordered diversity in a diversely disordered world. Such a verdict does not relegate intersex persons to the subhuman. Every body is subject to "death because of sin" (Rom. 8:10). Every mortal body needs life from the Spirit of Christ (Rom. 8:11). Everybody needs the restoration of *shalom*.

The need for restoration spurred us on to contemplate the theo-dramatic act of redemption in Chapter 5. Focusing on the first advent of Christ, I assessed the significance of his person and work for intersexuality. Attending to Christology proper, I sought to alleviate soteriological and anthropological concerns regarding Jesus' maleness by arguing that Jesus is *universally* human—thus all sexes are savable—and *particularly* male (not intersex)—thus no sex is necessarily second-class. All sexes, however sexed, find redemptive hope in a historically concrete male Messiah. Turning to consider Christ's work, redemptive newness in Christ neither replaces nor expands the creational structure of male and female. Rather, I submitted from 1 Corinthians 15 that the *act* of redemption in Christ restores the *stage* of creation by beginning to re-direct what was misdirected in the fall. From Matt. 19:12 and Gal. 3:28, redemption "now" concentrates on spiritual and social inclusion (valorizing the vocation of singleness), rather than any structural expansion toward SP. Yet bodies still groan and eagerly await their full and final redemption (Rom. 8:23), driving us on to contemplate the nature of redemptive newness for intersex embodiment in the consummation.

In Chapter 6, I concluded that arguments for intersex in heaven based upon appeals to Trinitarian person-*perichoresis*, the assumed normativity of Jesus' scars, or the exclusive elevation of our "body-story" plus "eccentric grounding" for numerical identity are biblically and theologically unwarranted. Constructively, I focused on 1 Cor. 15:35–58 to maintain that bodily transformation remains essential for heavenly inheritance (vv.50–53) and that such somatic change is contoured by creation (vv.35–49). If SD is part of the structure of creation, then we may expect its continuing existence in the ordered peace of the new creation. Indeed, given that death and its disordering decay will be swallowed up at the consummation (v.54), we may anticipate epistemic clarity regarding the sexed body. Thus, all bodies, however presently sexed, will likely be unambiguously male or female, restoratively transformed to the ordered *shalom* of the new creation. Nevertheless, this claim need not eliminate intersex identity in toto. Following Augustine's speculation on the eschatological embodiment of martyrs, God remains faithful to the goodness of historical particularity, for it attests to God's redeeming grace. This creates conceptual space to discern a certain fittingness to God "perhaps" (*fortasse*) inscribing the marks of virtue-cultivating impairments upon resurrected bodies.[2] Consequently, there may well be intersex conditions in heaven, not as "marks of deformity" (*deformitas*) but as "marks of honor" (*dignitas*), that testify to God's faithfulness. Thus, Augustine offers resources to read the "heavenly healing" of intersexuality not as the terroristic threat of "heavenly eugenics" but as the holistic hope of "heavenly eulogization."

II. Wearing Restoration-Transformation 3D Glasses

I have tracked and traced the sexed body through the theo-dramatic acts of creation to consummation. With the complete divine drama in view, I reiterate the strapline from Chapter 6 to summarize its coherence: "Consummation restoratively transforms creation." Correct intersex interpretation begins by recognizing that all created reality (including all humans, which includes all intersex persons) exists

---

2. Augustine, *Civ.* 22.19 (CCSL 48:839; WSA I/7:530).

within *this* divine drama. Knowing *what* (and *whose*) story we participate in and *where* we are within that story (i.e., which act plays on stage) clarifies which traits of sexed embodiment are structurally essential for human nature and which traits are accidental to the historical "direction" of the sexed body within a particular theo-dramatic act.

If the strapline of the story is "consummation restoratively transforms creation," then we read the story well when wearing a set of theological glasses that includes two lenses: one highlights restoration, the other accentuates transformation.[3] Like a pair of red and cyan lensed 3D glasses, the lenses of restoration and transformation interpret the image of intersexuality with vivid depth and enhancing clarity. The restoration lens accentuates the structural depth of the *stage*. It highlights humanity's creational structure as a sexuate correspondence between "male and female" that endures throughout the drama. The transformation lens focuses on the actors' performative direction within each theo-dramatic *act*. It helps us notice new characteristics as the performance moves from creation to consummation.

Both lenses are vital for accurate reading, but I have rendered the dynamic between the two as that of restoration modifying transformation—hence the strapline: "Consummation *restoratively transforms* creation." Reflecting the methodological approach in Chapter 1, and recalling comments from Chapter 6, this decision minimally looks to imitate the biblical pattern of foregrounding the story over the stage (the *where* over the *what*). But of course, the biblical story does not (indeed cannot) be performed without the stage. A literary foregrounding of the story need not background the inherent and indispensable value of the stage nor undermine its stability. The stage remains the external basis of the story, while the story is the internal basis of the stage. Stage without story is empty; story without stage is blind.[4] Indeed, the natural goods of the stage flower within the story through Christ the chief protagonist from creation and consummation. "Restoratively transforms" aims to capture this story-stage dynamic and so enhance the three-dimensional complexity and beauty of the divine drama.

With the restoration-transformation 3D glasses in place, I offer my interpretation of intersexuality. God made the sexed body in the event and intent of creation as a sexuate correspondence between "male and female." This structurally ordered peace was (spiritually, socially, and somatically) misdirected in the fall (spiritually and socially) redirected in redemption, and will be (somatically) transformed in the consummation.[5] Accordingly, one unavoidable conclusion is to read intersex conditions as physical impairments resulting from the fall. Given that humanity's creational structure includes a sexuate correspondence between "male and female,"

---

3. The chicken and egg dynamic between the divine drama and my proposed set of theological glasses may find an explanatory parallel in the hermeneutical spiral.

4. Michael Allen, ed., *T&T Clark Reader in John Webster* (London: T&T Clark, 2020), 143.

5. The spiritual and social renewal begun at Christ's first coming will also be complete in the consummation (cf. 1 Cor. 13:12).

intersex does not represent a metaphysical shift toward SP. Empirically observed in the present, intersex is a mix of male and female. Pre-consummation, epistemic ambiguity regarding one's true sex remains (at least from a human perspective). However, such metaphysical attention should not detract (nor distract) from the primary story—intersex Christians are individuals who *have been* redeemed spiritually and socially and *will be* transformed somatically at the consummation to sexed epistemic clarity. Augustinian reflection suggests that virtue-cultivating impairments may be eulogized as "marks of honor" that testify to God's faithfulness.

III. Cost-Benefit Analysis of Wearing Glasses

The interpretation of intersexuality that results from wearing restoration-transformation glasses raises an immediate pastoral objection: This position represents an insidious form of theological genocide because it eliminates intersex existence from the event and intent of creation and significantly reimagines intersex conditions in the new creation. In Lévinasian timbre, have I imposed SD as an abstract and totalizing ideal at the expense of the concrete face-to-face cry of the marginalized other?[6] This is an important concern, and innovationists have helpfully highlighted the concrete lived experiences of intersex people. Additionally, it is critical to consider carefully how one's proposal is *heard*, especially by those most affected. Nonetheless, both the restoration and transformation lenses remain theologically and pastorally beneficial.

A. Restoration Lens

Starting with the restoration lens and its focus on the *what* of creational structure, I restate from Chapter 3 that all humans are full bearers of God's image. Understanding the *imago Dei* in individual and not just collective terms means that each and every human person represents God's presence, however sexed.[7] First and foremost, all intersex individuals come from God and are objects of God's love. God defines who we are and who we can be. Thus, following Rowan Williams, "The reverence I owe to every person is connected with the reverence I owe to God, who brings them into being and keeps them in being."[8]

Moreover, I repeat from Chapter 4 that classifying intersex *conditions* as impairments consequent of the fall does not brand intersex *persons* as more

---

6. See Emmanuel Lévinas, *Totality and Infinity: An Essay on Exteriority*, trans. Alphonso Lingis, DuqSt 24 (Pittsburgh, PA: Duquesne University Press, 1969).

7. The Christological argument in Chapter 5 reaches the same conclusion about humanity's equal value. Since Jesus is universally human all sexes are savable. Since Jesus is male only in his historical particularity no sex is necessarily second-class.

8. Rowan Williams, *Being Disciples: Essentials of the Christian Life* (Grand Rapids: Eerdmans, 2016), 65.

fallen. A privative account of evil (affecting sexed form and function) combined with a robust commitment to God's providential common grace ensure that all postlapsarian bodies remain good in a deeply structural sense. As such, using the historically inflected term "intersex*ed*" may be more theologically accurate (and pastorally helpful) than the identitarian label of "intersex," for intersexed conveys a subtle distinction between the physical condition and the concrete person.[9] If the fall provides the provenance for intersex conditions, then the term intersexed guards the dignity of the person from being conflated with the defect of the condition.[10]

This, of course, does not mean that "male and female" are exempt from the fall. To claim otherwise is a "pious chimera."[11] Death disorders *all* postlapsarian bodies, even if that appears more visibly for some than others. Indeed, fixating on external physicality clashes with God's metric that "looks at the heart" (1 Sam. 16:7). In short, with its strong affirmation of the structural goodness of intersexed individuals, and its clearer ability to identify certain physical conditions that are resultant of the fall (whether as defect or dysfunction), the restoration lens possesses theological resources to avoid the charge of theological genocide.

Furthermore, there is an important category difference between the restoration lens' account of proper form and function and the stigmatization of anomalous conditions. History tells the tragic tale of how the former has been utilized to justify the latter. But historical correlation is categorically distinct from logical causation. As such, the concrete face of the other does not exert the kind of moral claim for SP that innovationists assume. Indeed, while innovationists sound the clarion call of justice, nothing about a metaphysical shift toward SP necessarily precludes the victimization of concrete others. Three sexes can still ostracize a fourth, fifth, or sixth sex. In which case, as Fellipe do Vale evinces, "[I]nstead of providing hope for intersex/DSD individuals who have experienced shame, such metaphysical revisions only paint a clearer target on their backs."[12]

More positively, the restoration lens' account of proper form and function possesses distinctly pastoral benefits, for it actively aids medical practitioners in their efforts to diagnose and care for intersexed persons. Conversely, as mentioned

9. For a similar attempt to define personal identity narrativally for the purposes of liberating individual agency (in contrast to static identarian names/labels that potentially feed shame and judgement), see Kelly M. Kapic, *You're Only Human: How Your Limits Reflect God's Design and Why That's Good News* (Grand Rapids: Brazos, 2022), 93.

10. In this sense "intersexed" shares benefits with DSD/VSD terminology. The term "intersexed" occurs in innovationist literature, but it does not appear to be employed in the way I am suggesting here, i.e., to highlight the distinction between the condition and the person. This is likely because the proposed distinction would be rejected.

11. Wesley Hill, "Afterword," in *Marriage, Scripture, and the Church: Theological Discernment on the Question of Same-Sex Union* (Grand Rapids: Baker Academic, 2021), 293.

12. do Vale, "Gender as Love," 326.

in Chapters 4 and 6, because some arguments for SP do not appear to provide the resources to ascertain defective bodily configurations in any normative sense, medical conditions associated with some forms of intersexuality (e.g., metabolic and endocrinological imbalances—sometimes life-threatening) could presumably go undiagnosed and untreated.[13] Yet if the potential tumor caused by genetic mosaicism is identified as such, then swift and apposite treatment can be given. But if genetic mosaicism is just one creational variation among many, then the risk of detrimental symptoms being missed (and worsening) increases. The innovationist case seeks to champion the cry of the marginalized, yet ironically lacks adequate resources to protect concrete intersexed lives. Worse, innovationist logic risks naively romanticizing impairments, thereby belying present struggles. Conversely, wearing theological glasses with a restoration lens helps us identify and affirm the goodness of creational structure, as well as interpret intersexuality in a way that upholds both the inherent theological value of intersexed persons and the pastoral imperative of protecting real lives through correct medical care.[14]

B. Transformation Lens

If the restoration lens offers valuable theological and pastoral benefits that avert the charge of theological genocide, can the same be said of the transformation lens? While the restoration lens accentuates the stability of creational structure, the transformation lens focuses our attention upon the direction of the divine drama. Conclusions drawn about the essential and accidental traits of sexed embodiment are necessarily situated (and so read) within the grand narrative of creation to consummation. This narrative emphasizes God's transformative work in Christ, foregrounding spiritual and social redemptive newness at Jesus' first advent and somatic newness at his second advent. The transformation lens stops us downplaying God's transformative purposes. It keeps us from settling for an over-realized eschatology that ends up minimizing the consummative life for which we have been made.

More positively, interpreting intersexuality through a transformation lens stresses that individual worth and identity are not exhausted by our sexed embodiment, but may be found in our spiritual status in Christ (cf. Col. 3:3–4). Recalling comments in Chapter 5 from Gal. 3:26–29, all Christians are first and foremost "children of God through faith" (v.26). Consequently, true justice is found and flourishes in communities comprised of individuals whose core identity rests "in Christ Jesus" (vv.26, 28). In such communities of grace, individual worth is not determined by one's perceived spiritual, social, or somatic capital. Rather,

---

13. For such imbalances, see Ellen K. Feder, "Imperatives of Normality: From 'Intersex' to 'Disorders of Sex Development,'" *GLQ* 15 (2009): 226.

14. Jennifer Anne Cox's caution is additionally *apropos*. We should beware agendas that use "intersex people as pawns for their political ends.... Using people this way undermines the humanity of intersex people" (*Intersex in Christ*, 36–7).

individual value is an equal *gift*—graciously bestowed by God and blood-bought by Christ—recognized and strengthened within the one body of Christ, a foretaste of consummation life. As such, the church should be *the* place of healing and wholeness for the stigmatized and broken.

Moreover, the consummative thrust of the transformation lens teaches that the ecclesial inclusion of intersexed individuals *as intersexed* is about holiness. True welcome of the other demands a willingness to be changed by the other, for church is the "place of transformation, of discipline, of learning, and not merely a place to be comforted or indulged."[15] We all need God's help to see others like God sees us, to move toward concrete face-to-face encounters, to give special honor to the seemingly less honorable, and to allow the indispensable contribution of the supposedly other to grow the body of Christ more into the image of Christ (1 Cor. 12:22–25; Eph. 4:15–16). As Julie Gittoes elaborates, the "blessing" of richer ecclesial "participation in Christ's humanity and priesthood" may be mediated through "the gift of . . . physical particularity," including individual embodiment.[16]

Accordingly, the transformation lens insists that intersexed persons are not theologically worse off than anyone else. Rather, the consummative direction of the divine drama casts a compelling vision of corporate holiness for all, however sexed. In an Augustinian key, such a vision appreciates the "strange vocation," and so unique contribution, of an intersexed individual's embodiment. Through bodies that are not clearly ordered to the opposite sex, God perhaps placards in a very concrete way the theological truth that humans are ultimately ordered to life with God. Viewing intersexuality through the transformative lens takes the spotlight off our sexed state and puts it rightly upon Christ to whom we journey—a timely word in our sex-saturated society. Thus, the transformation lens remains theologically and pastorally beneficial, for by foregrounding the direction of divine drama it comforts the unsettled other and unsettles comfortable others.

In summary, the dual-lensed restoration-transformation glasses are the product of (and a further aid to) a thick theological reading of the divine drama. The glasses attempt to capture something of both the coherence of the single divine drama (thereby combining a traditional emphasis on creation *and* an innovational stress on eschatology) and the dogmatic coherence between doctrinal loci (thus reflecting the coherence of the chief protagonist, our Triune God). Accordingly, such glasses remain theologically and pastorally beneficial for interpreting intersexuality, for they both clarify the enduring creational structure of humanity's sexuate correspondence (offering a theological account of the "natural" that undergirds apposite medical care), and they foreground the transformative direction for all

15. Richard B. Hays, *The Moral Vision of the New Testament: Community, Cross, New Creation: A Contemporary Introduction to New Testament Ethics* (San Francisco: HarperOne, 1996), 401.

16. Julie Gittoes, "Participation in the Body: The Gift of Physical Particularity," *IJST* 24 (2022): 313.

humans, however sexed, as we journey from creation to consummation (thus turning our introspective gaze up and onto Christ).

IV. Moving from Dogmatic Theology to Pastoral Theology

Even if one, like Agrippa (Acts 26:28), were almost persuaded by the biblical and theological logic of this dogmatic account of intersexuality, pastoral concerns regarding the ethical and aesthetic plausibility of the position may linger. The argument may be intellectually "true," but is it morally "good" and "beautiful"? In short, is the account livable and life-giving for real people, particularly the intersexed? The project thus far has been concerned with largely abstract matters, focusing on exegetical theology at the expense of wrestling with the daily concrete challenges facing intersexed individuals. Yet given the introductory concern to make an ecclesial (and evangelistic) contribution that is salutary, formative, and pastorally pertinent, I turn now to offer several ways one could move from dogmatic judgments concerning the concept of intersexuality to moral-pastoral care of concrete individuals.

One complex challenge facing intersexed individuals is marriage.[17] A traditional account of marriage emphasizes a heterosexual, monogamous, and covenantal partnership that is constituted by the individually necessary and jointly sufficient conditions of the couple exchanging the three goods of fidelity (*fides*), fruitfulness (*proles*), and indissolubility (*sacramentum*),[18] and being ordered toward the two ends of procreation and spousal union.[19] Yet can/should someone with CAIS (genotypically male; phenotypically female) get married? On the one hand, the conditions of fidelity, relational fruitfulness, a commitment to indissolubility, and the end of unitive love could be satisfied. But someone with CAIS remains infertile, unable to fulfill (regardless of their openness to) marriage's procreating and parenting ends. Further, the sign-character of heterosexual marriage, that points to Christ and his church (Eph. 5:32), would appear blurred. Thus, with not all conditions met, the implication is that intersexed individuals with CAIS cannot marry.[20]

---

17. Another challenging example: What if the best candidate to be an elder or pastor in a complementarian church is intersexed? For a creative exploration of this question in popular fiction, see Robert Harris, *Conclave* (London: Penguin Random House, 2017).

18. For the interrelation of these three goods named by Augustine, see Perry J. Cahall, "The Trinitarian Structure of St Augustine's Good of Marriage," *AugStud* 34 (2003): 223–32.

19. E.g., Matthew Levering, *Engaging the Doctrine of Marriage: Human Marriage as the Image and Sacrament of the Marriage of God and Creation* (Eugene, OR: Cascade, 2020); Belousek, *Marriage*.

20. Whether this logic could be extended to other intersexed conditions would need to be worked out on a case-by-case basis.

Nevertheless, rather than conclude with this pastorally blunt judgment, the theological glasses proposed thus far offer resources to reconsider the question of intersexuality and marriage without rejecting a traditional definition. While the restoration lens' focus on creational structure bolsters the heterosexual precondition of marriage (particularly as a creational ordinance), the transformation lens recalls God's miraculous empowerment for generation (highlighted by the matriarchal narratives in Genesis), reminding us that all procreation is indeed a miracle. Thus, someone with CAIS could possibly satisfy the *proles* condition by first being open to the miracle of physical healing, which would then provide the necessary sexuate correspondence for the subsequent miracle of generation.[21]

Further, the sign-character of marriage could be retained if it remains theologically legitimate for an intersexed individual to choose and stick with a gendered identity to then marry someone of the opposite sex. Of course, this raises complex questions about the ethics of choice, intent, and consent, compounded by the fact that gender identity is often chosen *for* intersexed persons at birth, a choice that may well be called into question at puberty.[22] While space precludes a robust analysis of such questions, it is sufficient to note that *if* identifying with a particular gender is theologically legitimate for intersexed individuals, then the sign-character condition for marriage could be satisfied.[23] The preceding thought-experiment offers good news for intersexed individuals who would love to be married *and* affirm the truthfulness of a traditional understanding of marriage.[24] Rather than trump "love" with "truth," the proposed theological glasses demonstrate potential to navigate the challenge of thinking through marriage and intersexuality with "truth in love" (Eph. 4:15).

21. This argument assumes that the *proles* condition for Christian marriage includes (at minimum) biological procreation. Space prevents assessing further the extent to which physical generativity in the new covenant has been expanded or replaced by evangelism and adoption, as well as whether it is possible to dissociate the procreative and unitive ends of marriage.

22. E.g., someone with 5-ARD (46,XY) may exhibit at birth "more female-appearing external genital organs but develop more typically male secondary sexual characteristics (facial hair, etc.) at puberty" (Petersen, *Guide to Intersex*, 72).

23. Decisions regarding the theological legitimacy of identifying with a certain gender could have interesting implications for trans* issues.

24. The moral reasoning above does not attempt to provide a complete answer to the question of whether intersexed persons can, or even should, marry. Given our post-resurrection, pre-consummation location within the divine drama, one should not neglect the high vocation of celibacy/singleness. See Jana Marguerite Bennett, *Water Is Thicker Than Blood: An Augustinian Theology of Marriage and Singleness* (Oxford: Oxford University Press, 2008).

V. Conclusion

This book has constructed a dogmatic account of intersexuality that offers a set of thick theological glasses through which to (self)interpret intersexed embodiment. Where traditionalists concentrate on creation and innovationists emphasize eschatology, this project has attended to the complete divine drama, whose macro-plot reveals "consummation restoratively transforming creation." The dual-lensed restoration-transformation glasses proposed above simultaneously clarify the abiding creational structure of humanity's sexuate correspondence and highlight the transformative direction of all humans, however sexed, as God guides us through the divine drama. Therefore, intersexuality need not be read as evidence for a metaphysical shift toward SP. More constructively, in God's providence, intersexuality may concretely placard the theological axiom that all humans, however sexed, are ultimately ordered to life with God. Indeed, following Augustinian theological reflection, intersexed conditions may well appear in the new creation, specifically as "marks of honor" that testify to God's enduring faithfulness and are praised as such.

Good theology humbly and prayerfully explicates God and the things of God. Given God reveals his manifold wisdom through the church (Eph. 3:10), good theology asks questions *from* the church and *for* the life of the church. I briefly demonstrated above how one might move from dogmatic judgments to pastoral care, considering the puzzle of intersexuality and marriage. Yet, even if one were to parse out for pastoral theology all the potential implications of the proposed dogmatic account of intersexuality, further steps remain for holistic pastoral care. While the *kenosis* of unambiguous sexed embodiment remains a misstep,[25] Susannah Cornwall's suggestion provokes the unambiguously sexed to recall God's kindness to them, stimulating both repentance (Rom. 2:4) and kindness to others (Eph. 4:32). As Nazianzen preached *c.* AD 370 to inspire love for homeless lepers, it is human "kindness" (φιλανθρωπία) that most clearly resembles Christ our head.[26] Such kindness could begin with simply taking the time (individually and collectively) to let go of privilege, listen, lament, and love our intersexed siblings. We need Christ to give us his "empathetic gaze" upon the wondrously wounded.[27] We need a humble willingness to be changed through concrete face-to-face encounters with the "strange vocation" (*mira vocatio*) of other others, so that the body of Christ may mature (Eph. 4:15–16), further placarding the manifold wisdom of God.

---

25. *Kenosis* "necessitates thinking ourselves beyond male-and-female, and reflecting this both in our theory and in our ecclesiological praxis" (Cornwall, *Sex and Uncertainty*, 233). E.g., refusing to indicate one's sex on official documentation.

26. Gregory of Nazianzus, "Oration 14," 8 (PG 35:868).

27. Brock, *Wondrously Wounded*, 33.

BIBLIOGRAPHY

Accord Alliance. "Our Mission." Cited November 3, 2021. https://www.accordalliance.org/about-accord-alliance/our-mission/.

Achermann, John C. and Ieuan A. Hughes. "Pediatric Disorders of Sex Development." In *Williams Textbook of Endocrinology*, edited by Shlomo Melmed, Kenneth S. Polonsky, P. Reed Larsen, and Henry Kronenberg, 893–963. 13th ed. Philadelphia, PA: Elsevier, 2016.

Allen, R. Michael. *The Christ's Faith: A Dogmatic Account*. TTCSST. London: T&T Clark, 2009.

Allen, R. Michael, ed. *T&T Clark Reader in John Webster*. London: T&T Clark, 2020.

Allen, Michael and Scott R. Swain. *Reformed Catholicity: The Promise of Retrieval for Theology and Biblical Interpretation*. Grand Rapids: Baker Academic, 2015.

Allen, Prudence. *The Concept of Woman*. 3 vols. Grand Rapids: Eerdmans, 1997.

Allison, Gregg R. *Embodied: Living as Whole People in a Fractured World*. Grand Rapids: Baker Academic, 2021.

Amy-Chinn, Dee. "Is Queer Biology a Useful Tool for Queer Theology?" *ThS* 15 (2009): 49–63.

Angel, Andrew R. *Intimate Jesus: The Sexuality of God Incarnate*. London: SPCK, 2017.

Anselm. *Basic Writings*. Translated by Thomas Williams. Indianapolis: Hackett, 2007.

Aquinas, Thomas. *Commentary on Romans*. Translated by Fabian R. Larcher. Green Bay, WI: Aquinas Institute, 2020.

Aquinas, Thomas. *Commentary on the Letters of Saint Paul to the Corinthians*. Edited by John Mortensen and Enrique Alarcón. Translated by Fabian R. Larcher. L/E 38. Lander, WY: Aquinas Institute, 2012.

Aquinas, Thomas. *Commentary on the Sentences III*. Translated by the Aquinas Institute. Green Bay, WI: Aquinas Institute, 2018–. https://aquinas.cc/la/en/~Sent.III.D12.Q3.A1.qa1.

Aquinas, Thomas. *Light of Faith: The Compendium of Theology*. Translated by Cyril Vollert. 3rd ed. Manchester, NH: Sophia Institute, 1993.

Aquinas, Thomas. *On Being and Essence*. Translated by Armand Maurer. 2nd rev. ed. Toronto: Pontifical Institute of Mediaeval Studies, 1968.

Aquinas, Thomas. *On Evil*. Translated by Richard Regan. Oxford: Oxford University Press, 2003.

Aquinas, Thomas. *Summa Contra Gentiles*. Translated by Laurence Shapcote. L/E 11–12. Green Bay, WI: Aquinas Institute, 2018.

Aquinas, Thomas. *Summa Theologiae*. Edited by John Mortensen and Enrique Alarcón. Translated by Laurence Shapcote. L/E 13–22. Lander, WY: Aquinas Institute, 2012.

Aristotle. *Generation of Animals*. Translated by A. L. Peck. LCL 366. Cambridge, MA: Harvard University Press, 2000.

Aristotle. *Poetics*. Translated by Stephen Halliwell. LCL 199. Cambridge, MA: Harvard University Press, 1995.

Aristotle. *Politics*. Translated by H. Rackham. LCL 264. Cambridge, MA: Harvard University Press, 1932.

Arnold, Bill T. and John H. Choi. *A Guide to Biblical Hebrew Syntax*. 2nd ed. Cambridge: Cambridge University Press, 2018.

Asher, Jeffrey R. *Polarity and Change in 1 Corinthians 15: A Study of Metaphysics, Rhetoric, and Resurrection*. HUT 42. Tübingen: Mohr Siebeck, 2000.

Asher-Greve, Julia M. "From La Femme to Multiple Sex/Gender." In *Studying Gender in the Ancient Near East*, edited by Saana Svärd and Agnès Garcia-Ventura, 15–50. University Park, PA: Eisenbrauns, 2018.

Ashford, Bruce Riley and Craig G. Bartholomew. *The Doctrine of Creation: A Constructive Kuyperian Approach*. Downers Grove, IL: IVP Academic, 2020.

Athanasius. *Contra Gentes and De Incarnatione*. Translated by Robert W. Thomson. OECT. Oxford: Clarendon, 1971.

Athanasius. *On the Incarnation*. Translated by John Behr. PPS 44b. Yonkers, NY: St Vladimir's, 2011.

Atkins, Margaret. "Pax." In vol. 4 of *A–L*, edited by Robert Dodaro, Cornelius Mayer, Christof Müller, 566–73. Basel: Schwabe AG, 2012–2018.

Augustine. *Answer to the Pelagians*. Edited by John E. Rotelle. Translated by Roland J. Teske. WSA I/23. Hyde Park, NY: New City, 1997.

Augustine. *Confessionum libri XIII*. Edited by Martin Skutella and Luc Verheijen. CCSL 28. Turnholti: Brepols, 1981.

Augustine. *De civitate Dei: Libri XI–XXII*. Edited by Bernard Dombart and Alphonse Kalb. CCSL 48. Turnhout: Brepols, 1955.

Augustine. *Enarrationes in Psalmos 101–109*. Edited by Franco Gori and Adiuvante Claudio Pierantoni. CSEL 95/1. Wien: OAW, 2011.

Augustine. *Marriage and Virginity*. Edited by David G. Hunter. Translated by Ray Kearney. WSA I/9. Hyde Park, NY: New City, 1999.

Augustine. *On Genesis: A Refutation of the Manichees, Unfinished Literal Commentary on Genesis, the Literal Meaning of Genesis*. Edited by John E. Rotelle. Translated by Edmund Hill. WSA I/13. Hyde Park, NY: New City, 2002.

Augustine. *On the Free Choice of the Will, on Grace and Free Choice, and Other Writings*. Edited by Peter King. CTHP. Cambridge: Cambridge University Press, 2010.

Augustine. *Sermons 184–229Z: On the Liturgical Seasons*. Edited by John E. Rotelle. Translated by Edmund Hill. WSA III/6. New Rochelle, NY: New City, 1993.

Augustine. *Sermons 306–340A: On the Saints*. Edited by John E. Rotelle. Translated by Edmund Hill. WSA III/9. Hyde Park, NY: New City, 1994.

Augustine. *Teaching Christianity*. Edited by John E. Rotelle. Translated by Edmund Hill. WSA I/11. Hyde Park, NY: New City, 1996.

Augustine. *The City of God: I–X*. Edited by Boniface Ramsey. Translated by William Babcock. WSA I/6. Hyde Park, NY: New City, 2013.

Augustine. *The City of God: XI–XXII*. Edited by Boniface Ramsey. Translated by William Babcock. WSA I/7. Hyde Park, NY: New City, 2013.

Augustine. *The First Catechetical Instruction*. Translated by Joseph P. Christopher. ACW 2. New York: Newman, 1978.

Augustine. *The Manichean Debate*. Edited by Boniface Ramsey. Translated by Roland J. Teske. WSA I/19. Hyde Park, NY: New City, 2006.

Augustine. *The Retractions*. Translated by Mary Inez Bogan. FC 60. Washington, DC: Catholic University of America Press, 1968.

Augustine. *The Trinity.* Edited by John E. Rotelle. Translated by Edmund Hill. 2nd ed. WSA I/5. Hyde Park, NY: New City, 2015.

Augustine. *Treatises on Various Subjects.* Translated by Mary Sarah Muldowney. FC 16. New York: Fathers of the Church, 1952.

Augustine. *Writings of Saint Augustine.* Translated by Denis J. Kavanagh. FC 5. New York: Cima, 1948.

Balthasar, Hans Urs von. *Theo-Drama: Theological Dramatic Theory.* 5 vols. San Francisco: Ignatius, 1988.

Bandstra, Barry L. *Genesis 1–11: A Handbook on the Hebrew Text.* BHHB. Waco, TX: Baylor University Press, 2008.

Barclay, John M. G. *Paul and the Gift.* Grand Rapids: Eerdmans, 2015.

Barrett, Matthew, ed. *Four Views on the Historical Adam.* Counterpoints. Grand Rapids: Zondervan Academic, 2013.

Barth, Karl. *Church Dogmatics: The Doctrine of Creation.* Vol. III/1. Edited by G. W. Bromiley and T. F. Torrance. London: T&T Clark, 2010.

Bauckham, Richard. *The Climax of Prophecy: Studies on the Book of Revelation.* Edinburgh: T & T Clark, 1993.

Bauer, W., F. W. Danker, W. F. Arndt, and F. W. Gingrich. *Greek-English Lexicon of the New Testament and Other Early Christian Literature.* 3rd ed. Chicago: University of Chicago Press, 1999.

Baumert, Norbert. *Antifeminismus bei Paulus? Einzelstudien.* FB 68. Würzburg: Echter, 1992.

Bavinck, Herman. *Christian Worldview.* Translated by Nathaniel Gray Sutanto, James Eglinton, and Cory C. Brock. Wheaton, IL: Crossway, 2019.

Bavinck, Herman. "Common Grace." Translated by Raymond Van Leeuwen. *CTJ* 24 (1989): 35–65.

Bavinck, Herman. *Reformed Dogmatics.* Edited by John Bolt. Translated by John Vriend. 4 vols. Grand Rapids: Baker Academic, 2003–2008.

Bavinck, Herman. *Reformed Ethics: Created, Fallen, and Converted Humanity.* Edited by John Bolt. Vol. 1. Grand Rapids: Baker Academic, 2019.

Bavinck, Herman. *The Wonderful Works of God: Instruction in the Christian Religion According to the Reformed Confession.* Translated by Henry Zylstra. Glenside, PA: Westminster Seminary Press, 2019.

Beale, G. K. *A New Testament Biblical Theology: The Unfolding of the Old Testament in the New.* Grand Rapids: Baker Academic, 2011.

Beattie, Tina. "Gendering Genesis, Engendering Difference. A Catholic Theological Quest." *STK* 92 (2016): 102–17.

Beauchamp, Paul. *Création et Séparation: Étude Exégétique du Chapitre Premier de la Genèse.* LD. Paris: Cerf, 2005.

Beauchamp, Paul. "מִין." In vol. 8 of *TDOT*, edited by G. Johannes Botterweck, Helmer Ringgren, and Heinz-Josef Fabry, translated by Douglas W. Scott, 288–90. Grand Rapids: Eerdmans, 1997.

Behr, John. *Irenaeus of Lyons: Identifying Christianity.* CTC. Oxford: Oxford University Press, 2013.

Belousek, Darrin W. Snyder. *Marriage, Scripture, and The Church: Theological Discernment on the Question of Same-Sex Union.* Grand Rapids: Baker Academic, 2021.

Belser, Julia Watts. "Priestly Aesthetics: Disability and Bodily Difference in Leviticus 21." *Int* 73 (2019): 355–66.

Benagiano, Giuseppe and Bruno Dallapiccola. "Can Modern Biology Interpret the Mystery of the Birth of Christ?" *JMFNM* 28 (2015): 240–4.

Bennett, Jana Marguerite. *Water Is Thicker Than Blood: An Augustinian Theology of Marriage and Singleness*. Oxford: Oxford University Press, 2008.

Berry, R. J. "This Cursed Earth: Is 'the Fall' Credible?" *SCB* 11 (1999): 29–49.

Bethmont, Rémy. "How Queer Can Christian Marriage Be? Eschatological Imagination and the Blessing of Same-Sex Unions in the American Episcopal Church." In *New Approaches in History and Theology to Same-Sex Love and Desire*, edited by Mark D. Chapman and Dominic Janes, 209–25. GSH. Cham, Switzerland: Palgrave Macmillan, 2018.

Bettenson, Henry and Chris Maunder, eds. *Documents of the Christian Church*. 4th ed. Oxford: Oxford University Press, 2011.

Bird, Michael F. "Salvation in Paul's Judaism?" In *Paul and Judaism: Crosscurrents in Pauline Exegesis and the Study of Jewish-Christian Relations*, edited by Reimund Bieringer and Didier Pollefeyt, 15–40. LNTS 463. London: T&T Clark, 2012.

Bird, Phyllis A. "'Male and Female He Created Them': Gen 1:27b in the Context of the Priestly Account of Creation." *HTR* 74 (1981): 129–59.

Blackless, Melanie, Anthony Charuvastra, Amanda Derryck, Anne Fausto-Sterling, Karl Lauzanne, and Ellen Lee. "How Sexually Dimorphic Are We? Review and Synthesis." *AJHB* 12 (2000): 151–66.

Block, Daniel I. "Marriage and Family in Ancient Israel." In *Marriage and Family in the Biblical World*, edited by Ken M. Campbell, 33–102. Downers Grove, IL: IVP Academic, 2003.

Bock, Darrell L. "Thinking Backwards About Adam and History." *TJ* 40 (2019): 131–43.

Boda, Mark J. *A Severe Mercy: Sin and Its Remedy in the Old Testament*. Siphrut 1. Winona Lake, IN: Eisenbrauns, 2009.

Boersma, Gerald P. "The Rationes Seminales in Augustine's Theology of Creation." *NV* 18 (2020): 413–41.

Boersma, Hans. *Seeing God: The Beatific Vision in Christian Tradition*. Grand Rapids: Eerdmans, 2018.

Bonhoeffer, Dietrich. *Ethics*. Edited by Clifford J. Green. Translated by Reinhard Krauss, Charles C. West, and Douglas W. Stott. DBW 6. Minneapolis, MN: Fortress, 2005.

Borden Sharkey, Sarah. *An Aristotelian Feminism*. HASNMA 1. Switzerland: Springer, 2016.

Bourbon, Florence. "La Femme Malade, Le Médecin Hippocratique et la Question du Genre." *Lalies* 32 (2012): 181–9.

Brandom, Robert. *Tales of the Mighty Dead: Historical Essays in the Metaphysics of Intentionality*. Cambridge, MA: Harvard University Press, 2002.

Brisson, Luc. *Le sexe incertain: Androgynie et hermaphrodisme dans l'Antiquité gréco-romaine*. 2ème éd. VdM. Paris: Belles Lettres, 2008.

Brock, Brian. "Augustine's Hierarchies of Human Wholeness and Their Healing." In *Disability in the Christian Tradition: A Reader*, edited by Brian Brock and John Swinton, 65–100. Grand Rapids: Eerdmans, 2012.

Brock, Brian. *Christian Ethics in a Technological Age*. Grand Rapids: Eerdmans, 2010.

Brock, Brian. *Disability: Living into the Diversity of Christ's Body*. PFL. Grand Rapids: Baker Academic, 2021.

Brock, Brian. *Wondrously Wounded: Theology, Disability, and the Body of Christ*. SRTD. Waco, TX: Baylor University Press, 2019.

Brock, Brian and Bernd Wannenwetsch. *The Therapy of the Christian Body: A Theological Exposition of Paul's First Letter to the Corinthians*. Vol. 2. Eugene, OR: Cascade, 2018.

Brookins, Timothy A. and Bruce W. Longenecker. *I Corinthians 10–16: A Handbook on the Greek Text*. BHGNT. Waco, TX: Baylor University Press, 2016.

Brown, Paul J. *Bodily Resurrection and Ethics in 1 Cor 15: Connecting Faith and Morality in the Context of Greco-Roman Mythology*. WUNT 2/360. Tübingen: Mohr Siebeck, 2014.

Brown, Peter. *The Body and Society: Men, Women, and Sexual Renunciation in Early Christianity*. 2nd ed. CCRel. New York: Columbia University Press, 2008.

Brownson, James V. *Bible, Gender, Sexuality: Reframing The Church's Debate on Same-Sex Relationships*. Grand Rapids: Eerdmans, 2013.

Budin, Stephanie Lynn. "Gender in the Tale of Aqhat." In *Studying Gender in the Ancient Near East*, edited by Saana Svärd and Agnès Garcia-Ventura, 51–72. University Park, PA: Eisenbrauns, 2018.

Budwey, Stephanie A. *Religion and Intersex: Perspectives from Science, Law, Culture, and Theology*. RNCTRTBS. Abingdon: Routledge, 2022.

Bultmann, Rudolf. "θάνατος." In vol. 3 of *TDNT*, edited by Gerhard Kittel, translated by Geoffrey W. Bromiley, 7–25. Grand Rapids: Eerdmans, 1965.

Burk, Denny. "Asking the Right Questions about Intersex Athletes: Part 1." *CBMW* (August 22, 2016). Cited November 19, 2020. https://cbmw.org/2016/08/22/asking-the -right-questions-about-intersex-athletes-part-1/.

Burk, Denny. "Asking the Right Questions about Intersex Athletes: Part 2." *CBMW* (August 23, 2016). Cited November 19, 2020. https://cbmw.org/2016/08/23/asking-the -right-questions-about-intersex-athletes-part-2.

Burk, Denny. *What Is the Meaning of Sex?* Wheaton, IL: Crossway, 2013.

Burnell, Peter. *The Augustinian Person*. Washington, DC: Catholic University of America Press, 2005.

Burrus, Virginia. "Carnal Excess: Flesh at the Limits of Imagination." *JECS* 17 (2009): 247–65.

Burrus, Virginia. "Queer Father: Gregory of Nyssa and the Subversion of Identity." In *Queer Theology: Rethinking the Western Body*, edited by Gerard Loughlin, 147–62. Malden, MA: Wiley-Blackwell, 2007.

Butchvarov, Panayot. "Metaphysics." In *The Cambridge Dictionary of Philosophy*, edited by Robert Audi, 661–4. 3rd ed. New York: Cambridge University Press, 2015.

Butler, Judith. *Gender Trouble: Feminism and the Subversion of Identity*. New York: Routledge, 1990.

Butner, D. Glenn. *Trinitarian Dogmatics: Exploring the Grammar of the Christian Doctrine of God*. Grand Rapids: Baker Academic, 2022.

Butticaz, Simon. *La crise galate ou l'anthropologie en question*. BZNW 229. Berlin: De Gruyter, 2018.

Bynum, Caroline Walker. *Resurrection of the Body in Western Christianity, 200–1336*. New York: Columbia University Press, 1996.

Cadenhead, Raphael A. *The Body and Desire: Gregory of Nyssa's Ascetical Theology*. CLA 4. Oakland, CA: University of California Press, 2018.

Cahall, Perry J. "The Trinitarian Structure of St Augustine's Good of Marriage." *AugStud* 34 (2003): 223–32.

Cahana, Jonathan. "Androgyne or Undrogyne? Queering the Gnostic Myth." *Numen* 61 (2014): 509–24.

Calder, Todd C. "Is the Privation Theory of Evil Dead?" *AphQ* 44 (2007): 371–81.

Calvin, John. *Institutes of the Christian Religion*. Translated by Henry Beveridge. Peabody, MA: Hendrickson, 2008.

Campbell, Constantine R. *Paul and the Hope of Glory: An Exegetical and Theological Study*. Grand Rapids: Zondervan Academic, 2020.

Carmichael, Calum M. *Sex and Religion in the Bible*. New Haven, CT: Yale University Press, 2010.

Carson, D. A. *Exegetical Fallacies*. 2nd ed. Carlisle: Paternoster, 1996.

Carson, D. A. "Partakers of the Age to Come." In *These Last Days: A Christian View of History*, edited by Richard D. Phillips and Gabriel N. E. Fluhrer, 89–106. Phillipsburg, NJ: P&R, 2011.

Charlesworth, James H., ed. "Martyrdom and Ascension of Isaiah." In *The Old Testament Pseudepigrapha*, translated by Michael A. Knibb, 2:143–76. 2 vols. Peabody, MA: Hendrickson, 2009.

Charlesworth, James H., ed. *The Dead Sea Scrolls: Hebrew, Aramaic, and Greek Texts with English Translations: Damascus Document, War Scroll, and Related Documents*. Vol. 2. PTSDSSP. Tübingen: Mohr Siebeck, 1994.

Childs, James M. "Eschatology, Anthropology, and Sexuality: Helmut Thielicke and the Orders of Creation Revisited." *JSCE* 30:1 (2010): 3–20.

Church of England. *Living in Love & Faith: Christian Teaching and Learning About Identity, Sexuality, Relationships, and Marriage*. London: Church House, 2020.

Ciampa, Roy E. and Brian S. Rosner. *The First Letter to the Corinthians*. PiNTC. Grand Rapids: Eerdmans, 2010.

Clemens, David M. "The Law of Sin and Death: Ecclesiastes and Genesis 1–3." *Them* 19 (1994): 5–8.

Clines, David J. A. "The Image of God in Man." *TynBul* 19 (1968): 53–103.

Clines, David J. A. *The Theme of the Pentateuch*. 2nd ed. JSOTSup 10. Sheffield: JSOT, 1997.

Coakley, Sarah. *God, Sexuality, and the Self: An Essay "On the Trinity"*. Cambridge: Cambridge University Press, 2013.

Coats, George W. *Genesis, with an Introduction to Narrative Literature*. FOTL 1. Grand Rapids: Eerdmans, 1983.

Collins, C. John. *Reading Genesis Well: Navigating History, Poetry, Science, and Truth in Genesis 1–11*. Grand Rapids: Zondervan Academic, 2018.

Collins, C. John. "The Place of the 'Fall' in the Overall Vision of the Hebrew Bible." *TJ* 40 (2019): 165–84.

Conway, Colleen M. *Behold the Man: Jesus and Greco-Roman Masculinity*. Oxford: Oxford University Press, 2008.

Cooper, Adam G. *Life in the Flesh: An Anti-Gnostic Spiritual Philosophy*. Oxford: Oxford University Press, 2008.

Cooper, John W. *Body, Soul, and Life Everlasting: Biblical Anthropology and the Monism-Dualism Debate*. Grand Rapids: Eerdmans, 2000.

Corcoran, Kevin, ed. *Soul, Body, and Survival: Essays on the Metaphysics of Human Persons*. Ithaca, NY: Cornell University Press, 2001.

Cornwall, Susannah. "All Things to All? Requeering Stuart's Eucharistic Erasure of Priestly Sex." In *Liturgy with a Difference: Beyond Inclusion in the Christian Assembly*, edited by Stephen Burns and Bryan Cones, 47–60. London: SCM, 2019.

Cornwall, Susannah. "Asking About What Is Better: Intersex, Disability, and Inaugurated Eschatology." *JRDH* 17 (2013): 369–92.

Cornwall, Susannah. "British Intersex Christians' Accounts of Intersex Identity, Christian Identity and Church Experience." *PracTheo* 6 (2013): 220–36.

Cornwall, Susannah. *Constructive Theology and Gender Variance: Transformative Creatures*. CIT. Cambridge: Cambridge University Press, 2023.

Cornwall, Susannah. "Faithfulness to Our Sexuate Bodies: The Vocations of Generativity and Sex." In *Thinking Again About Marriage: Key Theological Questions*, edited by John P. Bradbury and Susannah Cornwall, 62–81. London: SCM, 2016.

Cornwall, Susannah. "Intersex and the Rhetorics of Disability and Disorder: Multiple and Provisional Significance in Sexed, Gender, and Disabled Bodies." *JDR* 19 (2015): 106–18.

Cornwall, Susannah. "Laws 'Needefull in Later to Be Abrogated': Intersex and the Sources of Christian Theology." In *Intersex, Theology, and the Bible: Troubling Bodies in Church, Text, and Society*, edited by Susannah Cornwall, 147–71. New York: Palgrave Macmillan, 2015.

Cornwall, Susannah. *Sex and Uncertainty in the Body of Christ: Intersex Conditions and Christian Theology*. GTS. London: Equinox, 2010.

Cornwall, Susannah. "Sex Otherwise: Intersex, Christology, and the Maleness of Jesus." *JFSR* 30 (2014): 23–39.

Cornwall, Susannah. "'State of Mind' Versus 'Concrete Set of Facts': The Contrasting of Transgender and Intersex in Church Documents on Sexuality." *ThS* 15 (2009): 7–28.

Cornwall, Susannah. "The Future of Sexuality Debates in the Church: Shared Challenges and Opportunities for Theological 'Traditionalists' and 'Revisionists'." *ModB* 62 (2021): 10–23.

Cornwall, Susannah. "The Kenosis of Unambiguous Sex in the Body of Christ: Intersex, Theology and Existing 'For the Other'." *ThS* 14 (2008): 181–99.

Cornwall, Susannah. *Theology and Sexuality*. SCMCT. London: SCM, 2013.

Cornwall, Susannah. "Troubling Bodies?" In *Intersex, Theology, and the Bible: Troubling Bodies in Church, Text, and Society*, 1–28. New York: Palgrave Macmillan, 2015.

Cornwall, Susannah. *Un/Familiar Theology: Reconceiving Sex, Reproduction, and Generativity*. RTCAHD 1. London: Bloomsbury, 2017.

Cortez, Marc. "Election and Creation." In *The T&T Clark Handbook to Election*, edited by Edwin Chr. van Driel. TTCH. New York: Bloomsbury, forthcoming.

Cortez, Marc. *ReSourcing Theological Anthropology: A Constructive Account of Humanity in the Light of Christ*. Grand Rapids: Zondervan Academic, 2017.

Cortez, Marc. *Theological Anthropology: A Guide for the Perplexed*. London: T&T Clark, 2010.

Couenhoven, Jesse. "Augustine." In *T&T Clark Companion to the Doctrine of Sin*, edited by Keith L. Johnson and David Lauber, 181–98. London: Bloomsbury, 2016.

Couenhoven, Jesse. *Stricken by Sin, Cured by Christ: Agency, Necessity, and Culpability in Augustinian Theology*. Oxford: Oxford University Press, 2013.

Council on Biblical Manhood and Womanhood. *Nashville Statement: A Coalition for Biblical Sexuality* (2017). Cited November 3, 2020. https://cbmw.org/nashville -statement/.

Cox, James J., Lionel Willatt, Tessa Homfray, and C. Geoffrey Woods. "A SOX9 Duplication and Familial 46,XX Developmental Testicular Disorder." *NEJM* 364 (2011): 91–3.

Cox, Jennifer Anne. *Intersex in Christ: Ambiguous Biology and the Gospel*. Eugene, OR: Cascade, 2018.

Craig, William Lane. *In Quest of the Historical Adam: A Biblical and Scientific Exploration.* Grand Rapids: Eerdmans, 2021.

Crisp, Oliver. *Divinity and Humanity: The Incarnation Reconsidered.* CIT. Cambridge: Cambridge University Press, 2007.

Cross, Richard. "Aquinas on Physical Impairment: Human Nature and Original Sin." *HTR* 110 (2017): 317–38.

Daly, Todd T. W. "Gender Dysphoria and the Ethics of Transsexual (i.e., Gender Reassignment) Surgery." *E&M* 32 (2016): 39–53.

D'Anselme, Guillaume. "La convenance de l'incarnation masculine." *BLE* 121 (2020): 25–41.

Danylak, Barry. *Redeeming Singleness: How the Storyline of Scripture Affirms the Single Life.* Wheaton, IL: Crossway, 2010.

Das, A. Andrew. *Galatians.* St. Louis, MO: Concordia, 2014.

Das, A. Andrew. "Oneness in Christ: The Nexus Indivulsus Between Justification and Sanctification in Paul's Letter to the Galatians." *ConJ* 21 (1995): 173–86.

Daston, Lorraine and Katharine Park. *Wonders and the Order of Nature, 1150–1750.* New York: Zone, 2012.

Dauphinais, Michael, Barry David, and Matthew Levering, eds. *Aquinas the Augustinian.* Washington, DC: Catholic University of America Press, 2007.

Davidson, Richard M. *Flame of Yahweh: Sexuality in the Old Testament.* Peabody, MA: Hendrickson, 2007.

Davie, Martin. *Glorify God in Your Body: Human Identity and Flourishing in Marriage, Singleness and Friendship.* London: Lost Coin, 2018.

Davies, W. D. and Dale C. Allison. *A Critical and Exegetical Commentary on the Gospel According to Saint Matthew.* Vol. 3. ICC. Edinburgh: T&T Clark, 1997.

DeFranza, Megan K. "Good News for Gender Minorities." In *Understanding Transgender Identities: Four Views*, edited by James K. Beilby and Paul Rhodes Eddy, 147–78. Grand Rapids: Baker Academic, 2019.

DeFranza, Megan K. "Journeying from the Bible to Christian Ethics in Search of Common Ground." In *Two Views on Homosexuality, the Bible, and the Church*, edited by Preston Sprinkle, 69–101. Counterpoints. Grand Rapids: Zondervan Academic, 2016.

DeFranza, Megan K. "Rejoinder." In *Two Views on Homosexuality, the Bible, and the Church*, edited by Preston Sprinkle, 119–23. Counterpoints. Grand Rapids: Zondervan Academic, 2016.

DeFranza, Megan K. "Response to Justin Sabia-Tanis." In *Understanding Transgender Identities: Four Views*, edited by James K. Beilby and Paul Rhodes Eddy, 234–7. Grand Rapids: Baker Academic, 2019.

DeFranza, Megan K. *Sex Difference in Christian Theology: Male, Female, and Intersex in the Image of God.* Grand Rapids: Eerdmans, 2015.

Delitzsch, Franz. *Biblical Commentary on the Prophecies of Isaiah.* Translated by James Martin. Vol. 2. Grand Rapids: Eerdmans, 1949.

Dempster, Stephen G. *Dominion and Dynasty: A Biblical Theology of the Hebrew Bible.* NSBT 15. Leicester: Apollos, 2003.

DeVun, Leah. "Heavenly Hermaphrodites: Sexual Difference at the Beginning and End of Time." *PostM* 9 (2018): 132–46.

De-Whyte, Janice Pearl Ewurama. *Wom(b)an: A Cultural-Narrative Reading of the Hebrew Bible Barrenness Narratives.* BIS 162. Leiden: Brill, 2018.

Diller, Kevin. "Are Sin and Evil Necessary for a Really Good World? Questions for Alvin Plantinga's Felix Culpa Theodicy." *FP* 25 (2008): 87–101.

Dormor, Duncan. "Intersex in the Christian Tradition: Personhood and Embodiment." In *The Legal Status of Intersex Persons*, edited by Jens M. Scherpe, Anatol Dutta, and Tobias Helms, 105–63. Cambridge: Intersentia, 2018.

Douglas, Mary. *Purity and Danger: An Analysis of Concept of Pollution and Taboo*. RC. London: Routledge, 2005.

Douglas, Mary. "Sacred Contagion." In *Reading Leviticus: A Conversation with Mary Douglas*, edited by John F. A. Sawyer, 86–106. JSOTSup 227. Sheffield: Sheffield Academic Press, 1996.

Duby, Steven J. *God in Himself: Scripture, Metaphysics, and the Task of Christian Theology*. SCDS. Downers Grove, IL: IVP Academic, 2019.

Durand, Emmanuel. "Perichoresis: A Key Concept for Balancing Trinitarian Theology." In *Rethinking Trinitarian Theology: Disputed Questions and Contemporary Issues in Trinitarian Theology*, edited by Giulio Maspero and Robert J. Woźniak, 177–92. London: T&T Clark, 2012.

Ehrman, Terrence. "Disability and Resurrection Identity." *NBf* 96 (2015): 723–38.

Eiesland, Nancy L. *The Disabled God: Toward a Liberatory Theology of Disability*. Nashville, TN: Abingdon, 1994.

Ellison, Marvin Mahan. *Making Love Just: Sexual Ethics for Perplexing Times*. Minneapolis, MN: Fortress, 2012.

Ellul, Jacques. *The Humiliation of the Word*. Grand Rapids: Eerdmans, 1985.

Evdokimov, Paul. *Woman and the Salvation of the World: A Christian Anthropology of the Charisms of Women*. Translated by Anthony P. Gythiel. Crestwood, NY: St Vladimir's, 1994.

Fakhri, Omar. "Physicalism, Bodily Resurrection, and the Constitution Account." In *The Ashgate Research Companion to Theological Anthropology*, edited by Joshua R. Farris and Charles Taliaferro, 103–12. ARC. Farnham: Ashgate, 2015.

Faro, Ingrid. "The Question of Evil and Animal Death Before the Fall." *TJ* 36 (2015): 193–213.

Farris, Joshua Ryan. *The Soul of Theological Anthropology: A Cartesian Exploration*. RNCTRTBS. Abingdon: Routledge, 2017.

Feder, Ellen K. "Imperatives of Normality: From 'Intersex' to 'Disorders of Sex Development.'" *GLQ* 15 (2009): 225–47.

Feder, Ellen K. and Katrina Karkazis. "What's in a Name? The Controversy Over 'Disorders of Sex Development.'" *HCR* 38 (2008): 33–6.

Fee, Gordon D. *The First Epistle to the Corinthians*. Rev. ed. NICNT. Grand Rapids: Eerdmans, 2014.

Feldmeier, Reinhard. *God of the Living: A Biblical Theology*. Translated by Mark E. Biddle. Waco, TX: Baylor University Press, 2011.

Feuillet, A. *Le Christ, sagesse de Dieu, d'après les épîtres pauliniennes*. EBib. Paris: J. Gabalda, 1966.

Fischer, Georg. *Genesis 1–11*. HThKAT. Freiburg: Herder, 2018.

Fischer, John Martin. *Death, Immortality, and Meaning in Life*. FPS. New York: Oxford University Press, 2020.

Flemming, Rebecca. *Medicine and the Making of Roman Women: Gender, Nature, and Authority from Celsus to Galen*. Oxford: Oxford University Press, 2000.

Fortin, Timothy. "Finding Form: Defining Human Sexual Difference." *NV* 15 (2017): 397–431.

Foucault, Michel. *The History of Sexuality*. 3 vols. New York: Vintage, 1980.

France, R. T. *The Gospel of Matthew*. NICNT. Grand Rapids: Eerdmans, 2007.

Furnish, Victor Paul. *The Theology of the First Letter to the Corinthians*. NTT. Cambridge: Cambridge University Press, 1999.

Gagnon, Robert A. J. "Sexuality." In *Dictionary for Theological Interpretation of the Bible*, edited by Kevin J. Vanhoozer, Craig G. Bartholomew, Daniel J. Treier, and N. T. Wright, 739–48. Grand Rapids: Baker Academic, 2005.

Gagnon, Robert A. J. *The Bible and Homosexual Practice: Texts and Hermeneutics*. Nashville, TN: Abingdon, 2001.

Gagnon, Robert A. J. "Transsexuality and Ordination." *Robgagnon.net* (2007). Cited November 19, 2020. http://www.robgagnon.net/articles/TranssexualityOrdination.pdf.

Gaiser, Frederick J. *Healing in the Bible: Theological Insight for Christian Ministry*. Grand Rapids: Baker Academic, 2010.

Galen. *On Seed*. Translated by Phillip H. De Lacy. CMG V 3,1. Berlin: Akademie, 1992.

Galen. *On the Doctrines of Hippocrates and Plato: Second Part: Books VI–IX*. Translated by Phillip H. De Lacy. Vol. 2. 2nd ed. CMG V 4,1,2. Berlin: Akademie, 1984.

Galen. *On the Usefulness of the Parts of the Body*. Translated by Margaret Tallmadge May. Vol. 2. Ithaca, NY: Cornell University Press, 1968.

Gard, Paul R. *Human Endocrinology*. Bristol, PA: Taylor & Francis, 1998.

Garr, W. Randall. *In His Own Image and Likeness: Humanity, Divinity, and Monotheism*. CHANE 15. Leiden: Brill, 2003.

Gaventa, Beverly Roberts. "The Singularity of the Gospel Revisited." In *Galatians and Christian Theology: Justification, the Gospel, and Ethics in Paul's Letter*, edited by M. W. Elliott, Scott J. Hafemann, N. T. Wright, and John Frederick, 187–99. Grand Rapids: Baker Academic, 2014.

Geertz, Clifford. *The Interpretation of Cultures: Selected Essays*. New York: Basic, 1973.

Gentry, Peter J. "Kingdom Through Covenant: Humanity as the Divine Image." *SBJT* 12 (2008): 16–42.

Gertz, Jan Christian. *Das erste Buch Mose (Genesis): Die Urgeschichte Gen 1–11*. ATD 1. Göttingen: Vandenhoeck & Ruprecht, 2018.

Gil, Vincent E. *A Christian's Guide Through the Gender Revolution: Gender, Cisgender, Transgender, and Intersex*. Eugene, OR: Cascade, 2021.

Gittoes, Julie. "Participation in the Body: The Gift of Physical Particularity." *IJST* 24 (2022): 307–14.

Goldingay, John. *Old Testament Theology: Israel's Gospel*. Downers Grove, IL: IVP Academic, 2003.

Gondreau, Paul. "Disability, the Healing of Infirmity, and the Theological Virtue of Hope: A Thomistic Approach." *JMT* 6 (2017): 70–111.

Gondreau, Paul. "The 'Inseparable Connection' Between Procreation and Unitive Love (Humanae Vitae, §12) and Thomistic Hylemorphic Anthropology." *NV* 6 (2008): 731–64.

Gondreau, Paul. *The Passions of Christ's Soul in the Theology of St. Thomas Aquinas*. Providence, RI: Cluny Media, 2018.

Gondreau, Paul. "Thomas Aquinas on Sexual Difference: The Metaphysical Biology and Moral Significance of Human Sexuality." *ProEccl* 30 (2021): 177–215.

Gorringe, Timothy. *The Education of Desire: Towards a Theology of the Senses*. JAHLS. Harrisburg, PA: Trinity Press International, 2002.

Grabowski, John S. *Sex and Virtue: An Introduction to Sexual Ethics*. Washington, DC: Catholic University of America Press, 2003.

Grillmeier, Aloys. *Christ in Christian Tradition: Volume Two: From the Council of Chalcedon (451) to Gregory the Great (590–604): Part Two: The Church of*

Constantinople in the Sixth Century. Translated by John Cawte and Pauline Allen. London: Mowbray, 1995.

Gross, Julius. *Geschichte des Erbsündendogmas: Ein Beitrag zur Geschichte des Problems vom Ursprung des Übels*. 4 vols. München: Ernst Reinhardt, 1960.

Gross, Sally. "Intersexuality and Scripture." *ThS* 11 (1999): 65–74.

Gudbergsen, Thomas. "God Consists of Both the Male and the Female Genders: A Short Note on Gen 1:27." *VT* 62 (2012): 450–3.

Gundry-Volf, Judith M. "Beyond Difference? Paul's Vision of a New Humanity in Galatians 3:28." In *Gospel and Gender: A Trinitarian Engagement with Being Male and Female in Christ*, edited by Douglas A. Campbell and Alan J. Torrance, 8–36. STS 7. London: T&T Clark, 2003.

Gunton, Colin E. "The Indispensability of Theological Understanding: Theology in the University." In *Essentials of Christian Community: Essays for Daniel W. Hardy*, edited by David F. Ford and Dennis L. Stamps, 266–77. Edinburgh: T&T Clark, 1996.

Hadromi-Allouche, Zohar and Áine Larkin, eds. *Fall Narratives: An Interdisciplinary Perspective*. London: Routledge, 2017.

Hamilton, Victor P. *The Book of Genesis: Chapters 1–17*. NICOT. Grand Rapids: Eerdmans, 1990.

Hankinson, R. J. "The Man and His Work." In *The Cambridge Companion to Galen*, edited by R. J. Hankinson, 1–33. Cambridge: Cambridge University Press, 2008.

Hansen, Bruce. *All of You Are One: The Social Vision of Galatians 3:28, 1 Corinthians 12:13 and Colossians 3:11*. LNTS 409. London: T&T Clark, 2010.

Harding, Sarah. *Paul's Eschatological Anthropology: The Dynamics of Human Transformation*. ES. Minneapolis, MN: Fortress, 2015.

Hare, John. "Afterword." In *Intersex, Theology, and the Bible: Troubling Bodies in Church, Text, and Society*, edited by Susannah Cornwall, 197–209. New York: Palgrave Macmillan, 2015.

Hare, John. "Hermaphrodites, Eunuchs, and Intersex People: The Witness of Medical Science in Biblical Times and Today." In *Intersex, Theology, and the Bible: Troubling Bodies in Church, Text, and Society*, edited by Susannah Cornwall, 79–96. New York: Palgrave Macmillan, 2015.

Hare, John. "'Neither Male nor Female': The Case of Intersexuality." In *An Acceptable Sacrifice? Homosexuality and the Church*, edited by Duncan Dormor and Jeremy Morris, 98–111. London: SPCK, 2007.

Häring, Hermann. "Eschatologie." In *Augustin Handbuch*, edited by Volker Henning Drecoll, 540–7. 2nd ed. HT. Tübingen: Mohr Siebeck, 2014.

Häring, Hermann. "Malum." In vol. 3 of *Augustinus-Lexikon*, edited by Cornelius Mayer, 1111–21. Basel: Schwabe AG, 2004–2010.

Harper, Kyle. *From Shame to Sin: The Christian Transformation of Sexual Morality in Late Antiquity*. Cambridge, MA: Harvard University Press, 2013.

Harris, Robert. *Conclave*. London: Penguin Random House, 2017.

Harrison, Nonna Verna. "The Maleness of Christ." *SVTQ* 42 (1998): 111–51.

Harrison, Nonna Verna. "The Trinity and Feminism." In *The Oxford Handbook of the Trinity*, edited by Gilles Emery and Matthew Levering, 519–29. OH. Oxford: Oxford University Press, 2011.

Hart, Trevor A. *In Him Was Life: The Person and Work of Christ*. Waco, TX: Baylor University Press, 2019.

Hart, Trevor A. *Making Good: Creation, Creativity, and Artistry*. Waco, TX: Baylor University Press, 2014.

Hartke, Austen. "God's Unclassified World: Nonbinary Gender and the Beauty of Creation." *ChrCent* 135:9 (2018): 27–9.

Hartke, Austen. *Transforming: The Bible and the Lives of Transgender Christians.* Louisville, KY: Westminster John Knox, 2018.

Harvey, Susan Ashbrook. *Scenting Salvation: Ancient Christianity and the Olfactory Imagination.* TCH 42. Berkeley, CA: University of California Press, 2006.

Hawkesworth, Mary. "Sex, Gender, and Sexuality: From Naturalized Presumption to Analytical Categories." In *The Oxford Handbook of Gender and Politics,* edited by Georgina Waylen, Karen Celis, Johanna Kantola, and S. Laurel Weldon, 31–56. OH. Oxford: Oxford University Press, 2013.

Hays, Richard B. *The Moral Vision of the New Testament: Community, Cross, New Creation: A Contemporary Introduction to New Testament Ethics.* San Francisco: HarperOne, 1996.

Heaps, Jonathan and Neil Ormerod. "Statistically Ordered: Gender, Sexual Identity, and the Metaphysics of 'Normal.'" *TS* 80 (2019): 346–69.

Heard, Christopher. "The Tree of Life in Genesis." In *The Tree of Life,* edited by Douglas Estes, 74–99. TBN 27. Leiden: Brill, 2020.

Heeßel, Nils P. "Rechts oder links–wörtlich oder dem Sinn nach? Zum Problem der kulturellen Gebundenheit bei der Übersetzung von medizinischen Keilschrifttexten." In *Writings of Early Scholars in the Ancient Near East, Egypt, Rome, and Greece: Translating Ancient Scientific Texts,* edited by Annette Imhausen and Tanja Pommerening, 175–88. BZA 286. Berlin: de Gruyter, 2010.

Heil, John. *Philosophy of Mind: A Contemporary Introduction.* 4th ed. RCIP. New York: Routledge, 2020.

Helle, Sophus. "'Only in Dress?' Methodological Concerns Regarding Non-Binary Gender." In *Gender and Methodology in the Ancient Near East: Approaches from Assyriology and Beyond,* edited by Stephanie Budin, Agnès Garcia-Ventura, Adelina Millet, and Megan Cifarelli, 41–54. BMO 10. Barcelona: Universitat de Barcelona, 2018.

Henriksen, Jan-Olav and Karl Olav Sandnes. *Jesus as Healer: A Gospel for the Body.* Grand Rapids: Eerdmans, 2016.

Herdt, Gilbert H., ed. *Third Sex, Third Gender: Beyond Sexual Dimorphism in Culture and History.* New York: Zone, 1996.

Herring, Stephen L. *Divine Substitution: Humanity as the Manifestation of Deity in the Hebrew Bible and the Ancient Near East.* FRLANT 247. Göttingen: Vandenhoeck & Ruprecht, 2013.

Hess, Richard S. "Splitting the Adam: The Usage of 'Ādām in Genesis I-V." In *Studies in the Pentateuch,* edited by J. A. Emerton, 1–15. VTSup 41. Leiden: Brill, 1990.

Heß, Ruth. ""Es ist noch nicht erschienen, was wir sein werden": Biblisch-(de) konstruktivistische Anstöße zu einer entdualisierten Eschatologie der Geschlechterdifferenz." In *Alles in allem: Eschatologische Anstösse: J. Christine Janowski zum 60. Geburtstag,* edited by Ruth Heß and Martin Leiner, 291–323. Neukirchen-Vluyn: Neukirchener, 2005.

Hester, J. David. "Eunuchs and the Postgender Jesus: Matthew 19.12 and Transgressive Sexualities." *JNST* 28 (2005): 13.

Hester, J. David. "Intersex and the Rhetorics of Healing." In *Ethics and Intersex,* edited by Sharon E. Sytsma, 47–72. ILELNM 29. Dordrecht: Springer, 2006.

Hester, J. David. "Intersex(es) and Informed Consent: How Physicians' Rhetoric Constrains Choice." *TMB* 25 (2004): 21–49.

Hester, J. David. "Queers on Account of the Kingdom of Heaven: Rhetorical Constructions of the Eunuch Body." *Scri* 90 (2005): 809–23.

Hiebert, Val and Dennis Hiebert. "Intersex Persons and the Church: Unknown, Unwelcomed, Unwanted Neighbors." *JSIRS* 5 (2015): 31–44.

Hilary of Poitiers. *De trinitate.* Edited by Pieter Smulders. CCSL 62. Turnholti: Brepols, 1979.

Hill, Wesley. "Afterword." In *Marriage, Scripture, and the Church: Theological Discernment on the Question of Same-Sex Union,* 289–97. Grand Rapids: Baker Academic, 2021.

Hippocrates. *Diseases of Women.* Translated by Paul Potter. LCL 538. Cambridge, MA: Harvard University Press, 2018.

Hippocrates. *Hippocrates IV.* Translated by W. H. S. Jones. LCL 150. Cambridge, MA: Harvard University Press, 1998.

Hoch, Carl B. *All Things New: The Significance of Newness for Biblical Theology.* Ada, MI: Baker Academic, 1995.

Höhne, David A. *The Last Things.* CCTheo. Downers Grove, IL: IVP Academic, 2019.

Hollinger, Dennis P. "Creation: The Starting Point of an Ecclesial Ethic." In *Ecclesia and Ethics: Moral Formation and the Church,* edited by E. Allen Jones III, John Frederick, John Anthony Dunne, Eric Lewellen, and Janghoon Park, 3–20. TTCBS. London: T&T Clark, 2016.

Hollinger, Dennis P. *The Meaning of Sex: Christian Ethics and the Moral Life.* Grand Rapids: Baker Academic, 2009.

Holmes, Brooke. *Gender: Antiquity and Its Legacy.* Oxford: Oxford University Press, 2012.

Holmes, Christopher R. J. "Last Things." In *The Oxford Handbook of Reformed Theology,* edited by Michael Allen and Scott R. Swain, 609–20. OH. Oxford: Oxford University Press, 2020.

Holmes, Morgan, ed. *Critical Intersex.* QI. Farnham: Ashgate, 2009.

Holmes, Stephen R. "'Shadows and Broken Images': Thinking Theologically about Femaleness and Maleness." *Shored Fragments* (August 19, 2015). Cited February 26, 2019. http://steverholmes.org.uk/blog/?p=7538.

Holsinger-Friesen, Thomas. *Irenaeus and Genesis: A Study of Competition in Early Christian Hermeneutics.* JTISup 1. Winona Lake, IN: Eisenbrauns, 2009.

Homer. *Odyssey: Books 13–24.* Translated by A. T. Murray. LCL 105. Cambridge, MA: Harvard University Press, 1995.

Horn, Christoph. "Anthropologie." In *Augustin Handbuch,* edited by Volker Henning Drecoll, 479–87. 2nd ed. HT. Tübingen: Mohr Siebeck, 2014.

Hostoffer, Alexander D. "A Theory for the Metaphysical Foundation of the Complementarity of the Sexes." PhD, Washington, DC: The Catholic University of America, 2020.

Houck, Daniel W. *Aquinas, Original Sin, and the Challenge of Evolution.* Cambridge: Cambridge University Press, 2020.

Houck, Daniel W. "Natura Humana Relicta est Christo: Thomas Aquinas on the Effects of Original Sin." *ArV* 13 (2016): 68–102.

Hubing, Jeff. *Crucifixion and New Creation: The Strategic Purpose of Galatians 6.11–17.* LNTS 508. London: Bloomsbury, 2015.

Hütter, Reinhard. *Bound for Beatitude: A Thomistic Study in Eschatology and Ethics.* TRS 12. Washington, DC: Catholic University of America Press, 2019.

Hütter, Reinhard. *Dust Bound for Heaven: Explorations in the Theology of Thomas Aquinas.* Grand Rapids: Eerdmans, 2012.

Inbody, Tyron L. *The Many Faces of Christology.* Nashville, TN: Abingdon, 2002.

van Inwagen, Peter. "Possibility of Resurrection." *IJPR* 9 (1978): 114–21.

Irenaeus. *Against Heresies*. Translated by Alexander Roberts and James Donaldson. *ANF* 1. Buffalo: Christian Literature, 1885; reprint, Peabody, MA: Hendrickson, 2004.

Jamieson, R. B. *Jesus' Death and Heavenly Offering in Hebrews*. SNTSMS 172. Cambridge: Cambridge University Press, 2019.

Jeffery, Steve, Mike Ovey, and Andrew Sach. *Pierced for Our Transgressions: Rediscovering the Glory of Penal Substitution*. Nottingham: IVP Academic, 2007.

John of Damascus. "The Orthodox Faith." In *Saint John of Damascus: Writings*, translated by Frederic H. Chase, 165–406. FC 37. New York: Fathers of the Church, 1958.

John Paul II. *Man and Woman He Created Them: A Theology of the Body*. Boston, MA: Pauline, 2006.

Johnson, Elizabeth A. *She Who Is: The Mystery of God in Feminist Theological Discourse*. New York: Crossroad, 2002.

Johnson, Monte Ransome. *Aristotle on Teleology*. Oxford: Oxford University Press, 2005.

Jones, Beth Felker. "Embodied from Creation Through Redemption." In *Beauty, Order, and Mystery: A Christian Vision of Human Sexuality*, edited by Gerald Hiestand and Todd A. Wilson, 21–30. Downers Grove, IL: IVP Academic, 2017.

Jones, Beth Felker. *Marks of His Wounds: Gender Politics and Bodily Resurrection*. Oxford: Oxford University Press, 2007.

Jones, Beth Felker. *Practicing Christian Doctrine: An Introduction to Thinking and Living Theologically*. Grand Rapids: Baker Academic, 2014.

Jones, Charlotte. "Intersex, Infertility and the Future: Early Diagnoses and the Imagined Life Course." *SHI* 42 (2020): 143–56.

Jones, David Albert. *Approaching the End: A Theological Exploration of Death and Dying*. OSTE. Oxford: Oxford University Press, 2007.

Jones, David Albert. "Gender Identity in Scripture: Indissoluble Marriage and Exceptional Eunuchs." *SCE* 34:1 (2021): 3–16.

Julian of Norwich. *Revelations of Divine Love*. Translated by Barry Windeatt. OWC. Oxford: Oxford University Press, 2015.

Jung, Patricia Beattie. "Intersex on Earth as It Is in Heaven." In *Intersex, Theology, and the Bible: Troubling Bodies in Church, Text, and Society*, edited by Susannah Cornwall, 173–95. New York: Palgrave Macmillan, 2015.

Jung, Patricia Beattie. *Sex on Earth as It Is in Heaven: A Christian Eschatology of Desire*. Albany, NY: State University of New York Press, 2017.

Junius, Franciscus. *A Treatise on True Theology: With the Life of Franciscus Junius*. Translated by David C. Noe. Grand Rapids: Reformation Heritage, 2014.

Kahl, Brigitte. "No Longer Male: Masculinity Struggles Behind Galatians 3:28?" *JSNT* 79 (2000): 37–49.

Kapic, Kelly M. *You're Only Human: How Your Limits Reflect God's Design and Why That's Good News*. Grand Rapids: Brazos, 2022.

Karkazis, Katrina. *Fixing Sex: Intersex, Medical Authority, and Lived Experience*. Durham, NC: Duke University Press, 2008.

Keen, Karen R. *Scripture, Ethics, and the Possibility of Same-Sex Relationships*. Grand Rapids: Eerdmans, 2018.

Keener, Craig S. *Galatians: A Commentary*. Grand Rapids: Baker Academic, 2019.

Kelsey, David H. *Eccentric Existence: A Theological Anthropology*. 2 vols. Louisville, KY: Westminster John Knox, 2009.

Kelsey, David H. *Human Anguish and God's Power*. CIT. Cambridge: Cambridge University Press, 2021.

Kempf, Stephen. "Genesis 3:14–19: Climax of the Discourse?" *JOTT* 6 (1993): 354–77.

Kessel, Edward L. "A Proposed Biological Interpretation of the Virgin Birth." *JASA* 35 (1983): 129–36.

Kessel, Edward L. *The Androgynous Christ: A Christian Feminist View*. Portland, OR: Interprint, 1988.

Kilner, John F. *Dignity and Destiny: Humanity in the Image of God*. Grand Rapids: Eerdmans, 2015.

King, Helen. *The One-Sex Body on Trial: The Classical and Early Modern Evidence*. HMC. London: Routledge, 2013.

Kiuchi, Nobuyoshi. *Leviticus. AOTC 3*. Nottingham: Apollos, 2007.

Knust, Jennifer Wright. *Unprotected Texts: The Bible's Surprising Contradictions About Sex and Desire*. New York: HarperOne, 2011.

Koehler, Ludwig and Walter Baumgartner. *The Hebre Wand Aramaic Lexicon of the Old Testament*. Revised by Walter Baumgartner and Johann Jacok Stamm. Translated by M. E. J. Richardson. 5 vols. Leiden: Brill, 1994–2000.

Körner, Johanna. *Sexualität und Geschlecht bei Paulus: Die Spannung zwischen "Inklusivität" und "Exklusivität" des paulinischen Ethos am Beispiel der Sexual- und Geschlechterrollenethik*. WUNT 2/512. Tübingen: Mohr Siebeck, 2020.

Koyama, Emi and Lisa Weasel. "From Social Construction to Social Justice: Transforming How We Teach About Intersexuality." In *A Guide for Teachers in Women's, Gender and Queer Studies*, edited by Emi Koyama, 2–9. 2nd ed. Portland, OR: Intersex Initiative Portland, 2003.

Krannich, Conrad. *Geschlecht als Gabe und Aufgabe: Intersexualität aus theologischer Perspektive*. AngS 4. Gießen: Psychosozial-Verlag, 2016.

Kutzer, Mirja. "Mann/Frau (katholisch)." In *Handwörterbuch Theologische Anthropologie: Römisch-Katholisch/Russisch-Orthodox: Eine Gegenüberstellung*, edited by Bertram Stubenrauch and Andreï Lorgus, 74–83. Freiburg im Breisgau: Herder, 2013.

Laqueur, Thomas. *Making Sex: Body and Gender from the Greeks to Freud*. Cambridge, MA: Harvard University Press, 1990.

Laqueur, Thomas. "One Sex or Two." In *London Review of Books*. London: LRB, December 6, 1990. Vol. 12, no. 23, sec. Letters. Cited August 18, 2019. https://www.lrb.co.uk/v12/n23/letters.

Lawler, Michael G. and Todd A. Salzman. "Sex, Gender, and Intersex: Anthropological, Medical, and Ethical Critiques and Proposals." *ThS* 25 (2019): 205–26.

LeFebvre, Michael. *The Liturgy of Creation: Understanding Calendars in Old Testament Context*. Downers Grove, IL: IVP Academic, 2019.

Légasse, Simon. *L'Épître de Paul aux Galates*. Paris: Cerf, 2000.

Leick, Gwendolyn. "Too Young—Too Old? Sex and Age in Mesopotamian Literature." In *Sex in Antiquity: Exploring Gender and Sexuality in the Ancient World*, edited by Mark Masterson, Nancy Sorkin Rabinowitz, and James Robson, 80–95. RA. London: Routledge, 2015.

Leithart, Peter J. *Revelation 1–11*. ITC. London: Bloomsbury, 2018.

Levering, Matthew. *Aquinas's Eschatological Ethics and the Virtue of Temperance*. Notre Dame, IN: University of Notre Dame Press, 2019.

Levering, Matthew. *Engaging the Doctrine of Creation: Cosmos, Creatures, and the Wise and Good Creator*. Grand Rapids: Baker Academic, 2017.

Levering, Matthew. *Engaging the Doctrine of Marriage: Human Marriage as the Image and Sacrament of the Marriage of God and Creation*. Eugene, OR: Cascade, 2020.

Lévinas, Emmanuel. *Totality and Infinity: An Essay on Exteriority.* Translated by Alphonso Lingis. DuqSt 24. Pittsburgh, PA: Duquesne University Press, 1969.

Lewis, C. S. *Perelandra.* Scribner Classics ed. New York: Scribner, 1996.

Lincoln, Andrew T. *Born of a Virgin? Reconceiving Jesus in the Bible, Tradition, and Theology.* Grand Rapids: Eerdmans, 2013.

Litke, Wayne. "Beyond Creation: Galatians 3:28, Genesis and the Hermaphrodite Myth." *SR* 24 (1995): 173–8.

Lloyd, G. E. R. *Science, Folklore, and Ideology: Studies in the Life Sciences in Ancient Greece.* London: Duckworth, 1999.

Loader, William R. G. *Making Sense of Sex: Attitudes Towards Sexuality in Early Jewish and Christian Literature.* Grand Rapids: Eerdmans, 2013.

Loader, William R. G. *Sexuality and Gender: Collected Essays.* WUNT 458. Tubingen: Mohr Siebeck, 2021.

Lofgren, Mary Elizabeth Zagrobelny. "John Paul II's Theological Anthropology and the Intersexual Body." PhD diss., The Catholic University of America, 2020.

Löhr, Winrich. "Sündenlehre." In *Augustin Handbuch*, edited by Volker Henning Drecoll, 498–506. 2nd ed. HT. Tübingen: Mohr Siebeck, 2014.

Loraux, Nicole. *The Children of Athena: Athenian Ideas About Citizenship and the Division Between the Sexes.* Princeton, NJ: Princeton University Press, 1994.

Lorberbaum, Yair. *In God's Image: Myth, Theology, and Law in Classical Judaism.* New York: Cambridge University Press, 2015.

Loughlin, Gerard. "Gender Ideology: For a 'Third Sex' Without Reserve." *SCE* 31 (2018): 471–82.

Loughlin, Gerard. "Omphalos." In *Queer Theology: Rethinking the Western Body*, edited by Gerard Loughlin, 115–27. Oxford: Blackwell, 2007.

Lowe, Mary Elise. "Re-Embracing the Body of Jesus Christ: A Queer, Lutheran Theology of the Body of Christ." In *Lutheran Identity and Political Theology*, edited by Carl-Henric Grenholm and Göran Gunner, 117–33. CSR 9. Eugene, OR: Pickwick, 2014.

Lundberg, Tove, Peter Hegarty, and Katrina Roen. "Making Sense of 'Intersex' and 'DSD': How Laypeople Understand and Use Terminology." *P&S* 9 (2018): 161–73.

Luz, Ulrich. *Matthew 8–20: A Commentary on the Gospel of Matthew.* Translated by James E. Crouch. Vol. 2. Hermeneia. Minneapolis, MN: Augsburg, 2001.

Malatino, Hilary. *Queer Embodiment: Monstrosity, Medical Violence, and Intersex Experience.* ExpF. Lincoln: University of Nebraska Press, 2019.

Marchal, Joseph A. *Appalling Bodies: Queer Figures Before and After Paul's Letters.* New York: Oxford University Press, 2020.

Marías, Julián. *Metaphysical Anthropology: The Empirical Structure of Human Life.* Translated by Frances M. López-Morillas. University Park, PA: Pennsylvania State University Press, 1971.

Martin, Dale B. *Sex and the Single Savior: Gender and Sexuality in Biblical Interpretation.* Louisville, KY: Westminster John Knox, 2006.

Martin, Dale B. *The Corinthian Body.* New Haven, CT: Yale University Press, 1995.

Martin, Troy W. "The Covenant of Circumcision (Genesis 17:9–14) and the Situational Antithesis in Galatians 3:28." *JBL* 122 (2003): 111–25.

Maspero, Giulio. "La perichoresis e la grammatica teologica dei primi sette Concili ecumenici." *Theol* 4 (2020): 161–81.

Mathews, Kenneth A. *Genesis 1–11:26.* NAC 1A. Nashville, TN: Broadman & Holman, 1996.

Mawson, Michael and Samuel Tranter. "Guest Editorial: Apocalyptic Theology and Christian Ethics." *SCE* 34 (2021): 423–5.

Mayer, Cornelius. "Creatio, creator, creatura." In vol. 2 of *A-L*, edited by Cornelius Mayer, 56–116. Basel: Schwabe AG, 1996–2002.

McCall, Thomas H. *Against God and Nature: The Doctrine of Sin*. FET. Wheaton, IL: Crossway, 2019.

McCarthy, Margaret H. "Gender Ideology and the Humanum." *Comm* 43 (2016): 274–98.

McCaulley, Esau. *Sharing in the Son's Inheritance: Davidic Messianism and Paul's Worldwide Interpretation of the Abrahamic Land Promise in Galatians*. LNTS 608. London: T&T Clark, 2019.

McClain, Daniel Wade. "What (Not) to Do with the Trinity: Doctrine, Discipline, and Doxology in Contemporary Trinitarian Discourse." *AThR* 100 (2018): 603–17.

McConville, J. G. *Being Human in God's World: An Old Testament Theology of Humanity*. Grand Rapids: Baker Academic, 2016.

McDowell, Catherine L. *The Image of God in the Garden of Eden: The Creation of Humankind in Genesis 2:5–3:24 in Light of the Mīs Pî Pīt Pî and Wpt-R Rituals of Mesopotamia and Ancient Egypt*. Siphrut 15. Winona Lake, IN: Eisenbrauns, 2015.

McFarland, Ian A. "Rethinking Nature and Grace: The Logic of Creation's Consummation." *IJST* 24 (2022): 56–79.

McFarland, Ian A. *The Word Made Flesh: A Theology of the Incarnation*. Louisville, KY: Westminster John Knox, 2019.

McKnight, Scot. *The Letter to the Colossians*. NICNT. Grand Rapids: Eerdmans, 2018.

Meeks, Wayne A. "Image of the Androgyne: Some Uses of a Symbol in Earliest Christianity." *HR* 13 (1974): 165–208.

Melcher, Sarah J. "Disability and the Hebrew Bible: A Survey and Appraisal." *CBR* 18 (2019): 7–31.

Merrick, Teri. "Can Augustine Welcome Intersexed Bodies into Heaven?" In *Gift and Economy: Ethics, Hospitality and the Market*, edited by Eric R. Severson. Newcastle: Cambridge Scholars, 2012.

Merrill, Eugene H. "תום." In vol 2. of *NIDOTTE*, edited by Willem A. VanGemeren, 886–8. Grand Rapids: Zondervan Academic, 1997.

van der Merwe, Christo H. J., Jacobus A. Naudé, and Jan H. Kroeze. *A Biblical Hebrew Reference Grammar*. 2nd ed. London: T&T Clark, 2018.

Messer, Neil. *Flourishing: Health, Disease, and Bioethics in Theological Perspective*. Grand Rapids: Eerdmans, 2013.

Miles, Margaret R. *Augustine on the Body*. AARDS 31. Missoula, MT: Scholars, 1979.

Milgrom, Jacob. "Ethics and Ritual: The Foundations of the Biblical Dietary Laws." In *Religion and Law: Biblical-Judaic and Islamic Perspectives*, edited by Edwin Brown Firmage, Bernard G. Weiss, and John W. Welch, 159–92. Winona Lake, IN: Eisenbrauns, 1990.

Milgrom, Jacob. *Leviticus 17–22: A New Translation with Introduction and Commentary*. AB 3A. New York: Doubleday, 2008.

Mobley, Gregory. *The Return of the Chaos Monsters and Other Backstories of the Bible*. Grand Rapids: Eerdmans, 2012.

Moffitt, David M. *Atonement and the Logic of Resurrection in the Epistle to the Hebrews*. NovTSup 141. Leiden: Brill, 2011.

Mollenkott, Virginia R. *Omnigender: A Trans-Religious Approach*. Rev. and exp. Cleveland, OH: Pilgrim, 2007.

Moltmann, Jürgen. *God in Creation: A New Theology of Creation and the Spirit of God.* Minneapolis, MN: Fortress, 1993.

Moltmann, Jürgen. *The Coming of God: Christian Eschatology.* Translated by Margaret Kohl. Minneapolis, MN: Fortress, 1996.

Moo, Douglas J. *A Theology of Paul and His Letters: The Gift of the New Realm in Christ.* BTNT. Grand Rapids: Zondervan Academic, 2021.

Moo, Douglas J. *Galatians.* BECNT. Grand Rapids: Baker Academic, 2013.

Moo, Douglas J. *The Letter to the Romans.* 2nd ed. NICNT. Grand Rapids: Eerdmans, 2018.

Moog, Ute, Ute Felbor, Cristina Has, and Birgit Zirn. "Disorders Caused by Genetic Mosaicism." *DAI* 117 (2020): 119–25.

Moreland, J. P. *Body & Soul: Human Nature & the Crisis in Ethics.* Downers Grove, IL: IVP Academic, 2000.

Moss, Candida R. *Divine Bodies: Resurrecting Perfection in the New Testament and Early Christianity.* New Haven, CT: Yale University Press, 2019.

Moss, Candida R. "Heavenly Healing: Eschatological Cleansing and the Resurrection of the Dead in the Early Church." *JAAR* 79 (2011): 991–1017.

Moss, Candida R. and Joel S. Baden. *Reconceiving Infertility: Biblical Perspectives on Procreation and Childlessness.* Princeton, NJ: Princeton University Press, 2015.

Mühling, Markus. *T&T Clark Handbook of Christian Eschatology.* Translated by Jennifer Adams-Maßmann and David Andrew Gilland. London: Bloomsbury, 2015.

Mulder, Tara. "Flabby Flesh and Foetal Formation." In *Bodily Fluids in Antiquity*, edited by Mark Bradley, Victoria Leonard, and Laurence Totelin, 145–57. New York: Routledge, 2021.

Muller, Richard A. *Dictionary of Latin and Greek Theological Terms: Drawn Principally from Protestant Scholastic Theology.* 2nd ed. Grand Rapids: Baker Academic, 2017.

Mullins, Ryan T. "Some Difficulties for Amos Yong's Disability Theology of the Resurrection." *ArsD* 11 (2011): 24–32.

National Geographic Society. "Gender Revolution." *NatGeo* 231 (2017).

Nazianzus, Gregory of. *On God and Christ: The Five Theological Orations and Two Letters to Cledonius.* Translated by Frederick Williams and Lionel R. Wickham. PPS 23. Yonkers, NY: St. Vladimir's, 2002.

Nazianzus, Gregory of. "Oration 14." In *Opera omnia quae exstant*, edited by J.-P. Migne, 857–910. Patrologia Graeca 35. Paris: Migne, 1857.

Neusner, Jacob, ed. *Genesis Rabbah: The Judaic Commentary to the Book of Genesis: A New American Translation.* Vol. 1. BJS 104. Atlanta, GA: Scholars, 1985.

Neville, Richard. "Differentiation in Genesis 1: An Exegetical Creation Ex Nihilo." *JBL* 130 (2011): 209–26.

Niccacci, Alviero. *The Syntax of the Verb in Classical Hebrew Prose.* Translated by W. G. E. Watson. JSOTSup 86. Sheffield: Sheffield Academic Press, 1990.

Nyssa, Gregory of. *On the Making of Man.* Translated by H. A. Wilson. NPNF² 5. Buffalo: Christian Literature, 1893; reprint, Peabody, MA: Hendrickson, 2004.

Nyssa, Gregory of. *The Life of Saint Macrina.* Translated by Kevin Corrigan. Eugene, OR: Wipf & Stock, 2001.

Oakes, Edward T. *A Theology of Grace in Six Controversies.* Interventions. Grand Rapids: Eerdmans, 2016.

O'Brien, Michelle. "Intersex, Medicine, Diversity, Identity and Spirituality." In *This Is My Body: Hearing the Theology of Transgender Christians*, edited by Christina Beardsley and Michelle O'Brien, 45–55. London: Darton, Longman & Todd, 2016.

O'Brien, T. C. "Appendix 8: Original Justice." In *Summa Theologiae: Original Sin (1-2.81–85)*, vol. 26 of *Summa Theologiae*, translated by T. C. O'Brien, 144–53. London: Eyre & Spottiswoode, 1965.

O'Connor, Kathleen M. *Genesis 1–25A*. SHBC 1. Macon, GA: Smyth & Helwys, 2018.

O'Donovan, Oliver. *Begotten or Made?* Oxford: Clarendon, 1984.

O'Donovan, Oliver. *Church in Crisis: The Gay Controversy and the Anglican Communion*. Eugene, OR: Cascade, 2008.

O'Donovan, Oliver. *Entering into Rest*. ET 3. Grand Rapids: Eerdmans, 2017.

O'Donovan, Oliver. *Finding and Seeking*. ET 2. Grand Rapids: Eerdmans, 2014.

O'Donovan, Oliver. *Resurrection and Moral Order: An Outline for Evangelical Ethics*. Leicester: IVP Academic, 1986.

O'Donovan, Oliver. *Resurrection and Moral Order: An Outline for Evangelical Ethics*. 2nd ed. Leicester: IVP Academic, 1994.

O'Donovan, Oliver. *Self, World, and Time: An Induction*. ET 1. Grand Rapids: Eerdmans, 2013.

O'Donovan, Oliver. *The Desire of the Nations: Rediscovering the Roots of Political Theology*. Cambridge: Cambridge University Press, 1996.

O'Donovan, Oliver. *Transsexualism: Issues and Argument*. Cambridge: Grove, 2007.

Ollenburger, Ben C. "Creation and Peace: Creator and Creature in Genesis 1–11." In *The Old Testament in the Life of God's People: Essays in Honor of Elmer A. Martens*, edited by Jon M. Isaak, 143–58. Winona Lake, IN: Eisenbrauns, 2009.

Olyan, Saul M. *Disability in the Hebrew Bible: Interpreting Mental and Physical Differences*. Cambridge: Cambridge University Press, 2008.

O'Neill, Seamus. "Privation, parasite et perversion de la volonté: Une étude ontologique et psychologique de la doctrine augustinienne du mal." *LTP* 73 (2017): 31–52.

O'Reilly, Matt. *Paul and the Resurrected Body: Social Identity and Ethical Practice*. ESEC 22. Atlanta, GA: SBL, 2020.

Ortlund, Gavin. "Augustine on Animal Death." In *Evil and Creation: Historical and Constructive Essays in Christian Dogmatics*, edited by David Luy, Matthew Levering, and George Kalantzis, 84–110. SHST. Bellingham, WA: Lexham, 2020.

Ortlund, Gavin. *Retrieving Augustine's Doctrine of Creation: Ancient Wisdom for Current Controversy*. Downers Grove, IL: IVP Academic, 2020.

Osborne, Grant R. *Matthew*. ZECNT 1. Grand Rapids: Zondervan Academic, 2010.

Oswalt, John N. *Book of Isaiah: Chapters 40–66*. NICOT. Grand Rapids: Eerdmans, 1998.

Ovey, Michael. "The Cross, Creation and the Human Predicament." In *Where Wrath and Mercy Meet: Proclaiming the Atonement Today*, edited by David Peterson, 100–35. Carlisle: Paternoster, 2001.

Ozanne, Jayne. "LLF: That Video, Those Principles & a Call for a Public Inquiry." *ViaMedia.News* (November 23, 2020). Cited November 24, 2020. https://viamedia.news/2020/11/23/llf-that-video-those-principles-a-call-for-a-public-inquiry/.

Pailin, David A. *A Gentle Touch: From a Theology of Handicap to a Theology of Human Being*. London: SPCK, 1992.

Pannenberg, Wolfhart. *Systematic Theology*. Vol. 2. London: T&T Clark, 2004.

Pao, David W. *Acts and the Isaianic New Exodus*. WUNT 130. Tübingen: Mohr Siebeck, 2000.

Park, Katharine. "Cadden, Laqueur, and the 'One-Sex Body'." *MFF* 46 (2010): 96–100.

Park, Katharine and Robert A. Nye. "Destiny is Anatomy." *NewRe* 204 (1991): 53–7.

Parker, Julie F. "God as a Child in the Hebrew Bible? Playing with the Possibilities." In *T&T Clark Handbook of Children in the Bible and the Biblical World*, edited by Sharon Betsworth and Julie F. Parker, 155–77. TTCH. London: T&T Clark, 2019.

Paul, Ian. "Are We Sexed in Heaven? Bodily Form, Sex Identity and the Resurrection." In *Marriage, Family and Relationships: Biblical, Doctrinal and Contemporary Perspectives*, edited by Thomas A. Noble, Sarah K. Whittle, and Philip S. Johnston, 101–20. London: Apollos, 2017.

Pawl, Timothy. *In Defense of Extended Conciliar Christology: A Philosophical Essay*. OSAT. Oxford: Oxford University Press, 2019.

Pearcey, Nancy. *Love Thy Body: Answering Hard Questions about Life and Sexuality*. Grand Rapids: Baker Academic, 2018.

Peeler, Amy. *Women and the Gender of God*. Grand Rapids: Eerdmans, 2022.

Peled, Ilan. *Masculinities and Third Gender: The Origins and Nature of an Institutionalized Gender Otherness in the Ancient Near East*. AOAT 435. Münster: Ugarit-Verlag, 2016.

Pelikan, Jaroslav. *Credo: Historical and Theological Guide to Creeds and Confessions of Faith in the Christian Tradition*. New Haven, CT: Yale University Press, 2003.

Petersen, Jay Kyle. *A Comprehensive Guide to Intersex*. London: Jessica Kingsley, 2021.

Petri, Thomas. *Aquinas and the Theology of the Body: The Thomistic Foundations of John Paul II's Anthropology*. TRS 7. Washington, DC: Catholic University of America Press, 2016.

Pikramenou, Nikoletta. *Intersex Rights: Living Between Sexes*. Dordrecht: Springer, 2020.

Pinckaers, Servais. *The Sources of Christian Ethics*. Washington, DC: Catholic University of America Press, 1995.

Plantinga, Cornelius. *Not the Way It's Supposed to Be: A Breviary of Sin*. Grand Rapids: Eerdmans, 1995.

Plato. "Symposium." In *Complete Works*, edited by John M. Cooper, translated by Alexander Nehamas and Paul Woodruff, 457–505. Indianapolis: Hackett, 1997.

Preves, Sharon E. *Intersex and Identity: The Contested Self*. New Brunswick, NJ: Rutgers University Press, 2003.

Provan, Iain W. *Seriously Dangerous Religion: What the Old Testament Really Says and Why It Matters*. Waco, TX: Baylor University Press, 2014.

Punt, Jeremy. "Power and Liminality, Sex and Gender, and Gal 3:28: A Postcolonial, Queer Reading of an Influential Text." *Neot* 44 (2010): 140–66.

Raby, Elyse J. "'You Knit Me Together in My Mother's Womb': A Theology of Creation and Divine Action in Light of Intersex." *ThS* 24 (2018): 98–109.

Ramsey, Paul. "Human Sexuality in the History of Redemption." *JRE* 16 (1988): 56–86.

Raphael, Rebecca. *Biblical Corpora: Representations of Disability in Hebrew Biblical Literature*. LHBOTS 445. London: T&T Clark, 2008.

Rea, Michael C. *Metaphysics: The Basics*. TBas. London: Routledge, 2014.

Reeves, Michael and Hans Madueme. "Threads in a Seamless Garment: Original Sin in Systematic Theology." In *Adam, the Fall, and Original Sin: Theological, Biblical, and Scientific Perspectives*, edited by Hans Madueme and Michael Reeves, 209–24. Grand Rapids: Baker Academic, 2014.

Reinders, Hans S. "Life's Goodness: On Disability, Genetics and 'Choice.'" In *Theology, Disability, and the New Genetics: Why Science Needs The Church*, edited by John Swinton and Brian Brock, 163–81. London: T&T Clark, 2007.

Retief, Francois P. and Louise Cilliers. "Eunuchs in the Bible." *AcTSup* 7 (2005): 247–58.

Rettler, Bradley. "The General Truthmaker View of Ontological Commitment." *PhilS* 173 (2016): 1405–25.

Richards, Jay Wesley. "Can a Male Savior Save Women?" In *Unapologetic Apologetics: Meeting the Challenges of Theological Studies*, edited by William A. Dembski and Jay Wesley Richards, 156–75. Downers Grove, IL: IVP Academic, 2001.

Ricœur, Paul. *Time and Narrative*. Translated by Kathleen McLaughlin and David Pellauer. Vol. 1. Chicago: University of Chicago Press, 1984.

Ries, Julien. "The Fall." In vol. 5 of *ER*, edited by Lindsay Jones, 2959–70. 2nd ed. Detroit: Macmillan Reference USA, 2005.

Roberts, Christopher C. *Creation and Covenant: The Significance of Sexual Difference in and for the Moral Theology of Marriage*. New York: T&T Clark, 2007.

Rohr, Richard. *The Divine Dance: The Trinity and Your Transformation*. New Kensington, PA: Whitaker House, 2016.

Romero, Miguel J. "Aquinas on the Corporis Infirmitas." In *Disability in the Christian Tradition: A Reader*, edited by Brian Brock and John Swinton, 101–51. Grand Rapids: Eerdmans, 2012.

Rosenau, Hartmut. "Schöpfungsordnung." In vol. 30 of *TRE*, edited by Gerhard Müller, 356–8. Berlin: de Gruyter, 1976.

Roughgarden, Joan. *Evolution's Rainbow Diversity, Gender, and Sexuality in Nature and People*. 2nd ed. Berkeley, CA: University of California Press, 2004.

Ruello, Francis. *La christologie de Thomas d'Aquin*. ThH 76. Paris: Beauchesne, 1987.

Ruether, Rosemary Radford. *Sexism and God-Talk: Toward a Feminist Theology*. Boston, MA: Beacon, 1983.

Sabia-Tanis, Justin. "Holy Creation, Wholly Creative: God's Intention for Gender Diversity." In *Understanding Transgender Identities: Four Views*, edited by James K. Beilby and Paul Rhodes Eddy, 195–222. Grand Rapids: Baker Academic, 2019.

Sarisky, Darren. "The Ontology of Scripture and the Ethics of Interpretation in the Theology of John Webster." *IJST* 21 (2019): 59–77.

Sarisky, Darren. "Tradition II: Thinking with Historical Text—Reflections on Theologies of Retrieval." In *Theologies of Retrieval: An Exploration and Appraisal*, edited by Darren Sarisky, 193–209. London: Bloomsbury, 2017.

Sarna, Nahum M. *Genesis בראשית*. JPSTCP. Philadelphia, PA: Jewish Publication Society, 1989.

Sauter, Gerhard. *Eschatological Rationality: Theological Issues in Focus*. Grand Rapids: Baker Academic, 1996.

Sax, Leonard. "How Common Is Intersex? A Response to Anne Fausto-Sterling." *JSR* 39 (2002): 174–8.

Schafer, Steven. *Marriage, Sex, and Procreation: Contemporary Revisions to Augustine's Theology of Marriage*. PrinTMS. Eugene, OR: Pickwick, 2019.

Schaff, Philip. *The Creeds of Christendom: With a History and Critical Notes: The Evangelical Protestant Creeds with Translations*. Vol. 3. 6th ed. Grand Rapids: Baker Academic, 1983.

Schipper, Jeremy. *Disability Studies and the Hebrew Bible: Figuring Mephibosheth in the David Story*. LHBOTS 441. New York: T&T Clark, 2006.

Schipper, Jeremy. "Disabling Israelite Leadership: 2 Samuel 6:23 and Other Images of Disability in the Deuteronomistic History." In *This Abled Body: Rethinking Disabilities in Biblical Studies*, edited by Hector Avalos, Sarah J. Melcher, and Jeremy Schipper, 104–13. SemeiaSt 55. Leiden: Brill, 2007.

Schmid, Hans Heinrich. *Šālôm: Frieden im Alten Orient und im Alten Testament*. SBS 51. Stuttgart: KBW, 1971.

Schnabel, Eckhard J. *Der erste Brief des Paulus an die Korinther*. HTA. Wuppertal, Germany: R. Brockhaus, 2006.

Schnittjer, Gary Edward. *Old Testament Use of Old Testament: A Book-by-Book Guide*. Grand Rapids: Zondervan Academic, 2021.

Schrage, Wolfgang. *Der erste Brief an die Korinther*. Vol. 4. EKKNT 7. Düsseldorf: Benziger, 1991.

Schreiner, Patrick. *The Ascension of Christ: Recovering a Neglected Doctrine*. Snapshots. Bellingham, WA: Lexham, 2020.

Schroeder, Henry Joseph, ed. "Twelfth Ecumenical Council: Lateran IV 1215." In *Disciplinary Decrees of the General Councils: Text, Translation, and Commentary*, 236–96. St. Louis, MO: Herder, 1937.

Schüssler Fiorenza, Elisabeth. *In Memory of Her: A Feminist Theological Reconstruction of Christian Origins*. New York: Crossroad, 1994.

Seelbach, Larissa Carina. "Schöpfungslehre." In *Augustin Handbuch*, edited by Volker Henning Drecoll, 470–9. 2nd ed. HT. Tübingen: Mohr Siebeck, 2014.

Seely, Paul H. "The Meaning of Mîn, 'Kind.'" *SCB* 9 (1997): 47–56.

Seim, Turid Karlsen. "In Heaven as on Earth? Resurrection, Body, Gender and Heavenly Rehearsals in Luke-Acts." In *Christian and Islamic Gender Models in Formative Traditions*, edited by Kari Elisabeth Børresen, 17–41. STTA 2. Roma: Herder, 2004.

Seim, Turid Karlsen. "The Resurrected Body in Luke-Acts: The Significance of Space." In *Metamorphoses: Resurrection, Body and Transformative Practices in Early Christianity*, edited by Turid Karlsen Seim and Jorunn Økland, 19–39. Ekstasis 1. Berlin: de Gruyter, 2009.

Seitz, Christopher. "Sexuality and Scripture's Plain Sense: The Christian Community and the Law of God." In *Homosexuality, Science, and the "Plain Sense" of Scripture*, edited by David L. Balch, 177–96. Grand Rapids: Eerdmans, 2000.

Shaw, Jane. "Conflicts Within the Anglican Communion." In *The Oxford Handbook of Theology, Sexuality, and Gender*, edited by Adrian Thatcher, 340–57. OH. Oxford: Oxford University Press, 2015.

Shuster, Marguerite. *The Fall and Sin: What We Have Become as Sinners*. Grand Rapids: Eerdmans, 2004.

Shuttleworth, Sally. "Review of Making Sex: Body and Gender from the Greeks to Freud." *JHSe* 3 (1993): 633–5.

Simons, Patricia. *The Sex of Men in Premodern Europe: A Cultural History*. Cambridge: Cambridge University Press, 2011.

Sklar, Jay. "Sin." In *The Oxford Encyclopedia of the Bible and Theology*, edited by Samuel E. Balentine, 2:297–308. 2 vols. OEB. Oxford: Oxford University Press, 2015.

Sloane, Andrew. "'Male and Female He Created Them'? Theological Reflections on Gender, Biology and Identity." In *Marriage, Family and Relationships: Biblical, Doctrinal and Contemporary Perspectives*, edited by T. A. Noble, Sarah Whittle, and Philip Johnston, 223–36. London: Apollos, 2017.

Smith, Chris H. "Singles in the Family of God: An Ecclesial Account of Unmarried Devotion." PhD diss., Wheaton College, 2021.

Smith, David L. *With Willful Intent: A Theology of Sin*. Wheaton, IL: BridgePoint, 1994.

Smith, James K. A. "What Stands on the Fall?" In *Evolution and the Fall*, edited by William T. Cavanaugh and James K. A. Smith, 48–64. Grand Rapids: Eerdmans, 2017.

Soh, Debra. *The End of Gender: Debunking the Myths About Sex and Identity in Our Society*. New York: Threshold, 2020.

Sonderegger, Katherine. *Systematic Theology: Volume 2, The Doctrine of the Holy Trinity: Processions and Persons*. Minneapolis, MN: Fortress, 2020.

Song, Robert. *Covenant and Calling: Towards a Theology of Same-Sex Relationships*. London: SCM, 2014.

Sorč, Ciril. *Entwürfe einer perichoretischen Theologie*. TOW 5. Münster: Lit, 2004.

Southgate, Christopher. *The Groaning of Creation: God, Evolution, and the Problem of Evil.* Louisville, KY: Westminster John Knox, 2008.

Southgate, Christopher. *Theology in a Suffering World: Glory and Longing.* Cambridge: Cambridge University Press, 2018.

Sparks, Kenton L. *God's Word in Human Words: An Evangelical Appropriation of Critical Biblical Scholarship.* Grand Rapids: Baker Academic, 2008.

Sprinkle, Preston M. *Embodied: Transgender Identities, The Church & What the Bible Has to Say.* Colorado Springs, CO: David C Cook, 2021.

Spykman, Gordon J. *Reformational Theology: A New Paradigm for Doing Dogmatics.* Grand Rapids: Eerdmans, 1992.

Starr, James. "Does 2 Peter 1:4 Speak of Deification?" In *Partakers of the Divine Nature: The History and Development of Deification in the Christian Traditions,* edited by Michael J. Christensen and Jeffery A. Wittung, 81–92. Grand Rapids: Baker Academic, 2008.

Stavrakopoulou, Francesca. *God: An Anatomy.* London: Picador, 2021.

Steinmann, Andrew. *Genesis: An Introduction and Commentary.* Downers Grove, IL: IVP Academic, 2019.

Stewart, David Tabb. "Leviticus–Deuteronomy." In *The Bible and Disability: A Commentary,* edited by Sarah J. Melcher, Mikeal C. Parsons, and Amos Yong, 57–91. SRTD. Waco, TX: Baylor University Press, 2017.

Stewart, David Tabb. "Sexual Disabilities in the Hebrew Bible." In *Disability Studies and Biblical Literature,* edited by Candida R. Moss and Jeremy Schipper, 67–88. New York: Palgrave Macmillan, 2011.

Stock, Kathleen. *Material Girls: Why Reality Matters for Feminism.* London: Little, Brown, 2021.

Strack, Hermann Leberecht and Paul Billerbeck. *Kommentar zum Neuen Testament aus Talmud und Midrasch.* Vol. 1. 2nd ed. München: Beck, 1956.

Stump, Eleonore. *Aquinas.* London: Routledge, 2003.

Stump, J. B. and Chad Meister, eds. *Original Sin and the Fall: Five Views.* SMB. Downers Grove, IL: IVP Academic, 2020.

Sturm, Richard A. and Mats Larsson. "Genetics of Human Iris Colour and Patterns." *PCMR* 22 (2009): 544–62.

Swancutt, Diane M. "Sexing the Pauline Body of Christ: Scriptural Sex in the Context of the American Christian Culture War." In *Toward a Theology of Eros: Transfiguring Passion at the Limits of Discipline,* edited by Virginia Burrus and Catherine Keller, 65–98. TTC. New York: Fordham University Press, 2006.

Swancutt, Diane M. "'The Disease of Effemination': The Charge of Effeminacy and the Verdict of God (Romans 1:18–2:16)." In *New Testament Masculinities,* edited by Stephen D. Moore and Janice Capel Anderson, 193–233. SemeiaSt 45. Atlanta, GA: SBL, 2003.

Tabaczek, Mariusz. "The Metaphysics of Evolution: From Aquinas's Interpretation of Augustine's Concept of Rationes Seminales to the Contemporary Thomistic Account of Species Transformism." *NV* 18:3 (2020): 945–72.

Tanis, Justin. *Trans-Gendered: Theology, Ministry, and Communities of Faith.* Cleveland, OH: Pilgrim, 2003.

Tappenden, Frederick S. *Resurrection in Paul: Cognition, Metaphor, and Transformation.* ECL 19. Atlanta, GA: SBL, 2016.

Tennent, Timothy C. *For the Body: Recovering a Theology of Gender, Sexuality, and the Human Body.* Grand Rapids: Zondervan Academic, 2020.

Tertullian. "Against Marcion." In *Latin Christianity: Its Founder, Tertullian*, edited by Alexander Roberts and James Donaldson, 269–475. ANF 3. Peabody, MA: Hendrickson, 2004.

Thatcher, Adrian. *Gender and Christian Ethics*. NSCE 39. Cambridge: Cambridge University Press, 2021.

Thatcher, Adrian. *God, Sex, and Gender: An Introduction*. Chichester: Wiley-Blackwell, 2011.

Thatcher, Adrian. *Liberating Sex: A Christian Sexual Theology*. London: SPCK, 1993.

Thatcher, Adrian. *Redeeming Gender*. Oxford: Oxford University Press, 2016.

Thatcher, Adrian. "The One Sex Theory and Why It Still Matters." *Research Seminar in the Theology and Religion Department, University of Exeter*, November 2012. Cited August 5, 2020. http://www.adrianthatcher.org/lectures.php?id=44.

Thatcher, Adrian, ed. *The Oxford Handbook of Theology, Sexuality, and Gender*. OH. Oxford: Oxford University Press, 2015.

Thatcher, Adrian. *Thinking About Sex*. Minneapolis, MN: Fortress, 2015.

Thatcher, Adrian and Thomas Laqueur. *God, Sex and Gender: A Conversation on Adrian Thatcher's Redeeming Gender*. Berkeley, CA: Berkeley Center for the Study of Religion Colloquium, 2017.

Thiessen, Matthew. *Jesus and the Forces of Death: The Gospels' Portrayal of Ritual Impurity Within First-Century Judaism*. Grand Rapids: Baker Academic, 2020.

Thiselton, Anthony C. *The First Epistle to the Corinthians: A Commentary on the Greek Text*. NIGTC. Grand Rapids: Eerdmans, 2000.

Thomas, W. H. Griffith. *Principles of Theology: An Introduction to the Thirty-Nine Articles*. 4th ed. London: Church Book Room, 1951.

Tigay, Jeffrey H. *Deuteronomy* מירבד. JPSTCP. Philadelphia, PA: Jewish Publication Society, 1996.

Tillich, Paul. *The Courage to Be*. New Haven, CT: Yale University Press, 1952.

Tonstad, Linn Marie. *God and Difference: The Trinity, Sexuality, and the Transformation of Finitude*. GTS 17. New York: Routledge, 2016.

Toom, Tarmo. "Totus homo: Augustine on Resurrection." In *Resurrection and Responsibility: Essays on Theology, Scripture, and Ethics in Honor of Thorwald Lorenzen*, edited by Keith D. Dyer and David J. Neville, 59–75. Eugene, OR: Pickwick, 2009.

Toon, Peter. *Heaven and Hell: A Biblical and Theological Overview*. NelSBT. Nashville, TN: Thomas Nelson, 1986.

Torrance, Thomas F. *Incarnation: The Person and Life of Christ*. Edited by Robert T. Walker. Rev. ed. Downers Grove, IL: IVP Academic, 2008.

Torrell, Jean-Pierre. *Résurrection de Jésus et résurrection des morts: Foi, histoire et théologie*. Épi. Paris: Cerf, 2012.

Tranter, Samuel. *Oliver O'Donovan's Moral Theology: Tensions and Triumphs*. TTCETE. London: T&T Clark, 2020.

Treier, Daniel J. *Introducing Evangelical Theology*. Grand Rapids: Baker Academic, 2019.

Treier, Daniel J. *Lord Jesus Christ*. ZNSD. Grand Rapids: Zondervan Academic, forthcoming.

Treier, Daniel J. "Virgin Territory?" *ProEccl* 23 (2014): 373–9.

Treier, Daniel J. and Douglas A. Sweeney, eds. *Hearing and Doing the Word: The Drama of Evangelical Hermeneutics in Honor of Kevin J. Vanhoozer*. London: T&T Clark, 2021.

Trible, Phyllis. *God and the Rhetoric of Sexuality*. OBT. Philadelphia, PA: Fortress, 1978.

Trueman, Carl R. *The Rise and Triumph of the Modern Self: Cultural Amnesia, Expressive Individualism, and the Road to Sexual Revolution*. Wheaton, IL: Crossway, 2020.

Twombly, Charles C. *Perichoresis and Personhood: God, Christ, and Salvation in John of Damascus*. PrinTMS 216. Eugene, OR: Pickwick, 2015.

Twomey, Jay. "Stranger in a Stranger World: Queering Paul with Michael Faber's *The Book of Strange New Things*." In *Bodies on the Verge: Queering Pauline Epistles*, edited by Joseph A. Marchal, 267–88. SemeiaSt 93. Atlanta, GA: SBL, 2019.

Upson-Saia, Kristi. "Resurrecting Deformity: Augustine on Wounded and Scarred Bodies in the Heavenly Realm." In *Disability in Judaism, Christianity, and Islam: Sacred Texts, Historical Traditions, and Social Analysis*, edited by Darla Schumm and Michael Stoltzfus, 93–122. New York: Palgrave Macmillan, 2011.

do Vale, Fellipe. "Can a Male Savior Save Women? The Metaphysics of Gender and Christ's Ability to Save." *PC* 21:2 (2019): 309–24.

do Vale, Fellipe. "Cappadocian or Augustinian? Adjudicating Debates on Gender in the Resurrection." *IJST* 21 (2019): 182–98.

do Vale, Fellipe. "Gender as Love: A Theological Account." PhD diss., Southern Methodist University, 2021.

Vanhoozer, Kevin J. *First Theology: God, Scripture & Hermeneutics*. Downers Grove, IL: IVP Academic, 2002.

Vanhoozer, Kevin J. "Holy Scripture." In *Christian Dogmatics: Reformed Theology for the Church Catholic*, edited by Michael Allen and Scott R. Swain, 30–56. Grand Rapids: Baker Academic, 2016.

Vanhoozer, Kevin J. *Is There a Meaning in This Text? The Bible, the Reader, and the Morality of Literary Knowledge*. Grand Rapids: Zondervan Academic, 1998.

Vanhoozer, Kevin J. *The Drama of Doctrine: A Canonical-Linguistic Approach to Christian Theology*. Louisville, KY: Westminster John Knox, 2005.

Vanhoozer, Kevin J. and Daniel J. Treier. *Theology and the Mirror of Scripture: A Mere Evangelical Account*. SCDS. Downers Grove, IL: IVP Academic, 2016.

Vannier, Marie-Anne. *"Creatio," "Conversio," "Formatio": Chez S. Augustin*. Paradosis 31. Freibourg, Suisse: Éditions Universitaires, 1991.

Van Pelt, Miles V. "The Noahic Covenant of the Covenant of Grace." In *Covenant Theology: Biblical, Theological, and Historical Perspectives*, edited by Guy Prentiss Waters, J. Nicholas Reid, and John R. Muether, 111–32. Wheaton, IL: Crossway, 2020.

Viands, Jamie. *I Will Surely Multiply Your Offspring: An Old Testament Theology of the Blessing of Progeny with Special Attention to the Latter Prophets*. Eugene, OR: Pickwick, 2014.

Voß, Heinz-Jürgen. *Making Sex Revisited: Dekonstruktion des Geschlechts aus biologisch-medizinischer Perspektive*. Bielefeld: Transcript, 2010.

Walden, Wayne. "Galatians 3:28: Grammar Observations." *ResQ* 51 (2009): 45–50.

Walton, John H. *Ancient Near Eastern Thought and the Old Testament: Introducing the Conceptual World of the Hebrew Bible*. 2nd ed. Grand Rapids: Baker Academic, 2018.

Wang, Franklin. "A Holy People of YHWH: Deuteronomy's Vision of Israelite Identity." PhD diss., Wheaton College, 2020.

Ware, Bruce A. *The Man Christ Jesus: Theological Reflections on the Humanity of Christ*. Wheaton, IL: Crossway, 2013.

Warnke, Georgia. "Intersexuality and the Categories of Sex." *Hyp* 16 (2001): 126–37.

Wawrykow, Joseph P. *The Westminster Handbook to Thomas Aquinas*. Louisville, KY: Westminster John Knox, 2005.

Webster, John. *Christ Our Salvation: Expositions and Proclamations*. Bellingham, WA: Lexham, 2020.

Webster, John. *Confessing God: Essays in Christian Dogmatics II*. London: T&T Clark, 2005.

Webster, John. "Eschatology, Anthropology and Postmodernity." *IJST* 2 (2000): 13–28.

Webster, John. *God Without Measure: Working Papers in Christian Theology: God and the Works of God*. Vol. 1. TTCT. London: Bloomsbury, 2016.

Webster, John. *Holiness*. Grand Rapids: Eerdmans, 2003.

Webster, John. *Holy Scripture: A Dogmatic Sketch*. CIT. Cambridge: Cambridge University Press, 2003.

Webster, John. "'It was the will of the Lord to bruise him': Soteriology and the Doctrine of God." In *God of Salvation: Soteriology in Theological Perspective*, edited by Ivor J. Davidson and Murray Rae, 15–34. Farnham: Ashgate, 2011.

Webster, John. *The Culture of Theology*. Edited by Ivor J. Davidson and Alden C. McCray. Grand Rapids: Baker Academic, 2019.

Webster, John. *The Domain of the Word: Scripture and Theological Reason*. TTCT. London: T&T Clark, 2012.

Webster, John. "The Human Person." In *The Cambridge Companion to Postmodern Theology*, edited by Kevin J. Vanhoozer, 219–34. CCR. Cambridge: Cambridge University Press, 2003.

Webster, John. "Theologies of Retrieval." In *The Oxford Handbook of Systematic Theology*, edited by John Webster, Kathryn Tanner, and Iain R. Torrance, 583–99. OH. Oxford: Oxford University Press, 2007.

Wenham, Gordon J. *Genesis 1–15*. WBC 1. Nashville, TN: Thomas Nelson, 1987.

Wenham, Gordon J. *The Book of Leviticus*. NICOT 3. Grand Rapids: Eerdmans, 1979.

West, Christopher. *Our Bodies Tell God's Story: Discovering the Divine Plan for Love, Sex, and Gender*. Grand Rapids: Brazos, 2020.

Westenholz, Joan Goodnick and Ilona Zsolnay. "Categorizing Men and Masculinity in Sumer." In *Being a Man: Negotiating Ancient Constructs of Masculinity*, edited by Ilona Zsolnay, 12–41. SHANE. London: Routledge, 2017.

Westermann, Claus. *Genesis 1–11: A Continental Commentary*. Translated by John J. Scullion. Minneapolis, MN: Fortress, 1994.

White, Thomas Joseph. *Wisdom in the Face of Modernity: A Study in Thomistic Natural Theology*. FR. Ave Maria, FL: Sapientia, 2009.

Williams, Ronald J. *Williams' Hebrew Syntax. Revised and Expanded by John C. Beckman*. 3rd ed. Toronto: University of Toronto Press, 2012.

Williams, Rowan. *Being Disciples: Essentials of the Christian Life*. Grand Rapids: Eerdmans, 2016.

Williams, Rowan. *Grace and Necessity: Reflections on Art and Love*. Harrisburg, PA: Morehouse, 2005.

Williams, Rowan. "The Body's Grace." In *Theology and Sexuality: Classic and Contemporary Readings*, edited by Eugene F. Rogers, 309–21. BRMT. Oxford: Blackwell, 2002.

Williams, Rowan. *Why Study the Past? The Quest for the Historical Church*. Grand Rapids: Eerdmans, 2005.

Wirzba, Norman. "Creation Through Christ." In vol. 2 of *Christ and the Created Order: Perspectives from Theology, Philosophy, and Science*, edited by Andrew B. Torrance and Thomas H. McCall, 35–53. Grand Rapids: Zondervan Academic, 2018.

Witherington, Ben. *New Testament Theology and Ethics*. Vol. 2. Downers Grove, IL: IVP Academic, 2016.

Witherington, Ben. "Rite and Rights for Women-Galatians 3:28." *NTS* 27 (1981): 593–604.

Wolff, Michelle. "A Diptych Reading of Christ's Transfiguration: Trans and Intersex Aesthetics Reveal Baptismal Identity." *ThS* 25 (2019): 98–110.

Wolters, Albert M. *Creation Regained: Biblical Basics for a Reformational Worldview*. 2nd ed. Grand Rapids: Eerdmans, 2005.

Wolterstorff, Nicholas. *Practices of Belief: Selected Essays, Volume 2*. Cambridge: Cambridge University Press, 2010.

Wood, Jacob W. *To Stir a Restless Heart: Thomas Aquinas and Henri De Lubac on Nature, Grace, and the Desire for God*. TRS 14. Washington, DC: Catholic University of America Press, 2019.

Work, Telford. *Jesus—The End and the Beginning: Tracing the Christ-Shaped Nature of Everything*. Grand Rapids: Baker Academic, 2019.

Woznicki, Christopher. "Dancing Around the Black Box: The Problem and Metaphysics of Perichoresis." *PC* 22 (2020): 103–21.

Wright, N. T. "How Can the Bible Be Authoritative." *VE* 21 (1991): 7–32.

Wright, N. T. *The Resurrection of the Son of God*. COQG 3. Minneapolis, MN: Fortress, 2003.

Yadav, Sameer. "Christian Doctrine as Ontological Commitment to a Narrative." In *The Task of Dogmatics: Explorations in Theological Method*, edited by Oliver Crisp and Fred Sanders, 70–86. LATC. Grand Rapids: Zondervan Academic, 2017.

Yarbrough, Robert W. "Adam in the New Testament." In *Adam, the Fall, and Original Sin: Theological, Biblical, and Scientific Perspectives*, edited by Hans Madueme and Michael Reeves, 33–52. Grand Rapids: Baker Academic, 2014.

Yarhouse, Mark A. *Understanding Gender Dysphoria: Navigating Transgender Issues in a Changing Culture*. Downers Grove, IL: IVP Academic, 2015.

Yarhouse, Mark A. and Julia Sadusky. "Response to Megan K. DeFranza." In *Understanding Transgender Identities: Four Views*, edited by James K. Beilby and Paul Rhodes Eddy, 184–9. Grand Rapids: Baker Academic, 2019.

Yaron, Reuven. "The Climactic Tricolon." *JJS* 37 (1986): 153–9.

Yong, Amos. "Disability Theology of the Resurrection: Persisting Questions and Additional Considerations—A Response to Ryan Mullins." *ArsD* 12 (2012): 4–10.

Young, Frances M. *God's Presence: A Contemporary Recapitulation of Early Christianity*. CIT. Cambridge: Cambridge University Press, 2013.

Younger, K. Lawson. "The 'Contextual Method': Some West Semitic Reflections." In vol. 3 of *The Context of Scripture: Archival Documents from the Biblical World*, edited by William W. Hallo and K. Lawson Younger, xxxv–xlii. Leiden: Brill, 1997.

Younger, K. Lawson. "The Old Testament in Its Cultural Context: Implications of 'Contextual Criticism' for Chinese and North American Christian Identity." In *After Imperialism: Christian Identity in China and the Global Evangelical Movement*, edited by Richard R. Cook and David W. Pao. SCC. Eugene, OR: Pickwick, 2011.

Zeitlin, Froma I. *Playing the Other: Gender and Society in Classical Greek Literature*. Chicago: University of Chicago Press, 1996.

Zsolnay, Ilona, ed. *Being a Man: Negotiating Ancient Constructs of Masculinity*. SHANE. London: Routledge, 2017.

INDEX OF SELECTED AUTHORS

INDEX OF SELECTED SUBJECTS

INDEX OF SELECTED SCRIPTURE REFERENCES

INDEX OF SELECTED HEBREW, GREEK, AND LATIN TERMS